AF656750

Archaeology in the Third World

— A history of Indian Archaeology since 1947 —

Updating Indian Archaeology
(ISSN 0972-0642)

1. Archaeology of Mahūrbhañj; by Probodh Kumar Mishra (ISBN 81-246-0084-8)
2. Nālandā Mahāvihāra — Archaeology of an Indian Buddhist Site by Mary L. Stewart (ISBN 81-246-0218-2)

Updating Indian Archaeology, no. 3

Archaeology in the Third World

— A history of Indian Archaeology since 1947 —

Dilip K. Chakrabarti

DK PRINTWORLD

Publishers of Indian Traditions

Cataloging in Publication Data — DK

Chakrabarti, Dilip K. (Dilip Kumar), 1941–
Archaeology in the Third World.
(Updating Indian archaeology; no. 3)
Includes bibliographical references (p.)
Includes index.
ISBN 13: 9788124602171

1. Archaeology — India — History — 20th century. 2. Archaeology — Developing countries. 3. India — Antiquities. I. Title. II. Series: Updating Indian archaeology; no. 3.

ISBN 13: 978-81-246-0217-1 **ISBN 10: 81-246-0217-4**

First Published in India in 2003
Second Impression, 2012

© Author

All rights reserved. No part of this publication may be reproduced or transmitted in any form or by any means, electronic or mechanical, including photocopying, recording, or any information storage or retrieval system, without prior written permission of both the copyright owner, indicated above, and the publisher.

Published and printed by:
D.K. Printworld (P) Ltd.
Regd. office : '*Vedasri*', F-395, Sudarshan Park
(Metro Station: Ramesh Nagar)
New Delhi - 110 015
Phones : (011) 545-3975; 546-6019; *Fax* : (011) 546-5926
E-mail: indology@dkprintworld.com

Preface

THIS book is in continuation of my *A History of Indian Archaeology from the Beginning to 1947* (1988). There is also a major difference between the two. The earlier volume was concerned with the background and nature of archaeological discoveries in India from the sixteenth-eighteenth centuries AD onwards, and focussed essentially around the work of a few individuals. After the Archaeological Survey of India was founded in 1861, it became, with the exception of the chapter on pre-historic research, a history of the work done by this organisation which, in fact, was the only body entrusted with the task of archaeological research and conservation in the country during that period. Two points were carefully emphasised throughout that volume. First, there was a strong thread of continuity through the whole chronological spectrum. The discoveries of one period were linked, to a great extent, with the discoveries of the next. Secondly, such discoveries did not take place in an intellectual vacuum. There was a substratum of ideas throughout — the ideas which determined the interpretation of the discoveries and in fact, the discoveries themselves.

The volume was based only on the published material and aimed at dealing with the overall and evolving frame of archaeological research in pre-Independence India. Biographical exercises based on archival records and the historical analysis of individual themes fell outside its scope.

The present volume too is based only on the published sources and does not discuss the threads of individual themes, but there is a difference in approach between this and the earlier book. In the present-day Republic of India archaeology ceased to be an exclusively governmental activity and tried to become a part of the country's education system. No discussion of the history of Indian archaeology of this period can afford to ignore this issue. Similarly, there is an emerging and nationally important issue of 'heritage management'. In the pre-Independence phase the whole focus was on the conservation of individual monuments based on the principles of conservation enunciated by the Archaeological Survey in the early years of the twentieth century. As long as the population was much less than what it is today and as long as there was not much economic and political pressure on land, this purely governmental 'conservation approach' perhaps served the country well. With the burgeoning population and all that it entails in a democratic set-up, it is perhaps time to widen the scope of this approach and initiate a national debate on the archaeological aspects of the country's heritage issue. Some of these aspects will be considered in this volume.

As is well-known, religious fundamentalism has become a factor in the problem of the preservation of monumental heritage of south Asia. On a general level we shall try to understand some complexities of this issue.

Finally, it is important that we realise that there is an ever-widening gulf of difference between the archaeological research in the First World and that in the Third World. It is true that these two research traditions have never been monolithic or homogeneous. At the same time, it would be taking an ostrich-like position to deny that there is a very noticeable difference between them. As India is a part of the Third World, it is our responsibility in the present context to understand how the post-Independence Indian situation highlights some common features of Third World archaeology.

In recent years there has been an increased interest in the history of Indian archaeology, a biographical and archival approach being one of its features. There is still a vast field waiting for such studies. For instance, there is as yet nothing available on the organisation, activities and research orientations of the government archaeology departments of the 'native' states, some of whom had elaborate archaeological set-ups on the model of the British Indian set-up. Besides, there should be analytical biographies of people like R.L. Mitra, R.G. Bhandarkar, R.D. Banerji, B.L. Indraji and others in the background of the emergence of a consciousness of the ancient past in modern India.

Such detailed studies can, of course, be undertaken only within a general framework of the subject's development. Both in this and the earlier volume I have tried to establish this framework.

As an ordinary foot-soldier of Indian archaeology since the mid-1960s I have been both a witness of, and participant in, various developments and situations which find a place in this book. My observations on them may not be acceptable to all but I do hope that I have tried to portray the ground reality as best as I could understand.

Dr Nayanjot Lahiri sent me some information regarding a reference and a copy of the Indian UGC circular discussed in the section on the place of archaeology in Indian education (chapter 3). Mr. Deep Kanta Lahiri Choudhury drew my attention to a Bengali book available in the Cambridge University Library — *Bharat Bhraman* which was written and published by his great-great grandfather Dharani Kanta Lahiri Choudhury.

Contents

To
the memory of
Sri Sushil Kumar Sanyal
(1917 — 1967)

&

Srimati Sulata Sanyal
(1924 — 2001)

1

The Quest for New Horizons, 1947-73

THE BEGINNING, 1947-52

The Evidence of *Ancient India* 4 to 8

In 1947 there were three compulsive issues before Indian archaeology. First, with the famous sites of Mohenjo-Daro and Harappa gone to Pakistan, it was time to think of the possibility of locating Indus civilization sites in the territorial limits of the new 'India'. There were already strong indications in this direction : Rangpur in the Kathiawar peninsula of Gujarat, Kotla Nihang Khan in the eastern Panjab foothills, Aurel Stein's discovery of the Indus sites in the dried-up Hakra valley of Cholistan, which had implications for the upward extension of this valley in the Bikaner area of Rajasthan, and finally, K.A.A. Ansari's survey of some sites in the Saharanpur area (for Ansari's survey, Lahiri and Sharma, In press). Secondly, there was the question of a hiatus between the end of the Indus civilization and the beginning of the early historic cities of the Ganga plain. Mortimer Wheeler brought the issue of this 'hiatus' into sharp relief, mainly through his work at Harappa and the subsequent writings. Thirdly, after the establishment of the 'Prehistory Branch' of the Survey under Wheeler, it became imperative to turn one's gaze to prehistory as well.

In retrospect, it is interesting to find that within the first few years of its existence the new Archaeological Survey of India published two volumes trying to assess what was known about the archaeology of the new country at that point. These publications, one in 1950 and another in 1953, were as neat an attempt at 'stock-taking' as was possible under the circumstances, suggesting a clear urge to move forward. One cannot help feeling respect for the people at the helm of the Survey during that period both for their academic understanding and honesty of purpose.

The initial credit has to go to Mortimer Wheeler whose Director Generalship of the Survey ended in 1948. Partition is first mentioned in the editorial notes of the 1947-48 issue of *Ancient India 4* (Wheeler 1948a). The Archaeological Survey of India remained unchanged in the new India except losing much of the old Frontier Circle and some portions of the old Eastern Circle. These 'lost' areas became the responsibility of the new Pakistan Department of Archaeology which was assembled from the Muslim staff of the former Archaeological Survey. Pakistan gained Mohenjo-Daro, Harappa and Taxila among the major sites, but India ended up by having most of the major Islamic monuments of the subcontinent. Wheeler tried to explain the concentration of the Muslim population at two ends of the Gangetic plain — the north-western region and the eastern half of Bengal — as an effect of the vastness of Indian geography which did not lend easily to the formation of more Muslim nuclei than these two. This was not much of a geographical explanation, but one notes here a concern to understand the past and the present of the subcontinent in terms of its physical expanse.

The important part of Wheeler's formulation was that there had to be a shift of research interest in the new India from the north-west to the Gangetic plain on the one hand and the Peninsular India on the other. This particular issue of *Ancient India* itself seems to have pointed the way : an article on megaliths by Gordon Childe (1948) trying to configure the south Indian megaliths in the context of the general Euro-Asian distribution of megaliths, a detailed report on his excavations at Brahmagiri and Chandravalli in the modern Karnataka by Wheeler himself (1948b), and an analysis of the excavated terracottas from the Gangetic early historic site of Ahichchhatra by V.S. Agrawala (1948).

The editorial notes of *Ancient India 5* were written by Niranjan Prasad Chakravarti who succeeded Wheeler as the Director General on 30 April 1948. With a Ph.D. in Indian epigraphy from Cambridge University, he became the chief epigraphist of the Survey before becoming Joint Director General during Wheeler's Director Generalship. He highlighted the issue of archaeology in the Indian princely states in the changed circumstances. There were about 550 such states in British India, comprising 48 per cent of the total area of the subcontinent and 27 per cent of its population. Although the issue of running the archaeological affairs of these states was not firmly decided when Chakravarti wrote these notes, it was clear by that time that the Archaeological Survey of India would have to take control of their archaeology, implying in turn a considerable expansion of its activities including conservation. The second point mentioned by him is also important. The draft of the new Constitution of India kept archaeology as a central subject but mentioned only the ancient and historical monuments, sites and remains of 'national importance' which were declared as such by 'Parliament by law'. In his opinion it was only proper that 'thousands of monuments all over India which are only of regional importance' should be under the 'care and patronage of the Provincial Governments'. He drew attention to the interest already displayed by some of these governments in 'starting their own archaeological departments'. Whereas he felt that this 'growing interest in archaeology' was to be welcomed and that 'very valuable work in ground-survey and in listing of sites and monuments' could be done by the provincial officials, he was against 'any large amount of decentralisation' in the field of archaeological excavations and explorations. Planning, according to him, should be done on an all-India basis, and thus 'be the responsibility of the Central organisation', although the States would have their due share in this process.

> Local patriotism is not to be discounted but must be subordinated to the interests of science, and the paltry resources that are available for archaeological pursuits cannot be frittered away on diverse aims and for uncertain results. — Chakravarti 1949 : 3

It is apparent that according to Chakravarti the 'interests of science' would be best served by allowing the Survey total control of explorations and excavations. Even in the context of the period, it was not a happy or even positive attitude and reflected a mind-set which considered archaeological research in the newly independent India as the basic prerogative of the central government. This was, in fact, in total contrast to Wheeler's interest in making archaeology in India broadbased beyond the confines of a government department, and underlined a determination on the part of the Director General to keep the pre-Independence organisational structure of archaeological research in India intact even after Independence.

In his article on 'Archaeological fieldwork in India : planning ahead' Wheeler more or less repeats his opinions expressed in 1947-48 (Wheeler 1948a), but from the point of view of later developments it is important to draw attention to what he emphasised as 'the absolute necessity for completing the written report of one season's work before resuming field-work in the next'.

> If need be, a whole season's digging must be postponed to enable this essential task to be accomplished. . . . Complete and punctual publication must be the invariable rule; no excuse whatsoever can condone deferment. — Wheeler 1949 : 11

Two other articles of this issue of *Ancient India* are important in heralding two later developments. V.D. Krishnaswami, the first official prehistorian of the Survey, had already published a broad assessment of Indian prehistory in *Ancient India 3* (Krishnaswami

1947). In his article on the 'megalithic types of south India' (Krishnaswami 1949) in *Ancient India 5* he undertook an excellent classificatory exercise which remains basically valid even today. In a sense, this is related to Gordon Childe's earlier article on 'megaliths' as an archaeological problem. On the other hand, Krishnaswami draws attention to the prevalence of a living megalithic custom in north-east India, contrasting it with the archaeological remains of megaliths in the south. In contrast to the north-eastern memorials which are not directly associated with graves and — according to the anthropological opinions he cited — 'moved with the great Austronesian migration in the movement of the Austro-Asiatic races westwards into Peninsular India' (Krishnaswami 1949 : 42), the south Indian megaliths were invariably burials associated with the Iron Age and suggested links with 'the Mediterranean megalithic culture in their architectural features and "port-holes", etc.'. His theoretical conclusion was that 'several megalithic waves must have reached India both from the West and the East'. (Krishnaswami 1949 : 36)

B.B. Lal's report on the Sisupalgarh excavations in Orissa (B.B. Lal 1949) was also indicative of the shape of things to come. The excavation was undertaken not to throw light on one of the most important early historic cities of the region but to trace the northward extension of the rouletted ware which was found at Arikamedu and considered as an indicator of Roman trade. This ware was in fact found in the excavations at this site, but as far as the details of its basic features are concerned, the entire emphasis lay on taking a section across the defences, relating it to a section in the habitational area and clearing a gateway. It was an excellent exercise in digging up a town site on the model of what Wheeler articulately expressed later in *Archaeology from the Earth*. (Wheeler 1954) Considering that the whole thing was done between April and June 1948 and the report published in 1949, it was an admirable technical piece of archaeology. The problem lay with the mind-set which assumed that the need for further work at the site was over.

Ancient India 6 was also edited by Chakravarti as the Director General. By this time the sharing of powers between the Centre and the States in archaeological affairs was accepted in the Constitution, and their 'respective spheres of jurisdiction' were defined as follows :

1. Union : 'Ancient and historical monuments and records and archaeological sites and remains, declared by Parliament by Law to be of national importance'; and

2. State : 'Ancient and historical monuments and records other than those declared by Parliament to be of national importance'.

3. Besides these two categories, both the Union and the States will have concurrent jurisdiction over 'archaeological sites and remains other than those declared by Parliament by law to be of national importance'. — Chakravarti 1950 : 1

As far as the responsibility of conservation of monuments was concerned, the division of responsibility between the Centre and the States was clear, but it is apparent that in the matter of 'archaeological sites and remains' the responsibility was concurrent. As the Director General of the Survey saw it,

> The implications are significant, for it means that the Centre will not be absolved of all responsibility in this direction and can assert itself whenever it feels that a State, either through negligence or by following wrong methods and policies of exploration, is acting detrimentally to the sites and remains in its jurisdiction. — Chakravarti 1950 : 1

A fear of conflict of interest between the Centre and the States was not far from Chakravarti's mind, although as the Director General he offers the states all co-operation.

> For good or evil, the monopoly of the Centre has been broken, though it remains to be seen how the States take to their new task. Many States may not be prepared to shoulder the additional responsibility immediately. To them we assure all help : consistent with our limited resources, we shall be glad to tend to the monuments which are now legitimately their charge; we shall, again consistent with the limited facilities available, train their archaeologists, so that they can eventually take charge of their responsibility with confidence and credit. To such States as can undertake their antiquarian functions forthwith we offer all co-operation. Given goodwill and mutual understanding, no occasion for conflict of interest between the Union and the States need arise, and it should not be at all difficult to formulate principles and policies and to start healthy conventions which will stimulate archaeological activities throughout India on sound lines.
>
> — Chakravarti 1950 : 3

One is not sure if the Director General liked the very thought of the idea of having the powers of the Survey curtailed in any way; he is trying to make a point for the primacy of the Survey in all disputed matters. But it is also interesting that he is willing to offer all possible help to the states and thinking of formulating principles and policies which will help the cause of archaeology in the country.

There are two historically significant articles on prehistory in *Ancient India 6*. The article by K.R.U. Todd (1949) basically studied the microlithic industry in and around Bombay, but made the important point that it was 'subsequent to the blade and burin horizon found at Khandivli, located on the surface of the upper gravel'. The article by

Colonel D.H. Gordon also dealt with the microlithic industries but on a wider scale, reaching the very interesting conclusion that

> a greater part of Peninsular India was in a microlith-using mesolithic or neolithic stage of culture from relatively remote times and continued in this manner of living while chalcolithic urban or semi-urban cultures spread over the great river-valleys of the north.
>
> — Gordon 1950 : 85

This paper is full of various other insights and one would draw attention to his observations on the possibility of an early beginning of a stone axe culture at Burzahom/Burzhama in Kashmir.

In the matter of application of scientific techniques to archaeological remains, S.S. Ghosh's identification of the wood of an inscribed wooden pillar of the second century AD from Kirari near Bilaspur in Chhattisgarh as *Madhuca latifolia* is among the first publications of this type in Independent India (S.S. Ghosh 1950). Similarly, T.R. Gairola's chemical analysis of the composition of the red paint, lime-washes and plasters on the Konarka temple and some temples of Bhuvaneshwar are also among the first publications of this kind. Gairola's publication (Gairola 1950) further indicates that the tradition of archaeological chemistry built up by Mohammad Sana Ullah in the Survey in the pre-Independence years did not die out with Partition.

Ancient India 7 (1951) was edited by Madho Sarup Vats who had taken over as the Director General on 30 June 1950 from Chakravarti, who continued for further two years as the 'Adviser' to the Department. In his 'notes', Vats harps on the extension of the Survey's responsibility in relation to the states and the consequent realigning of the boundaries of the Survey's 'Circles'. The latter, he added, was 'calculated to bring about a clearer visualisation of the local archaeological problems and better planning on a regional basis over the whole of India'. (Vats 1951 : 1) He also pointed out the need to maintain a common standard of conservation all over India. Explorations too were necessary, not merely for sites and underground remains but also for epigraphical wealth. The loss of Mohenjo-Daro and Harappa could be made up by undertaking explorations in Rajasthan and Cutch, as geographically an extension of the Indus civilization might naturally be expected in these areas. As we shall see later, by 1952 A. Ghosh's survey in the Sarasvati-Drishadvati valley in Bikaner had already yielded Indus sites, and further east, Vats speaks of an 'eastern variety of that culture' and also draws attention to the isolation of Painted Grey Ware around Delhi. Further, he reports the discovery of a 'late pre-historic culture' involving black-on-red painted pottery and microliths in western

India. The rapidity with which the broad picture of a proto-historic India began to emerge is striking.

Meanwhile, B.B. Lal (1951) published an analysis of the Gangetic valley 'copper hoard' implements, suggesting an association of an 'ill-fired, thick, ochre-washed pottery' with the specimens from the upper Ganga plain. The article was thoroughly documented and illustrated and thus highlighted the significance of the find of such implements in the context of the Ganga valley. He at least put clear emphasis on their Ganga valley identity, 'with a possible southward extension across the Vindhya and Kaimur ranges'. In the eastern section of this valley A. Ghosh (1951) outlined the possibility of a horizon before the beginning of early history at Rajgir. Prehistory was moving forward too, and in *Ancient India 7* the article on the lithic tool-industries of the Singrauli basin in the old Mirzapur district sets out the form of the contemporary and subsequent pre-historic studies in India : a detailed regional investigation with emphasis on sites, stratigraphy and typology. The distinction offered by Hallam Movius between the pebble-based 'chopper-chopping industry' and the biface industry used to be quite seriously taken by the investigators of the period, and one finds V.D. Krishnaswami and K.V. Soundara Rajan (1951) trying to argue the case of Singrauli as a 'meeting place of the (chopper-chopping) Sohan' and (biface) 'Madras' industries. The archaeological science scene also was encouraging, K.A. Chowdhury and S.S. Ghosh's analysis of the plant remains from Wheeler's 1946 excavations at Harappa (Chowdhury and Ghosh 1951), and Gairola's mathematical analysis of the weights of the punch-marked coins from the Barwani hoard of such coins from central India (Gairola 1951) being two good examples of this kind from this period. It is the Gairola article which for the first time pointed out that the average weight of the punch-marked coins (3.43 gm in the case of the Barwani hoard) was equivalent to 'four times the smallest weight-unit (.86×4 = 3.44 gm) of the Harappa culture'.

M.S. Vats continued to be the editor of *Ancient India 8* (1952). He began by pointing out that the Survey in the post-Partition phase actually increased its control of territory in terms of square miles, which happened because of the addition of the various princely states which now became parts of 'India' : '11.2 lakh square miles instead of 7.3 lakh square miles in undivided India'. Twenty of the 150 sites plotted in the Sarasvati-Drishadvati valley were declared to be of

> characteristic Harappa culture, the existence of which finally establishes the eastward spread into the Indian Union of that culture which had been surmised previously by the

> discoveries made by me at Kotla Nihang Khan near Rupar in Ambala District of Panjab.
> — Vats 1952 : 1-2

The discovery of the Painted Grey Ware at Hastinapur and other sites was 'helpful in narrowing down the interval of time between the early historic and the Harappa cultures which still remains a Dark Period of Indian history'.

Vats concludes his 'notes' in this issue with a positive and inspiring attitude :

> Every effort is being made to bridge, or at any rate narrow down, the gulf of time in the Dark Period referred to, and to this end operations are being extended over northern India and the peninsula to corroborate or modify the sequence of the early cultures of India.
> — Vats 1952 : 2

Soundara Rajan (1952) continued his Stone Age studies, this time in the context of Giddalur in the Kurnool district of Andhra. The implementiferous localities were well described along with their sequence and tool typology. The work in the Giddalur area was a part of the Archaeological Survey of India work with F.E. Zeuner in 1948-49, which was led by Zeuner and Krishnaswami. B.K. Thapar's work at the megalithic urn-burial site of Porkalam (B.K. Thapar 1952) in the Cochin area of Kerala followed the megalithic excavation methods perfected by Wheeler at Brahmagiri. K.A. Chowdhury and S.S. Ghosh (1952) identified 6 tree specimens in the wood remains from Sisupalgarh, arguing that there had been no change in the climate of this locality for the last 2000 years because all these trees still grew there. Dr. B.B. Lal, the Archaeological Chemist of the Survey of the period, published a detailed scientific analysis of some excavated glass specimens from Ahichchhatra, Nalanda, Arikamedu and other sites (Dr. B.B. Lal 1952) and M.G. Dikshit (1952) undertook a typological analysis of the early historic beads from Ahichchhatra.

In 1952 India completed 5 years of Independence, and we have been following so long only the course of events reflected in the most important publication of Indian archaeology of the period, *Ancient India*. At this point we may turn back and consider the evidence furnished by other relevant publications.

Monographs on Prehistory

There were at least three monographs on prehistory between 1947 and 1952, even if one ignores V.D. Krishnaswami's attempt at synthesis in 1947 (Krishnaswami 1947) : N.K. Bose and D. Sen's *Excavations in Mayurbhanj* (1948) Zeuner's *Stone Age and Pleistocene*

Chronology in Gujarat (1950a), and H.D. Sankalia's *The Godavari Palaeolithic Industry* (1952). It was also in 1948 that B. Subbarao published his *Stone Age Cultures of Bellary* (1948). Prehistory of Karnataka came to be discussed by Sankalia, Subbarao and R.V. Joshi (1950). Sankalia's work on Gujarat prehistory dates from before Independence, but the microlithic industry of Langhnaj, which was excavated by him in north Gujarat, was discussed by Zeuner in 1952. What is also interesting is that the study of prehistory now spread outside the Survey, with Bose and Sen, Sankalia, Subbarao and Zeuner coming from Calcutta, Poona, Baroda and London universities, respectively.

Developments in Protohistory

More important strides were taken in protohistory. M.G. Dikshit excavated in 1947 the site of Rangpur in the Kathiawar peninsula of Gujarat, which is now considered as an indisputably Harappan site. By 1952 A. Ghosh surveyed the remains of about 25 sites along the dry bed of the Ghaggar in Bikaner. Another major break-through took place in central India and Maharashtra (Sankalia 1951) where a clear chalcolithic horizon came to be identified. Lal excavated Rajpur Parsu in 1949 identifying an ochre-washed ware which he also found at the lowest level of Hastinapur in 1950-52. Before he undertook excavations at Hastinapur he published a paper in 1950, carefully identifying the significance of the Painted Grey Ware which he had found by that time in the surface explorations (Lal 1950). This is a paper which has not lost its analytical appeal after all these years. No clear progress had been made in eastern India, but E.C. Worman (1949) argued in detail about the southeast Asiatic affinity of certain east Indian neolithic tool-types. In south India Wheeler's work at Brahmagiri was carried forward by Subbarao (1948) at Sanganakallu in Bellary. In the field of early historic archaeology no positive progress seems to have been made during this period.

Comments

What is significant in retrospect is the rapidity with which the archaeology of the newly independent India took strides, especially in the fields of prehistory and protohistory, during the first five years of its existence. One would, in fact, go to the extent of arguing that in the domains of prehistory and protohistory this period set the frame of future researches in India. The theoretical framework remained simple; it was all a question of determining the 'authorship' of particular cultures and the multiple waves of people from different directions to explain these authorships. In his explanation of the authors of the 'copper hoards' of the upper Ganga plain, Lal attributed them to the racial category of 'Proto-Australoids'. It was not certainly an archaeological explanation but made the whole thing understandable in terms of the postulated racial framework of the country. Krishnaswami was happy with the idea of various racial and linguistic migrations to south India to explain his megalithic burial types. What stands out is the number of discoveries in certain important directions and attempts to understand them in terms of the prevalent historical, racial and linguistic frameworks.

ANCIENT INDIA 9 (1953)

Ancient India 9, published in 1953 under the editorship of A. Ghosh, the Director General who came into office on March 2 of that year, was technically supposed to mark the fifty years of the Archaeological Survey of India since John Marshall became the Director General in 1902. In a sense that was an apt date to count the fifty years from, because it was only in 1902 (21 February) that the Survey was put on a properly organised and comprehensive footing. It was also since that date that the Survey has had a continuous existence. What is also important about this volume is the natural way in which the Survey lays claim to its institutional heritage. The Archaeological Survey of India of the new truncated India was the natural successor of the old Survey which in its origins goes back to 1861 when the Government of India entrusted Alexander Cunningham with the responsibility of conducting archaeological surveys. The new government of India did not downgrade the Survey into an ordinary government 'department' as Pakistan did.

A. Ghosh's editorial notes were both dignified and inspiring.

> In the following pages we have only indicated where we stand today after a striving for five decades through circumstances seldom affluent and at times definitely critical. It is not out of a feeling of self-approbation and complacence that we offer this number to our readers; on the contrary we desire our Jubilee to be the occasion for an assessment of our worth by the competent. To ourselves, this is a moment for self-criticism and resolve.
>
> — Ghosh 1953 : 1

As Ghosh saw it, the Survey was the custodian of 'the national heritage of the land', and in 1953 it was time not merely for self-assessment but also for looking into the future.

> Let us also look forward to an age of increased opportunities, of greater activities and of still harder toil, always with the consciousness that what little has been achieved is only a fraction of what remains to be achieved. — Ghosh 1953 : 1

Although Ghosh declares the past and the present role of the Survey as the custodian of the national heritage of the land, he uses this occasion to acknowledge thankfully the contribution made by people from outside the organisation. He mentions the contribution made by the officers of the Geological Survey of India to the study of Indian prehistory, the sincere and successful efforts of the various princely states to preserve the monuments in their care, the research undertaken by the scholars of Indian epigraphy to illuminate many dark corners of Indian history, and the organisation and development of different museums which, although greatly supported by the Survey in various ways, were not always under its direct jurisdiction. According to him, the activities of the Survey have 'sometimes inspired and have been usefully supplemented by the efforts of sister-organisations and individuals' and he thought that on the occasion of the jubilee of the continued existence of the Survey for the fifty years, 'it would be uncharitable to forget them and not to give them their due recognition'.

The role of the Indian universities in archaeological fieldwork was always extremely limited, if not virtually absent, in the pre-Independence days. In the early 1920s Calcutta University under D.R. Bhandarkar who, after a career as a senior officer of the Survey, was then the Charmaichael Professor of ancient Indian history at the university, did only one year's excavations at Paharpur but failed to continue it. The Asutosh Museum of Fine Arts of this university undertook excavations at the early historic site of Bangarh in Bengal (modern West Bengal) in 1937-41 and 1951. In the 1940s N.K. Bose and D. Sen of its Department of Anthropology initiated pre-historic research in the Mayurbhanj area of Orissa in the 1940s,which culminated in a monograph in 1948. In the 1940s the Deccan College of Poona University under H.D. Sankalia began pre-historic research in Gujarat and Maharashtra and he was soon followed by Baroda University under B. Subbarao who at that stage worked in the Bellary area of Karnataka. However, both Sankalia and Subbarao were also interested in historical archaeology with Sankalia excavating Brahmapuri with M.G. Dikshit in 1945-46 and Subbarao excavating Baroda in the early 1950s. In 1948 Allahabad University under G.R. Sharma began excavating the famous early historic site of Kausambi. In a sense, there was a limited but increased amount of participation by the Indian universities in archaeological research after 1947. Ghosh did not ignore the point. He, in fact, wrote that it was a 'happy augury' that the relationship between the Survey and the universities had been 'one of perfect understanding and co-operation'.

In his editorial of 1953 the newly appointed Director General made two further points. As a general policy the primary objective was to 'complete the general outline of the archaeological picture of India' before trying to fill in, 'except incidentally', the regional details. Secondly, among the associated cultural problems he categorically mentioned the migrations of the Austro-Asiatics and Aryans to India. According to him, it was 'vital to Indian archaeology to learn whether the material remains in India pertaining to the period that saw the immigration of the Aryans have analogues in the countries that they are believed to have traversed before they reached and settled in India'.

This concern to find archaeological correlates for the generally prevailing assumptions of India's language history strongly coloured V.D. Krishnaswami's and B.B. Lal's treatment of the progress of pre-historic and proto-historic researches in this volume. They were also joined by K.R. Srinivasan and N.R. Banerjee in their survey of south Indian megaliths. According to Krishnaswami (1953 : 78) the association of shouldered hoe with Austro-Asiatic languages was inescapable.

> A characteristic feature of this language-group is the erection of the megalithic menhirs. The close parallels between megalithic rituals of the Bastar Maria Gonds, Austro-Asiatic hill-tribes of Orissa and Chhota Nagpur and the Nagas and Khasis of Assam provide evidence for a generic connection between all these manifestations of megalithic culture concentrated in the tribes of well-developed agricultural civilizations characterized by the use of hoes.
> — Krishnaswami 1953 : 78-79

Lal was more tentative in his approach, but because the issue touched the Aryans, his hypothesis regarding the Painted Grey Ware became more well known. His report on Hastinapur was not published till 1955 but the work was done in 1950-52, and on that basis he wrote the following which he himself considered 'highly provisional'.

> . . . many of the sites containing the Painted Grey Ware, e.g. Hastinapura, Ahichchhatra, Kampil, Barnawa, Panipat, Baghpat, Tilpat, Mathura, etc. are associated with the story of the *Mahabharata*. The date of the *Mahabharata* war has been suggested by Pargiter, on probable grounds, to be *circa* 950 B.C., which falls well within the Painted Grey Ware period at Hastinapura. It would seem, therefore, that the Ware was associated with the early settlers at these sites, viz. The Pauravas, Panchalas, etc., who formed the Aryan stock in India.
> — B.B. Lal 1953 : 97

To be fair to Lal, he was aware that trying to interpret archaeological data 'in terms of ethnical movements and literary traditions' was the 'greatest risk' one could ever run.

In 1950 and 1952 two seasons of megalithic excavations were undertaken by Banerjee at Sanur in Chingleput District near Madras. In 1953 he combined with K.R. Srinivasan to offer a survey of the south Indian megalithic types and all that has been inferred about them. They discussed the possibility of the builders of the south Indian megaliths being speakers of the Dravidian language family or belonging to the 'Dravidian race', and they hoped that with the further studies of the megalithic skeletal material 'we shall perhaps get nearer to the solution of the problem'. (Srinivasan and Banerjee 1953: 114)

Thus, although there was a clear resolve to fill up the outline of the general archaeological picture of India at the dawn of Independence, there was also an equal resolve to interpret the archaeological data in terms of all the ethnic and linguistic postulates of India's history.

The chapter on the exploration of historical sites by Y.D. Sharma (1953) had not really much new to offer except notes on Sisupalgarh in Orissa, Brahmapuri in Maharashtra (Sankalia and Dikshit 1952), Tripuri, Amreli, Bahal, Maheshwar and Nasik. At the last five places the occupation began with a chalcolithic horizon and thus clearly established the chalcolithic antecedence of the early historic occupation in these areas of Madhya Pradesh, Gujarat and Maharashtra.

On the whole, *Ancient India 9* is still an indispensable volume, containing as it does a detailed stock-taking of what had so far been achieved in Indian archaeology. This stock-taking covered not merely the results of archaeological excavations and explorations in Indian prehistory, protohistory and early history but also epigraphical research on both ancient and mediaeval India, the development of museums, the structure and history of conservation work, the notable milestones in the pursuit of archaeological chemistry and scientific studies, and finally, two substantive articles on the history of the Archaeological Survey of India, both of which were based on the archival sources. In retrospect, the comments by B.B. Lal, the Archaeological Chemist, on the work done by the Archaeological Survey of India in this field are interesting :

> . . . the Archaeological Survey of India did not lag behind in the application of the methods of archaeological chemistry to archaeological problems, and intensive analytical work done during the last thirtysix years has produced important and interesting results.
>
> — B.B. Lal 1953 : 200

What is also interesting is the contrast between *Ancient India 9* and an earlier publication of this kind, *Archaeology in India* which was published in 1950 and carries a preface by the then Minister of Education, Humayun Kabir (1950). It was intended, as Kabir wrote, 'to cover in a short compass the various aspects of Indian archaeology' for the use of general readers in India and abroad. The topics which were dealt with included 'the story of Indian archaeology' (N.P. Chakravarti), pre-historic and proto-historic explorations (B.B. Lal), historical sites (A. Ghosh), *stupa* and temple architecture (K. Deva), Islamic architecture (M.A. Husain), sculpture and painting (V.S. Agrawala), conservation (M.S. Vats and A. Ghosh), chemical preservation (B.B. Lal), Sanskrit and Prakrit inscriptions (B.Ch. Chhabra and N.L. Rao), Muslim inscriptions (M.A. Husain), and 'greater India' (V.S. Agrawala). The tone of the volume is a little subdued, which is hardly surprising because of the fact that it was put together within two/three years of Partition, but the scholarship of the articles involved still endows it with some usefulness. Chakravarti took care to emphasise that the civilization of the subcontinent, despite Partition, had been one throughout the ages and the study of the history and archaeology of India and Pakistan were interdependent. V.S. Agrawala compared India's position on the cultural map of Asia to a wheel whose spokes radiated in all directions : Iran and Afghanistan on the west, Central Asia, Tibet and China on the north, Burma/Myanmar, Thailand, Indo-China and Indonesia on the east, and Sri Lanka on the south. This theme of 'greater India' subsequently dropped out of the Archaeological Survey of India publications, but in 1949-50 it was quite natural to try to find one's place in Asia.

THE PERIOD FROM 1954 to 1965

It is essentially an arbritary segment of time, but a number of major developments may be said to have taken place during this period. First, the annual review of archaeological research in India, *Indian Archaeology — a Review*, began to be published from the 1953-54 season onwards. Pending full-length reports, this is the most important annual archaeological publication of the country. Secondly, this was the period in which the essential outline of Indian prehistory and protohistory in all its geographical areas emerged in a reasonably coherent fashion. In 1962 H.D. Sankalia's *Prehistory and Protohistory in India and Pakistan* (Sankalia 1962) was the first clear statement in this regard. It was based on a number of detailed reports on some major central Indian, Deccanese and south Indian sites. He himself played a lead role in the publication of these reports, although the tradition of publishing reports in *Ancient India* continued. Thirdly, there were certain thematic studies of the newly emerging archaeological data during this period, the early phase of which was dominated by the publication of Bendapudi Subbarao's *The Personality of India* (1956, 1st edn.-1958, 2nd edn.). Towards the end of this period the major studies were *The Neolithic Cattlekeepers of the Deccan, a Study of the Deccanese Ashmounds* by Frank Raymond Allchin (1963) and *The Iron Age in India* by N.R. Banerjee (1965). Fourthly, this was the period when archaeology as a distinct subject was inducted into a few universities with the support of the University Grants Commission. Along with this one must consider the fact that by this time there was a large-scale establishment of Directorates/Departments of Archaeology at the level of the State or provincial governments.

We shall discuss each of these strands of development separately here but to begin with, it might be useful to continue to highlight the significance of the successive volumes of *Ancient India*.

Ancient India 10-11 to 18-19

Ancient India 10-11 (1954 and 1955) was largely devoted to the report on the Hastinapur excavations by Lal (1954-55). This work, as A. Ghosh (1954-55) pointed out in his editorial notes, was related to the long-aired concern with 'the Dark Age' between the end of the Harappans and the beginning of the historical period. This report has been justly famous in Indian archaeology for a number of reasons. First, this showed the complete profile of occupation in this part of the upper Doab between the Ochre-Coloured Pottery (OCP) level and the late mediaeval period, with some breaks in occupation. The OCP level was linked to the pottery found by Lal himself at sites like Rajpur Parsu and brought into the range of acceptability the hypothesis that this level was associated with the Copper Hoards from the Doab. This in itself was a major step forward. Secondly, the find of both punch-marked and cast copper coins in the early phase of the Northern Black Polished Ware (NBPW) at the site threw light on an intriguing problem of ancient Indian history. Similarly, the long stratigraphic profile obtained at Hastinapur was a firm indicator of the chronological position of different types of Gangetic valley antiquities. Thirdly, the report was accompanied by an analysis of its bone and plant remains. The bone study was done by Bhola Nath, Vertebrate Zoologist of the Department of Anthropology, Government of India. Bones of horse were identified in the Painted Grey Ware (PGW) level, along with the bones of domestic humped cattle, Indian domestic buffalo, domestic sheep and domestic pig. A large number of bones belonged to younger animals and bore definite cut marks by sharp instruments, suggesting that their meat was eaten. The plant remains were studied by K.A. Chowdhury and S.S. Ghosh of the Forest Research Institute, Dehradun, and the most important aspect was perhaps the identification of domesticated rice in the PGW level. Rice husks were found in the mud plaster and as the housing material wild cane occurred extensively in this level. What is significant is that the economic picture of proto-historic inner India began to fall in place through studies like these. Besides, copper and glass from the PGW level were analysed. Fourthly, the Hastinapur report was accompanied by detailed lists of the explored PGW and NBPW sites, giving these two cultural levels a definitive focus in the archaeology of the country. The Hastinapur excavation itself was a quest to establish the regional vertical profile. The job was thus limited in scope but it was well done, and the standard of the report was in no way inferior to the reports which had hitherto been published in *Ancient India*.

Eventually, however, only one of its periods, i.e., the PGW level, monopolised the limelight. That happened because of its suggested association with the Aryans in general and the *Mahabharata* in particular. The way this hypothesis was put forward both by the Director General in his editorial notes and by the excavator in his report ensured that it became one of the most commonly cited hypothesis in the subsequent period. To be fair to Ghosh, Lal and other protagonists of this view, it was not the first time that the Aryan theory was being brandished in Indian archaeology; equally weak (and perhaps irrelevant) assumptions of this kind had already been made regarding the Cemetery H Pottery of Harappa, miscellaneous copper objects of the Indo-Iranian borderlands and the Copper Hoards of the Ganga valley.

Ghosh's chain of reasoning was the following : the PGW was not something which was connected with any other known archaeological culture of India, and thus it was reasonable to suppose that 'its authors did not spring out of the Indian soil'. On the other hand, the distribution of this pottery was 'co-terminous with the land Brahmavarta and Brahmarshi-desa, held holy in the Aryan literature and watered by those sacred rivers the virtues of which the Aryans were eloquent about'. The date of the pottery around *c.* 1100 BC was no less significant. If the traditional date of the entry of the Aryans to India at *c.* 1500 BC was accepted, then this would be the tentative date by which the people moving from the north-west would arrive at the head of the Ganga-Yamuna plain. Apart from the fact that the distribution of the pottery was in the holiest area of early Hinduism, there was absolutely nothing acceptable in Ghosh's chain of argument. An M.A. in Sanskrit from Allahabad University, he was certainly familiar with some authentic books on the history of Sanskrit literature, and that itself should have told him that this date of 1500 BC as the date of the Aryan migration to India was nothing more than a supposition. Besides, even in the context of the 1950s it was hasty to assume that any archaeological horizon which was not previously discovered meant that 'its authors did not spring out of the Indian soil'.

The excavator himself, another M.A. in Sanskrit from Allahabad University, went to great lengths to put forward the *Mahabharata* or Pauranic correlates of the PGW. We have already taken note of his view regarding its Aryan affiliation; as far as the *Mahabharata* is concerned, Hastinapur no doubt was the Kuru capital, and in the flood-scar of the PGW deposit at the site towards the end of the level he found a corroboration of the Pauranic legend that the Kuru capital was shifted to Kausambi after Hastinapur.

It was indeed unfortunate that the first major report of the excavations of a Doab site in Independent India decided to make the Aryans its central issue. In the same issue of *Ancient India* D.H. Gordon (1954-55) refused to take the PGW earlier than 650 BC but Gordon himself was as much a believer in the Aryan theory as others were; according to him, however, their homeground had first to be identified in the north-west. This was also the volume of *Ancient India* which saw the publication of one of the studies undertaken by Sunder Lal Hora (1954-55), the Director of the Zoological Survey of India, on the art of angling and pisciculture in ancient India.

The focus of *Ancient India 12* (1956) was on prehistory and the south Indian megalithic studies. The article by F.E. Zeuner and Bridget Allchin (1956) on the microlithic industry of the *teris* or coastal dunes of the southern section of the Tamil Nadu coast examined the chronology of these microliths in terms of old shore lines. The exploration for megaliths in the Chingleput district of the same state led N.R. Banerjee (1956) to speculate about their 'racial basis', and that was something in which he was also joined by his Director General, A. Ghosh (1956). Ghosh admitted that 'race, language and archaeological culture need not necessarily go hand in hand' but still, 'a discovery in any one of these fields should be examined for its possible implications on other fields'. H.D. Sankalia's article 'Animal Fossils and Palaeolithic Industries from the Pravara basin at Nevasa, District Ahmadnagar' (Sankalia 1956) laid down for many years the ideal and basic form of palaeolithic studies in India. His section along the left bank of the Pravara near 'Hathi' or elephant well with a number of gravels defined the implementiferous gravel deposits along the Peninsular Indian rivers. Prehistory of the Kangra valley was the theme of Lal's paper here (1956), faithfully copying the terrace-based mode of study worked out in the Soan valley of the former Panjab by H. de Terra and T.T. Paterson. Y.D. Sharma (1956) examined the rock-cut 'megalithic' caves of Cochin in Kerala. Incidentally, Y.D. Sharma, a Ph.D. in Sanskrit from Oxford, did not get involved too much in the murky water of 'megalithic orgin' and remained satisfied only by referring to the earlier theories. B.B. Lal's scientific analytical study of about 18 bronze images from Nalanda in eastern

India was a major study of its kind (1956). In the same vein, T.R. Gairola's technical study of the Bidri Ware (1956) was important.

Apart from Gairola's (1957) technical note on the preservation of a textile and a miniature painting, *Ancient India 13* was devoted exclusively to B.K. Thapar's report on Maski, a proto-historic to early historic site in the Raichur Doab of Karnataka, which he excavated in 1954 (Thapar 1957). Its basic significance, as perceived both by the excavator and his Director General, was that it extended the Brahmagiri succession of neolithic-chalcolithic, megalithic and early historical further north, with a view to linking it up with the chalcolithic cultures which by that time had begun to emerge in Maharashtra and central India.

Ghosh's editorial notes (1957) bear two points, both of which deserve notice. He mentions that for a proper perception of the newly researched archaeological material on chalcolithic sites it was important that the different excavators got an opportunity to study and analyse the material excavated by others. The issue, according to him, had become 'all the more imperative today than ever before' because the monopoly of the Survey in excavations was 'happily, a thing of the past', with 'many an expert hand' turning the soil to produce rich archaeological harvests. The following statement by Ghosh is historically significant, especially from the point of view what has been happening in the recent past.

> A direct result of the disappearance of the monopoly is the necessity for co-ordination among field-workers, and it is gratifying that this is realized by all. Exhibitions of excavated material and conferences among workers, which have now become a regular annual feature in the country, are helping in the acquaintance of one another's activities and are providing a forum for the discussion of archaeological problems and for stock-taking.
>
> — Ghosh 1957 : 1-2

As far as one make out, Ghosh is here referring to the system of holding the annual meetings of the Central Advisory Board of Archaeology under the auspicies of either the Survey or the Ministry of Education of which the Survey was a part. The documents related to these meetings are not available in published forms, and all that one informally knows is that this Board (CABA) comprised members from the Survey, the universities, a few other 'learned institutions' and the State-level government archaeology departments. It was for the first time that its meetings were referred to as 'regular features' by the Director General in an official publication of the Archaeological Survey. It is somewhat incredible that the Director General did not consider it worthwhile to make the structure of this important national Board and its activities more public than a general, almost casual, reference.

Secondly, while admitting that the building up of the vertical profiles of archaeological culture-succession in different parts of India would take a lot more time, Ghosh wrote, apparently for the first time after Independence, of the necessity of undertaking horizontal excavations at selected sites.

> What the objectives of horizontal excavations for the next few years should be is abundantly clear : to lay bare the relics of the newly-discovered cultures comprehensively, so that they can be viewed as the components of a coherent unit, as the trees constituting the wood, which is at present not seen. Without horizontal excavation, the early man will never reveal himself to us in his fulness, and our knowledge of the culture to which he belonged will remain circumscribed by the limitations imposed by the dimensions of the trench.
>
> — Ghosh 1957 : 3

Another point worth noting in this 'editorial' by Ghosh is the issue of collaborating with the Deccan College in the exploration for palaeoliths in the upper Beas valley and the need for geochronological studies, for which, he wrote, that the Chemical Branch of the Survey was being equipped.

The Maski report itself followed the model of reports published in *Ancient India* and offered comprehensive documentation followed by reports on animal — remains by Bhola Nath, pollen-analysis by Vishnu-Mittre of the Birbal Sahni Institute of Palaeobotany, Lucknow, and plant — remains by K.A. Chowdhury and S.S. Ghosh. B.K. Thapar's own discussion on the chronology of the site and the cultures involved was confused.

Ancient India 14 (1958) contained two major articles on prehistory, one by B.B. Lal on his excavations at the microlithic site of Birbhanpur (West Bengal) in 1954 and 1957 (1958) and the other by K.V. Soundara Rajan (1958) on his study of the pre-historic sequence in the Nagarjunakonda valley in Andhra in 1956. Both the articles were enriched by detailed local observations and in the case of the Birbhanpur one, accompanied by the mechanical, microsopic and chemical analyses of the soil samples of the site by B.B. Lal. who put the microlith-using culture of this site at the beginning of the Holocene. Another contribution by Lal (1958) to this issue was a scientific examination of some glass specimens from Arikamedu.

A. Ghosh's editorial notes (1958) in *Ancient India 14* discuss the provisions of the Ancient Monuments and Archaeological Sites and Remains Act of 1958. This was modelled on the Act of 1904 which underwent some modifications in the wake of the Government of India Act of 1935. Whereas the 1904 Act assigned the responsibility of the protection of monuments, etc., to the provincial governments, these functions were assigned in 1935 to the central government as Archaeology was then made a central or federal subject. There was a major amendment in 1932, allowing the sanction of license to 'outside agencies' for excavations of protected sites (this made possible E.J. Mackay's excavations at Chanhudaro) and the control of mining, quarrying, blasting and other related mining operations at or near protected monuments. The 1958 act too was based on the model of the 1904 Act, but it gave powers to the central government to take steps to include a site in the 'nationally protected' category or remove it from that. Some powers under the act were also transferred from the district administration to the Survey officers. The government was also granted some powers over the owners of monuments if they refused to enter into an agreement with the government. The Act further authorised the Survey to undertake excavations in unprotected areas and made provisions for compensation to the owner of the excavated land both for the damage done to the land and the excavated antiquities, with the provision that the value of the excavated antiquities would not take their historical or antiquity value into consideration. The Act laid down that the state governments could not authorise anybody to excavate an archaeological site anywhere without the approval of the central government or the Survey. Interestingly, the antiquity law, which prescribed that any object more than a hundred years old could not be exported without a license issued by the central government for the purpose, also applied to the 'share of a person who excavates a site of national importance with a license and who intends to take his share out of India'. The principle was that any antiquity considered by the government to be of national importance would be retained in India, and 'that of the rest the excavator will be allowed to have such a portion of the antiquities as is sufficient, in the opinion of the government, to recompense him for the expenditure incurred by him on the excavation'. (Ghosh 1958 : 3) What is clear is that the Act of 1958 clearly made allowance for excavations conducted by foreign archaeologists of nationally protected sites and the repatriation of a share of the excavated antiquities by them.

Ancient India 14 also published a detailed analysis of the Pallava architecture of south India between the latter half of the sixth century and the first half of the tenth century by K.R. Srinivasan (1958), thus reasserting the tradition of architectural studies by the Survey's officers.

The editorial notes by Ghosh (1959) in *Ancient India 15* are specially important because he discusses the first radiocarbon dates in Indian archaeology — those from the University of Pennsylvania (Navdatoli) and the British Museum (Utnur) — and the significance of such dates in fixing up the comparative stratigraphy of the excavated Indian archaeological sites. He also examined how the radiocarbon dates fitted in the known framework of the archaeological cultures, noting with some satisfaction that 'the priority of the Sanganakallu-Pikhlihal-Utnoor culture to the Navdatoli-Jorwe-Nevasa, now established by Carbon-14 dates' was in 'full consonance with archaeological inferences'. This issue contained a detailed report on the excavations of megaliths at Sanur in the Chingleput district in 1950 and 1952 by N.R. Banerjee and K.V. Soundara Rajan (1959). The tradition of the architectural studies was continued by Krishna Deva (1959) in the context of Khajuraho, but perhaps the most important report of this issue was that on the rock-cut caves of Pitalkhora by M.N. Deshpande (1959). The cave was reported earlier but it was for the first time that the significance and the details of such a cave were subjected to a meticulous scholarly exercise with excellent plans and illustrations in Independent India. In the 'technical section' of this issue J.C. Nagpal and O.P. Agrawal (1959) analysed the composition of a stucco head found by Aurel Stein in the ruins of a shrine outside the walls of Kara-Khoto in southern Mongolia.

Ancient India 16 was due to be published in 1960 but got delayed by two years, being eventually published in 1962. The Director General (Ghosh) apologised to its readers for the inconvenience caused to them. It is in this issue of *Ancient India* that one learns for the first time of the introduction of archaeology in the Indian universities on a comparatively wide scale. The Director General is not specific in his discussion but he alludes to the introduction of pre-historical archaeology papers and provisions of field-training in some universities. He also mentions the support of the Indian UGC in this connection.

Ghosh begins his editorial notes of *Ancient India 16* by citing Wheeler who wrote in *Ancient India 1* (1946) that one of the conditions of the progress of archaeological research in India was that archaeology should cease to be a purely governmental activity and be a part of 'the liberal activities of the universities and learned societies of India'. Before he joined the War and later came to India, Wheeler was one of the main persons behind the establishment of the Institute of Archaeology of London University. He was an academic and fully aware of how archaeology could be turned into an academic discipline only in the portals of educational institutions. On the other hand, Ghosh was a

Government of India bureaucrat, and however committed he was to the cause of Indian archaeology, it was unlikely that he could view the subject through the eyes of a teacher and academic. In fact, he seemed to be fairly worried when he wrote the following paragraph.

> Archaeology being essentially a field-science, a love for the field has to be inculcated in its students. The scholarly atmosphere of the universities, admirably suitable as it is for developing an academic outlook, may not necessarily provide the required background for the field-life that a student of archaeology should be prepared to take up subsequently. It would be well if from the very outset the teacher of archaeology takes adequate steps to create the right surroundings for his students. — Ghosh 1962 : 2

To create a powerful alternative to whatever archaeological training was then about to be imparted to the students at the universities, the Survey created in October 1959, under its own control, a training school for potential archaeologists. At the end of a 20-month-period (originally 15 months) the students would be trained essentially in the excavation methods and conservation and get a diploma. The sanctioned number of students was ten. The archaeological bureaucrats of India were not willing to share their power of control with the universities, although that was the time when the idea of a National Institute of Archaeology in India as an autonomous academic body could be mooted and accepted.

There were three major articles in this issue of *Ancient India* : B.B. Lal's study of pottery graffiti (1962), V.D. Krishnaswami's analysis of the neolithic pattern of India (1962) and H.B. Sarkar's article on the excavated Buddhist monuments of Nagarjunakonda (1962). One cannot be sure if Lal achieved anything specific in his analysis of the pottery graffiti, and Sarkar's article incorporated a substantive amount of the relevant excavated data from Nagarjunakonda which was excavated by the Survey between 1954 and 1960. Krishnaswami's article broke new grounds by taking a vast sweep of the emerging data on the early farming communities of the sub-continent, and if any part of this article was wholly useless, that is the section on eastern India, but that is because there was no serious excavation in eastern India during that period. Krishnaswami's concluding observations are still worth quoting :

> The picture I have outlined above is largely speculative, and the most that I hope for is that it will ultimately stimulate discussion. But one thing is clear : without being unduly influenced by a *mirage orientale* for the neolithic origin of India, we have evolved our own neolithic pattern of India, influenced partly by a west-Asian neolithic culture, by the

> Harappa culture and by the south-east Asian neolithic culture, the rest of autochthonous origin.
>
> — Krishnaswami 1962 : 64

The technical section of this volume contained a note by T.R. Gairola (1962) on the preservation of a miniature painting and a tempera wall-painting.

Ancient India 17 in 1961 announced in its editorial notes the holding of the Centenary celebration of the Archaeological Survey of India in 1961, which was accompanied by an International Conference on Asian Archaeology. Although there was in 1964 a publication on the model of *Ancient India 9 — Archaeological Remains, Monuments and Museums* — the Proceedings of the International Conference have remained unpublished.

R.V. Joshi's elaborate article on the stone-age industries of the Damoh area, Madhya Pradesh (1961) followed the model which had by this time become standard in the study of Indian prehistory, and B.B. Lal and S.B. Lal (1961) published the details of their analytical work on the Birbhanpur soil profile. R. Sengupta undertook a comprehensive study of the problems of conservation in the Ellora caves, and K.V. Soundara Rajan published a speculative study of what he called 'pebble, core and flake cultures of India'.

The joint issue *Ancient India 18* and *19* was published in 1963 and coincided with R.B. Foote's discovery of a handaxe in India. Ghosh's editorial notes (1963) were devoted to the work of Foote and his contemporaries in the field of Indian prehistory. The most important article of this issue was by S.R. Rao (1963) on his 'Excavation in Rangpur and other Explorations in Gujarat' which put the Harappan studies on a very secure footing in this part of India and has remained since then an anchor-point of such studies in Gujarat. Whether we agree with some of his conclusions or not, this has remained a fundamental study, especially in view of the fact that a clear picture of transition from the mature Harappan to the late Harappan phase (marked by the presence of Lustrous Red Ware in Gujarat) was argued in detail for the first time in the context of the Indus civilization studies in India. What was also significant was that the basic distribution of the Harappan sites in Gujarat was adequately worked out, highlighting their southward extension right up to the Tapti valley. This report marked S.R. Rao as one of the most important archaeologists in the context of the Indus studies. The Rangpur report was also accompanied by technical studies on metal, plants and animals by B.B. Lal, S.S. Ghosh and Krishna Lal, and Bhola Nath respectively.

B.B. Lal (1963) tried to examine the implications of radiocarbon dates in Indian proto-historic archaeology with some reference to the emerging picture of a comparative stratigraphy between the relevant excavated sites. There were only a few radiocarbon dates available by then on the Indian sites, but this was the first paper to deal with the impact of the radiocarbon dates on Indian archaeology. B.B. Lal (1963) put up a definitive technical section on the chemical preservation of ancient objects, which is even now the most definitive attempt of this kind undertaken by an Indian archaeological chemist. The second convocation address of the School of Archaeology of the Archaeological Survey of India by a Calcutta University academic Niharranjan Ray (1963) did not specifically address any significant archaeological problem of the country, deciding to dwell on some generalities instead.

Till 1965 the publication of *Ancient India* was, with only one exception, regular and its contents faithfully reflect the diverse contents and developments of archaeology in India. It was a departmental publication of the Archaeological Survey of India, and it is not a matter of surprise that it was edited by the Director General himself and bore his editorial notes. The editorial notes throw light on the official archaeological perception of the time when they were written.

However, as we have pointed out before, *Ancient India* cannot be our only governmental source of study during this period. A perusal of the contents of the successive volumes of *Indian Archaeology — a Review* is equally important.

The Publication of *Indian Archaeology — A Review* (*IAR*)

The first issue of *Indian Archaeology — a Review* was entitled *Indian Archaeology 1953-54 — a Review* and edited by A. Ghosh. It was published in 1954 itself — an astonishing feat in view of what has happened to this publication in recent years — and bore the sub-title 'Report of the Director General of Archaeology in India on the occasion of the tenth meeting of Central Advisotry Board of Archaeology, 1954'. The background of this publication, according to Ghosh (1954) was the following :

> A body, called the Central Advisory Board of Archaeology, was formed by the Government of India in 1945 with the intention of associating scholars and learned institutions in India with the activities of the Department and to get their advice about its betterment. Nine meetings of the Board have taken place and the successive Directors General have placed their reports before the Board giving the salient features of the activities of the Department and of the advance of archaeology in general in the country. In the last meeting of the Board held in 1953 it was suggested that reports on these lines should be printed and widely circulated in future, so that they could be accessible to the world at

> large. This useful suggestion of the Board has now been worked upon, and this publication, the first of a series, is the result thereof.
> — Ghosh 1954 : iv

As is well known, the successive volumes of *IAR* are the most important window on the season by season archaeological field-activities in modern India and also on the diverse activities of the Archaeological Survey of India. The 1954 issue was divided into 12 sections : general, excavations, epigraphy, preservation of monuments, archaeological chemistry, museums, archaeological gardens, important discoveries, treasure-trove, departmental publications, training and programme for the current year. These sections were not uniform every year; in 1955 itself there were only 10 sections. The sections which were dropped in 1955 were two : 'training' and 'programme in the current year'.

Considering the significance of these two sections which went missing not only in the 1955 issue but in all other subsequent issues, it is important to comment on them.

The fact that Wheeler arranged for the training of various university deputees in the excavation methods is well known. From *IAR 1953-54* (p. 41) it appears that this practice of imparting 'training in fieldwork to the nominees of different universities and other bodies' continued and that this training took place not merely at the major Survey excavation camp of the year but also at other Survey camps. This was a laudable system (the present author can personally vouch for its benefits, being a student trainee from Calcutta University in the Kalibangan camp in 1963-64) and to some extent the practice continues even now, depending on the attitude of the Survey excavator concerned. In recent years the excavator of Dholavira has been generous in this regard. However, with the establishment of a regular 'School of Archaeology' under the direct control of the Survey, this practice has lost its importance. Further, one hears that the possession of a 'diploma' from this School has become a mandatory qualification for recruitment to the Survey and certainly a 'desirable qualification' in other archaeology-related appointments. What has been ignored is that this situation has led to a serious undermining of university-level qualifications in Indian archaeology. A great part of the curriculum of the Survey school is devoted to the normal academic aspects of Indian archaeology : prehistory, protohistory, sculpture, architecture, coins, inscriptions, etc., which are also taught comprehensively in the universities. Some universities also try to introduce the students to excavation methods by making them trench supervisors in their own excavations. The only thing which is not covered by the university curricula is 'conservation' (structural and chemical), but then the work of conservation is an 'in-house' requirement of the Archaeological Survey of India and its cause may best be served by running a conservation school for the 'in-house trainees'. Banaras Hindu University runs, for instance, a 2-year/1-year diploma/certificate vocational level post-M.A. courses in Archaeology. Exclusive emphasis on what to all intents and purpose has become an unnecessarily lengthy and expensive in-house training school of the Survey has not turned out to be a good development in Indian archaeology. It may also be remembered that the government departments do not have the necessary attitude to run formal academic programmes which lead to recognised degrees/diplomas. For instance, it is not an uncommon practice in the Survey's archaeology school to compress the programme of a series of lectures by an invited lecturer from outside Delhi into a day or two. The quality of teaching is the first casualty in such situations. There have also been cases where such lecturers from outside Delhi had cut short even this hurried schedule so that he/she could catch a particular plane or train to return home. The need of basic academic discipline cannot be said to weigh heavily on the minds of the School management or its lecturers. The pre-School system of taking in university trainees in the Survey excavations for complete seasons was a much better and far less expensive way of increasing the number of trained archaeologists in the country.

The *IAR 1953-54* section of 'programme for the current year' calls for open admiration. This is the last time (and perhaps for the first time as well) that the Survey was laying bare its programme of action for a particular year to that year's meeting of the nation-wide members of the Central Advisory Board of Archaeology (CABA) and thus to the Indian public as well. Among the programmes enumerated in the 1953-54 issue, it is stated that 'the Circles will, as far as possible, undertake small excavations at important sites within their jurisdiction'. This feature too has continued till today, although one would say that with the creation of about five 'Excavation Branches' in recent years, the importance of the excavation work by 'Circles' has to some extent decreased. From the point of view of regional archaeology in India this is not a happy situation.

It is also in this issue that one is informed about the creation of a 'special project' at Nagarjunakonda for a period of five years. The area was to be submerged due to the construction of a dam as a part of the Nandikonda project.

Excavations

The sites excavated between 1953 and 1965 and briefly reported in the relevant issues of *IAR* may be listed in the following chart.

Chart 1.1 : Excavated sites in *IAR 1953-54* to *IAR 1964-65*

Site	*Year*	*Nature*	*State*	*Status*	*Agency*	*Person*
Birbhanpur	53-54,56-57	mesolithic	West Bengal	Published	ASI	B.B. Lal
Rupar	53-55	Harappan	Panjab	Unpublished	ASI	Y.D. Sharma
Rangpur	53-55	Harappan	Gujarat	Published	ASI	S.R. Rao
Maheshwar	53-54	neo-chalco	M.P.	Published	D. Coll	Sankalia *et al.*
Langhnaj	53-54,63-64	mesolithic	Gujarat	Published	D. Coll	Sankalia *et al.*
Maski	53-54	neo-chalco	Karnataka	Published	ASI	Thapar
Rajgir	53-55,57-59 61-63	early hist	Bihar	Unpublished	ASI	unknown
Kausambi	53-65	early hist	U.P.	only 57-59 Published	Allah. Univ	G.R. Sharma
Kumrahar	53-55	early hist	Bihar	Published (53)	K.P.J.Inst	Altekar-Mishra
Vadnagar	53-54	early hist	Gujarat	Unpublished	Baroda Un	unknown
Jagatgram	53-54	early hist	U.P.	Unpublished	ASI	unknown
Salihundam	53-54	early hist	Andhra	Unpublished	ASI	unknown
Pallavamedu	53-54	historic	Tamil Nadu	Unpublished	ASI	unknown
Sirpur	53-56	historic	Chhattisgarh	Unpublished	Sagar Un	M.G. Dikshit
Bhinmal	53-54	early med	Rajasthan	Unpublished	Raj. State	unknown
Mumma Khan	53-54	historic	J&K	Unpublished		unknown
Nevasa	54-56,59-61	neo-chalco	Maharashtra	Published	D.Coll	Sankalia *et al.*
Bara & Salaura	54-55	Harappan	Panjab	Unpublished	ASI	Y.D. Sharma
Lothal	54-60,61-63	Harappan	Gujarat	Published	ASI	S.R. Rao
Prakash	54-55	neo-chalco	Maharashtra	Published	ASI	Thapar
Purana Qila	54-55	early hist	Delhi	Unpublished	ASI	unknown
Ahar	54-56		Rajasthan	Unpublished	R. State	R.C. Agrawala
	61-62	neo-chalco		Published	Decc.Coll	Sankalia *et al.*
Nagda	55-56	neo-chalco	M.P.	Published	ASI	N.R. Banerjee
Ujjain	55-58,64-65	early hist	M.P.	Unpublished	ASI	N.R. Banerjee
Kanauj	55-56	early hist	U.P.	Unpublished	ASI	K.K. Sinha
Kunnatur	55-58	megalithic	Tamil Nadu	Unpublished	ASI	Krishnaswami B. Saran
Nagarjunakonda	54-61	early hist	Andhra	Unpublished	ASI	B. Sub'nyam
Pataliputra	55-56	early hist	Bihar	Published	KPJ Inst	B.P. Sinha, L.A. Narain
Mathura	54-55	early hist	U.P.	Unpublished	ASI	B. Saran
Tamluk	54-55	early hist	West Bengal	Unpublished	ASI	M.N. Deshpande
Tildah	54-55	early hist	West Bengal	Unpublished	Cal Univ	K.G. Goswami
Amrithamang	54-55	megalithic	Tamil Nadu	Unpublished	ASI	N.R. Banerjee
Kotturu	54-55	early hist	Andhra	Unpublished	ASI	R.C. Kar

Site	*Year*	*Nature*	*State*	*Status*	*Agency*	*Person*
Karian	54-55	early med	Bihar	Unpublished	KPJ Inst	unknown
Bhatinda Fort	54-55	mediaeval	Panjab	Unpublished	ASI	unknown
Alamgirpur	58-59	Harappan	U.P	Unpublished	ASI	Y.D. Sharma
Amaravati	58-59	early hist	Andhra	Unpublished	ASI	unknown
Bahal	56-57	neo-chalco	Maharashtra	Unpublished	ASI	M.N. Deshpande
Baragaon	56-57	neo-chalco	U.P	Unpublished	ASI	unknown
Chandraketugarh	56-65	early hist	W. Bengal	Unpublished	Cal Univ	K.G. Goswami
Chittor Fort	58-59	mediaeval	Rajasthan	Unpublished	ASI	unknown
Daimabad	58-59	neo-chalco	Maharashtra	Unpublished	ASI	S.R. Rao
Dhanora	56-57	megalithic	Chhattisgarh	Unpublished	ASI	unknown
Gollathagudi	58-59	early med	Andhra	?	Unknown	unknown
Indragarh	58-59	early med	M.P.	Unpublished	Unknown	unknown
Jadigenahalli	56-57	megalithic	Karnataka	Unpublished	Unknown	unknown
Jajmau	56-58	early hist	U.P.	Unpublished	Unknown	unknown
Lakhnesward.	56-57	early hist	U.P.	Unpublished	Unknown	unknown
Lal Kot	57-59,60-61	mediaeval	Delhi	Unpublished	Unknown	unknown
Prabhas Pat	55-57	Harappan	Gujarat	Unpublished	Guj. State	R.P. Pandya
Q.Rai Pithora	57-58	mediaeval	Delhi	Unpublished	ASI	unknown
Rajghat	57-58,60-65	early hist	U.P.	Published	BHU	A.K. Narain
Rojdi	57-59,62-65	Harappan	Gujarat	Unpublished	Guj State	Nanavati
Sonpur	56-57,59-62	neo-chalco	Bihar	Published	Bihar State	B.P. Sinha B.S. Varma
Ter	57-58	early hist	Maharashtra	Unpublished	Unknown	Unknown
Unchgaon	56-57	mediaeval	U.P.	Unpublished	Unknown	Unknown
Utnur	58-59	neo-chalco	Andhra	Published	Andhra Sta.	F. Allchin
Vaisali	58-62	early hist	Bihar	Published	Bihar State	B.P. Sinha, S.R. Roy
Yelleswaram	57-59 60-65	megalithic	Andhra	Published	Andhra Sta.	A.W. Khan
Broach	59-60	early hist	Gujarat	Unpublished	ASI	K.V.S. Rajan
Devnimori	59-63	historic	Gujarat	Published	MSU, Baroda	Subbarao
Awra	59-60	early hist	M.P.	Unpublished	MP State	H.V. Trivedi
Manoti	59-60	neo-chalco	M.P.	Unpublished	MP State	H.V. Trivedi
Bahurupa-Sawalda	59-60	neo-chalco	Maharashtra	Unpublished	ASI	R.V. Joshi
T. Narasipur	58-60,61-62, 64-65	neo-chalco	Karnataka	Unpublished	Karn. State	Sheshadri
Ratnagiri	57-61	historic	Orissa	Published	ASI	D. Mitra
Gilund	59-60	neo-chalco	Rajasthan	Unpublished	ASI	B.B. Lal

Site	*Year*	*Nature*	*State*	*Status*	*Agency*	*Person*
Kesarapalli	61-62	neo-chalco	Andhra	Unpublished	ASI	H.B. Sarkar
Mukhalingam	61-62	historic	Andhra	Unpublished	ASI	Raghavachari
Antichak	60-65	historic	Bihar	Unpublished	Bihar State	B.P. Sinha
Nagal	61-62	neo-chalco	Gujarat	Unpublished	ASI	K.V.S. Rajan
Shamlaji	61-62	historic	Gujarat	Unpublished	MSU,Baroda	Subbarao
Burzahom	60-63,64-65	neo-chalco	J&K	Unpublished	ASI	T.N. Khazanchi
Adamgarh	60-61	pre-historic	M.P	Published	ASI	R.V. Joshi
Eran	60-65	neo-chalco	M.P	Unpublished	Sagar Univ	K.D. Bajpai
Chandoli	60-61	neo-chalco	Maharashtra	Published	Decc. Coll.	S.B. Deo
T'kambuliyur	61-63	historic	T Nadu	Unpublished	Madras Univ	Mahalingam ?
Kaundanpur	61-62	historic	Maharashtra	Published	Mah. State	M.G. Dikshit
Junapani	61-62	megalithic	Maharashtra	Unpublished	ASI	Thapar
Kuchai	61-62	neo-chalco	Orissa	Unpublished	ASI	Thapar
Udayagiri	61-62	historic	Orissa	Unpublished	ASI	D. Mitra
Kalibangan	60-65	Harappan	Rajasthan	Unpublished	ASI	B.B. Lal B.K. Thapar
Sohgaura	61-62	neo-chalco	U.P.	Unpublished	G'khpur Uni	G.C. Pande
P'Rajar Dhibi	61-65	neo-chalco	W. Bengal	Unpublished	W.B. State	P.C. Dasgupta
Dharanikota	62-65	historic	Andhra	Unpublished	ASI	V. Ramayya
D'Hading	62-64	neo-chalco	Assam	Unpublished	Gauh.Univ	T.C. Sharma
D'pani Than	62-63	historic	Assam	Unpublished	As.State	?
B'rajgarh	62-63	early hist	Bihar	Unpublished	ASI	R. Singh
Chirand	62-65	neo-chalco	Bihar	Unpublished	Bihar State	B.S. Verma
Dwaraka	62-63	historic	Gujarat	Unpublished	Guj State Decc. Coll.	Nanavati Sankalia
Bilawali	62-63	early hist	M.P.	Unpublished	ASI	V.K. Mishra
Gudiyam	62-64	pre-historic	T. Nadu	Unpublished	ASI	K.D. Banerjee
Kav'pattanam	62-65	historic	T. Nadu	Unpublished	ASI	S.R. Rao
Nagari	62-63	historic	Rajasthan	Unpublished	ASI	K.V.S. Rajan
Bairat	62-63	early hist	Rajasthan	Unpublished	ASI	N.R. Banerjee
At'khera	62-65	neo-chalco	U.P.	Published	Alig. Univ	R.C. Gaur
Bhainsaur	62-63	pre-historic	U.P.	?	Allah. Univ	R.K. Varma
B'millia-B'ra	62-63	megalithic	U.P.	Unpublished	BHU	A.K. Narain
Kakoria	62-63	megalithic	U.P.	Unpublished	BHU	A.K. Narain
Prahladpur	62-63	neo-chalco	U.P.	Published	BHU	A.K. Narain

Site	*Year*	*Nature*	*State*	*Status*	*Agency*	*Person*
R'badi-danga	62-65	historic	W Bengal	62-63 Pub	Cal Univ	S.R. Das
Pochampad	63-65	megalithic	Andhra	Unpublished	Andh.State	A.W. Khan
Buxar	63-64	early hist	Bihar	Unpublished	Bihar State	B.P. Sinha
Barudih	63-64	neo-chalco	Bihar	Unpublished	Cal Univ	D. Sen
Nagara	63-65	historic	Gujarat	Published	MSU Baroda	R.N. Mehta
Desalpur	63-64	Harappan	Gujarat	Unpublished	ASI	K.V.S. Rajan
Besnagar	63-65	early hist	M.P.	Unpublished	ASI	M.D. Khare
Alagarai	63-64	historic	T. Nadu	?	Madras Univ	Mahalingam ?
Tekk'kota	63-64	neo-chalco	Karnataka	Published	Decc. Coll.	Sankalia
Hemmige	63-64	neo-chalco	Karnataka	Published	K'State	M.H. Rao
Sugh	63-64	historic	Haryana	Unpublished	P'ab Univ	?
Noh	63-65	neo-chalco	Rajasthan	Unpublished	Raj State	R.C. Agrawala
Kotia	63-64	megalithic	U.P.	Unpublished	Allah. Univ	G.R. Sharma
Mainahai	63-64	historic	U.P.	Unpublished	Allah. Univ	G.R. Sharma
Ahichchhatra	63-65	early hist	U.P.	Unpublished	ASI	N.R. Banerjee
Lalitpur	63-64	pre-historic	U.P.	Unpublished	ASI	R.V. Joshi
Lekhahia	63-64	pre-historic	U.P.	Unpublished	Allah. Univ	G.R. Sharma
Ambkheri	63-64	neo-chalco	U.P.	Unpublished	ASI	M.N. Deshpande
Bargaon	63-64	neo-chalco	U.P.	Unpublished	ASI	M.N. Deshpande
Hath'Pahar-	63-64	megalithic	U.P.	Unpublished	Allah. Univ	G.R. Sharma
Kamauli	63-64	historic	U.P.	Unpublished	BHU	A.K. Narain
Mahiṣdal	63-64	neo-chalco	W. Bengal	Unpublished	ASI	R.P. Das
Nanur	63-64	neo-chalco	W. Bengal	Unpublished	ASI	R.P. Das
Goswamik'da	63-64	historic	W. Bengal	Unpublished	WB State	Dasgupta
Saradkel	64-65	historic	Jharkhand	Unpublished	ASI	S.C. Ray
Jahanpanah	64-65	mediaeval	Delhi	Unpublished	ASI	K.M. Srivastava M.C. Joshi
Modhera	64-65	early med.	Gujarat	Unpublished	ASI	R. Sub'nyam
Rani-ki-Vav	64-65	early med.	Gujarat	Unpublished	ASI	R. Sub'nyam
Kayatha	64-65	neo-chalco	M.P.	Published	V'kram Uni	W'kankar
Att'pakkam	64-65	pre-historic	T. Nadu	Unpublished	ASI	K.D. Banerjee
Paiyampalli	64-65	neo-chalco	T. Nadu	Unpublished	ASI	SR Rao
Urayur	64-65	early hist	T. Nadu	Published	Madras Univ	Mahalingam ?
Songaon	64-65	neo-chalco	Maharashtra	Published	Decc. Coll.	S.B. Deo
Kupgal	64-65	neo-chalco	Karnataka	Published	Decc. Coll.	M'dar-R'guru
S'kallu	64-65	neo-chalco	Karnataka	Published	Decc. Coll.	M.S.N. Rao
Anagwadi	64-65	pre-historic	Karnataka	Published	Decc. Coll.	R.S. Pappu

Site	Year	Nature	State	Status	Agency	Person
Kovalli	64-65	pre-historic	Karnataka	Published	Decc. Coll.	R.S. Pappu
Hallur	64-65	neo-chalco	Karnataka	Published	Decc. Coll.	M.S.N. Rao
Kenduli	64-65	historic	Orissa	Unpublished	Orissa State	K.N. M'patra
Autha	64-65	early hist	Haryana	Unpublished	ASI	K.M. Srivastava
Masaon	64-65	early hist	U.P.	Unpublished	Sans.Un.B'ras	R.B. Narain
Haraipur	64-65	neo-chalco	W. Bengal	Unpublished	ASI	R.C. Kar

Attention may be drawn to some major aspects of the foregoing chart. First, out of about 144 sites excavated between 1953 and 1965, about 105 sites have remained unpublished in detail even today. It is impossible to claim, in view of this fact, that the Indian excavators were ever seriously concerned with the publication of their work in detail. Secondly, the excavators who defaulted on this crucial aspect of their work belong to all the organisations involved in the excavations conducted during this period, but most of them belong to the Archaeological Survey of India (about 58 out of about 105 unpublished excavations). This is not because of any innate limitation of the Survey excavators but because of the simple fact that they conducted a very large percentage of the excavations done during this period. If any institution comes honourably out of our simple test, that is the Deccan College, Poona. Thirdly, even where the excavations have been considered published, not all of them are in fact fully published. Kausambi (U.P.) and Rajbadi-danga (West Bengal) have remained basically unpublished with the exception of only a handful of seasons. This is an important point to remember. As far as the Harappan sites are concerned, only Lothal and Rangpur have been published among the sites where excavations began before 1965. Fourthly, if one goes through the list of the defaulting excavators, one will find many 'famous' archaeologists of the country, and one will also realise that the non-publication of reports never stood in their way to fame, power and career-advancement. As far as the Survey is concerned, the responsibility for this situation must be put squarely on the Director General, members of the CABA and eventually the concerned Ministry. As far as the universities and State governments are concerned, the responsibility goes to the leadership of those organisations.

Among the brief reports published in *IAR* up to 65 we have not considered the issue of reports on explorations, neither is it particularly necessary to do so. But one thing stands out : very few exploration reports have been published in any other form except the form in which they appear in *IAR*, which means that no analytical work has ever been done on them.

One may further point out that the publication of *IAR* which was regular up to the 1960-61 issue (published in 1961 itself) began to get delayed by a few years from the 1961-62 issue onwards : '1961-62' published in 1964, '1962-63' in 1965, '1963-64' in 1967, '1964-65' in 1969 and '1965-66' in 1973.

In the context of our discussion on the evidence of *Ancient India* we have drawn attention to A. Ghosh's assertion that it was difficult to inculcate proper aptitude for fieldwork among the students/trainees in the academic atmosphere of the universities. Secondly, he was also apprehensive about the quality of archaeology as a science being diluted by its induction in the universities. It is interesting to note that by 1965 the bulk of his own Department's fieldwork remained unpublished and unanalysed.

Notwithstanding such limitations, Indian archaeology made considerable progress between 1953 and 1965, and it is possible to trace it in the pages of the successive issues of *IAR*. The most noticeable feature was the extent to which the pre and proto-historic roots of India's history were worked out virtually all over the land. The essential framework of India's pre-historic stratigraphy and typology was laid down during this period which also witnessed the highlighting of the proto-historic background of the early historic period of the Ganga plain and the peninsula. The ease and rapidity with which the Indian archaeologists of the period made the Indus civilization a large and secure part of the modern India's ancestry also call for unqualified praise. It is not that early historic and later studies were neglected. Kausambi, Chandraketugarh, Nagarjunakonda, Patna, Vaisali, Rajbadi-danga, Antichak, Devnimori, Kaveripattinam, etc., come readily to mind among the excavated sites of the historic levels. The orthodox archaeological fieldwork was also accompanied by the discoveries of a large number of inscriptions, monuments and sculptures, the organisation of new museums and the expansion of the already existing ones. There is a careful annual listing of the various conservation programmes undertaken by the Survey in every issue of *IAR*. The 1965-66 issue of *IAR* also witnessed the first reporting on the 'architectural survey of temples' conducted by the Survey, and apparently by this time a Temple Survey Project was in place.

Other Publications

One may begin by pointing out that the post-Independence expansion of archaeological activities in India led to a sharper emphasis on the significance of archaeological data as a source of ancient Indian studies and a general widening of the scope of understanding the material basis of life in ancient India. The publications of different categories of artefacts including houses, lithic and metal objects, pottery, human and animal remains, plant and wood remains, etc., in various archaeological reports gradually led to a consideration of excavated data of this kind in addition to the usual literary sources. H.D. Sankalia (1960) for instance, discussed the evidence of 'houses and habitations through the ages' in India almost exclusively on the basis of the excavated data, but more significantly, the technical reports by specialist scholars in the well-published excavation reports of the period led to an increased historical consciousness in this regard. The technical studies by K.A. Chowdhury, S.S. Ghosh, Bhola Nath and B.B. Lal have already been referred to, and along with their publications one must consider the significance of the well-documented technical data studied by scholars like Vishnu Mittre on the early plant economy of Navdatoli and A.N. Gulati on the early history of silk in India in the reports on the central Indian and Deccanese proto-historic sites (cf. Sankalia, Subbarao and Deo 1958, Sankalia, *et al.* 1961).

On the other hand, this trend is a natural corollary of the increased archaeological activities in the country and does not necessarily throw light on its history of archaeology. More relevant to the latter issue is a study of the basic approaches and ideas embedded in the representative major publications of the period.

The archaeological research tradition of Calcutta and Poona universities dates from before 1947. One does not know when archaeology was introduced in the Maharaja Sayajirao University of Baroda, but in 1951-52 it conducted excavations at Akota in the periphery of the city, took into consideration the various finds of antiquities in its different residential localities, invited special contributions from the specialist numismatists, art-historians and historians on the character and significance of the related finds, and published in 1953 a report entitled *Baroda through the Ages* (*being the report of an excavation conducted in the Baroda area 1951-52*) as the publication number 1 of the M.S. University Archaeology Series. What emerged was a carefully conducted study of the history of Baroda city and area, integrating both archaeological and literary data. Bendapudi Subbarao, 'Reader and Head of the Department of Archaeology', was the author of this study which set an excellent example of the archaeological approach to the study of the history of a living Indian city. Apart from the later topographical studies by R.N. Mehta of the same department of some pre-Mogul Muslim and Mogul period Gujarati cities like Surat and Cambay (Mehta 1974, 1975) this approach pioneered by Subbarao has basically remained neglected.

In the beginning of his report Subbarao refers to the miscellaneous finds of antiquities from different areas of Baroda and then asks :

> We have described the various finds from different parts of Baroda. Then what is their inter-relationship and their place in the general history of Baroda ? To connect these loose threads, we must know the sequence of events and assign the various objects to their proper places. — After knowing sufficiently about Baroda, the next question, which arises naturally, is the place of Baroda in the Cultural History of Gujarat and the rest of India.
>
> — Subbarao 1953 : 7-8

To establish this 'place' or the links with the other parts of Gujarat and the country, he emphasised the importance of ceramic evidence, and in fact, one of the highlights of the report was a study of the types, age and distribution of Red Polished Ware of the first three centuries AD. Rightly or wrongly, this ceramic type has been linked to the Indo-Roman trade of the period, but far more significant than such technical contributions was the report's emphasis on the building up of a continuous — and as far as practicable, a total — history of the place.

*B. Subbarao's **The Personality of India** and D.H. Gordon's **Prehistoric Background of Indian Culture***

This concern for totality is amply manifest in Subbarao's *The Personality of India, a Study in the Development of Material Culture of India and Pakistan*, which was first published in 1956 as the publication number 3 of the M.S. University archaeology series.

As stated in the preface, he set himself two tasks, one to 'study and correlate the physical and the cultural regions from the point of view of Archaeology', and the second, 'correlation in space and time of the archaeological sequence in different parts of the country'. The second part is now dated, but the first part, being a quest to explain India's cultural diversity and 'differential development' in terms of Indian physical geography, still retains a methodological interest. In his chapter on the geographical factors in Indian archaeology, he shows himself deeply influenced by the chapter on history in O.H.K. Spate's *India and Pakistan, a Regional Geography* (1954) and F.J. Richards' article on the geographic factors in Indian archaeology in 1933 (1933). Spate called the major river valleys 'perennial nuclear regions'; Subbarao calls them 'areas of attraction'. He also looks at the distribution of tribal groups in modern India and finds a 'close relation between the thick jungle and rain forests and the main centres of the so-called primitive tribes'. He calls them 'areas of isolation'. In between these areas of 'attraction' and 'isolation' he finds a third geographical category of 'areas of relative isolation' which, according to him, were away from the 'main trans-continental communications' and whose 'isolation was broken up slightly later than the areas of attraction'. In his first category he places Panjab, the area between the Sutlej and the Yamuna and between the Simla foothills and the dried-up Ghaggar course in Rajasthan, Ganga plain, Malwa, Maharashtra, Karnataka and Tamil Nadu. The second category is taken up by the thickly forested highland belts, whereas the third category includes Sind, Marwar, Gujarat, Konkan, Kerala and Assam. Elsewhere I have commented in detail on this historical-geographical classification proposed by Subbarao (Chakrabarti 1988b, 1999), but the point here is not the validity/invalidity of this classification but the fact that somebody at that point was seriously interested in understanding the flow of India's multilinear cultural development in terms of her geography and archaeology. One feels that he did not think carefully about the implications of dividing the physical geography of the country in terms of three clear-cut historical and culrtural divisions. He was fully aware of the fact of tribal-Hindu continuum in Indian history. He cited Iravati Karve's work on *Kinship Organization in India* and apparently agreed with her opinion that 'the primitives have almost all the social institutions and elaborations of the non-primitive, while the Hindus actively share all the beliefs of the primitives'. (Subbarao 1956 : 66) He was further aware that the so-called tribal areas were the main resource-bearing areas of the country and this probably 'enabled a harmonious development of the higher cultures of the plains and the lower cultures of the hills and forests, maintaining each other's economy and institutions without much interference'. (*ibid*)

Subbarao (1956: 73) had a firm faith in the correlation between the Indian archaeological and literary data. He believed that Lal's premise of the PGW — makers being Aryans were 'the first sure but faltering steps' in this direction. According to him, it was only a matter of time 'till the names of some of our legendary kings enshrined in our literature appeared from under the earth'. He also had a firm belief in the story of the Aryan colonisation of India. Regarding Orissa, for instance, he writes that its wide alluvial plains were 'colonised by adventurous Aryan groups from the Gangetic valley and central India'. (Subbarao 1956 : 63)

The second edition of this book was published in 1958 and incorporated more archaeological data and perhaps a more elaborate reference to the distribution of various Indian language families.

D.H. Gordon's *The Prehistoric Background of Indian Culture* was published in 1958 incorporating a lifetime of interest in archaeology, especially the microliths and rock-paintings of the subcontinent. Towards the end of his career Colonel Gordon was the British Resident in the court of Mysore. This has become a connoiseur's book with time, full of interesting observations, signs of close familiarity with the material and the ground, inclination to ride rough shod over opposing opinions and an unshakeable faith in what he himself saw and believed. It may be interesting for those currently interested in discovering caste system in the Indus civilization to know that it was Colonel Gordon who thought of the existence of 'pre-Aryan brahmanas in the Harappan cities'. One of the highlights of his observations on the 'Copper Hoards' of the Ganga-Yamuna Doab was that 'the principal copper mines that supplied the Ganga-Yamuna Doab were in Rajputana', this being a conclusion with which I fully agree. He also realised that the Gungeria Hoard of Balaghat marked a merchant's trail and that the findspot lay in the 'only gap in the hills on a front of many hundred miles'. The importance of this book lies mainly in the fact that in 1958 somebody made an active case for establishing a pre-historic background of Indian culture and integrating that background with what was then understood as the essential framework of Indian history.

*H.D. Sankalia's **Prehistory and Protohistory in India and Pakistan** and the Research Materials in the Background*

In 1962 H.D. Sankalia published his *Prehistory and Protohistory in India and Pakistan* (*PPIP*) along with his *Indian Archaeology Today* (*IAT*) published earlier in the same year. It is these publications which bear a much more accurate reflection of the total state of Indian archaeology of that period than any other publication we can think of, including the major excavation reports of Navdatoli and Nevasa which were in fact out before 1962 and authored by Sankalia himself and his associates. Whereas *PPIP* is concerned with the details of prehistory and protohistory, *IAT* is more comprehensive and includes historical material as well.

The aim of *PPIP*, as stated in the preface, was to offer a critical review of the pre-historic and proto-historic branches of archaeology in the subcontinent with an emphasis on the 'careful collection of material' and separation of the conclusions from the facts. He was already unhappy with the state of publications of many excavations briefly announced in *IAT* :

> These announcements, however welcome and excellent in their own way, can never take the place of full, or even interim, well-written, definitive reports. Unfortunately the latter

> are not available in a number of cases. And it is doubtful, if many will ever see the light of the day; or if published after years, they will be as good as still-born.
>
> — Sankalia 1962 : xii

A striking example of the benefits of archaeology spreading to the universities under the care of suitable and committed teachers is this book by Sankalia :

> Every exploration by a pupil has given the author an opportunity to study new sites in different regions of India, such as Bellary, Karnatak, Kurnool, Malwa, Rajputana, Gujarat, the Punjab, Orissa, and Bengal. Thus it is the team work and co-operation which has helped the writer to produce this work. — Sankalia 1962 : xiii

The 'introduction' gives an insight into some of the core beliefs of Sankalia. To begin with, he had no doubt about India's position at the periphery of the cultural spread arising in west Asia :

> These civilizing forces having entered India either from the north-west and/or west marched along the main lines of communication, their progress depending upon their inherent vitality as well as on the strength of the opposing natural and man-made forces.
>
> — Sankalia 1962: iii

For 'physio-cultural divisions' he accepted Subbarao's scheme and ideas, although he thought that archaeological excavations would be able to settle the point whether the present-day tribals were comparatively recent settlers in the areas they occupied or had been there since time immemorial.

Terminology occupied some of his thoughts, with the uneven pace of the sub-continent's development taking a major place in his mind. Palaeoliths were not present everywhere even outside the major alluvial plains; early palaeolithic was, according to him, absent in a number of areas including western Rajasthan and middle palaeolithic was not present in all palaeolithic areas either. In the case of the mesolithic he could be more direct : although a term of 'stratigraphic, chronological, typological and economic significance', 'mesolithic' did not have universal validity in India, 'nor can we equate in time or content the various Mesolithic Cultures of India, either with each other within India or with any outside India'. (Sankalia 1962 : xx) He was aware that polished stone axes were not an invariable feature of the Indian neolithic and the chalcolithic had all the features of the neolithic with the addition of copper in small quantities. The Indus civilization was a true Bronze Age civilization, and iron was introduced in some parts of northern India only as late as the fourth-sixth centuries BC, with the use of microliths still continuing in 'the hilly forested regions of Central India and Andhra and Assam'.

The 'Indian' section of his chapter I (Lower Palaeolithic Culture) begins with Olaf Prufer's discovery of palaeoliths in the Nalagarh area of the Sirsa valley, a tributary valley of the Sutlej in 1951. This discovery was followed up by D. Sen's work in the area (1955). In about the same time Y.D. Sharma reported 'Late Soan' tools from Daulatpur in the Beas valley (*IAR 1954-55* : 58). For the Beas-Banganga valleys in the neighbouring Kangra Sankalia relied on B.B. Lal's report which we have mentioned earlier. In each of these cases the emphasis was on an attempted correlation between river terraces and stone tools, apparently a continuation of the H. de Terra and T.T. Paterson model worked out in the context of the Potwar plateau in the 1930s. In Uttar Pradesh the base-line was the report by Krishnaswami and Soundara Rajan on the Singrauli basin, but by this time Allahabad University under G.R. Sharma located a palaeolithic site at Bariyari in the Banda district. In Bihar a reference was made to some pre-1947 discoveries, but the major focus was on D. Sen's finds in the Roro valley near Chaibasa (Singhbhum) where Sen (Sen and Ghosh 1960) reported a stratigraphic profile in addition to terraces. Further references were made to the find of tools near Nimdih (Sinha 1951) in eastern Singhbhum and at Bhimbandh (N.K. Bose *et al.* 1960) near Munger. In West Bengal the highlight was Krishnaswami's survey of the submerged Kangsavati valley (*IAR 1960-61*) where lower palaeolithic tools were recovered from a thick gravel bed. The Burhabalang valley of Mayurbhanj in Orissa was surveyed for palaeolithic tools by N.K. Bose and D. Sen (1948), but for Orissan prehistory Sankalia could depend on G.C. Mohapatra's *The Stone Age Cultures of Orissa* (1962), a Ph.D. thesis which he himself supervised. Mohapatra's survey of five Orissan districts (Dhenkanal, Sundargarh, Sambalpur, Keonjhar and Mayurbhanj) established not merely a rich assemblage of palaeolithis in this region but also a succession of industries correlated to two gravels in a two-fold cycle of gravel-silt succession. In addition to Soundara Rajan's reports on palaeoliths at Giddalur and Nagarjunakonda, Sankalia depended for Andhra on N. Isaac's Ph.D. thesis *Stone Age Cultures of Kurnool* (1960), which was supervised by him. This area too produced a succession of tool-bearing gravels, clays and silts. For Tamil Nadu he had to depend mainly on pre-1947 work, although some references were made to stray discoveries in the neighbouring Andhra areas of Tirupati, Nellore, etc. No palaeoliths were yet found in Kerala and in Karnataka the modern framework was provided by R.V. Joshi's work *Pleistocene Studies in the Malaprabha Basin* (1955) based on his Ph.D. dissertation at Deccan College under Sankalia. The gravel-silt cycle was established in this region too. By this time the most important pre-historic section studied by Sankalia and his colleagues in Maharashtra was at Nevasa (gravel > silt > gravel > silt > fine loose gravel), although the solitary discoveries made in the Mula, Bhima, Tapti and Wardha valleys were taken into account along with S.C. Malik's work in Bombay and Satara (1959). In Maharashtra an important aspect was the discovery of *Bos namadicus*, *Elephas namadicus* and rhinoceros in association with tool-bearing gravels at Nandur Madhmeshwar, Kalegaon and Nevasa. F.E. Zeuner's report (1950) on the Sabarmati valley and his own earlier reports formed his base-line in Gujarat. In Madhya Pradesh Sankalia and Subbarao worked out the following sequence at Maheshwar on the Narmada : cemented pebbly gravel > pinkish silt > less cemented pebbly gravel > pink silt > smaller trap gravel > brownish silt > kankary sandy gravel and silt > Black Soil, gravels I, II and III (numbered from the bottom upwards) being implementiferous. About 13 types of extinct mammals including wild elephant, ox and horse were found to be contemporary with early tool remains in the Narmada valley. In the Chambal basin in Malwa the basic data and sequence (cemented pebble gravel > yellowish silt > fine well-cemented gravel) were provided by A.P. Khatri's Deccan College Ph.D. thesis *Stone Age Cultures of Malwa* (1958). In Rajasthan V.N. Misra's Deccan College Ph.D. thesis *The Stone Age Cultures of Rajputana* (1961, 1967) provided the basic ground in the Banas, Gambhiri, Luni and Berach valleys. By this time palaeolithic discoveries came to be made around Delhi and in Lalitpur, Jhansi, etc., in Uttar Pradesh.

Chapter 2 of *PPIP* bore the title 'Middle Palaeolithic Cultures of India'. Based on the carefully worked-out stratigraphical sequence and the associated tool-types, which has been mentioned in the preceding section, Sankalia here established the special and evolved character of the lithic industry found in the less cemented and finer gravel deposits separated usually by an intervening silt deposit from the basal cemented gravel which was the general Peninsular stratigraphical context of the lower palaeoliths. He discusses the issue of its nomenclature : Middle Stone Age or Middle Palaeolithic, and eventually he opted for 'Middle Palaeolithic' because of its stratigraphic position, preference for fine-grained stone types (cf. jasper and chert) as raw material and its character as a 'flake industry' as opposed to the biface tradition of the lower palaeolithic. The regional evidence was discussed in detail, the discussion being accompanied by descriptions and illustrations of individual tool-types such as scrapers, points and borer.

In *PPIP* the upper palaeolithic as a distinct stage is not established. Sankalia was aware of the problem and occasionally he raises the issue but apparently finds the evidence available to him at that time unconvincing. He was also sceptical of the existence of a mesolithic stage in India (chapter 3) :

> Nowhere in India microliths immediately overlie the Palaeolithic and underlie the Neolithic. It is therefore not true to say that we have got definitely mesolithic cultures comparable to those in Europe or Africa, either in time or content or stratigraphy.
>
> — Sankalia 1962 : 126

He then went on to describe the typology and modes of occurrence of microlithic tools in India mostly on the basis of the surveys by his students in Maharashtra, Andhra, Madhya Pradesh, Orissa and Rajasthan, but also highlighting the work in the coastal dune belt of Tamil Nadu, Singrauli basin of Uttar Pradesh and the Durgapur area of West Bengal. The most important part of this chapter was a detailed discussion on the site of Langhnaj (Mehsana district, north Gujarat) excavated by him and his colleagues. A detailed map was produced to show the distribution of 'Langhnaj microlithic industry' in the different river valleys of the mainland Gujarat. The Langhnaj stratigraphy which showed a 'pure microlithic culture with most of the human skeletons and animal remains like rhinoceros' giving way to a period with 'old pottery, microliths and mace-head or ring-stone' was considered to begin from a period earlier than, or contemporary with, the Indus civilization at Rangpur, i.e., *c.* 2500 BC Microliths of 'Langhnaj type' were found below the earliest Indus civilization level at Rangpur.

The questions of climate and origin came back at the end of the chapter. A climate drier than the present was postulated, and regarding the origin, the possibility that microliths could evolve from the earlier 'blade and burin industry' or even from the middle palaeolithic complex was admitted, although with the cautionary note that nowhere was such an evolution available stratigraphically.

Chapter 4 was about the 'neolithic and chalcolithic cultures'. The criticism he makes of Krishnaswami's scheme of 'neolithic pattern of India' is that 'it does not make a sharp distinction between the Neolithic and the Chalcolithic cultural stages of man's development'. (Sankalia 1962 : 152) He offered his own scheme of five categories : pure neolithic with only ground tools (Assam. Bihar, Bengal, Kashmir); neolithic-chalcolithic with ground and blade tools, hand made pottery and wattle-and-daub huts (north Karnataka, early Baluchi cultures and north Gujarat); chalcolithic with blade tools, wheelmade and mostly painted pottery, and wattle-and-daub houses (north Karnataka, Maharashtra and Malwa); chalcolithic-Bronze Age with blade tools, wheelmade pottery, copper and bronze tools, burnt-brick houses (Sind, Panjab and Saurashtra) and finally, chalcolithic or Bronze Age with wheelmade pottery, copper and bronze (?) tools, no stone tools and wattle-and-daub houses on stone foundations (Ganga-Yamuna Doab and south-east Rajasthan).

This is a very illogical and unnecessary scheme, but it also shows an effort to make some sense of the newly emergent picture of proto-historic India. One can pass over in silence his discussion on the Indus civilization and the proto-historic cultures, which is detailed and highlights the panorama of the newly discovered pre-historic village life of south-east Rajasthan, Malwa and Maharashtra. The issues of 'racial origins', 'authorship' and 'Iranian or West Asiatic influence' were never far from his mind, and behind all of these, there was a fervent desire to impart veracity to the Indian Vedic and Pauranic traditions. The Malwa Ware of Navdatoli could have been 'brought and made popular by the Haihayas or one of the branches of the Yadavas' or the Painted Grey Ware could be identified not merely with the Aryans but also specifically 'with one of the tribes of the Aryans viz., the Bharatas who occupied the Ganga-Yamuna valley'.

His overriding concern was with what he called 'Iranian penetration'. The footed goblets and channel-spouted vessels from Maheshwar-Navdatoli suggested 'some kind of connection between Eastern Iran or Western Asia and Central India'. To these he added the goblets in the Lustrous Red Ware from Rangpur.

> I believe that the influences which spread to the Narmada valley might have continued in wave after wave after the earlier waves reached Narmada. Other waves followed with slightly different pottery traditions and it is this that we find at Rangpur and other sites in Saurashtra like Somnath and elsewhere, and as far down at Piklihal in Karnatak, along with the ground stone axes. — Sankalia 1962 : 281

Occasionally he also contradicted himself. He also thought that

> the bearers of the Nevasa-Navdatoli culture as well as of the Copper Hoard belonged to indigenous tribes, such as Nishadas, Pulindas, Savaras, some of whom though now quite primitive might have made, 3000-4000 years ago beautiful painted pottery and even copper tools and weapons. — Sankalia 1962 : 225

The first edition of Sankalia's *Indian Archaeology Today* was also published in 1962 and followed more or less the same ground, with additional sections on megaliths, early history, epigraphy and numismatics. An important aspect of this work is his emphasis on the importance of co-ordinated archaeological planning. He believed that archaeological problems should be tackled at the successive levels of region, nation and the world. 'For the solution of the Aryan problem' he suggested joint excavations by the universities and the governments of India, Pakistan and Iran. For solution of the problems of national importance, 'such as the civic life of the early historic period' he recommended horizontal excavations of some major city sites by the combined strength of the universities and other institutions.

Indian Prehistory : 1964

Two years after the publication of *PPIP* the Deccan College organised a seminar (24-31 May 1964) on Indian prehistory and protohistory under a project sanctioned by the University Grants Commission. The proceedings were edited by V.N. Misra and M.S. Mate and published under the title of *Indian Prehistory : 1964* in 1965. The volume carried a preface by Sankalia (1965) who defined the three broad aims of the seminar : to discuss a few important problems of Indian prehistory and protohistory which had been highlighted by the work done after Independence; to bring together young and old scholars so that the emergent problems could be discussed threadbare; and finally, to place the new data before the world. Sankalia's definition of the third objective is worth quoting in full, because the situation he complains about is still with us.

> The third objective was to place before the scholars at large the latest happenings in Indian prehistory and protohistory. For it would appear that excepting a few scholars in Russia, scholars elsewhere do not care to acquaint themselves with Indian publications and hence theories and views decades old are 'dished out' to the world in publications which claim to speak on world prehistory. It is hoped that the publication of the proceedings of the seminar would help to remove this deliberate neglect of Indian prehistory.
>
> — Sankalia 1965 : vii

The printed lists of 'delegates' and 'student delegates' are interesting and suggest a clear bias for the Archaeological Survey, the Deccan College and its ex-students and the university departments and other institutions with which the Deccan College interacted or 'networked'. In this sense this seminar was also an announcement of the emergence of the Deccan College as a power-centre in Indian archaeology.

The topic which was first discussed was the status of the Soan river lithic industry as a separate culture and linked to the fact that pebble tools were being found in various parts outside the 'Soan zone'. None of the discussants, with the exception perhaps of R.V. Joshi, had any secure grounding in geology or geomorphology or in fact, in any branch of the natural sciences, and thus all their pronouncements were generally valueless even at the time when they were made. Basically they were discussing if the Indian data permitted the visualisation of two palaeolithic typo-technological traditions in the subcontinent. They did not reach any conclusion, but the discussions touched at some point A.P. Khatri's claim of the find of a pure pebble-based 'Oldowan' industry at the base of the lithic sequence of the Narmada valley (Khatri 1962), suggesting the evolution of hand-axe industry from a pebble-base. The hypothesis has since then been revived by J. Armand (1979) on the basis of his excavations at the Durkadi Nala, but in 1964 there was a strong onslaught against Khatri by Misra (Misra and Mate 1965 : 10-11), which possibly ensured that Khatri was no longer acceptable in archaeological institutions of the country.

The second major topic was Vishnu Mittre's review of the pleistocene stratigraphy of India with reference to the pollen stratigraphy of the Lower Karewa formation in Kashmir. He placed the Plio-Pleistocene boundary in the subcontinent at the base of the Pinjor beds in the Siwaliks, and if one has to point out the significant bits in the ensuing discussion, one has to draw attention to the comment by Gudrun Karve-Korvinus (Misra and Mate 1965 : 31-34) that the yardstick of judging the old cemented bouldery gravel as 'old' should not be based only on the usually known fact that 'the bouldery gravel is bouldery and hard-cemented and lies at the bottom'. According to S.N. Rajaguru (*ibid* : 26), the tectonic factor should be taken into consideration while studying coastal terraces or sedimentation sequences.

The third topic was constituted by Sankalia's essay on the 'middle stone age', which, following the pattern of *PPIP*, established the typo-technological and stratigraphical distinctiveness of this industry dominated by scrapers, points and borers on flakes. He was astute enough to realise on the basis of his field-observations that long chalcedony blades that he found on the surface at Nevasa could constitute a different and later industry. V.N. Misra argued eloquently (*ibid* : 46-47) in favour of using the term 'middle palaeolithic' in the place of the 'middle stone age'. A.K. Ghosh (*ibid* : 49) thought, on the basis of his field-data from Singhbhum, that the flake-based middle stone age industry was stratigraphically followed by a flake-blade industry in the Singhbhum sequence. He was willing to call the former 'middle palaeolithic' and the latter 'upper palaeolithic'.

As the fourth topic of discussion V.N. Misra reviewed the data on the mesolithic phase, arguing both for its true post-Pleistocene antiquity and continuity into the historic period. The most significant aspect of the ensuing discussion was the report on the microlithic sites and associated rock-paintings of Mirzapur (*ibid* : 73-79) in Uttar Pradesh by R.K. Varma and G.R. Sharma of Allahabad University. G.R. Sharma reported the results of excavations in the rockshelter of Lekhahia.

B.K. Thapar's essay, as the fifth topic, on the neolithic problem in India focussed on Kashmir, south India and east India and reported in some detail the new excavated finds from Burzahom (Kashmir) and Kuchai (Orissa), besides drawing attention to the ongoing typological neolithic research in Assam. The subsequent discussion hardly raised any interesting point.

As the sixth topic A. Ghosh wrote perhaps the most important and still relevant paper of this volume : 'The Indus civilization : its origins, authors, extent and chronology'. He drew extensively on the results of the first few seasons of excavations at Kalibangan, highlighting the significance of what he described as the Sothi substratum of this civilization. The other sections of the paper are not particularly edifying. He was still interested in knowing how the Harappan skeletons were to be 'racially affiliated', but citing S.S. Sarkar's opinion (1964) that there was a population continuity from the Harappan times in the present-day Sind, Panjab and Gujarat, he argues that 'this, if true, is a complete blow to any idea of a homogeneous Harappan people'. On chronology he accepts Wheeler's date of 2500 BC as the date of its beginning whereas for its end he depends mostly on the radiocarbon dates from the late levels of the mature Harappan culture at Lothal and thinks that the end took place between 1900 and 1700 BC. The discussions which followed substantially amended and elaborated Ghosh's framework. M.A. Dhaky argued that the Indus civilization survived 'for some centuries further' in Gujarat after it came to an end in the Indus valley proper. M.N. Deshpande established the Harappan affiliation of Ambkheri ('degenerate Harappan') and Bargaon ('late Harappan') in the Saharanpur district of U.P. S.R. Rao underlined the possible existence of 'indigenous people' in Gujarat before the Harappans and regional differences in their religious beliefs and social customs. Y.D. Sharma listed some new sites in Panjab and the Doab. B.K. Thapar dwelt on the variety of pottery fabrics from the pre-mature-Harappan Kalibangan. D.P. Agrawal (1964) repeats the argument he published elsewhere that the chronological framework of this civilization, as obtained from its newly emergent radiocarbon dates, agreed with the evidence supplied by archaeology. R.C. Gaur drew attention to his excavations at Atranjikhera near Aligarh in U.P. V.S. Wakankar underscored the presence of Harappan pottery at Manoti in Mandasore of M.P. This site on the Chambal river subsequently got submerged in the water of the Gandhi Sagar project.

The seventh essay of the book, B.K. Thapar's article on the 'relationship of the Indian chalcolithic cultures with west Asia' failed to establish any framework of such relationships, and the commentators hardly fared any better. In a remarkably puerile and long-winded discussion on 'the Iron Age in India' (the eighth essay of the book), based on his Calcutta University Ph.D. thesis which was subsequently published as a book (Banerjee 1965), N.R. Banerjee concluded that the early Iron Age in India could be 'dated between circa 800 BC and 200 BC, and the prime responsibility for introducing it in India and spreading it far and wide within the subcontinent can be tentatively fixed on the Aryan endeavour' (Misra and Mate 1965: 199) His dating of the Painted Grey Ware was criticised by R.C. Gaur on the basis of his work at Atranjikhera.

As the ninth essay Sankalia speculated on the 'traditional Indian chronology and C-14 dates of excavated sites' and could not offer any clear picture or even a coherent logical frame. The tenth essay was by B.B. Lal on the use of soil-studies as 'environmental and chronological tools' in archaeology. The final essay of the volume, Sankalia's 'archaeology and education' failed to raise any crucial issue related to the problem in India.

Some New Developments

Outside the orbits of the Deccan College and the Archaeological Survey of India F.R. Allchin of Cambridge University published in 1963, *Neolithic Cattle-Keepers of South India, a Study of the Deccan Ashmounds*. After a grounding in Indian history and literature at the School of Oriental and African Studies of London University, Allchin shifted his interest to Indian archaeology, deciding to follow in the footsteps of R.B. Foote in south India. Two excavation reports were published (Allchin 1960, 1961), preceded by a number of papers dealing with the details of the south Indian neolithic culture. Of the two excavated sites — Piklihal and Utnur — Piklihal was a neolithic site of the region, whereas Utnur was more specifically an ashmound. traditionally associated with the same neolithic complex. The main interest of the work lies in its methodology. Having defined the archaeological problem of ashmounds, he offers the basic archaeological evidence from Utnur including its section, pottery, stone tool industry, animal remains, other objects and analytical data on the composition of ash in this and other such mounds. He then considers the evidence of place-names and the tradition about these mounds in the same region. The study of the place-names was representative, and it was possible to conclude that the evidence of place-names and folk-lore associated 'the ashmounds with some sort of cattle-penning practice'. Further, in a survey of modern cattle-keeping in the Deccan and central India he noted the custom of cattle-penning and the accumulation of cow-dung in such pens. This was followed by a study of what he called 'pastoral elements in folk religion', basically the festivals associated in some way with the cattle and their keepers known under various names in different parts of India.

Certain seasonal festivals like *Divali*, *Holi* and *Pongal* were highlighted in this context. He then turned back to the archaeological evidence and traced the history of repeated burnings at the thirty-odd ashmounds which had been investigated both by him and other workers. The important point is his conclusion : 'all the evidence indicates that the unique ash formation process began and ended within the life cycle of the Deccan Neolithic culture'. (Allchin 1963 : 175) To interpret this evidence he cites the association of fire and cattle in the festivals of *Holi*, *Divali* and *Pongal*.

> We now wish to propose our hypothesis. There is sufficient practical value in the periodical burning of the cattle-pens to warrant the necessary risk in celebrating certain great seasonal festivals in them. Thus every year at the time of the seasonal migrations, which today among the Gollas are regarded as breeding-expeditions, a bonfire ceremony took place in the Neolithic cattle-pens, in much the same way as lamps are lighted in the modern cow-pens and cow-sheds at Holi and Divali. Probably the ceremony involved the cattle being driven through a moderate fire of dung, lighted in the centre of the pen. Our view is that it would be regarded as auspicious, particularly when the pen was in need of reconstruction, if the resulting fire got out of control and caught the whole mass of dung. One may expect that the rite would be accompanied by other kinds of cattle participation, decoration and processions, the choice of royal or king bulls, perhaps driving through mango topes and the *Margapali* rite, sports, etc. —Allchin 1963 : 176-77

Later research has shown that the formation of the Deccanese ashmounds need not have been exclusively neolithic, nor can they be the products of a single universal factor. However, Allchin's explanation, based on his intimate familiarity with the land and its rituals, has still to be considered as one of the viable explanations. The point is that in 1963 it was an attempt to infuse some ethnographic warmth in an important segment of Indian prehistory.

Among the miscellaneous publications of the period one may mention Sourindranath Roy's *The Story of Indian Archaeology 1784-1947* (1961) which was based on the two chapters on the history of the Archaeological Survey of India and the events leading to the establishment of the Survey. In 1964 B.B. Lal offered an account of *Indian Archaeology since Independence*, and a major item of interest in this book which carries a foreword by the Prime Minister Lal Bahadur Sastri, is his reference to the Survey excavations in Nepal (the early historic site of Tilaura Kot and the temple site of Kudan (*c*. AD 1000) in 1961-62 and in Nubia in the same year. The Tilaura Kot work was published by Debala Mitra (1972) but the Nubia work done by Lal lies unpublished. Here he drew attention to the significance of archaeological research in the neighbouring countries from the

Indian point of view and he suggested the setting up of permanent Indian Archaeological Missions for the purpose.

THE PERIOD FROM 1966 to 1973

Ancient India 20-21 (1967), *22* (1973)

Only two issues of *Ancient India* were published during this period. The 20th and 21st numbers were issued as a combined volume, with B.K. Thapar's (1967) report on his excavations at Prakash as its major feature. Among its other features the most important one was D.K. Sen's (1967) criticism of the old trend of racial identifications of the excavated records from Indian sites. The 22nd issue which was due in 1966 was published only in 1973 and primarily contained articles on Nepal. There was no satisfactory explanation of the delay by the editor of this issue, M.N. Deshpande who apologised for the inordinate delay in the publication and added that it would be their endeavour to bring out the subsequent issues as early as possible. No issue has appeared since then.

Excavations

The following chart tries to offer a comprehensive listing of the excavated sites during this period. The data are derived entirely from *IAR*.

Chart 1.2: Excavated sites in *IAR 1965-66* to *IAR 1972-73*

Site	*Years*	*Nature*	*State*	*Status*	*Inst.*	*Person*
Khuntitoli	65-66	historical	Bihar	Unpub.	ASI	S.C. Ray
Buxar	65-66	historical	Bihar	Unpub.	State Dept	B.P. Sinha
Modhera	65-66	temple	Gujarat	Unpub.	ASI	J.P. Joshi
Sejakpur	65-66	temple	Gujarat	Unpub.	ASI	J.P. Joshi
Burzahom	65-73	neolithic	Kashmir	Unpub.	ASI	T.N. Khazanchi
Tripuri	65-71	historical	M.P.	Unpub.	Sagar Uni	K.D. Bajpai ?
Besnagar	65-66	historical	M.P.	Unpub.	State Dept	M.D. Khare
Pondi-Neyveli	65-66	pre-historic	T. Nadu	Unpub.	ASI	K.D. Banerjee
K'vripatt'nm	65-67/70-74	historical	T. Nadu	Unpub.	ASI	K. Deva
Urayur	65-66,67-68	historical	T. Nadu	?	Madras Uni	T.V. Mahalingam ?
Kausan and Paithan	65-66	historical	Maharashtra	Unpub.	State Dept	M.G. Dikshit
Halingali	65-66	neolithic	Karnataka	Unpub.	State Dept	A. Sundara
Terdal	65-66	chalco	Karnataka	Unpub.	State Dept	A. Sundara
Udayagiri	65-66	historical	Orissa	Unpub.	State Dept	A. Joshi
Sugh	65-66	historical	Panjab	Unpub.	Panjab Uni	B.C. Chhabra
Noh	65-72	chalco	Rajasthan	Unpub.	State Dept	R.C. Agrawala

Site	Years	Nature	State	Status	Inst.	Person
Kalibangan	65-69	Harappan	Rajasthan	Unpub.	ASI	B.B. Lal-B.K. Thapar
Khalaua	65-66	chalco	U.P.	Unpub.	ASI	J.P. Gupta
Atranjikhera	65-69	chalco	U.P.	Pub	Alig.Mus. Uni	R.C. Gaur
Masaon	65-66,67-68 70-71	historical	U.P.	Unpub.	Kashi San.Uni	R.B. Narain
Burogaon	65-66	temple	U.P.	Unpub.	ASI	Y.D. Sharma
Kashipur	65-6/70-72	historical	U.P.	Unpub.	ASI	Y.D. Sharma
Rajghat	65-67/68-69	historical	U.P.	Pub.	BHU	A.K. Narain
Chandraketugarh	65-67	early hist	W.Bengal	Unpub.	Cal.Univ	Roychowdhury
Peddabankur	67-69/70-73	historical	Andhra	Unpub.	State Dept	A.W. Khan
Selbalgiri-2	67-68	pre-historic	Meghalaya	Unpub.	Gau.Uni.Anth	T.C. Sharma
Jalukbari	67-68	historical	Assam	Unpub.	Gau.Uni.Anth	T.C. Sharma
Dhatva	67-68	iron	Gujarat	?	MSU Baroda	K.T.M. Hegde
Kayatha	67-68	chalco	M.P.	Unpub.	Vikram Uni	V.S. Wakankar
Paiyampalli	67-68	neolithic	T.Nadu	Unpub.	ASI	S.R. Rao
Champaner	70-73	historical	Gujarat	Unpub.	MSU Baroda	R.N. Mehta
Chirki Nala	66-70	pre-historic	Maharashtra	Pub.	D.Coll	G. Corvinus
Khapa and Takalghat	67-69	megalithic	Maharashtra	Pub.	Nagpur Uni	S.B. Deo
Ter	66-69	historical	Maharashtra	Unpub.	State Dept	?
Pandharpur	67-68	historical	Maharashtra	Unpub.	D.Coll	M.S. Mate M.K. Dhavalikar
Tilwara	67-68	microlithic	Rajasthan	Pub.	D.Coll	V.N. Misra
Bagor	67-70	microlithic	Rajasthan	Unpub.	D.Coll	V.N. Misra
Sarai Mohana	67-68	early hist	U.P.	Unpub.	BHU	A.K. Narain
Tulsipur	67-68	chalco	W. Bengal	Unpub.	ASI/Sydney	J. Birmingham
Battavallam	68-69	pre-historic	Andhra	Unpub.	ASI	K.D. Banerjee
Ambari	68-69/70-71	historical	Assam	Unpub.	Gau.Uni.Anth	T.C. Sharma
Chirand	68-73	neolithic	Bihar	Unpub.	State Dept	B.P. Sinha
Daulatpur	68-69	Harappan	Haryana	Unpub.	Kuruk. Uni	U.V. Singh, S. Bhan
Cheraman	68-69	historical	Kerala	Unpub.	ASI	K.V.S. Rajan
Piparia	68-69	temple	M.P.	Unpub.	Sagar Uni	K.D. Bajpai
Gangapur	68-69	megalithic	Maharashtra	Pub.	Nagpur Uni	S.B. Deo
Inamgaon	68-71,72-73	chalco	Maharashtra	Pub.	D.Coll	M.K. Dhavalikar *et al.*
Khangkui	68-69	pre-historic	Manipur	Unpub.	State Dept	O.P. Singh
Hunur	68-69	megalithic	Karnataka	Unpub.	ASI	S.R. Rao
Budhitittu	68-69	neo/meg	Karnataka	Unpub.	ASI	K.V.S. Rajan
Sanghol	68-73	Harappan	Panjab	Unpub.	State Dept	T.S. Talwar, R.S. Bisht
Korkai	68-69	megalithic	T.Nadu	Unpub.	State Dept	R. Nagaswamy
Lal Qila	68-70,71-72	chalco	U.P.	Pub.	Alig.Mus. Uni	R.C. Gaur
Bhitari	68-70/71-72	temple	U.P.	Unpub.	BHU	K.K. Sinha
Rajbadidanga	66-67/68-69					

Site	*Years*	*Nature*	*State*	*Status*	*Inst.*	*Person*
	71-73	historical	W.Bengal	Unpub.	Cal.Univ	S.R. Das
Bhattiprolu	69-70	*stupa*	Andhra	Unpub.	ASI	R. Subrahmaniyam
Purana Qila	69-73	historical	Delhi	Unpub.	ASI	B.B. Lal B.K. Thapar M.C. Joshi
Malvan	69-70	Harappan	Gujarat	Pub.	ASI/Camb.	J.P. Joshi F.R. Allchin
Champa	69-73	historical	Bihar	Unpub.	Patna Univ.	B.P. Sinha
Martand	69-70	temple	Kashmir	Unpub.	ASI	T.N. Khazanchi
Craganore	69-70	temple	Kerala	Unpub.	ASI	K.V.S. Rajan
Pauni	68-70	*stupa*	Maharashtra	Pub	Nagp U/ASI	S.B. Deo, J.P. Joshi
Kanheri	69-70	historical	Maharashtra	Unpub.	ASI	S.R. Rao
Pachad	69-71	pre-historic	Maharashtra	ASI	ASI	R.V. Joshi
Theur	69-70	chalco	Maharashtra	Unpub.	ASI	S.R. Rao
Kanchipuram	69-73	historical	T.Nadu	Madras Uni ?		T.V. Mahalingam ?
Kaseri	69-70	proto-historic	U.P.	Unpub.	Delhi U/ASI	Romila Thapar K.N. Dikshit
Sarai Nah.Rai	69-70/71-73	microlithic	U.P.	Pub.	Allh Uni	G.R. Sharma
Manwan	69-70	historical	U.P.	Unpub.	State Dept	?
Golconda	70-73	mediaeval	Andhra	Unpub.	State Dept	A.W. Khan
Hashmatpet	70-71	megalithic	Andhra	Unpub.	Birla In. Hyd	M.L. Nigam
Billa Surgam	70-71	pre-historic	Andhra	Unpub.	ASI	R.V. Joshi
Gollathagudi	70-73	temple	Andhra	Unpub.	State Dept	?
Gazulabanda	70-71	*stupa*	Andhra	Unpub.	State Dept	?
Sonpur	70-71	chalco	Bihar	Pub.	State Dept	B.S. Varma
Kankarbagh	70-71	early hist	Bihar	Unpub.	ASI	B.K. Thapar M.C. Joshi
Chandigarh	70-71	Harappan	Panjab	Unpub.	ASI/State	?
Surkotada	70-72	Harappan	Gujarat	Pub.	ASI	J.P. Joshi
Karna-ka-Tila	70-73	Harappan	Haryana	Unpub.	Kuruk. Uni	U.V. Singh, S. Bhan
Navdatoli Preh.	70-71	pre-historic	M.P.	Pub.	D.Coll	J. Armand
Mahurjhari	70-72	megalithic	Maharashtra	Pub.	Nagpur Uni	S.B. Deo
Hathkhamba	70-71/72-73	pre-historic	Maharashtra	Unpub.	ASI	B.P. Bopardikar
Banavasi	70-71	historical	Karnataka	Unpub.	Mys.U/State	?
Sisupalgarh	70-71	historical	Orissa	Unpub.	State Dept	A. Joshi
Pallavamedu	70-71	historical	T.Nadu	Unpub.	State Dept	R. Nagaswamy
Vasavasamudram	70-71	historical	T.Nadu	Unpub.	State Dept	R. Nagaswamy
Perur	70-71	historical	T.Nadu	Unpub.	ASI	K.V.S. Rajan
Malaiyamputtu	70-71	temple	T.Nadu	Unpub.	ASI	K.V.S. Rajan
Ukkirankottai	70-71	historical	T.Nadu	Unpub.	ASI	K.V.S. Rajan
Piprahwa	70-73	historical	U.P.	Pub.	ASI	K.M. Srivastava
Allahpur	70-71	proto-historic	U.P.	Unpub.	Delhi U/ASI	Romila Thapar
Prabhas Patan	70-71	chalco	Gujarat	?	D.Coll	H. Sankalia

Site	Years	Nature	State	Status	Inst.	Person
Tumain	71-73	historical	M.P.	Pub.	Sagar Uni	K.D. Bajpai
Jaderua	71-72	historical	M.P.	Unpub.	Jiwaji Uni	B.B. Lal K.P. Nautiyal
Bhimbetka	71-73	pre-historic	M.P.	Unpub.	Vikram Uni	V.S. Wakankar V.N. Misra
Sastevadi	71-72	proto-historic		Unpub.	ASI	S.R. Rao
Vadgaon, etc.	71-73	historical	Karnataka	Unpub.	State Dept	M.S.N. Rao A. Sundara
Nagar	71-72	historical	Karnataka	Unpub.	ASI	S.R. Rao
Koldihawa	71-72	proto-historic	U.P.	Unpub.	Allh Uni	G.R. Sharma
Takiaper	71-72	historical	U.P.	Unpub.	Allh Uni	G.R. Sharma
Chandavaram	72-73	historical	Andhra	Unpub.	State Dept	?
Chidu-Chumri	72-73	historical	Arunachal	Unpub.	State Dept	Y. Raikar
Malinithan	72-73	historical	Arunachal	Unpub.	State Dept	L.N. Chakravarty
Balirajgarh	72-73	historical	Bihar	Unpub.	State Dept	S.R. Roy
Bhojasala	72-73	historical	M.P.	Unpub.	ASI	V.K. Tiwar
Bhokardan	72-73	historical	Maharashtra	Pub.	Nagpur Uni	S.B. Deo
Patne	72-73	pre-historic	Maharashtra	Pub.	ASI	S.A. Sali
Asurgarh	72-73	historical	Orissa	Unpub.	Samb.Uni	N.K. Sahu
Jodhpura	72-73	chalco	Rajasthan	Unpub.	State Dept	R.C. Agrawala
Jiwangarh	72-73	historical	U.P.	Unpub.	ASI	R.P. Sharma
Bharatpur	72-73	chalco	W. Bengal	Unpub.	ASI/Burd U.	S.C.Roy-S. Samanta

Out of a total of about 112 excavated sites between 1965/66 and 1973, comprehesive and detailed reports have so far been available for only 19. The publication schedule of *IAR* was interesting too.

IAR-65-66 was edited by A. Ghosh before he retired, but the volume could be published only in 1973 when M.N. Deshpande was the Director General of the Survey. B.B. Lal took over as the Director General from Ghosh on 7 February 1968, and curiously, *IAR 1967-68* was published in 1968 itself. The contents of *IAR 68-69* fell in the Lal regime but it was published in 1971. The contents of the 69-70 issue also fell in the Lal regime but its publication took place in 1973. In 1970-71 M.N. Deshpande was the Director General and the issue of that year was published in 1974. The 71-72 issue, also under Deshpande's Director Generalship, was out in 1975, and the 72-73 volume, edited under the Director Generalship of Deshpande, could be out only in 1978. One can also easily detect 'famous' names in the list of unpublished excavations, giving once more general credence to our opinion that Indian archaeology has never been serious about the publication of its reports.

Other Publications

Puratattva, *Bulletin of the Indian Archaeological Society*

One of the major developments of this period was the establishment of the Indian Archaeological Society. This Society was established in 1967-68 with its organisational centre in Banaras Hindu University, Banaras. The first issue of its bulletin was published in the same year, carrying an editorial note. The editors were A.K. Narain (Banaras) M. Sheshadri (Mysore) and S.B. Deo (Nagpur, Pune). The Assistant Editors were P.C. Pant and P. Singh, both from Banaras. It may be put on record here that Professor A.K. Narain played a leading role in its start and perhaps wrote the editorial note himself. While drawing attention to the tremendous expansion of archaeological activities in the country since Independence, he underlines the need for a co-ordinating body which can give a sense of organisation and proper direction :

> It should further serve as a suitable forum for academic discussions and thus provide opportunities to the archaeologists of the various parts of this vast country to exchange views on the diverse problems. With these primary objectives in mind, the Indian Archaeological Society has been formed, somewhat on the lines of similar institutions in other countries.

The journal was named *Puratattva* ('knowledge of the old or past'), and one of its stated aims was to 'try to bring about a worthwhile collaboration between the archaeologists in the field and natural scientists working in the laboratory'. An important methodological article of the first issue was by P.C. Pant (1967-68) on the need for precision and uniformity in discussing the typology of pre-historic tools. This was based on F. Bordes' and others' studies of palaeolithic tools. Another important article was by I.K. Sharma (1967-68) on the possibility of a chalcolithic assemblage with painted pottery in Andhra.

The publication of *Puratattva* and the headquarter of the Indian Archaeological Society were shifted from Banaras to Delhi with the sixth issue of the journal in 1972-73. The leadership of this organisation was then assumed by S.P. Gupta and K.N. Dikshit of the National Museum.

A number of miscellaneous publications appeared in the scene during this period. The newly discovered archaeological data slowly began to find their way into history books. For instance, in his *Cities of Ancient India* B.N. Puri (1966) aimed at giving a historical and archaeological picture of sites of political and religious importance. However, there were some specifically archaeological publications. Archaeological data were the main source of study in Purushottam Singh's analytical review (Singh 1970) of *Burial Practices in Ancient India (a study in the eschatological beliefs of early man as revealed by archaeological sources)*. Although essentially focussed on Baluchistan and the Indus valley, *The Roots of Ancient India, the Archaeology of Early Indian Civilization* (Fairservis 1971) briefly discussed some 'Indian' data. L. Leshnik (cf. 1966) tried to understand the implications of chalcolithic discoveries in central India in the light of the ethnographic framework of the present villages of the area. He also published extensively on the mortuary practices of south Indian megaliths during this period, which was published in a comprehensive form in 1974 (Leshnik 1974).

Bridget and F.R. Allchin's ***The Birth of Indian Civilization***

The highlights of the late 1960s were the publications of two books : *The Birth of Indian Civilization. India and Pakistan before 500 B.C.* by Bridget and F.R. Allchin (1968) and *Indian Civilization, the Formative Period* by S.C. Malik (1968). An important feature of the Allchins' book is that it was published in the widely circulated and easily accessible Pelican series, being the second book on Indian archaeology in this famous series, the first being Stuart Piggott's *Prehistoric India* (1950) which still retains some value as the expression of opinions on the south Asian scene by this distinguished archaeologist. The Allchin volume does not allow for the existence of any major phase corresponding to the upper palaeolithic blade and burin industries of Europe and western Asia. It accepted the three-fold division of the *early*, *middle* and *late* Stone Ages, corresponding to the chopper-biface, flake and microlithic industries respectively. The terms *neolithic* and *chalcolithic* largely overlapped and were used in combination, although they admitted the existence of primary neolithic phases in Baluchistan, Kashmir and south India and a general chalcolithic phase spreading from Baluchistan to various parts of the subcontinent. Further, they thought that the late Stone Age industries of India were 'associated with people much like the modern "tribal" groups in more remote regions who live (or lived until less than a century ago) primarily by hunting and gathering, only sometimes augmenting this by trading with more advanced communities or by going out to work for them'. (B. and F.R. Allchin 1968 : 95) This approach is something which Bridget Allchin earlier developed in her *The Stone Tipped Arrow* (1966) using a substantive amount of Indian data. Although the importance of sites like Kot Diji, Amri, Kalibangan, etc., in understanding the genesis of the Indus civilization was well understood by this time, they do not seem to be sure of the purely indigenous development of this civilization. They were further in favour of considerably shortening its chronology, allowing it only

400 years (2150-1750 BC) to flourish. In retrospect, what is incredible is their detailed discussion on each and every bit of isolated 'west Asiatic' finds in the north-west to try to offer an archaeological evidence of the Aryan invasions at the end of this civilization.. Interestingly, they admit the possibility that even its 'initial impetus may have been due to Indo-European speaking peoples'. (B. and F.R. Allchin 1968 : 144) They also thought that archaeology was on the threshold of pinning down the authors of the *Rigveda* (p. 156). Their discussion of the neolithic-chalcolithic settlements beyond the Indus system was clearly flawed in the sense that they made a distinction between the 'neolithic' of Kashmir, south and east India and the 'chalcolithic' cultures from Kathiawar to the Deccan and the east coast. The chalcolithic cultures were put under the rubric, 'the expansion of post-Harappan settlements'. This was a clear attempt to understand Indian proto-historic data in terms of a neat succession of stages, which was a complete defiance of the complexities of Indian geography. The Aryan question intruded here too. When the chalcolithic cultures are found 'to the east of the geographical region of the Rigveda, they may either indicate pre-Aryan settlements, or settlements of Aryans who had arrived and dispersed before the arrival of those who brought the Rigveda'. (B. and F.R. Allchin 1968 : 206) That the question of the archaeological identification of 'Aryans' was never far from their mind is also suggested by their preoccupation to trace the origin of the south Indian neolithic tradition to various influences from the north-west, including its human physical types which in all cases are supposed to 'fall within a "Caucasoid" or "Mediterranean" range'.

The section on the beginning of iron-working tradition in the subcontinent accepted N.R. Banerjee's postulate without demur : the Hittites of Anatolia provided the earliest and original focus of iron-metallurgy and its dissemination to the subcontinent was attributed to the penetration of Aryan horsemen into the land. The Painted Grey Ware level of the Ganga-Yamuna Doab was ascribed unquestioningly to the phase of the later Vedic literature. In the case of the Iron Age burrial complex of megaliths of south India an attempt was made to combine the Indo-European tradition with sundry other influences, both indigenous and foreign.

> The south Indian graves appear as a developing complex with several strains of influence combining in them. First, some grave types are reminiscent of those of Central Asia, Iran or the Caucasus, and could well represent traits brought from these areas by Indo-European speaking immigrants. Next, some appear as developments of the indigenous Neolithic-Chalcolithic burial customs of the Deccan. A third series points to influences from outside India, and comparable types may indicate the source of the influences.

> Thus, stone cist graves, with and without port-holes, aqre found in the Levant, and on the coasts of south Arabia. Pottery sarcophagi occur in Mesopotamia and the Persian Gulf region during the late centuries B.C., and legged urns identical to Indian types are reported from the Yemen. The same regions provide evidence of rock-cut caves with shaft-like entrances, in forms strikingly reminiscent of those of the Malabar coast. Strictly speaking not all these examples are dated with any precision, and therefore they can scarcely provide a firm basis for comparisons; but they suggest that during the first millennium B.C. India received them as influences by dints of maritime contacts with the Middle East. A fourth stream also cannot be excluded, being the possibility of local developments in peninsular India itself : the stone alignments appear to belong to this class.
>
> — B. and F.R. Allchin 1968 : 230

What is clear is that even in the late 1960s it was almost impossible for many scholars to think clearly of the rapidly increasing archaeological data from various parts of the country in terms of the country itself. The basic points of chronology, specificities of comparisons, etc., did not matter; the movement of Aryans and other people from west Asia was an article of faith, and remained the basic way of accounting for the newly discovered archaeological facts.

The analytical chapters of this volume — 'patterns of settlements', 'economy and agriculture', 'craft and technology' and 'art and religion' — by and large escaped the compulsions of the Aryan premise and still retain some value.

S.C. Malik's ***Indian Civilization : the Formative Period***

S.C. Malik's book was published in 1968 under the auspicies of the Indian Institute of Advanced Study, basically a Government of India set-up in the not-too-well-maintained former viceregal palace in Simla. The Institute was established in 1965 (or around that period) to give people fellowships and other facilities to conduct research in the Humanities and social sciences, apparently under the assumption that facilities for conducting such research were missing in the Indian universities. In practice, this may be interpreted as a place where the politicians or people close to the important politicians can oblige their favourite academics with Directorships and where the Directors can oblige their friends by inviting them to spend some time in the cool of the Simla hills and hold seminars to which they in turn are allowed to invite people belonging to their own networks. On the whole, this is supposed to be a place where the dirt and noise of the Indian universities are not allowed to intrude and the academic invitees play the role of sophisticated '*sahibs*/

memsahibs' in their chosen fields. In fact, Malik's book faithfully echoes the atmosphere of the Institute where it was written.

Malik was a graduate of Delhi University from its Anthropology department where prehistory was — and still, is — marginally taught and which makes no other provision for its students to be introduced to the historical dimensions of the country. He did orthodox field-studies in the Bombay and Satara areas of Maharashtra and eventually joined the Department of Archaeology, M.S. University of Baroda, having spent some time in the meanwhile in the Institute of Archaeology of London University. Subsequently he spent a year under the Fullbright programme at Chicago University. It is important to appreciate this background of Malik because he emphasises throughout the book that Indian archaeology should be based more on anthropology than anything else. His main contention in 'introduction' is that the past archaeological research in India led to 'little interpretative results in terms of any social science approach (such as the processual concepts of "how" and "why") because relatively few professional archaeologists in India have come into it by way of anthropology'. (Malik 1968 : 3) Towards the end of the 'introduction' Malik states the aim of his work : 'The simple aim is to stimulate interest in the development of different approaches to the study of archaeology rather than to present any definitive results.'

In the chapter entitled 'the background' Malik begins by providing a historical sketch of the development of archaeological research in India on the basis of secondary sources. He then takes up for analysis Krishnaswami's article in *Ancient India 9*, Sankalia's *PPIP* and *Indian Prehistory — 1964*. His basic criticism of all these publications bears a common theme : 'interpretations are frequently based on conjectural and imaginative statements rather than on either any social science generalizations or ethnographic fact'. (Malik 1968 : 34)

The next major part of the book is devoted to a study of the 'formative period of Indian civilization', by which he means the Harappan and non-Harappan cultures of the subcontinent. By introducing us to some concepts like 'function', folk-society, peasant society, great and little traditions, etc., he sets out to do essentially a study of interactions between the Harappan civilization and the non-Harappan chalcolithic cultures and within the Harappan civilization itself. This was a perfectly valid exercise but that was also something which any orthodox archaeologist could easily undertake without Malik's anthropological proforma. He then takes up the problem of socio-cultural inferences based on some Harappan evidence. The arguments in this section lead to the hypotheses that the Harappans had a broad subsistence base helped by small-scale canal-based irrigation and that 'the central agency of Harappan society must have served many different functions, such as the social, political and economic ones, in addition to the religious one. (Malik 1968 : 105) The most important part of the book deals with the premise that some features of the Harappan society 'appear to be very familiar in terms of the characteristic institutions by which Indian society (Style) is distinguished from any other society' : the institution of caste, the genealogical means of the perpetuation of caste status by birth and the importance given to the memorisation process. Regarding the origins of the civilization, Malik believes in the process of indigenous origins where 'the ancestors of the people inhabiting the urban areas must have had a long history of the development of the specific form of social organisation and integration in this very area and region'. (Malik 1968 : 112) The process of Harappan urbanisation was rightfully seen as 'the transformation of the indigenous folk and peasant societies into a "primary civilization" '. Its spread too was visualised not as 'colonization' or 'political expansion' but as 'the permeations of the socio-economic and socio-cultutal systems of Harappan society'. This 'permeation' came to include not merely secondary urban areas but also the villages which were parts of the contemporary redistributive urban economy. He argues that even after the disappearance of Harappan cities, the Harappan style of life came to be preserved in the villages and small towns through the preservation, for instance, of its caste-class structure, genealogical descent-reckoning, and the presence of an 'instititionalised resident stranger who is the representative of the urban "elite" but who now becomes a part of the village structure'. This is the most important and original section of Malik's work and certainly a major attempt to visualise the Harappan civilization in terms of an indigenous and Indian framework. When it comes to his attempted integration of the civilization into an alien 'Aryan' framework, it is a different matter altogether. The section on 'culture areas, regionalism and archaeology' is based on Subbarao's discussions in *The Personality of India* and adds that the current or past socio-cultural and political phenomens of India had long-range antecedents 'because of the long continuity of India's traditional society, culture and civilization'. In the final section, 'conclusion', it is argued that the 'static' approach of Indian archaeology should yield to the 'dynamic' one.

We have pointed out the contribution of Malik's book to the understanding of the Indus civilization, but this is the only area where he seems to have bothered with some detail. Otherwise, his entire exercise is didactic, but it is didacticism of a kind which bears no relationship with the grass-roots realities of Indian archaeology. Here he is not concerned at all with the way archaeology was progressing in post-Independence India or how it was structured. He shows no concern with the marginal place of archaeology in the scheme of Indian education. His main concern is that Indian archaeology should be more 'sophisticated'. He does not dare move out of the sacred Aryan-non-Aryan scheme of Indian archaeology; as long as anthropological formulae derived from the Euro-American literature are dutifully cited by Indian archaeologists and historians, he is happy. He would have been taken more seriously if he had shown some interest in pursuing some of the anthropological ideals he espouses in this book in the field.

General Developments

In 1973 S.R. Rao, the excavator of Lothal, published an account of Lothal and the Indus Civilization (Rao 1973) with a foreword by Mortimer Wheeler. In the foreword Wheeler writes about the inadvisability of putting too much trust on the uncorrected radiocarbon dates : 'the often-repeated nonsense about the Indus Civilization dating from, say 2100 to 1700 BC must be forgotten'. Here he admitted, especially in view of the unexcavated levels of Mohenjo-Daro, that the beginning of the mature form of this civilization could go back 'to or beyond 2500 BC'. The main text by Rao has a number of implications from the point of view of some later developments in Indian archaeology. He discusses the primary data in terms of a number of 'provinces' — the central province of the Indus valley, the western province of Baluchistan, the eastern province of Rajasthan and Uttar Pradesh and the southern province of Gujarat. He puts the Panjab-Haryana sites in the central province. When he wrote this book the Haryana sites were mostly undiscovered. The emphasis remained on the Lothal data with an outline of the basic features of the settlement and its stratigraphy. He consistently referred to Lothal as a large port-city of the Harappans. The other chapters of the book dealt with farming and industry, arts and crafts, social life, trade and transport, Indus script, religion, disposal of the dead, authorship, chronology, origin and 'end and devolution'. In the chapter on authorship the physical data of the excavated skeletons was interpreted in terms of the orthodox racial classifications. The presence or absence of the Aryans was a major issue, and according to him (Rao 1973 : 160) 'more than one ethnic group including the pre-Vedic Aryans' were responsible for evolving this civilization. In the chapter on script he makes a distinction between the signs of the mature phase and those of the late phase, comparing the 'Late Harappan Script with the Phoenician and South Semetic writings'. He accepts the attribution of the value of 'a' to the famous 'jar/cup sign' of the Indus script, and confining himself to 15 consonants and 5 vowels derived from this sign, he found it possible to read personal names and titles in nearly 25 seals from Lothal, Harappa and Mohenjo-Daro. It should be remembered that the phonetic values on the analogy of Semetic signs played the most important role in Rao's claim of decipherment of 'all the twenty alphabets of the Late Harappan Script and a few more in the mature Harappan script'. The final conclusion was that 'the early syllabic-cum-alphabetic writing of the Indus people was disciplined into an alphabetic system by 1500 B.C. They spoke an Indo-European language which shows close affinity to Indo-Aryan in vocabulary, semantics and phonology'. (Rao 1973 : 133) The Vedic gods and rituals including the Yogic practices were invoked to explain some seal motifs and terracottas. Thus, the Aryans occupied a fair amount of Rao's thought in his analysis of the Indus civilization. This may be one of the reasons why he highlighted, sometimes uncritically, the similarities of some Indus artefacts (cf. terracottas) with Egyptian, Syrian and other west Asiatic specimens. In the field of religion he thought that 'the religion of the Indus people was the lineal progenitor of Hinduism' (Rao 1973 : 137) and he cites with satisfaction T.N. Ramachandran's opinion that 'the similarity of the Indus valley and Rigvedic conceptions is close and consequently certain'. He also feels that there could be differences in the religious beliefs of the Indus civilization people in different areas. In the case of Lothal he draws attention to the absence of 'any cult-scene or a divinity' on the seals from the site which do not possess 'even the Brahmani bull'. He argues that 'the worship of the god Siva and the phallus were unknown in Saurashtra'. On the other hand, he highlights the finds of 'fire-altars' both at this site and Kalibangan. He accepted the flood-theory of G.F. Dales and R.L. Raikes ands argued that natural disasters of various kinds led to the downfall of the civilization and the dispersal of its people to various peripheral areas including the Ghaggar valley and the Ganga-Yamuna Doab. Regarding its origin, he argued in favour of an essentially autochthonous origin :

> there is no doubt that the pre-Harappan inhabitants of the Indus valley must have taken at least a few centuries, not a couple of generations, as suggested by Ghosh, to completely change over from an illiterate rural economy to a highly industrialized urban civilization.
>
> — Rao 1973 : 175

He further accepted Wheeler's date of *c.* 2500 BC for the beginning of this civilization, rejecting arguments to bring it down to 2300 BC. He believed, quite rightly, that this late date went against 'the impressive evidence of seals and other objects found in well-dated levels of Mesopotamian cities'.

In view of his excavations at Rangpur and Lothal, publication of their reports and basic mapping of Harappan sites in Gujarat, S.R. Rao's contribution to the study of the Indus civilization has to be ranked much higher than that of any of his Archaeological Survey contemporaries. This is the reason why some of his ideas in this context needed specific mention. This book by Rao also highlights that by the early 1970s the Indus studies were in a kind of flux. On the one hand, the idea of continuity from an early Harappan stage or still earlier stages in Baluchistan was getting increasingly clear, but on the other hand there was still a fair amount of confusion about the way in which the civilization was linked to later developments. The short radiocarbon chronology offered by D.P. Agrawal (1964) did not suggest a long-drawn process of 'beginning' and 'end', and Agrawal's (1965) assertion that his uncalibrated radiocarbon chronology fitted in the scheme of archaeological evidence of Indus-west Asiatic contacts made matters worse. By 1973 R.H. Brunswig made his point about the implications of calibration on the Indus civilization radiocarbon dates, but those implications had not yet sunk in when Rao published his book. The 1960s were also the time when the 'massacre theory' of the decline or end of the civilization was challenged, with the idea of natural disasters slowly gaining ground. Rao's is the first major Indian publication which tried to stabilise, so to speak, the somewhat confusing situation of the Indus studies of that period with reference, primarily, to the data from India, especially Lothal. He did not put the Aryans away; he tried to incorporate them in the fabric of the Indus civilization. Some parallels between Indus representations and the rituals and/or divinities suggested by the Vedic religion have long been noted by Indian scholars including M.S. Vats who interpreted the painted designs on the Cemetery H pottery from Harappa in terms of the Vedic funerary ceremonies. Rao incorporated this strand of analysis in his book, going to the extent of claiming that the language spoken by the Harappans belonged to the Indo-Aryan family.

There were two other major single-authored books during this period : D.P. Agrawal's *Copper-Bronze Age in India* (1971) and A. Ghosh's *The City in Early Historic India* (1973). As the archaeologist in charge of the radiocarbon laboratory, first in the Tata Institute of Fundamental Research, Bombay, and then in the Physical Research Laboratory, Ahmedabad, D.P. Agrawal must be considered, along with his scientist colleague Sheela Kusumgar, the two most visible people behind the acceptance and dissemination of radiocarbon dates and their significance in Indian archaeology. In this book, however, he was concerned with the metallurgical analysis of a representative range of Indian proto-historic copper-bronze artefacts and their explanation in the archaeological contexts. It is not that archaeometallurgical studies in the subcontinent began with Agrawal; such studies can be traced back to the nineteenth century and great credit should be given in this connection to Mohammad Sanah Ullah and his successors (such as B.B. Lal) in the post of Chief Archaeological Chemist in the Archaeological Survey of India. However, Agrawal once again highlighted the general issues of this branch of study in the light of some fresh analytical studies that he himself undertook on some proto-historic samples of both the Harappan and non-Harappan varieties. His major emphasis, apart from the actual results of metal analysis, was on what he called the ecological backgrounds of the archaeological cultures which yielded the samples. Even in the context of the early 1970s Agrawal's treatment of both archaeological chronology and ecology was straight-jacketed, almost amounting to environmental determinism. Further, his book made no allowance for the tremendous breadth and diversity of copper metallurgical traditions of pre-industrial India. But on the whole, this book suggested the renewal of an old concern in Indian proto-historic archaeology, aided by the new tool of radiocarbon dating and new techniques like atomic absorption spectometry.

A. Ghosh's book on the early historic cities marked the beginning of specific interests in the process and phenomenon of urban growth as a theme of research in Indian archaeology. This slim volume, written in Ghosh's post-retirement days at the Institute of Advanced Study, Simla, was, like the earlier volume of Malik from the same Institute, not much based on the empirical data of different phases in different parts of the subcontinent. That had to wait till a revised version of the present author's Ph.D. thesis (Calcutta University, 1972-73) on the archaeological perspective of the Harappan and early historic urban centres of India was published many years later (Chakrabarti 1995). Both Ghosh's book and the present author's dissertation were in a sense rooted in the specifically archaeological interest in the general theme of urbanisation which had been noticeable since the early 1960s. In India this interest was reflected by H.D. Sankalia's paper in the volume *Courses toward Urban Life* edited by R.J. Braidwood (1962). The archaeological scholarship of the time was divided between the technological school of Gordon Childe and the Chicago school of Orientalists who emphasised the primacy of social-institutional changes. The present author reviewed the basic pattern of Indian data in the light of this controversy and agreed with the latter school (Chakrabarti 1972-73). In his comments on the present author's paper in 1972-73 in *Puratattva 6* A. Ghosh supported the conclusions of this paper. One of the concerns of his book was to assess the archaeological data on the early historic Indian cities in the light of the ten urban traits listed in Childe's 1950 paper on the Urban Revolution in *Town Planning Review*. He agreed that there was a break in the history of Indian urbanism between the end of the Harappan civilization and the beginning of History in the Gangetic plain. He did not neglect the probable role of the Achaemenids in the beginning of the urban process in the north-west when they extended their empire up to the Indus valley. If anything in this book betrays Ghosh's concern with the text-based image of ancient India, that is his implicit acceptance of the hypothesis of Aryan migration to India. He clearly expressed his belief that the Painted Grey Ware culture represented the later Vedic Aryans. That was also something he accepted in his editorial notes in *Ancient India 10-11*. It was not that the Aryan premise was entirely unchallenged in the early 1970s. In 1968 the present author offered a detailed review of the Aryan hypothesis in Indian archaeology and argued that none of the theories offered made any logical sense and were in fact mutually contradictory (Chakrabarti 1968). However, Ghosh, like many of his generation of Indian archaeologists, had to discover archaeological evidence of Aryan migrations to India.

In the early 1970s there were also a number of edited volumes in the field of Indian archaeology. *Potteries in Ancient India* edited by B.P. Sinha (1969) was, in fact, published in 1969 and concerned more with the Gangetic valley types like OCP, PGW, NBP, etc., than with the types from other regions. In 1972 S.B. Deo (1972) edited a volume entitled *Archaeological Congress and Seminar Papers* and based on the papers at the 4th annual session of the Indian Archaeological Society in Nagpur in 1970. Such annual sessions and attached seminars, funded wholly by the national organisations of different kinds, became increasingly a common feature of Indian academia, and whether the proceedings were published or not depended on the efficiency and commitment of their participants and organisers. For instance, the Institute of Advanced Study in Simla organised a conference on the Indus civilization in the autumn of 1977 but its organiser B.B. Lal, who spent a significant number of his post-retirement years as a 'fellow' of this institute and eventually its director, was unable to publish its proceedings. However, Deo believed in the importance of timely publications, and some papers published in this volume still retain a historical value. For instance, R.K. Pant's paper on 'the tool-marks as vital technological and functional data' is the first paper in the Indian context on the micro-wear analysis of stone tools and Suraj Bhan's paper on the 'changes in the course of the Yamuna and their bearing on the proto-historic cultures of Haryana' opens up a new chapter in the history of the Harappan studies in the Indo-Gangetic divide. Similarly, J.P. Joshi's paper on his Harappan explorations in Kutch is of pioneering significance in that context. Apart from documenting a greatly increased number of new Harappan sites in Kutch, which was achieved by following the old caravan routes between Kutch and Sind, this paper highlights the feasibility of overland connections between these two areas. Until then the prevalent idea was that the Harappans reached Saurashtra only by sea. K.T.M. Hegde who had hitherto conducted technical analyses of some proto-historic metal artefacts and the slip of NBP wrote a summary paper on his work under a rather curious title, 'physics and chemistry in Indian archaeology'. Vishnu Mittre's paper on 'palaeobotany and the environment of early man in India' and the subsequent exchange between him and Gurdeep Singh put certainly Singh's famous postulate of 'cerealia pollen' in the profiles of Rajasthan salt lakes in an interesting light. H.D. Sankalia offers a review of 'the chalcolithic cultures of India' and commented that the problem of their 'authorship' was more vital than their archaeological aspects. According to him this problem of authorship raised the following questions :

(i) Do these cultures represent indigenous people or peoples ?

(ii) Who could they be ?

I. Indo-Aryans,

II. Pre-Aryans or non-Aryans, speaking the Munda, Kol, Ho, or the Gondi, that is the Austro-Asiatic and Dravidian languages,

III. Are these cultures Gangetic or do they belong to the old lateritic plateau ? (Deo 1972: 156)

The Association of South Asian Archaeologists in Western Europe was founded in 1970 'to provide a forum for scholars based in Europe who specialise in the pre-historic and historic archaeology of the subcontinent and its Iranian and Burmese borderlands'. (Hammond 1973) It held its first international conference in Cambridge in 1971, with its proceedings being published in 1973. (Hammond 1973) The published volume carried a foreword by Mortimer Wheeler who wrote the following :

> If in the recent conference there was a weakness, it lay in the less than adequate representation of this scholarship actually from the Orient, no doubt due in part to inadequate or inadequately organised means of travel.

This weakness still continues; in fact the south Asian participation in this biennial conference, which has a commendable regularity of expensive publications reporting Euro-American archaeological research in the subcontinent (mostly Pakistan where the number of 'foreign' missions working is larger than the rest of the subcontinent), has been marginal. The Indian participation has always been limited to a handful of people who love to attend conferences of any kind and one or two 'important' people whose travel costs are borne by the organisers of the conference. Even the impact of their publications in India has been less than what it should have been because of the comparative rarity of articles on India in them and of their high prices in terms of Indian rupees. The prices would have been much cheaper if they were published in India. But, as an unstated purpose of these volumes is to hold aloft the banner of Euro-American power in south Asian archaeology, they cannot obviously be published in India. It is to the credit of Bridget Allchin that she organised the publication of a single volume in India, which made that particular volume widely available in the Indian university libraries. It is also curious that the volume published in 1973 or those published later nowhere comments on the general absence of any kind of south Asian archaeological studies in the Euro-American set-up. The general tendency is to lay the blame at the door of the Government of India which has been reputedly hesitant in giving 'permits' to foreign archaeological expeditions, but a more correct explanation is that the scheme of Indian studies in the Western universities is ruthlessly dominated by unsavoury Indologists of various shades who have not the most marginal interest in the material features of the ancient Indian past. On the whole, these volumes are the main, if not the only, vehicles of publication of the work done by 'foreign' missions in Pakistan. As far as Indian archaeology is concerned, their effect has been marginal.

Radiocarbon Dating and a Neglected Blue-print of Archaeological Science

We have already drawn attention to the beginning of radiocarbon dating in India, first at the Tata Institute of Fundamental Research (TIFR), Bombay, and then at the Physical Research Laboratory (PRL), Ahmedabad. The radiocarbon laboratory of the TIFR was set up by a physicist, D. Lal, in 1961-62, with the support of Homi Bhava who is rightfully considered the 'father' of India's Atomic Energy Programme. Although D.P. Agrawal and A. Ghosh do not mention the fact in their joint preface to the volume entitled *Radiocarbon and Indian Archaeology* (1973), the beginning of radiocarbon dating in the country was made first in the Bose Institute of Science, Calcutta sometime in the late 1950s. The scientist concerned was Shyamadas Chatterjee, an eminent Indian physicist in his own right. The dating was done on a piece of wood from the remains of the famous timber palisade of Pataliputra and reported in a Calcutta science journal called *Science and Culture*. S.D. Chatterjee subsequently shifted to the physics department of Jadavpur University of Calcutta, and it was there that he undertook the dating of a charcoal sample from the West Bengal proto-historic site of Pandu Rajar Dhibi. The dating arrived at was 1012 +/- 120 BC (half-life of 5568 years). The dating was subsequently published in a brief and incomplete report on the excavations at this site by the West Bengal

Directorate of Archaeology (Dasgupta 1965). However, the radiocarbon dating did not eventually take off in Calcutta, and the TIFR and PRL deserve all credit for introducing this technique to Indian archaeology in an organised and systematic fashion. A special word of credit should also go to D.P. Agrawal who joined as the Secretary of the Radiocarbon Committee of the Institute and was expected to act as a kind of liaison man between the archaeologists and the scientists. However, he soon took on the mantle of an active researcher in the fields of archaeometallurgy, quaternary investigations and radiocarbon dating and directed specific attention of the archaeological community to the historical possibilities of archaeological science in India. One does not have to agree with the theories offered by him to admit the historical importance of his role.

To mark the first decade of active archaeological science work of the TIFR laboratory, the laboratory organised an international symposium in March 1972 to study the impact of radiocarbon dating in India and related scientific work in archaeology. Apart from a handful of non-Indian scholars, the delegates were predominantly from the Archaeological Survey of India and the Deccan College, which adequately reflected the prevailing power-structure of Indian archaeology. The proceedings which were published in 1973 (Agrawal and Ghosh 1973) carried a 'foreword' by M.G.K. Menon, one of the policy-making physicists of India. Menon adequately deals with the academic background of the setting up of a radiocarbon laboratory in the TIFR :

> Experimental work in the areas of cosmic ray physics and nuclear physics, and a wide variety of electronic techniques have been the background for much of the work at the Tata Institute of Fundamental Research since its inception. Arising from this was the development of the geophysics research programmes based on radiochemical and low-level counting techniques; these were developed for the detection of naturally occurring radioisotopes and their use for studying a variety of phenomena in the earth sciences. It was clear that all of the expertise and background necessary to set up and to operate successfully a radiocarbon laboratory existed at this Institute.
>
> At the time the laboratory was set up, there were only a few isolated radiocarbon ages obtained from Indian archaeological horizons through samples sent abroad. This was both expensive and time consuming; and clearly not available for large scale dating in Indian archaeology. Homi Bhava therefore decided to set up at this Institute a radiocarbon laboratory as a service facility for Indian archaeology. — Agrawal and Ghosh 1973 : vi

Menon goes on to emphasise that radiocarbon is only one of the physical techniques available for archaeological research :

> We must not forget that many more physical methods are becoming available which are extremely powerful in their own way; and I see no reason why Indian archaeological research should not use these in a significant way and enrich itself. —*Ibid* : vii

He then briefly alludes to the potential of a host of destructive and non-destructive tools of physical analysis of a whole range of materials, and comments :

> These various techniques exist in the country in some form or the other (rudimentary or advanced) in various universities and institutes, for research on aspects of physics and chemistry. Some of this research is not very important or first-rate in itself, but the technique is there. And if one make the concerned research worker realize that by adapting these techniques for use with archaeological specimens, results can be obtained of much greater significance and importance, then a great deal would have been achieved. The basic problem is of getting the archaeologists and physical scientists together. . . . I hope that archaeologists will begin to appreciate the significance of these objective physico-chemical methods and interest physical scientists in joining hands with them. Since both categories of research workers exist in India, I look forward to an era of successful and exciting co-operation. —*Ibid* : viii

This 'era of successful and exciting co-operation', which Menon hopes for, is still a very far cry in Indian archaeology. However, Menon's 'foreword' still remains the best blue-print for the development of archaeological science in India. The fact that it has not yet got beyond the blue-print stage or the fact that this blue print itself has been pushed into a dusty corner of the shelf is a serious negative reflection on the Indian archaeologists and historians and the power structures that operate behind them.

Only a handful of papers had anything to do with archaeological science. A line of investigation which came in for close attention was the environment of early man, almost exclusively in western India. The science papers which are historically significant were contributed by R.K. Iyer on 'neutron activation analysis', by Sheela Kusumgar on the problem of errors in radiocarbon dating, by S.B. Lal on the geochronology of lateritisation, by G.G. Mujumdar on the technical studies of ancient pottery and by Venkatavaradan on the potential of archaeological inferences from human hair. S.C. Malik undertook a long didactic exercise about the models and social relevance in Indian archaeology without giving a single case-study of the relevance of his 'models' or their 'social usage', but his basic honesty of purpose puts it on a far superior level than the pious platitudes of Indian historians like those of Romila Thapar (1973) on the relevance of archaeological data to the study of Indian history. The main theme of Malik's article is a call to redefine our archaeological research goals in the context of the emerging values of modern India :

> Those who wish to know India's past 'objectively' without involvement, and claim to pursue self-evident 'truth' are really *status quo* people who do not wish India to change. And, not only that, they wish to perpetuate their own ideas and those of the 'vested' interests, even if at times, unconsciously. — Agrawal and Ghosh 1973 : 375

To us, 'involvement' is the key word, and in retrospect, one wishes Malik himself were to give some more evidence of 'involvement' in Indian archaeology. The opinion of '*status quo* people' mentioned by Malik was cogently put forward by H.D. Sankalia (*ibid*). In an analysis of 'radiocarbon dates in India, their consistency and cultural implications' he reaches the following conclusion :

> Thus, according to the evidence presented here on the strength of C14 dates, pottery, grains, oil-seeds and human skeletons, a slow and gradual diffusion of cultures from western Asia, in wave after wave, was responsible for the growth and development of various regional cultures of India from *c.* 3000 B.C. to 500 B.C., i.e. from the Neolithic-Chalcolithic period to the Early Iron Age (or the Megalithic of south India). These western cultural and biological impacts have never altogether ceased. Time and again during historical times, these influences have poured in or filtered through, depending upon the force of the immigrant culture or people, causing various changes in the racial stock, religions, dress and ornaments of the local elements. . . . There remain the various Chalcolithic and Neolithic Cultures of central India, south India and eastern India. No specific labels have been suggested for these people. However, it seems to be certain that these people had some Iranian or western Asiatic blood in them. They might be described anatomically, as Mediterranean or Europoid, according to one's predilection. . . .
>
> — Agrawal and Ghosh 1973 : 215-16

In the Indian archaeology of the early 1970s I do not know of a more forthright and comprehensive 'racial' and 'colonial' model of the ancient Indian past than the above-mentioned analysis of the Indian archaeological situation by H.D. Sankalia.

CONCLUDING REMARKS ON INDIAN ARCHAEOLOGY, 1947-73

It is undeniable that Indian archaeology greatly expanded its base in the wake of Independence. To claim that it was an abrupt process of expansion would be wrong. In many ways this expansion was rooted in the archaeology of the preceding years. The possibility of Harappan discoveries in Panjab, Gujarat, Rajasthan, and perhaps even the upper portion of the U.P. Doab, was already understood, and what was needed in the post-Independence years was a deliberate quest. We have seen how that quest bore rich fruits. The seeking of proto-historic roots of historical Indian cultures was a recognised research aim after the excavations at Brahmagiri, and committed persons everywhere began to discover hitherto unperceived dimensions of Indian protohistory. Krishnaswami's article on Stone Age India in *Ancient India 3* introduced the Indian archaeological community at large to the scope and significance of stone tool discoveries in the land. It is not that these discoveries were welcomed with open arms all over India. As a young student in Calcutta of the early 1960s the present author is fully aware of how the Calcutta academic establishment refused to accept the pre-historic and proto-historic discoveries initiated in the State of West Bengal by the Director of its State archaeology, P.C. Dasgupta. To some extent, it was due to the exuberant and occasionally wild claims made by the Director, but to a great extent it was due to the sheer cussedness and envy on the part of the local university set-up. The general academic response to the first flush of pre-historic and proto-historic discoveries in various parts of the country perhaps deserves a fuller study, but I suspect that they were not greeted very effusively in the general Indian academic scene related to historical studies. Where the archaeologists themselves showed their commitment to the point of coming out with full reports on their discoveries, the reception was no doubt genuine and warm, notwithstanding some initial hesitation. In the early years at least the Archaeological Survey of India played a stellar role; the Director Generals till A. Ghosh's retirement had a national perspective and were educated enough to possess an awareness of the outstanding archaeological problems of the country as a whole. In retrospect, one also finds it difficult to accuse them of being openly supportive of their individual castes and regions. Not all the Director Generals of the post-Ghosh years have been casteist or regionalist, but some of them have certainly been vitiated by these feelings, which has no doubt played havoc with the general morale of the Survey officers. To some extent I would put the responsibility squarely on the shoulders of the early Director Generals themselves for ignoring to lay down a comprehensive recruitment policy for the Archaeological Survey of India, the largest recruiting organisation of Indian archaeology. The recruitment to the Survey has always been through 'interviews' which in the Indian context has mostly meant manipulations based on caste and region, especially in a field like archaeology where job opportunities are severely restricted. The old principle of recruiting 'scholars' was soon discarded, and this slowly led to a situation where the academic record of the recruitee ceased to be a matter of concern. Secondly, the early Director Generals should have tried to get rid of some aspects of the pre-1947 policy. For instance, the publication policy ought to have been considerably liberalised. What Indian archaeology needed — or needs even now — is a spate of easily produced publications containing the basic documentation of the works done. An ideal model would have been the Geological Survey of India publications with their 'ordinary' paper and ordinarily printed pages and illustrations. Besides, one does not have to be a 'scholar' to write down clearly what one has done in the field. The quest for mythical scholarly reports has not done the Survey any good, especially when 'scholars' have been in singularly short supply among its recruits.

One of the most important developments in the field of Indian archaeological studies during this period was the regularisation of archaeology as an academic discipline in some Indian universities. The establishment of separate university departments under the rubrics of 'Department of Archaeology' or 'Department of Ancient Indian History, Culture and Archaeology' with financial support from the Indian University Grants Commission was a major step forward, and to some extent one would have been justified in hoping for a greatly increased profile of archaeological studies and research in the Indian universities after this very positive support from the UGC. The universities which figured in this context were Pune, Baroda, Lucknow, Madras, Calcutta, Banaras, Sagar and Allahabad. This process of development began around 1960. In Calcutta there were eight 100-mark papers divided into 16 'halves' of 50-mark each. They ran like this: elements of physical and ancient historical geography of India; ethnology, history of archaeology, principles and methods of archaeology, prehistory of India, protohistory of India, palaeography, epigraphy, numismatics, iconography, sculpture and painting, architecture, Mesopotamian history, Mesopotamian archaeology, methods of conservation, and practicals including an interview. With variations, this was the general pattern of syllabus of archaeology in the few universities where Archaeology was introduced as a recognised academic subject. These Departments — it is important to point out — came with a ready package : a separate building, one-off grant for equipment including surveying, drawing, photographic and camping equipment, recurrent grants for annual excavations and explorations, and a number of academic and non-academic posts including those of administrative staff, surveyor-draughtsman, photographer, museum curator, etc. For the students there was a compulsory requirement of fieldwork for 12 weeks in 2 years, and the field-notebooks had to be submitted during the 'practical' test. It was virtually impossible to claim that the UGC was not adequately supportive of Archaeology in the universities.

The newly-created Departments of Pune and Baroda made the most of this new opportunity. By 1960 they, under the leadership, respectively, of Sankalia and Subbarao, had an active archaeological field-programme, with — as we have earlier noted — a rich record of important publications. Historically speaking, the study of ancient India was comparatively new at these places, and one would think that their already-working archaeology groups could move forward without any major constraint. Under the leadership of G.R. Sharma Allahabad too had a long-standing archaeological programme at Kausambi, and had, by the early 1970s, expanded into pre-historic and proto-historic investigations of the eastern fringe of the Vindhyas. Under the leadership of A.K. Narain Banaras Hindu University began to excavate the remains of ancient Banaras at Rajghat. The publication record of Allahabad and Banaras was not impressive in the early years, but the very fact that they were involved in such famous ancient Indian cities as Kausambi and Varanasi redounded to their credit. The situation was somewhat different in the other places. In Calcutta, Lucknow and Madras, for instance, the study of ancient India was well-rooted, and archaeology in these places meant primarily an extension of ancient Indian studies with the freshly added elements of prehistory, protohistory, conservation, excavations and explorations. Calcutta had an earlier background of archaeological investigations, but those investigations used to be conducted by the university's museum of 'Fine Arts' under the leadership of a Sanskrit language teacher who participated in the Mohenjo-Daro and Ahichchhatra excavations. The university's Anthropology department had a long-standing interest in prehistory, but the pre-historians were not familiar with the techniques of excavation. Thus, there were teething problems in Calcutta's archaeology programme, and the new Department's reluctance to publish its reports did not help matters. What has been said about Calcutta can be said about Lucknow and Madras too. These three Departments were dominated right from the start by people whose major field was 'ancient India', and it is doubtful if they ever came to terms with archaeology. Among the early university departments Sagar certainly deserves a place, but regrettably their long years of excavations at the important chalcolithic site of Eran in central India did not lead to any substantive publication.

By the early 1970s the UGC had limited resources for archaeology, and the bulk of the grants went to places who could show good results for their early years. By now the question of personal influences also came in, and one would think that by this time the weak departments were well on their way of becoming weaker. The university expansion of archaeological studies on the M.A. level was not accompanied by any change in the B.A. stage of historical studies, at least not for a long time. This restricted the opportunities for job in this new subject, and consequently the students' response was lukewarm.

What was happening on the provincial government levels during this period was no less interesting. All the major 'States' had their separate Archaeology directorates/ departments by the early 1970s. What they did with them depended exclusively on the enthusiasm and leadership of the 'directors' of these new units. Interestingly, they too began with complete packages, space, equipment and staff being laid on fairly generously. Being government departments they had better budgets than university departments. Some departments (cf. Andhra and partly Bihar) were more forthcoming with publications, but other departments remained satisfied with brief accounts in *IAR*, which did not greatly increase their reputation or morale. Before long, many of them became moribund, functioning not as an academic research organisation but as another bureaucracy-ridden minor government department.

By this time Indian archaeology also made bold attempts to lay the foundations of an increased collaboration between archaeologists and scientists. Part of it was already there. The Archaeological Survey of India had always kept alive its interest in archaeological chemistry, and to this interest was now added the facility of a radiocarbon laboratory. The implications of both archaeo-botany and archaeo-zoology were well realised, and although the number of people involved was small, publications kept coming out, leading in turn to a better awareness of the possibilities of scientific analysis of the excavated archaeological material. By 1973 Menon's blue-print for the development of archaeological science in India was available for everybody to read. However, right from the beginning, archaeological science found no place in the scheme of the universities. The newly established university archaeology set-ups had some posts for a few categories of archaeological science, notably in chemistry, botany and zoology. Most of these posts were eventually converted into general archaeological positions, and the very few posts that remained could not do a lot because of a serious shortage of funds. Again, Deccan College under H.D. Sankalia was an exception. The Baroda department too showed serious concern with archaeological chemistry. Banaras had a marginal interest in chemistry but this was not allowed to develop in any way.

While pointing out the major elements of progress in Indian archaeology between 1947 and 1973 we have thought it proper to put some emphasis on the inhibiting factors as well and the general situation behind such factors.

It is also intriguing that till 1973 the major explanatory framework of Indian archaeological universe was in terms of race and language, and the diffusion of such racial and language groups from west Asia. In 1972 I.K. Sharma made a rather valiant effort to add south-east Asia in a big way as a source of such diffusionary impulses. However, dissident voices began to be heard from about this time; alternative ways began to be explored, and Malik (1973) went to the extent of drawing attention to the perpetuation of 'colonial research stereotypes and fallacies'. The very fact that such concerns began to be expressed in Indian archaeology was in a large measure due to the induction of the subject in the universities. We have seen that the university level archaeology in India had some inhibiting factors right from the beginning, but despite all these handicaps archaeology became recognised, by the early 1970s, as an academic subject in the country with its inevitable concomitant of challenges and counter-challenges and altogether a much greater air of freedom. Whatever might have been our comments on the various seminar proceedings we have discussed in this chapter, these were milestones in the general progress of the subject in the country. Their significance as milestones will be better realised if one remembers that it was the first time that scholars from different parts of the country were coming together to discuss archaeological issues.

This, of course, in no way lessened the grip of bureaucracy in archaeological research in India, and nowhere is the tone of bureaucratic and self-seeking attitude of the Indian archaeological Establishment more sanctimonious and complacent than in the editorial notes written by Ghosh in *Ancient India 20-21* which otherwise is devoted to B.K. Thapar's (1967) report on Prakash and D.K. Sen's comments on the study of Indian excavated skeletal remains in terms of 'races'. In his notes Ghosh mentions that the Government of India appointed in 1965 an Archaeological Review Committee with Mortimer Wheeler as Chairman and Professors H.D. Sankalia, Niharranjan Ray and S. Nurul Hassan as members. The committee assembled from 15 March to 1 April 1965, holding its meetings and inspections in Delhi, Kalibangan, Hyderabad, Kondapur and Agra. It submitted its 22000-word report to the Minister of Education on 2 April. The report, divided into 20 chapters and 2 appendices, lauded, without any reservation, the work done by the Archaeological Survey of India.

> The Committee wishes to make one thing clear at the outset : namely, its complete faith in the integrity, liveliness and devotion of the Survey's staff. . . . It is fair to say that in no part of the world is there at the present time a better understanding than in India of the basic techniques of modern scientific excavation. . . . The Survey remains, and will remain, the only institution capable of sustained and major enterprises of the kind (in the field of excavation). The Survey is responsible for sustaining the national standard in this increasingly scientific branch of research. . . .
>
> — Ghosh 1965 : 1-2

Mortimer Wheeler's loyalty to the Survey, an organisation he once served, is well known, and in the Indian archaeological world the cases of septuagenarian and octogenarian former officers of the Survey trying to derive some political mileage by waving long-forgotten testimonials from Wheeler are not unknown. It is, however, incredible that the three senior Indian academics who were Wheeler's fellow-members of the Committee forgot that no academic discipline ever thrived outside the portals of universities and that no single organisation could ever be considered responsible for holding aloft the standard of a particular academic discipline in the country. It is also incredible that these people ignored the fact that by 1965, i.e., the year in which they drew up their report, archaeological excavations in India were reduced to mere routine publicly funded activities which very few people were interested in publishing in detail.

This is the last Government of India committee on archaeology that one has reliable information about. There have been other committees since then but their deliberations and recommendations are unpublished. One does not even know why these committees were set-up in the first place. It is, of course, unlikely that they were set-up with the general improvement of Indian archaeology in mind. Whatever one has come to know about these archaeological committees in recent years has led to the impression that they are set up only when something has to be pushed through the government channels for the personal or departmental benefit of some individuals. They are also invariably filled up by people who will eagerly sign on the dotted lines.

2

New Issues and Perspectives 1974 to the Present

THE YEAR 1974

H.D. Sankalia's *Prehistory and Protohistory of India and Pakistan* and the New Researches It is Based on

From our point of view the most important event of 1974 was the publication of *Prehistory and Protohistory of India and Pakistan* (cited hereafter as *PPOP*) by Sankalia. This was no doubt a revised and enlarged edition of his 1962 publication *PPIP*, but just as the earlier work dealt with the basic scaffolding of the subcontinent's prehistory and protohistory on the basis of the ongoing research, this work too gave a ready access to this knowledge, highlighting the field-investigations that had taken place in the meanwhile. The theoretical scheme remained unchanged. India was still considered 'to be on the periphery of the culture spread in relation to Western Asia'. (p. 7) Although there was a reference to Grahame Clarke's opinion that the 'invasion hypothesis' was overemphasised in British archaeology and should leave some scope for 'explanation in terms of indigenous evolution' (fn 14c, p.7), nothing was done to emphasise this approach in the volume. In its chapter on 'lower palaeolithic cultures' there was a detailed discussion on the Terra-Paterson work in the Soan valley, as before, but in the context of Indian Panjab there are now discussions on R.V. Joshi's and G.C. Mohapatra's explorations in the Kangra area (Joshi 1968, Mohapatra 1966) and Mohapatra's work near Chandigarh and in the adjacent Siwaliks. (Mohapatra 1966) An important step forward was Sankalia's own find of some lower palaeolithic tools in what he argued to be a lower pleistocene context. The find was not supported by R.V. Joshi's and others' work in the same area (Joshi *et al.* 1974), but in view of the recent claims of lower pleistocene palaeolithic finds in Ladakh, Panjab Siwaliks and elsewhere, this report by Sankalia is important. In the central Narmada valley, S.G. Supekar's Ph.D. thesis in the Deccan College (1968) acted as the base-line of Sankalia's discussion. The section on Uttar Pradesh was expanded beyond the Singrauli basin by taking into consideration the Allahabad University's work in Banda, Hamirpur, the Belan valley and the adjacent areas of Madhya Pradesh, such as Rewa. In the case of these more recent discoveries in U.P. he emphasised the need of working out a detailed stratigraphy aided by excavations which would throw light on the evolution of tool-types in this region. The Garo hill region was mentioned in the context of the north-east, although we would straightaway reject his support for T.C. Sharma's hypothesis of a lower palaeolithic industry in Meghalaya. In Bihar the new results were provided by A.K. Ghosh's work on Singhbhum (1970), B. Narayan's work in the Jethyan valley near Rajgir and his own work in the Bhimbandh area of the Kharagpur hills in Munger. He disagreed with Ghosh's subdivisions of the Singhbhum lower palaeolithic. For West Bengal he depended mostly on A.K. Ghosh's fresh work in the region and the discoveries of various types of stone tools made by the Directorate of Archaeology, Government of West Bengal, in the western part of the State. In Orissa the lower palaeolithic framework was still dependent on the earlier Mayurbhanj work by Bose and Sen and Mohapatra's broader survey, but he also made a reference to K.C. Tripathy's unpublished dissertation on the lithic industries of south-western Orissa (Tripathy 1980). In Andhra he found new material in two Deccan College Ph.D. theses : *Stone Age Cultures of Nalgonda* (S.N. Rao 1966) and *Stone Age Cultures of Chittoor District* (M.L.K. Murty 1966). In Tamil Nadu he could refer to K.D. Banerjee's excavation in the Gudiyam cave and survey from Chennai to Nellore. In Karnataka he cited Z.A. Ansari's find of pebble tools at Nittur (Ansari 1970) and K. Paddayya's find of a lower palaeolithic industry comprising tools made predominantly of limestone at Gulbal. In Maharashtra the major new finds came from the Wardha-Banganga valley, the Mula-Mutha valley in Pune, Chirki-Nevasa, R.S. Pappu's work in the upper Krishna valley (Pappu 1974), S.A. Sali's work in Dhulia, and miscellaneous researches in Konkan including Goa and a few other areas. In Gujarat the major new researches in the lower palaeolithic covered the Bhadar and Bukhi valleys. The discussion on the lower palaeolithic in Madhya Pradesh was dominated by the situation in the Narmada valley (for a new publication Wainright 1966) which had a consistent history of Deccan College interest in the area. Among the new works cited in the context of Madhya Pradesh are the Ph.D. theses of Rameshwar Singh (1965) and Nissar Ahmed (1966). Several other areas also were considered mainly on the basis of *IAR* reports. In Rajasthan V.N. Misra's work (1967) formed the base-line. The division between the Soanian pebble tools and the Madrasian handaxe industries continued to excite Sankalia's attention in the new volume too, and he also found space to devote a section to the contemporary flora and fauna.

It is in this book that the term 'middle palaeolithic' is used in lieu of the earlier term 'middle stone age'. The general range of literature is about the same as the literature on the lower palaeolithic, but the discussion on the stratigraphy and typology of middle palaeolithic tools is now far more assured than their treatment in the 1962 volume. Further, both palaeontological data and radiocarbon dates have been given due consideration here. The geographical areas which have been covered within modern India are Maharashtra, Karnataka, Andhra, Tamil Nadu, West Bengal, Bihar, Uttar Pradesh, Madhya Pradesh, Gujarat and east Panjab. In conclusion he argued that the Indian middle palaeolithic industry had

> many typological parallels with cultures called Levalloiso-Mousterian, Mousterian (with varying traditions), and treated under the heading Middle Palaeolithic, in Western Europe, Western and Central Asia, Northern Africa and those placed in the Middle Stone Age in Africa, south of the Sahara. — Sankalia 1974 : 205

In the chapter on the upper palaeolithic its occurrence as a blade-and-burin industry embedded in a particular stratigraphic profile in different areas has been adequately highlighted, particularly with reference to M.L.K. Murty's work in the Kurnool caves which led to the discovery of a distinct range of bone tools and S.A. Sali's work at Patne which led to a detailed stratigraphy showing the transformation of various upper palaeolithic tool-types leading eventually to a full-fledged mesolithic industry. The significance of the burin element in this industry was underscored by M.L. Murty's work at Renigunta :

> The number of burins (131 : 16.24 per cent of the finished forms) is the largest so far found anywhere in the Indian subcontinent, and not only they are varied but match the European and Western Asiatic types in size as well as in shape. — Sankalia 1974 : 210

Patne showed different phases of the upper palaeolithic between the middle palaeolithic and the mesolithic, in addition to the presence of ostrich shells both in the middle palaeolithic and the upper palaeolithic. His conclusion was :

> India satisfies, therefore, the two basic requisites for the existence or recognition of a Stone Age cultural phase known as the Upper Palaeolithic. Geological evidence is supported by archaeological data. What it still lacks is the evidence of a rich art tradition. . . . Even this, just a hint, is now provided by the engraved ostrich shell at Patne.
>
> — Sankalia 1974 : 230

The major new additions to the chapter on the mesolithic were provided by the excavations at Sarai Nahar Rai, Adamgarh and Bagor, the works of G.R. Sharma (1973), R.V. Joshi (1966) and V.N. Misra (1973) respectively. The full reports on Sarai Nahar Rai and Bagor remain unpublished; the one on Adamgarh was published later (Joshi 1978).

In the chapter on 'neolithic and chalcolithic cultures' Sankalia does not change his theoretical framework from that of his earlier publication (Sankalia 1962), preferring to go by such terms as 'pure neolithic' (east India and northern India comprising Kashmir and Panjab), 'neolithic-chalcolithic' (southern India comprising western Andhra, Karnataka and Tamil Nadu), early Baluchi cultures and eastern Rajasthan), 'chalcolithic' (Andhra, Karnataka, Maharashtra and Madhya Pradesh), 'chalcolithic and Bronze Age cultures' (Sind, Panjab, Kutch, Saurashtra and northern Rajasthan), 'Copper-Bronze Age cultures' (Ganga-Yamuna Doab and south-east Rajasthan) and 'Early Iron Age' (Ganga-Yamuna Doab, Bihar, West Bengal, Madhya Pradesh, north Karnataka and probably Rajasthan, Saurashtra and Maharashtra and Panjab). Among other things it is interesting to note that 'Early Iron Age' is put in a chapter headed 'neolithic-chalcolithic cultures'. The typology of undated 'neolithic' tools from Assam is discussed following T.C. Sharma's Ph.D. thesis (1966) and his excavations at Daojali Hading which has remained undated and basically unreported. The excavated material from all parts of the subcontinent are scrupulously discussed in this chapter, especially the assemblages from Madhya Pradesh and Maharashtra where the Deccan College workers were most active. The section on Inamgaon in Maharashtra incorporates the results of the first phase of excavations at the site, which began under the directorship of Sankalia himself. Different sections of this chapter remained unintegrated and need careful but separate readings. One of the important sections here is the one on religion in the context of the Maharashtra chalcolithic. His comment that 'the Indus script and language cannot contain all that is found in the Rigveda, Puranas and the Mahabharata' (p. 386) is particularly relevant in the context of some recent attempts to decipher this script. His detailed discussion on the dockyard at Lothal is important too; at the end of a long summing-up he regards the brick-built basin provisionally as dock (p. 374).

In the final chapter on 'general conclusions' he argues that in the absence of climatic, faunal or floral evidence the archaeologist in India has to use the

> traditional or conventional methods viz. try to explain the changes in tool typology as due to (a) new cultural influences, (b) fresh arrivals of men, and further if the data permit suggest (i) invasion, (ii) colonization or (iii) symbiosis of the new and indigenous elements.
>
> — Sankalia 1974 : 549

He unequivocally believes that the neolithic-chalcolithic cultures of India

> are in a way 'colonization' by a people of higher cultures, who seem to have migrated (in small numbers) to India from Western Asia. Except the shape or form of their huts all the rest — pottery, stone tools, and lithic blades, the burial practices were foreign inspired. . . . Their skeletons show mixed primitive and advanced physical features, because, as it happened in later history, the foreigners soon got mixed with the indigenous population.
> — Sankalia 1974 : 544

He also makes an attempt to correlate archaeological chronology to the hypothetical chronology of the Puranic texts.

This book — or, the second edition of his *PPIP* published in 1962 — by Sankalia clearly demonstrates that the fresh discoveries in various areas of the subcontinent and in various fields did not mean that he developed a new attitude to the past represented by these discoveries in which he himself and his students played undeniably a crucial role during this period. His treatment of the Indian proto-historic data, despite his emphasis on the total lifeways of the relevant communities, continued to remain bogged in terminological confusions as well as in a kind of compulsive urge to find in them a reflection of Indian Pauranic tradition. His last major publication, except the Inamgaon report jointly with M.K. Dhavalikar and Z.A. Ansari, was *New Archaeology: Its Scope and Application to India* (Sankalia 1977). By 'new archaeology' he meant only an emphasis on lifeways and the increasing numbers of techniques.

What distinguished Hasmukh Dhirajlal Sankalia from his contemporary university archaeologists in India was his single-minded and relentless commitment to the development of his subject in the institution he served. Nothing except archaeology could seriously touch him in life, and he certainly lived in full the role model of a traditional Indian *guru*. In fact, he is the only true *guru* Indian archaeology has been able to throw up since Independence. This does not mean that he could not be cranky and confused, if not downright wild, on occasions. His blunt emphasis on the derivation of most of the things Indian from the West or his implicit faith in the historical veracity of Indian tradition suggests the grip of Hindu Aryanism and orthodoxy over him, although he was a deeply secular and liberal person in his professional life. On the whole, my generation of Indian university archaeologists has been able to look upon him, with considerable affection and respect, as a true teacher of our subject during our formative years. Quite rightly his biography figures in one of the volumes on 'the great archaeologists' of the world (Murray 1999, vol. 2).

The Coming of Age of Radiocarbon Dating in India

The radiocarbon dating came of age in India in 1973-74, especially with the publication of *Prehistoric Chronology and Radiocarbon Dating in India* jointly by D.P. Agrawal and Sheela Kusumgar (1974). Chapter 1 is 'introduction' and Chapter 2 gives an outline of the scientific basis and techniques of radiocarbon and other methods of scientific dating. Chapter 3 discusses Stone Age chronology mainly with reference to the limited number of dates from a handful of 'middle stone age', 'late stone age' and 'neolithic' sites. Various archaeological issues including typological data are summarised in this context. Under the heading of 'chronology of chalcolithic cultures' (chapter 4) they tabulate mainly the dates available mainly for the Indus civilization and the related sites and the neolithic-chalcolithic levels of Rajasthan, central India, Maharashtra, etc. The problem with this chapter is a dogmatic emphasis on their supposed correlation with the archaeological data. For instance, they think that the short chronology suggested by them for the Indus civilization ('2300-200 BC for the Nuclear Harappan and *c.* 2200-1700 BC for the Peripheral Harappan' — p. 103) entirely agrees with the evidence provided by the archaeological data on cross-dating between this civilization and Mesopotamia :

> the only reliable contacts which have chronological value are confined to the Sargonoid (*c.* 2350 BC) and Isin-Larsa (*c.* 2000 BC) periods. This puts a lower limit of *c.* 2350 BC on the Harappan beginnings.
>
> —p. 100

In the process of building up this argument they show a complete lack of concern to go into the depth of archaeological data. The same may, in fact, be said about the handling of archaeological data throughout this volume. They accept Sankalia's argument that the chalcolithic levels of south-east Rajasthan, Malwa and central India were related to earlier painted pottery cultures of Iran, and similarly N.R. Banerjee's argument that the Aryans introduced iron in India are given support. Among other problems, the Painted Grey Ware of the Doab is not considered earlier than the ninth-eighth century BC, and the earliest NBP is put in the fifth century BC. Their general conclusions, as stated in 'epilogue' (Agrawal and Kusumgar 1974 : 154-55) are the following :

(1) An 'admixture' of the chopper-chopping and handaxe industries may 'indicate a relatively late date of the Early Stone Age in India'.

(2) The West Asian 'Mousterian and allied dates are antecedent to the Indian M.S.A. (Middle Stone Age)'.

(3) 'This trend continues in the early neolithic times'.

(4) 'In the chalcolithic period again, we find that the West Asian copper technology and other cultural influences have a temporal precedence over the Indo-Pak subcontinent. And these traits seem to have reached north-west and Central India from these. Though for the Copper Hoards Culture we may have to look to S.E. Asia for inspiration'.

(5) 'Again, the Iron Age and the iron technology seem to have been inspired by the west, especially Iran. In this diffusion, one may also recognise the part played by the movements of the Indo-Aryans. The Indian megalithism too has close parallels with Yemen and South Arabia'.

There was an appendix 'on the calibration of C-14 dates' where they write of the uncertainties of the calibration method and think that we should be satisfied with a radiocarbon calender which need not be equated with historical eras.

The problem with this publication was that the authors, while putting forward the available radiocarbon dates for various phases and sites of Indian pre-historic, proto-historic and early historic archaeology, expected their readers to accept not merely their superficial and hyper-diffusionist approach to archaeological data but also believe that the radiocarbon calender which is not a historical calender supported their historical assumptions.

It may be added that in 1977 Sankalia published an abridged edition of this work under the title *Prehistory of India*.

THE PERIOD FROM 1975 to 1981

Publications

Some Major Books of the Period

This is an arbitrary but convenient division to highlight the general trend of writings before the publication of two important general books on the subcontinental prehistory and protohistory — B. and F.R. Allchin's *The Rise of Civilization in India and Pakistan* (1982) and D.P. Agrawal's *The Archaeology of India* (1982). The general framework and discoveries are easier to peg on such comprehensive publications, and this is one of the main reasons why we earlier discussed both the editions of Sankalia's *Prehistory and Protohistory* — in some detail.

Among the books, the major publications of the period were *The Prehistory and Palaeogeography of the Indian Desert* by B. Allchin, A. Goudie and K.T.M. Hegde (1978) and two edited volumes — *Ecology and Archaeology of Western India* (eds. D.P. Agrawal and Pande 1977) and *Essays in Indian Protohistory* (Agrawal and Dilip K. Chakrabarti 1979). The first volume is distinctive in two main ways. First, it wanted to determine the pattern of occupation over a very large but related region — virtually the whole of the arid zone of the subcontinent and showed its evolving pre-historic picture, focussing mostly on the upper palaeolithic and the mesolithic. Secondly, the related soil profiles were chemically and morphologically examined in all cases to build up a general idea of the varying extent of aridity or its absence throughout prehistory. The papers of the second volume also underline the significance of an environmental approach to the archaeology of mainly Gujarat and Rajasthan. The problem of the coastal miliolite formation in parts of Saurashtra and its significance in understanding the palaeolithic occupation of the region were examined in detail, possibly for the first time, in this volume. The third volume was intended to bring together articles which would give a comprehensive perspective of Indian protohistory, and from that point of view the volume was a success. Attempts at literary correlations were carefully kept out of this volume. An additional feature of the volume was a critique of the way archaeology was conducted in India of the late 1970s and how the different university 'history departments' of the country were inadequate to provide both infrastructure and scientific basis of archaeological studies.

In 1979 there was another volume, *Source-Book of Indian Archaeology, Volume I,* (eds. F.R. Allchin and Dilip K. Chakrabarti 1979) which consisted of excerpts from some representative writings on a few selected themes of Indian archaeology (background; early methods; geography, climate and early man; domestication of plants and animals) and was intended to offer a historical perspective of how the ideas regarding these issues developed in Indian archaeology and how the subject itself developed.

Among the other books before 1982 one has to mention Vibha Tripathi's useful synthesis of the archaeological data on the Painted Grey Ware level of northern India, although one would say that the volume was too much under the influence of the idea that this pottery was related to the Aryans (Tripathi 1976). In the same vein one should draw attention to G.L. Possehl's *Indus Civilization in Saurashtra* (1980) which was based on his field-study of Harappan settlements in the Ghero-Kalubhar valley of Saurashtra. This is perhaps the first book in the Indian context to raise consciously the issues of 'settlement archaeology'.

Early Issues of Puratattva, Bulletin of the Indian Archaeological Society

There were also other areas in which one can detect certain changes in the general approach to Indian archaeological studies. *Puratattva*, bulletin of the Indian Archaeological Society was shifted from Banaras to Delhi where S.P. Gupta became its editor. Its fourth issue (1970-71) reproduced an article by Gurdip Singh, originally published in 1971 in *Archaeology and Physical Anthropology in Oceania* : 'the Indus valley culture (seen in the context of post-Glacial climate and ecological studies in north-west India)'. Although Gurdip Singh's pollen analytical model of climatic fluctuations between general aridity and wetness between pre-8000 BC and 1800-1500 BC in the north-west India, which was derived from his study of the profiles of salt lakes of western Rajasthan, would now need modification (cf. Enzell *et al.* 1999 in N. Lahiri ed. 2000; Misra 1984 in *ibid.*), this article had a major impact on the Indian archaeological scene because it adequately highlighted the possibilities of pollen analytical approach in the Indian context. *Puratattva 5* printed the proceedings of a seminar held by the Indian Archaeological Society on 11 May 1971 to discuss threadbare two major pottery types of Gangetic India : Ochre-Coloured Pottery (OCP) and NBPW. The relationship between the Late Harappans and the OCP occupied a lot of attention. It was for the first time that pottery types came in for detailed scrutiny in Indian archaeology from the point of view of their archaeological and historical implications. The publication was accompanied by a detailed bibliography and many illustrations of these pottery types. In the editorial notes of *Puratattva* 7 B.K. Thapar (1974) tried to counter the criticism of the Archaeological Survey of India in the 'Report of the Estimates Committee of the Lok Sabha' during that period. The main criticism rested — justly — on the non-publication of excavation reports. Thapar who became the Director General after M.N. Deshpande wrote rather pompously that promptness was not the only merit of an excavation-report; 'it has to be sound and adequately published as well'. Without trying to have a close look at the shortcomings of the Survey he decided to point out the limitations of the archaeology departments in the universities and the states.

> . . . there is a marked imbalance in the growth of field archaeology in these universities; some of these have fully equipped Departments for undertaking explorations and excavations, while others have neither adequate expertise nor the proper equipment for such a work. Yet, there is another category where archaeology is taught but not practised. The position of the State Departments of Archaeology is no better : out of a total of

twenty-one states, only sixteen have so far set up Departments of Archaeology.
— Thapar 1974

Puratattva 8 (1975-76, published in 1978) is important because some of its articles are related to a number of major issues and show the emergence of new trends. R.V. Joshi's and A.R. Marathe's article, 'Metrical analysis of handaxes from Chirki-on-Pravara (western Maharashtra, India)', and V.N. Misra's article, 'The Acheulian Industry of Rock Shelter IIIF-23 at Bhimbetka, Central India : A Preliminary Study' both introduce on an extensive scale quantitative aspects of the analysis of lithic industries. As Bhimbetka report lies unpublished, the details offered by Misra on its Acheulian industry and stratigraphy are doubly important. Secondly, on the basis of the first six reasons of excavations between 1968 and 1975 at Inamgaon Dhavalikar offered a picture of 'settlement archaeology of Inamgaon' and was followed by Vishnu Mittre and R. Savithri who described the 'ancient plant economy 'of the site. The orientation of these articles will be apparent from the following remark by Dhavalikar (1978 : 54):

> What we have tried to make out is not the settlement pattern in the accepted sense of the term, but rather the community pattern. The concentration of the houses of the craftsmen along the western periphery of the settlement and the location of the houses of men of means in the central part demonstrate that it was a class structured society and that we have here the beginning of the *varna* system which later becomes the distinguishing feature of the Hindu society.

The point is not whether Dhavalikar is right or wrong, but the fact that attention is now being focussed on such possible implications of the excavation results is important.

Thirdly, there was a substantive section on 'archaeology and tradition' with articles from a number of people including Sankalia. They were all eager to explain the Indian proto-historical data in terms of either 'Later Vedic Aryans' (R.S. Sharma) or the Puranic lineages of cultures (R. Thapar). Sankalia contributed a piece on 'pre-historic colonization in India : archaeological and literary evidence' where he wrote, among various other jumbled things, the following :

> . . . one has to recognize that this is an ancient land, where the traditions have survived in a distorted form, and therefore the traditional accounts — both Vedic and Puranic — do contain a grain of truth which we must endeavour to discover by long and continuous sieving.
> — Sankalia 1978 : 85

As I have elsewhere (Chakrabarti 1988b) discussed the issue of archaeology-literature correlation in the Indian context, I shall not make detailed comments on the articles of this section, but in retrospect, it is interesting to reflect that the textual scholarship of these enthusiasts for finding a reflection of India's traditional history in Indian archaeological record did not extend much beyond F.E. Pargiter's reconstruction in *The Ancient Indian Historical Tradition*. The only discordant note of this section was struck by M.C. Joshi (1978) who had the honesty to admit that all such interpretations were subjective and based on distorted evidence. A case for investigating the archaeological basis of the epics was made by B.B. Lal (1978).

Fourthly, it was also in this issue of *Puratattva* that there was a beginning of a close examination of the archaeological data related to India's contact with west Asia. The archaeological item for consideration was 'Reserved Slip Ware' which had hitherto been supposed to be an import from West Asia in the context of the Indus civilization. A detailed review of the relevant archaeological evidence both in west Asia and the subcontinent leads to the conclusion that 'there is not a scrap of reasonable archaeological evidence to interpret the Indus finds as evidence of any link with Mesopotamia'. (Chakrabarti 1978)

A New Look at the Problems of the Beginning of Iron in India and her Contact with West Asia

In 1976 the problem of the beginning of iron was re-assessed (Chakrabarti 1976) leading to a number of postulates which were important in the context of the time. The evidence of the earliest iron-smelting in central and south India was earlier than the corresponding evidence in the north-western part of the subcontinent. Iron entered the productive system of India by *c.* 800 BC. The distribution of iron ores suitable for pre-industrial smelting and pre-industrial smelting tradition itself overlaps with that of the early centres of the use of iron in the subcontinent. Both ores and pre-industrial smelting occur particularly extensively in central and south India which are also the earliest archaeological centres of Indian iron metallurgy. The first iron tool types in India do not show any similarity with the west Asiatic iron tool types of that age. There was a steady continuity between the early and contemporary pre-industrial traditions of India's iron metallurgy. And finally, there was nothing sacred about the idea of dissemination of iron technology from a single centre like Anatolia where the Hittites are credited with the discovery. These points led to the premise that India was a separate and possibly independent centre of the manufacture of early iron. This paper and related publications which later culminated in a book (Chakrabarti 1992) took the study of the early history of metals, especially iron, away from its erstwhile diffusionist and Aryanist frame and made it the focus of an integrated study of all kinds of relevant data — literary, archaeological, geological, archaeometallurgical and ethnographic data.

Meanwhile M.D.N. Sahi (1979) highlighted the significance of the occurrence of both iron objects and slag in the so-called 'chalcolithic' context at Ahar, and J.G. Shaffer (1978) widely circulated a then unpublished paper drawing attention to the occurrence of iron artefacts in the Bronze Age context of Said Qala Tepe, Mundigak and Deh Morasi Ghundai and its implications in the understanding of early iron technology in south Asia. He also argued for an indigenous development of iron technology in the region.

There was a detailed examination of the entire range of archaeological data on the contact between the Indus civilization and Mesopotamia in a seminar on the Indus civilization in the Indian Institute of Advanced Study in Simla in October 1977. The paper was widely circulated by its author and culminated much later in a book (Chakrabarti 1990). The examination of the concerned evidence was detailed leading to an ordering of the evidence and its implications for the Indus chronology, external trade and its routes. The phenomenon of trade began critically to be examined by Indian archaeologists from now on, and in the Indus context another publication before 1982 was by Shereen Ratnagar (1981), although she put more emphasis on anthropological speculations than on a close examination of the primary evidence. A fresh re-examination of the Indus civilization's contact with west Asia was also initiated by E.C.L. During-Caspers and her study of the etched carnelian beads in this context deserves note (During-Caspers 1971). In 1979 Shashi Asthana (1979) examined the evidence of Indus contact with the Kirman area of Iran, and S.P. Gupta (1979) undertook a detailed archaeological study of India's pre-historic and proto-historic links with central Asia.

The Start of ***Man and Environment****, Bulletin of the Indian Society for Prehistoric and Quaternary Studies*

In 1977 another archaeological society was formed under the name of 'Indian Society for Quaternary and Prehistoric Studies' with its headquarter in the Deccan College, Pune. An annual bulletin began to be published from 1977 onwards, and in comparatively recent years it has become bi-annual. The main person behind the publication of the new Society's journal *Man and Environment* in 1977 and for several years after that was S.P. Gupta who persuaded Mr. Mittal of B.R. Publishing Corporation to finance its publication. After some years it began to receive grants from the Indian Council of Historical Research and the Archaeological Survey of India, and the responsibility of distribution was taken up by Mr. Indra Mohan Sharma of Books and Books, another Delhi publisher. In the late 1980s, after the journal got a very large grant from the Ford Foundation, the responsibility of its publication was taken over by a group of scholars in Pune and the Deccan College, and in recent years it has been functioning well as a kind of in-house journal of that institution.

The new trends, the beginning of which one could notice in *Puratattva* in the mid-and-late 1970s, became more accentuated with the publication of *Man and Environment* which began to value environment-based articles right from its beginning. In the first issue of the new journal there was a separate section on Inamgaon with primary emphasis on the pattern of settlement, and faunal and skeletal remains, with contributions from Dhavalikar, Sankalia and G.L. Badam, among others. It was also in this issue that there was an attempt to seek a geographical frame for the analysis of India-west Asia relations (Chakrabarti 1977). It was argued on the basis of political and economic data that the whole region between the Oxus valley or the southern part of central Asia and the Indus valley, including the eastern rim of Iran belonged to a single economic and political interaction zone. The implication of this hypothesis was then examined in the context of Indian archaeology. Among other things, it was asserted that Sankalia's arguments in favour of contacts between the chalcolithic cultures from south-east Rajasthan to the Deccan and different sites in Iran and elsewhere made no geographical or cultural sense at all.

New Trends in Pre-historic Studies and Floral, Faunal and Skeletal Analyses

Some recent trends of Indian pre-historic studies began to crystallise during this period. The understanding of Indian Pleistocene fauna became much easier after the publication of G.L. Badam's *Pleistocene Fauna of India with Special Reference to the Siwaliks* (1979). K. Paddayya (1978) began to think of 'new research designs and field-techniques in the palaeolithic archaeology of India' as a preliminary step towards his subsistence-system approach to the data gathered from the Hunsgi-Baichbal valley of Karnataka. M.L.K. Murty (1981) published an ethnographic model of 'hunter-gatherer eco-systems and archaeological patterns of subsistence behaviour' on the data from his field-study area in Andhra. This settlement-subsistence approach to Indian pre-historic data is to a great extent rooted in Jerome Jacobson's publications on palaeolithic occupation floors (Jacobson 1970), early Stone Age habitation sites in eastern Malwa (Jacobson 1975) and investigations of Late Stone Age cultural adaptations in the central Vindhyas (Jacobson 1980). Jacobson wrote his dissertation on the Vindhyan microlithic sites in 1970 in

Columbia University, and although it was not published as a book, his publications on the prehistory of the Vindhyan region mark him out as a distinguished subcontinental archaeologist. In 1979 he also published a review of the theoretical developments and status of Indian archaeology where he showed a clear grass-roots understanding of the new theoretical trends of that period (Jacobson 1979). Statira Guzder (1980) published her Deccan College Ph.D. thesis on *Quaternary Environment and Stone Age Cultures of the Konkan, Coastal Maharashtra*, almost as the culmination of a long-standing Deccan College interest in the prehistory of that region.

The study of excavated faunal remains and skeletal studies have long formed a distinct part of Indian archaeological reports in the form of appendices contributed by specialist scientists who usually belonged to the Zoological Survey of India and Anthropological Survey of India. By the late 1970s both these studies showed signs of coming into their own. The main result was a better integration of both archaeozoology and skeletal biological studies with archaeology, pointing to new dimensions of their contributions to the past cultures. Certain scholars have played major roles in this process. In the field of archaeozoological studies a leading role during this period was played by K.R. Alur (1973) who is noted for his contributions to the study of animal bones from various south Indian neolithic and other sites and also for his work on the Allahabad University material in the Vindhyas. He tried to take the study of archaeological faunal remains beyond the mere identifications of animals : 'the only way to know about the animals that lived in the pre-historic period is to learn to interpret the bone fragments in terms of their size, strength and mode of living'. The Indian archaeozoological studies of the period were also helped by a number of papers in *Archaeoozoological Studies* (Clason ed. 1975). M.L.K. Murty's study (1975) of the 'late Pleistocene fauna of Kurool caves of Andhra' was oriented towards reconstructing the environmental situation of their upper palaeolithic context. He also underlined the significance of the occurrence of *Ovis* during late Pleistocene times in this region in the context of sheep domestication in Peninsular India. P.K. Thomas who has since then been playing a lead role in Indian archaeozoological studies reviewed the faunal data from a few excavated mesolithic sites such as Adamgarh, Bagor, etc., and underscored the fact of animal domestication in India going back to the mesolithic period (Thomas 1975). Similarly, Paddayya (1975) discussed the faunal background of the south Indian neolithic culture with reference to their significance in understanding the patterns of economy and food, and ecology. In 1974 A.K. Sharma reviewed the occurrence of horse in the context of the Indus civilization sites like Harappa, Kalibangan, Malvan and Surkotada and drew attention to Alur's identification of horse bones from the neolithic-chalcolithic context at Hallur in Karnataka.

The early excavation reports had no doubt separate sections on the study of the excavated human remains, and the emphasis there was not merely on the relevant physical measurements but also racial identifications. Although D.K. Sen who was a physical anthropologist and the Director of the Anthropological Survey of India pointed out the fallacy of many such identifications as early as 1964 (Sen 1964), the reports which began to appear in the 1960s and 1970s faithfully continued the earlier trend to seek races in the archaeological record and draw cultural conclusions from those races. We have already seen how Sankalia in both the editions of his *PPIP* freely used racial categories to understand the mesolithic and later cultures. The tradition still continued strongly in the writings of Dhavalikar (cf. 1979a, 1979b). The person who has played the most important role in bringing about a basic reorientation of studies of excavated skeletons at Indian sites is K.A.R. Kennedy whose *The Physical Anthropology of the Megalith-Builders of South India and Sri Lanka* (1975) did not look at 'race' but at different important physical variables including the element of population continuity. Kennedy (1980) soon offered an exhaustive review of the skeletal studies which had hitherto taken place in south Asian archaeology.

Although Vishnu Mittre (1989, for a list of his important publications) had been active in the field of archaeobotany for a long time before this period and in fact slowly took up the main responsibility of this line of investigation in India, there were two developments in the field by the late 1970s. One was the fact of flotation which began to be widely practised in Indian excavations from this period onward and soon led to a quantum leap in the availability of the data. This is well reflected in the publications of the period (cf. Kajale 1977a, 1977b). Secondly, there was the addition of two or three researchers in the field, notably M.D. Kajale and K.S. Saraswat, both of whom soon assumed importance as archaeobotanists of national significance. That like archaeo-zoology, archaeobotany too was something more than the identification of wood and crop remains was adequately highlighted in the Indian context by *Evolutionary Studies in World Crops, Diversity and Change in the Indian Subcontinent* (Hutchinson ed. 1974).

The Impact of Prehistoric Researches in the Belan Valley and Ganga Plain under G.R. Sharma

The find of domesticated animals in the so-called 'mesolithic' contexts of Bagor and Adamgarh, and the claims of cerealia-like pollens in a setting of pieces of charcoal in the pollen profile of the salt lakes of Rajasthan brought into focus, at least to some extent, the problem of the beginning of agriculture in India. However, the publication which brought the entire issue into fore was the publication of *Beginnings of Agriculture* by G.R. Sharma *et al.* (1980), which basically comprised the excavation reports on Chopani-Mando, Mahadaha and Mahagara. Chopani-Mando and Mahagara are in the Belan valley while Mahadaha is in the Ganga plain in Pratapgarh. The combined evidence is supposed to show a transition from hunting and food-gathering mesolithic to food-producing and animal-domesticating neolithic in the Belan valley in the eastern fringe of the Vindhyas. The other major sites which were excavated during this period but remained unreported in detail included Sarai Nahar Rai (Pratapgarh) and Koldihawa (Belan valley). The details of the archaeology of this area and their dates and uncertainties do not concern us here. What is important is that G.R. Sharma (1980) could make the following claim :

> Within the chronological frame-work provided by C-14 dates for the terminal Upper Palaeolithic reading 17765 +/- 340 B.C. and for the Pre-Neolithic 8080 +/- 115 B.C. and the early Neolithic levels reading 6570+/-210 B.C. and 5540+/240 B.C., the totality of evidence furnished by these excavations and explorations in the Belan valley (Vindhyas) and the Ganga valley . . . developing sequence of lithic tools from the beginnings of the Epi-Palaeolithic to the Neolithic, presence of potential animal domesticates in the Palaeolithic and Mesolithic, evidence of wild sheep/goat in the Pre-Neolithic levels of Mahagara in 9th-8th millennium B.C. and their complete domestication in 7th-6th millennium B.C. . . . evidence of wild rice in the Advanced Mesolithic (Proto-Neolithic) and its cultivation in the Neolithic, all present a continuous story of human achievements beginning with the Epi-Palaeolithic, maturing through the Mesolithic and ultimately culminating into the new transformation that heralded the beginnings of the Neolithic with its new economy, the basis of which was provided by domestication of animals and plants, especially the cultivation of rice (*Oryza sativa*). This transformation was achieved in a small compact area of 12 sq. km in the valley of the Belan and was an indigenous development.
>
> — Sharma 1980

In a number of ways this was a claim of extraordinary historical significance in the annals of post-Independence Indian archaeology. Whereas the people of the two major power-centres of Indian archaeology — the Archaeological Survey of India and the Deccan College — had kept an extraordinarily large chunk of their finds focussed on such issues as the Aryans, the archaeological veracity of Indian tradition and 'pre-historic colonisation of India', an archaeologist from Allahabad University tried to demonstrate the relevance of alternative dimensions. Whether one agreed with him or not was a different matter altogether. Secondly, by working rather intensively on a limited area, the members of the Allahabad group under G.R. Sharma — V.D. Mishra, R.K. Varma, B.B. Mishra,

D. Mandal, J.N. Pal and J.N. Pandey, to give the full list of these formidable field-workers — could argue in detail about the stratigraphic and typological continuity of its archaeological sequence right from the lower palaeolithic upward. Thirdly, it established this section of the Vindhyas and the Pratapgarh part of the Ganga plain as one of the crucial areas of ancient south Asia. That there was an archaeological India beyond the Indus civilization and the Aryans was demonstrated unequivocally for the first time by this phase of research in Allahabad University. Fourthly, these excavations, especially the ones in Pratapgarh, led to the discovery of a substantive number of mesolithic skeletons, greatly increasing the total number of pre-historic skeletal finds in the country. Finally, the assemblages themselves were broad-based, with traces of various activity areas and extensive evidence of tool manufacture at every stage. The cattle pens and circular huts of the advanced mesolithic level at Chopani Mando, for instance, very much sharpened the image of 'mesolithic India'.

Concerns with History of Technology and Mediaeval Archaeology

The publication of *Aspects of Ancient Indian Technology* by H.C. Bharadwaj (1979) of Banaras Hindu University covered his own technical studies on different groups of ancient objects : chemical analysis of glasses (5 glass beads from the early historic level of Rajghat and 4 glass specimens from Bhitari of the fourth-fifth century AD); scientific examination of the slip of the NBP, chemical and metallographic examination of copper-based objects (5 copper objects from early historic Rajghat, 5 copper coins of *c.* 300 BC-AD 100 — two from Taxila, and one each from Rajghat, Mathura and Ayodhya); chemical and metallographic examination of four silver punch-marked coins from Taxila, one silver coin of the ninth century AD Rajghat and one fifteenth century silver coin; scientific and metallographic examination of an alleged gold punch-marked coin and 4 Gupta period gold coins; and finally, chemical and metallographic examination of six early historic iron objects from Rajghat and two pieces of iron slag of the same period from Rajghat. The range of data was obviously limited and could not lead to wide-ranging general conclusions. It may be put on record that professionally Bharadwaj was the archaeological chemist of the Department of Ancient Indian History, Culture and Archaeology of Banaras Hindu University.

R.N. Mehta's *Mediaeval Archaeology* (1979) displayed the first general awareness of the need to take field-archaeological methods to the study of Indian mediaeval history. Mehta was an archaeology professor in M.S. University, Baroda. He had already published the results of his 'archaeological, topographical and toponymical' studies of some later cities of Gujarat, such as Surat (Mehta 1974) and Khambat/Cambay (Mehta 1975). In 1979 he defined 'mediaveal archaeology' of India as the study of 'the material remains of the period from about the twelfth century to about the end of the eighteenth century in their manifold aspects'. This is also one area of Indian archaeological study where many topographical features can be seen, rather easily in many cases, on the surface, and the study of local place-names can play an important role in the identification of these features. The literary sources of this period are much more detailed and diverse than the literary sources of the ancient period, but even here archaeology can play a significant role : 'the mediaeval archaeologist has to function on an interdisciplinary level to throw additional new light on the known history and open up further fields of data and interpretation'. (Mehta 1979 : 77) He takes up the case-study of some documents related to the mediaeval history of Gujarat and the topographical features of the town-planning of two famous city-sites of the period — Champaner and Surat.

The study of mediaeval archaeology has not yet made an effective beginning in India outside the domain of general architectural studies, and the basic examples of such work that one can cite are the Archaeological Survey of India and Aligarh Muslim University excavations at the Mogul emperor Akbar's short-lived capital at Fatehpur Sikri, the study of the town-planning and houses of the Mogul capital of Shajahanabad by the Archaeological Survey of India, some miscellaneous studies of the material remains of the period by the historians of Aligarh Muslim University, an ongoing study of the remains of Gaur and Pandua under the sponsorship of the Directorate of Archaeology, Government of West Bengal, and the prolonged work at Vijayanagara by the Archaeological Survey of India, Karnataka State Archaeology Department and an international group of archaeologists. Among these the Vijayanagara work has been much in focus, mainly due to the extensive literature it has generated. The problem with this work is that it has not been integrated into the overall archaeology of the region in which this site is located. As things stand, the archaeology of Vijayanagara seems to stand as a kind of academic island. Credit for bringing 'mediaeval archaeolgy' within the focus of Archaeological Survey of India interests belongs to S. Nurul Hasan, an Aligarh Muslim University mediaeval historian who became the Indian minister in charge of education in the early 1970s. However, it is worth pointing out that the Archaeological Survey of India already possessed a long-standing and well-organised section for the study of inscriptions written in Arabic and Persian. These inscriptions constitute the primary source-material of Indian archaeology during the mediaeval period.

Excavations

The data incorporated in the following table is taken mostly from *IAR 1973-74* to *IAR 1982-83*.

Chart 2.1: Excavated Sites in *IAR 1973-74* to *IAR 1982-83*

Site	*Years*	*Nature*	*State*	*Status*	*Inst.*	*Person*
Mottupalli	73-74	historical	Andhra	Unpub.	State Dept	?
Palampet	73-74	temple	Andhra	Unpub.	State Dept	K.V. Rao
Antichak	73-80,81-82	historical	Bihar	Unpub.	ASI	B.C. Verma
Bakraur	73-74	historical	Bihar	Unpub.	ASI	K.M. Srivastava
Aphsad	73-82	historical	Bihar	Unpub.	State Dept	P.C. Prasad
Mkhdm mosq.	73-74	historical	Delhi	Unpub.	ASI	T.N. Khazanchi
Pambarwan	73-74	historical	J & K	Unpub.	ASI	?
Burzahom	73-74	neolithic	J & K	Unpub.	ASI	S. Lal
Harwan	73-74	temple	J & K	Unpub.	ASI	L.K. Srinivasan
Vadagaon	73-78	historical	Karnataka	Unpub.	State Dept	M.S.N. Rao
Banahalli	73-74	neolithic	Karnataka	Unpub.	ASI	K.V.S. Rajan
Bhokardan	73-74	early hist	Maharashtra	Pub.	Nagpur Uni	S.B. Deo
Yesar	73-74	pre-historic	Maharashtra	Unpub.	D.Coll/ASI	Deo-Bopardikar
Nanganallur	73-74	temple	T. Nadu	Unpub.	ASI	K.V.S Rajan
Gingi Fort	73-74	historical	T. Nadu	Unpub.	ASI	K.V.S. Rajan
Kaveripattin-	73-74,77-78	historical	T. Nadu	Unpub.	ASI	K.V.S. Rajan
Anand Bhvn	73-74	historical	U.P.	Unpub.	Allh Uni	G.R. Sharma
Koldihawa	73-74,75-76	neolithic	U.P.	Unpub.	Allh Uni	G.R. Sharma
Piprh/Gnwria	73-77	early hist	U.P.	Pub.	ASI	K.M. Srivastava
Virabhadra	73-75	early hist	U.P.	Unpub.	ASI	N.C. Ghosh
Jajmau	73-77	early hist	U.P.	Unpub.	State Dept	R.C. Singh ?
Mathura	73-77	early hist	U.P.	Unpub.	ASI	M.C. Joshi
Bharatpur	73-75	chalcolithic	W. Bengal	Unpub.	Burd.U/ASI	S.K. Mukherjee
Tamluk	73-74	early hist	W. Bengal	Unpub.	ASI	S.K. Mukherjee
Amaravati	74-75	early hist	Andhra	Unpub.	ASI	I.K. Sharma
Golconda	73-75	mediaeval	Andhra	Unpub.	State Dept	?
Dhulikatta	74-77	early hist	Andhra	Unpub.	State Dept	?
Kadambapur	74-75	megalithic	Andhra	Unpub.	State Dept	?
Satanikota	74-75,77-80	early hist	Andhra	Pub.	ASI	N.C. Ghosh
Gollathagudi	73-75	temple	Andhra	Unpub.	State Dept	?
Chandavaram	73-76	historical	Andhra	Unpub.	State Dept	?
Ambari	74-75	historical	Assam	Unpub.	Gau U Anth	T.C. Sharma
Champa	74-77,82-83	early hist	Bihar	Unpub.	Patna Uni	B. Narayan

Site	Years	Nature	State	Status	Inst.	Person
Balirajgarh	74-75	early hist	Bihar	Unpub.	State Dept	S.R. Ray
Rajgir	74-75	early hist	Bihar	Unpub.	ASI	V.K. Misra
Karvan	74-76	historical	Gujarat	Unpub.	ASI	W.H. Siddiqi
Hunsgi	74-76,77-78	prehistory	Karnataka	Pub.	D.Coll	K. Paddayya
Muttalavadi	74-75	neolithic-meg	Karnataka	Pub.	State Dept	A. Sundara
Machad	74-75	megalithic	Kerala	?	MSU Baroda	K. George
Malhar	74-76,77-78	early hist	M.P.	Pub.	Sagar Uni	K.D. Bajpai
Bhimbetka	74-77,81-82	prehistory	M.P.	Unpub.	D.Coll	V.N. Misra
Daimabad	74-79	chalcolithic	Maharashtra	Pub.	ASI	S.A. Sali
Ter	74-75	historical	Maharashtra	Unpub.	D.Coll/Mrd.U	S.B. Deo-T. Pathy
Inamgaon	74-75,77-83	chalcolithic	Maharashtra	Pub.	D.Coll	M.K. Dhavalikar
Raibania	74-75	temple	Orissa	Unpub.	State Dept	?
Kuruma	74-77	historical	Orissa	Unpub.	State Dept	?
Kanchipuram	74-76	historical	T. Nadu	?	Madras Uni	?
Jakhera	74-76	chalcolithic	U.P.	Unpub.	Aligrh M.Uni	M.D.N. Sahi
Sohgaura	74-75	chalcolithic	U.P.	Unpub.	Gkhpur Uni	S.N. Chaturvedi
Keesaragutta	75-77,78-79, 80-81	historic	Andhra	Unpub.	State Dept	?
Polakonda	75-77	neolithic	Andhra	Unpub.	State Dept	?
Katragarh	75-80	early hist	Bihar	Unpub.	State Dept	S.R. Ray
Nalanda	75-80,81-83	temple	Bihar	Unpub	ASI	various
Prabhas Patan	75-77	Harappan	Gujarat	?	D.Coll/State	Ansari *et al.*
Champaner	74-76	historical	Gujarat	Unpub.	MSU Baroda	R.N. Mehta
Bhagwanpura	75-76	Harappan	Haryana	Pub.	ASI	J.P. Joshi
Kasital	75-76	chalcolithic	Haryana	Unpub.	ASI	J.P. Joshi
Hampi	75-77,78-83	historical	Karnataka	ASI/ State	various	various
Besnagar	75-77	early hist	M.P.	Unpub.	ASI	M.D. Khare
Mahagara	75-76,77-79, 82-83	neolithic	U.P.	Pub.	Allh Uni	G.R. Sharma
Panchoh	75-76	chalcolithic?	U.P.	Unpub.	Allh Uni	G.R. Sharma
Mandhal	75-77	historical	Maharashtra	Unpub.	Nagpur Uni	A.M. Sastri
Mismagiri	75-76	prehistory	Meghalaya	Unpub.	Gau U. Anth	T.C. Sharma
Ranipur-Jhar	75-76	historical	Orissa	Unpub.	State Dept	?
Sittanavasal	75-76	megalithic	T. Nadu	Unpub.	ASI	K.S. Ramachandran
Batesvara	75-76	early hist	U.P.	Pub.	ASI	J.S. Nigam
Dupadu	76-77	historical	Andhra	Unpub.	State Dept	?
Budigepally	76-77	neo-mega	Andhra	Unpub.	State Dept	?
Nelakondapal	76-78	historical	Andhra	Unpub.	State Dept	?
Agirapalli	76-77	megalithic	Andhra	Unpub.	State Dept	?

Site	*Years*	*Nature*	*State*	*Status*	*Inst.*	*Person*
Jonnawada	76-77	megalithic	Andhra	Unpub.	State Dept	?
Siri Fort	76-77	mediaeval	Delhi	Unpub.	ASI	Raghubir Singh
Daulatpur	76-78	Harappan	Haryana	Unpub.	Kuruk Uni	U.V. Singh
Manda	76-77	Harappan	J & K	Pub.	ASI	J.P. Joshi
Hallur	76-77	neo-mega	Karnataka	Pub.	State Dept	M.S.N. Rao
Kalyadi	76-77	copper mine	Karnataka	Unpub.	ASI	S.R. Rao
Raisen Fort	76-77	historical	M.P.	Unpub.	ASI	M.D. Khare
Apegaon	76-77	chalcolithic	Maharashtra	Pub.	D.Coll	S.B. Deo
Kathpalon	76-77	Harappan	Panjab	Pub.	ASI	J.P. Joshi
Nagar-Dhaderi	76-77	Harappan	Panjab	Pub.	ASI	J.P. Joshi
Ghuram	76-77	Harappan	Panjab	Unpub.	State Dept	?
Kallupatti	76-77,79-80	megalithic	T. Nadu	Unpub.	ASI	L.K. Srinivasan
Appukallu	76-77,79-80	megalithic	T. Nadu	Unpub.	Madras Uni	K.V. Raman
Ayodhya	76-77,79-80	early hist	U.P.	Unpub.	ASI/IIAS	B.B. Lal
Rambagh	76-77	Mediaeval	U.P.	Unpub.	ASI	S.C. Roy
Birdpur	76-77	early hist	U.P.	Pub.	ASI	K.M. Srivastava
Dongalasani	77-78	temple	Andhra	Unpub.	State Dept	?
Chagatur	77-79	megalithic	Andhra	Unpub.	State Dept	?
Uppalapadu	77-79	megalithic	Andhra	Unpub.	State Dept	?
Peddamarrur	77-78	megalithic	Andhra	Unpub.	State Dept	?
Chandahadin	77-78	early hist	Bihar	Unpub.	ASI	S.C. Roy
Chr-Kutubpur	77-78	neolithic	Bihar	Unpub.	ASI	R.S. Bisht
Zekhada	77-78	Harappan	Gujarat	?	MSU Baroda	R.N. Mehta
Kanewal	77-78	Harappan	Gujarat	Unpub.	MSU Baroda	R.N. Mehta
Pabumath	77-79,80-81	Harappan	Gujarat	Unpub.	State Dept	?
Semthan	77-79,80-81	early hist	J & K	Unpub.	ASI	R.S. Bisht
Tarsang	77-78	prehistory	Gujarat	Unpub.	MSU Baroda	V.H. Sonawane
Chandravalli	77-78	neo-mega	Karnataka	Unpub.	ASI	V.K. Misra
Naikund	77-8,79-80	megalithic	Maharashtra	Pub.	D.Coll/State	S.B. Deo
Panhalekazi	77-78,79-80	rockcut cave	Maharashtra	Unpub.	ASI	L.S. Rao
Sanghol	77-78, 80-81	Harappan	Panjab	Unpub.	State Dept	G.B. Sharma
Mallappadi	77-78	megalithic	T. Nadu	Unpub.	Madras Uni	K.V. Raman
Mahadaha	77-79	mesolithic	U.P.	Pub.	Allh Uni	G.R. Sharma
Sringaverpur	77-83	historical	U.P.	Pub.	ASI/IIAS	B.B. Lal
Vamulapadu	78-79	early hist	Andhra	Unpub.	ASI	N.C. Ghosh
Kudaveli	78-79,82-83	historical	Andhra	Unpub.	ASI	N.C. Ghosh
Tadakanahalli	78-79	megalithic	Karnataka	Unpub.	State Dept	M.S.N. Rao
Bhdj Asram	78-79,82-83	early hist	U.P.	Unpub.	ASI/IIAS	B.B. Lal
Pariar	78-79	chalcolithic	U.P.	Unpub.	ASI/IIAS	B.B. Lal

Site	*Years*	*Nature*	*State*	*Status*	*Inst.*	*Person*
Hullikalu	78-79	neolithic-meg	Andhra	Pub.	State Dept	?
Chinnamarrur	78-80	neo-chalco	Andhra	Unpub.	State Dept	?
Pagidigutta	78-79	chalco-mega	Andhra	Unpub.	State Dept	?
Calingapatnam	77-80	historical	Andhra	Unpub.	ASI	K. Krishnamurthy
Anhilwada	78-79	historical	Gujarat	Unpub.	MSU Baroda	?
Taraghda	78-79	Harappan	Gujarat	Unpub.	State Dept	?
Agroha	78-81	historical	Haryana	Unpub.	State Dept	?
Balu	78-80	Harappan	Haryana	Unpub.	Kuruk Uni	Singh-Bhan
Dangwada	78-80,82-83	chalcolithic	M.P.	Pub.	Vikram Uni	V.S. Wakankar
Mahurjhari	78-79	megalithic	Maha.	Pub.	Nagpur Uni	S.B. Deo
Arni	78-79	historical	Maha.	Unpub.	Nagpur Uni	A.M. Sastri
Mottur	78-79	megalithic	T. Nadu	Unpub.	ASI	L.K. Srinivasan
Kallerimalai	78-79	megalithic	T. Nadu	Unpub.	Madras Uni	K.V. Raman
Moradhwaj	78-81,82-83	historical	U.P.	Unpub.	Garhwal Uni	K.P. Nautiyal
Hulaskhera	78-83	historical	U.P.	?	State Dept	?
Ranihat	78-79	early hist	U.P.	Unpub.	Garhwal Uni	K.P. Nautiyal
Nandalur	79-80	historical	Andhra	Unpub.	State Dept	?
Rajahmundry	79-81	historical	Andhra	Unpub.	State Dept	?
Siddarajalin-gapuram	79-80	prehistory	Andhra	Unpub.	State Dept	?
Budidapaddu	79-80	megalithic	Andhra	Unpub.	State Dept	?
Karapakala	79-80	neolithic ?	Andhra	Unpub.	State Dept	?
Rangapuram	79-80	temple	Andhra	Unpub.	State Dept	?
Karnachaura	79-80	historical	Bihar	Unpub.	State Dept	?
Valabhi	79-80	Harappan ?	Gujarat	Unpub.	MSU Baroda	V.H. Sonawane
Dwaraka	79-80	historical	Gujarat	Unpub.	ASI	S.R. Rao
Bhaghor	79-80,81-83	prehistory	M.P.	Pub.	Allh Uni	G.R. Sharma-J.D.Clark
Ghagaria	79-80	prehistory	M.P.	Pub.	All h Un	G.R. Sharma-J.D.Clark
Nakjar-Khurd	79-80	prehistory	M.P.	Pub	Allh Uni	G.R. Sharma-J.D.Clark
Patpara	79-80	prehistory	M.P.	Pub.	Allh Uni	G.R. Sharma-J.D.Clark
Nagra	79-82	temple	Maha.	Unpub.	State Dept	Jamkhedkar
Poluvanpatti	79-80	historical	T. Nadu	Unpub.	State Dept	R. Nagaswamy
Kovalanpattal	79-80	megalithic	T. Nadu	Unpub.	State Dept	R. Nagaswamy
Gangkndchlpm	79-80	historical	T. Nadu	Unpub.	State Dept	R. Nagaswamy
Amahata	80-81	megalithic?	M.P.	Unpub.	State Dept	?
Bankadagarh	80-81	temple	Orissa	Unpub.	State Dept	?
Boregaon	80-81	megalithic	Maha.	?	?	?
Chirand	80-81	neo-chalco	Bihar	Unpub	Patna Uni	?
Didwana	80-84	prehistory	Rajasthan	Unpub.	D.Coll	V.N. Misra

Site	*Years*	*Nature*	*State*	*Status*	*Inst.*	*Person*
Indari	80-81	neolithic	U.P.	Unpub.	Allh Uni	G.R. Sharma
Indolakidhani	80-81	prehistory	Rajasthan	Unpub.	D.Coll	V.N. Misra
Khajuraho	80-83	temple	M.P.	Unpub.	ASI	?
Kheradih	80-81	chalcolithic	U.P.	Unpub.	BHU	K.K. Sinha
Munhai	80-81	chalco-megal	M.P.	Unpub.	BHU ?	?
Nandur	80-83	early hist	M.P.	Unpub.	State Dept	?
Pagara	80-81	historical	M.P.	Unpub.	?	?
Paisra	80-81	prehistory	Bihar	Pub.	BHU	P.C. Pant, V. Jayaswal
Ramapuram	80-83	chalcolithic	Andhra	Unpub.	ASI	Narasimhaiah
Raygad	80-81	historical	Maha.	Unpub.	?	?
Runija	80-81	chalcolithic	M.P.	Unpub.	?	?
Singh Bhgnpur	80-81	early hist	Panjab	Unpub.	?	?
Singi Talav	80-83	prehistory	Rajasthan	Unpub.	D.Coll	V.N. Misra
Sunari	80-81	early hist	Rajasthan	Unpub.	?	?
Surpan	80-81	historic	Gujarat	Unpub.	?	?
Vaddamanu	81-83	historic	Andhra	?	Birla Arch Inst. Hyder.	T.V.G. Sastry
Muravkonda	81-82	prehistory	Andhra	?	D.Coll	R.S. Pappu
Taradih	81-83	neo-chalco	Bihar	Unpub.	State Dept	A.K. Prasad
Gufkral	81-82	neolithic	J & K	Unpub.	ASI	A.K. Sharma
Gilaulikhera	81-82	chalcolithic	M.P.	Unpub	Prachya Nktn, Bhopal	R.K. Sharma
Kunjhun	81-82	neolithic	M.P.	Pub. ?	Allh Uni	G.R. Sharma-J.D.Clark
Rampur	81-82	prehistory	M.P.	Published	Allh Uni	G.R. Sharma-J.D.Clark
Udayasvara	81-82	temple	M.P.	Unpub.	?	?
Daulatabad	80-82	historic	Maharashtra	?	D.Coll	M.S. Mate
Khairwada	81-82	megalithic	Maharashtra	?	State Dept	?
Adiyamankottai	80-82	hist	T. Nadu	Unpub.	Madras Uni	?
Rajbadidanga	81-82	historic	W. Bengal	Unpub.	Cal Uni	?
Gandluru	82-83	neolithic	Andhra	Unpub.	Nagarjuna Uni	B.R. Subrahmanyam
Kudavdi	82-83	temple	Andhra	Unpub.	ASI	I.K. Sarma
Papanasi	82-83	temple	Andhra	Unpub.	ASI	I.K. Sarma
Rojdi	82-83	Harappan	Gujarat	Pub.	State/Penn U	G.L. Possehl
Goraj	82-83	temple	Gujarat	Unpub.	ASI	B.M. Pande
Banki	82-83	prehistory	M.P.	Unpub.	Allh Uni	G.R. Sharma
Medhauli	82-83	prehistory	M.P.	Unpub.	Allh Uni	G.R. Sharma
Phulbani	82-83	prehistory	Orissa	?	D.Coll	S.B. Ota
Rohira	82-83	Harappan	Panjab	Unpub.	State Dept	G.B. Sharma
Gutturmalai	82-83	megalithic	T. Nadu	Unpub.	Madras Uni	K.V. Raman

Site	*Years*	*Nature*	*State*	*Status*	*Inst.*	*Person*
Kambarmedu	82-83	megalithic	T. Nadu	Unpub.	ASI	?
Malari	82-83	cave burial	U.P.	Unpub.	Garhwal Uni	K.P. Nautiyal
Bharat Mandir	82-83	historic	U.P.	Unpub.	Garhwal Uni	K.P. Nautiyal
Panduwala	82-83	historic	U.P.	Unpub.	Garhwal Uni	K.P. Nautiyal
Thapli	82-83	PGW	U.P.	Unpub.	Garhwal Uni	K.P. Nautiyal
Ballal Dhipi	82-83	historic	W. Bengal	ASI	unpublished	?

It is possible that some sites excavated during this period were not reported in *IAR*. For instance, the Birla Archaeological and Cultural Research Institute of Hyderabad excavated the proto-historic and later site of Veerapuram (Sastri, Bai and Rao 1984) and the Department of History, Delhi University excavated a Black-and-Red Ware site called Bahiri in 1982 (Chakrabarti and Hasan 1982). Similarly, the site of Kakrehta (Rupnath) was excavated by Jabalpur University, although it does not appear to have been listed in *IAR* (Sharma and Mishra 1992).

Out of the present list of about 191 excavated sites during this period, most of them (about 145, if not more) still remain unpublished. Even among those which are considered published, there are discrepancies in the scale of reporting. For instance, the site of Malhar excavated by Sagar University under K.D. Bajpai was reported in a monograph (Bajpai and Pandey 1978), and the site is generally considered 'published'. However, this 'report' is in the form of a brief article both in Hindi and English and unaccompanied by any site-plan or section drawing. The only illustrative material it contains is only a set of photographs, not all of which are of excavated specimens. On the other hand, the site is of massive proportion and surrounded by a well-preserved, high mud rampart. This is certainly the most impressive fortified early historical city in the Chhattisgarh or south Kosala region. The report does not do any justice to the site or the work done here. There is perhaps no point in trying to apportion blame for an almost complete or all-pervasive indifference to the need of publishing in detail the results of publicly funded excavations. A look at the preceding chart gives a comprehensive idea of the individual defaulters and the defaulting institutions. It might interest us to note that some organisations and/or people have not bothered to publish the results of their excavations ever in their lives. No question has ever been asked of the way these organisations and individuals have functioned. Whether the organisations/departments belong to the central and state governments or to the universities is immaterial; no university except Poona University/Deccan College possesses a consistent track record of publication, and even in the case of the Deccan College the record is not without some serious lapses.

Emerging Trends

Constraints

The pull of the earlier trends was still very strong in the mid to the late 1970s. Seeking the archaeological roots of Indian tradition — whether it was in the Vedas or in the epics — was still a basic motive-force of Indian archaeological research. Equally compelling was the notion to seek the roots of everything Indian from west Asia and, to a lesser degree, from south-east Asia. It seems that the Indian educated class had an innate repulsion against the idea of being 'aborigines'; they had to call themselves migrants from foreign lands ! It was also true that archaeology did not become rooted deeper into Indian psyche during this phase; the central Survey considerably increased its size and the scope of its activities; the provincial departments/directorates organised themselves as smaller copies of the central Survey, and archaeology became a generally accepted part of the Indian university activities in a number of cases. On the whole, archaeology still remained a remote thing, enmeshed in bureaucracy and an all-pervasive lethargy to analyse the field-data and publish them.

Prehistory

Once one accepts these limitations, one finds some new trends. For instance, there was a drift from the earlier stratigraphical and typological approach to prehistory. The problem of environmental setting of the pre-historic assemblages slowly came to the fore, and along with this emerged a quest for both geochronological and radiocarbon dating. There was also slow induction of thermoluminiscent dating (Agrawal, Bhandari and Singhvi 1979). The importance of finding primary sites was now registered strongly in the minds of the working prehistorians. Excavations at Hunsgi, Paisra, Bhimbetka, Baghor and other areas in Sidhi (M.P.) and Belan valley (U.P.), and the beginning of excavations at Didwana, Singi Talav, etc., in western Rajasthan brought about a different perspective of palaeolithic India. The discovery of bone tools in the upper palaeolithic assemblage of the Kurnool caves was also an important factor in bringing about this changed perspective. After excavations at Baghor, Adamgarh and the host of sites in the Belan valley and Pratapgarh area there was a different perspective for the mesolithic phase too. The introduction of a 'settlement-subsistence' approach also made pre-historic studies a little more worthwhile from the point of view of India's general economic and developmental history. This approach also heightened the need for a sharper focus on ethno-archaeological investigations in the related areas. Although the detailed report on the

Deccan College pre-historic investigation in western Rajasthan is still awaited, its multi-disciplinary — specifically soil science oriented — approach was a major step forward. The Allchin-Goudie-Hegde survey of the entire arid zone of Gujarat and Rajasthan, supplemented by extensive geographical formulations based on the chemical analysis of the relevant soil samples initially showed the way. Microwear studies of lithic assemblages made their appearance (cf. R.K. Pant 1979) and the typo-technological studies of stone tools became more sophisticated (cf. Semans 1981).

Protohistory

In the field of the Indus studies this was the phase in which the entire stretch from the Kalibangan section of Rajasthan to the Simla foothills and the upper Doab gained a special significance of its own (cf. Bhan and Shaffer 1978). This was also the phase when the issue of the interrelatedness of the Late Harappans and the makers of the OCP came strongly to the fore, providing a new insight into the transformation of the Indus civilization in the upper part of the Ganga-Yamuna Doab. The excavations at Bhagwanpura and related sites which showed an interlocking of the late Harappan and the PGW levels changed our perception of the proto-historic archaeology of this region. Further, the association between the 'Copper Hoards' and the OCP was proved at Saipai and R.C. Agrawala's work in Rajasthan (1979, 1980a, 1980b) led to a new perception of the metallurgical significance of the Aravalli zone. In Gujarat this was the time for the late Harappans to emerge into view with all their shades of difference; the excavations at sites like Rojdi, Zekhada, Kanewal, etc., played a leading role in this regard. Finally, the fact that the Daimabad excavations and the earlier explorations in the Dhulia district of Maharashtra identified late Harappan levels of occupation in the interior of the Deccan drove home the point that the Indus civilization could no longer be studied apart from the issue of its interaction with, and impact on, the neolithic-chalcolithic cultures of inner India. In eastern India the earlier identification of a neolithic level was consolidated by this time by the discoveries from Chechar-Kutubpur and Taradih. The picture of neolithic-megalithic transition and continuity in south India was a very important development in its own context. Early historical archaeology did not make any positive progress, mainly because of the sporadic character of investigations and lack of detailed publications. By this time there was also a clearly expressed perception of the need to harness archaeological methods to investigate the material remains of mediaeval India. A consciously formulated approach to understand the Indian archaeological sequence in terms of indigenous developments was markedly visible during this phase too. The cases where this approach was worked out were those of the beginning of iron in India and the geographical and archaeological parameters of India's interrelations with west and central Asia.

THE YEAR 1982

D.P. Agrawal's *The Archaeology of India*

D.P. Agrawal is more at home in the technicalities of dating, metallurgical analysis and palaeoclimate and less in historical and archaeological data. However, his book *The Archaeology of India* (1982) tried to provide a clear update on the developments which took place since the publication of Sankalia's *PPOP* in 1974. Whatever specific science-based research was done during this period in prehistory and protohistory was also aptly synthesised by him. Although the importance of a geographical approach is made clear by him in the introduction (chapter 1), the way he organises his data, following basically the Three Age system, does not do justice to the intricate relationship between geographical zones and archaeological cultures of the subcontinent. It surely does not unravel a geographical story. Unfortunately he also believes in ecological and technological determinism and does not pay sufficient attention to the possible complexities of the situation. For instance, he accepts what he thinks is the testimony provided by the Indian epics on the deep forest cover of the Ganga valley but does not ask himself if the testimony was complete in itself and could be treated as a piece of historical information of a certain age, and if so, of which age. He then goes on to argue on the basis of such nebulous 'testimony' that deep forests of the Ganga plain could be cleared only when iron implements began to be used to cut down forests. He thinks of 'large-scale deforestation and drainage of swamps before the beginning of the early historic period in the Ganga valley. He commits two serious mistakes in this case. First, he does not critically examine his literary sources — in this case, the Indian epics — and secondly, he prefers to ignore the very extensive evidence of pre-iron settlements in the valley. The point is that he glosses over the basic realities of both environment and archaeology to drive an apparently innocuous ecological point home. The same can be said about his dependence on Gurdip Singh's interpretation of the pollen sequence of the Rajasthan salt lake profiles which pointed to a phase of climatic amelioration during the early Harappan and Harappan periods. The fact that the issue of Harappan climate may depend on the examination of more variables in a much larger area does not seem to appeal to him.

In the chapter on 'palaeolithic cultures' he rightly points out that most of the reported palaeolithic tools are from secondary contexts and do not denote anything more than 'occurrences'. One of the positive aspects of this chapter is that it discusses the problem of plio-pleistocene boundary, especially in the Siwaliks. This was the period when Agrawal's Kashmir Palaeoclimate Project was taking shape and this is reflected by his reference to the onset of deglaciation in Kashmir around 15000 BP. In the case of Rajasthan reference was made both to Gurdip Singh's pollen sequence and the climatic sequence built by Bridget Allchin, Andrew Goudie and K. Hegde. In the case of Saurashtra three marine transgressions at about 5000 BP 35000 BP and 130000 BP were mentioned, along with the significance of miliolite formations for the dating of palaeoliths in coastal Saurashtra. In central India the excavations of the Acheulian deposit in Bhimbetka rock-shelter III-F-23 provided the central focus. The significance of the fossilised fauna was discussed both in the contexts of the Belan valley and Maharashtra. In the north-east claims of palaeolithic finds were uncritically accepted. Discussion of the south Indian palaeoliths highlighted the upper palaeolithic finds of the Kurnool caves. Only a few radiocarbon dates from middle palaeolithic contexts are cited.

Chapter 4 discusses the 'mesolithic cultures' which he takes to mean 'all microlith-using cultures', despite the facts which he himself cites :

> . . . in India microliths have been used from the Mesolithic to the historical times. Some of the microlithic cultures were perhaps Neolithic in the economic sense.
>
> — Agrawal 1982 : 57

An important chapter of the book is the one on 'pre-historic art' where he discusses the evidence from Kashmir and central India on the basis of the publications of B.M. Pande and Y. Mathpal respectively.

In chapter 6 ('the first farming cultures') he lumps together the stratified and dated archaeological material from Baluchistan, Kashmir and south India and the unstratified and undated material from the north-east. The Indus civilization and related cultures are discussed next, highlighting the bracket of 2300-2000 BC for the 'nuclear Mature Harappan'; for its end he puts emphasis on climatic changes. In his discussion on 'chalcolithic cultures' he wisely admits that 'no ethnic equations need be based on the mere bicolour of the black-and-red ware' (Agrawal 1982 : 211), although in the chapter on the Iron Age he considered it prudent to devote a section to 'the Aryan problem'. In the case of the Gandhara Graves he thinks that some pottery types suggest 'some Indo-Aryan association'.

Finally, Agrawal concludes that 'most of the new technologies — right from the early palaeolithic to the Iron Age' have a late start in India and 'cultural influences, during various periods, can be traced to West Asia, China, Central Asia and Southeast Asia'. The emphasis is not on interaction but on 'influences' from those directions. From this point of view, he does not move far away from Sankalia's model of 'colonisation' of the land in various periods.

Bridget and F.R. Allchin's *The Rise of Civilization in India and Pakistan*

Bridget and Raymond Allchin's *The Rise of Civilization in India and Pakistan* (1982) was an expanded and updated version of their earlier publication *The Birth of Indian Civilization*. In the chapter on 'pre-historic environments' they drew heavily on the Allchin-Goudie-Hegde work in Gujarat and Rajasthan and on the work of Helen Rendell in the Potwar plateau which completely changed the terrace-based approach of de Terra and Paterson. This is the first time that the Terra-Paterson stratigraphy of the Soan valley, which had hitherto formed the cornerstone of all discussions on Indian prehistory was discarded, and for this reason alone, this chapter has some historical significance. One of the major features of their chapters on prehistory is an emphasis on the diversity of site locations and the steady element of stratigraphic and technological continuity between the various stages of the palaeolithic and between the upper palaeolithic and the mesolithic. The mesolithic chapter was enriched by references to the modern hunting-gathering communities like the Veddahs and the Chenchus. In all cases where the pre-historic industries were discussed there was a complete command of the primary materials involved. One of the perceptive comments is that 'the religion of modern hunting communities must have been invaded by and become closely integrated with that of neighbouring people at many different stages'. (Allchin and Allchin 1982 : 93) Although the chapter on 'the first agricultural communities' discusses Baluchistan, Kashmir, Ganga plain, the north-east and south India together, a major part of the chapter is devoted to the new discoveries at Mehrgarh, which were by and large ignored by D.P. Agrawal (1982). The chapter on the 'early Indus' civilization underscores the point that the 'Early stage must be seen as the formative period, the stage of incipient urbanism'. (Allchin and Allchin 1982 : 164-65) The two chapters on the 'mature Indus civilization' offer a substantial summary of the evidence, including a reference to Shortughai, the significance of which was inexplicably bypassed by D.P. Agrawal (1982). The discussion on the Indus chronology is far less decisive, but they make references to the importance of MASCA calibrations and the possibility that the Indus-Mesopotamia trade 'goes back well before 2500 BC'.

The chapter on 'the aftermath of the Indus civilization in the Indus and Ganges systems' is oriented to the authors need to locate some archaeological traces of the Aryans, and to this end various Iranian and central Asian analogies are brought in for the miscellaneous copper-bronze artefacts from the north-west, pottery of the Gandhara Graves, Cemetery H pottery and even the pottery of Bara and Mitathal. Even the cairn graves of Mogul Ghundai in Baluchistan, which are indisputably from the late centuries BC, have been given a date early in the first millennium BC. The 'aftermath' in Peninsular India has a more objective focus, including a detailed description of the Daimabad hoard of bronzes which, unlike D.P. Agrawal (1982), they are willing to admit as proto-historic. The significance of Ganeshvar in the Aravallis as a metallurgical site is also properly analysed, despite the search for parallels of the Khurdi hoard from the Nagaur district of Rajasthan in Iran. The discussion on south India has gained from their close familiarity with the area and its archaeological and ethnographic material. In the chapter on 'the arrival of Indo-Aryan speaking people and the spread of the Indo-Aryan languages' it is argued that

> we would expect there to have been at least two main periods of Indo-Aryan migration into north-western India and Pakistan, the first or early period dating from around 2000 B.C., and the second some six centuries later. — Allchin and Allchin 1982 : 301

As for archaeological correlates, they find an early 'pre-Vedic' movement in the Gandhara graves, although no positive evidence is cited except a vague and uncritical reference to the parallels for their material culture in the Caucasus, north Iran and southern central Asia. In the Harappan fire-altars of Kalibangan they find 'an indication of culture contact between an early group of Indo-Aryans and the population of the still flourishing Indus civilization'. (Allchin and Allchin 1982 : 303) The rest is uncertain, driven mostly by an uncontrolled desire to discover 'Aryans' in the Indian archaeological record from Gujarat and Panjab to south India. The Iron Age data are discussed in the penultimate chapter and in the context of the south Indian graves the conclusion is that its principal elements 'suggest contact with some external source, and this, it seems clear, must be derived from the direction of the Caucasus, Iran and Central Asia'. (Allchin and Allchin 1982 : 342) Soon archaeology takes leave, and we are treated to the assertions of the following kind :

> This complex of traits may be associated ultimately with the 'Kurgan' burial complex which has been related to the early Indo-European speaking peoples, and whose diffusion appears often to coincide strikingly with the spread of Indo-European languages into areas where previously they were not known. — Allchin and Allchin 1982 : 342-43

An early date for the beginning of the use of iron in India is accepted in this chapter. The quest for Indo-Aryans, Dravidians, Mundas and others colours the concluding chapter ('subcontinental unity and regional diversity') too.

Protohistory

In 1982 R.K. Sharma (1982) edited *Indian Archaeology, New Perspectives* which had a special focus on the protohistory of Madhya Pradesh. Two major articles, one by V.S. Wakankar on 'chalcolithic Malwa' and the other by Giriraj Kumar on 'house-planning in the chalcolithic Malwa', are major repositories of information on the chalcolithic remains of the region. Such regional focus was then rare in Indian archaeology, although a beginning in this direction was made by the Madhya Pradesh government directorate of archaeology and museums which had begun to its own journal called *Puratan* in about this period. It is possible that the Andhra Pradesh State directorate had founded a journal called *Itihas* in a somewhat earlier period. Suman Pandya (1982) contributed an important paper on her surface observations at Dholavira to the volume edited by R.K. Sharma.

Another event of 1982 was the publication of *Harappan Civilization. A Contemporary Perspective* which was edited by G.L. Possehl. In his introductory article he argues that the archaeological sites and settlement patterns should be read within their own context and comments on the settlement pattern of Harappan sites and their 'domains'. Regarding the settlement pattern his main argument is that the way in which the resources needed by the Harappans were dispersed over a wide area from the Oxus valley to the Deccan 'drove the optimum position for the settlements away from one another'. (Possehl 1982 : 19) According to this approach, Lothal could be seen as an outlier of Mohenjo-Daro — 'a settlement daughtered-off to capture the resources from a very specific terrain'. His reliance on Ratnagar's characterisation of Harappa as a 'gateway city' — a major procurement centre where transportation functions and facilities outweighed the importance of manufactures there — led him astray because a subsequent painstaking analysis of the excavated archaeological material from Harappa (Lahiri 1990) easily identified it as a major manufacturing centre. The definition of the 'domains' does not aim for geographical precision; the 'eastern domain' has been defined to include 'Panjab, Haryana, northern Rajasthan, western Uttar Pradesh, even Jammu and Kashmir' and thus becomes too wide a term to be of specific use. Vishnu Mittre (1982) also writes of the 'need for a new approach' and argue that short-term environmental fluctuations can be important in the life of a settlement and that it is important to reconstruct the entire environmental context of each site without entering the debate about wet or dry climates.

Among the points which J.G. Shaffer (1982) submits as examples of his reconsideration of the Harappan culture, two are important: the primacy of an internal trading network, and the fact that the differential ratio of copper to the other alloying materials of the relevant Harappan artefacts 'may reflect functional variations'. Regarding the primacy of internal trading network, his opinion is worth quoting :

> What I do maintain is that external exchange networks did not have the same socioeconomic significance in the Mature Harappan context that they did in Mesopotamia or the Iranian Plateau, and that for the Mature Harappan Culture, the development and maintenance of internal networks is a critical issue for understanding the cultural processes at work in the greater Indus valley. — Shaffer 1982 : 48

This is supported by the present author's opinion regarding the extent of Harappan external trade (Chakrabarti 1977) :

> . . . if one has to make a comment on the archaeological evidence of the external trade of the Harappan civilization, one has to admit that the total evidence is not as impressive as the general discussions on the problem lead one to believe. Quite expectedly the Harappans were familiar with their neighbouring areas to the west up to Mesopotamia, but the available archaeological evidence does not carry the impression that the Indus flotillas were constantly sailing up the Persian Gulf or that the Indus caravans were particularly dense on the west Asian highways.

The depth of internal trading network in the Indus context has subsequently been adequately highlighted by Nayanjot Lahiri's research (1992). In his paper in the present volume the present author (Chakrabarti 1982) drew attention to the pre-Sargonic date of the beginning of the mature Harappan contact with Mesopotamia, with obvious implications for the date of the beginning of this civilization. The artefact type which figured principally in this discussion was long barrel-cylinder carnelian beads, the significance of which had until then been ignored in the contemporary literature. Among the Indian participants of the conference, the proceedings of which form this volume, some read papers on the results of their excavations, and as those reports are unlikely to be published in detail in future, these conference papers are important. In this category one should place R.S. Bisht's paper on his excavations at Banwali between 1974 and 1977, R.C. Agrawala's and Vijay Kumar's paper on the Ganeshwar-Jodhpura culture of Rajasthan, Y.D. Sharma's paper on the Harappan complex in the Indian section of the Sutlej valley and K.N. Dikshit's paper on Hulas and the late Harappan complex in western Uttar Pradesh (Bisht 1982, Agrawala and Kumar 1982, Y.D. Sharma 1982, K.N. Dikshit

1982). S.A. Sali (1982) provided a specific focus on the late Harappan level at Daimabad, and as he points out, 'the final form of the transformed Harappan Culture in south and central India as a whole' needs future investigations. The late Harappan level at Daimabad also figures in Dhavalikar's article in the same volume, where he establishes the link between thids level and the famous Daimabad bronzes. Y.M. Chitalwala's paper on the distribution of the Harappan settlements in Kutch and Saurashtra (Chitalwala 1982) is based on his close familiarity with the sites and their immediate geography. The paper has a special importance because of its analysis of the geographical location of Dholavira — 'an entrepot for the Harappans coming from Sind across the Great Rann'. Vishnu Mittre and R. Savithri (1982) examine the food economy of the Harappans, a distinctive part of their approach being the environmental analysis of crops. They argue that 'environmental variability, much as is seen today, also existed in Harappan times'. Further, the cultivation of wheat, barley, gram and *Pisum arvense* or field-pea outside the Harappan distribution area in the subcontinent was a result of contact with the Harappans. D.P. Agrawal and R.K. Sood (1982) believe that around 3000 BC the climate was wetter than before in Rajasthan and there was an onset of aridity around 1500 BC. This was no doubt in line with Agrawal's environmental determinism. K.T.M. Hegde *et al.* (1982) undertook a detailed technical study of Harappan steatite microbeads, and considering the number of non-Harappan sites where such beads have been found, this article is important for comparative purposes. J.R. Lukacs' study of the dentition of the Mohenjo-Daro and Harappa skeletons in this volume was in line with his earlier studies of dentition of chalcolithic skeletons (Lukacs 1978). A.K. Sharma (1982) provided an account of the Harappan cemetery of Kalibangan, with some interesting observations. For instance, he points out that

> Except in one case, all the extended burials exposed so far have yielded very poor burial furnishings. Does this point to the fact that these burials belonged to a particular section of the society, with the other section or sections practising some other mode of disposal of the dead or even had a separate cemetery ? — A.K. Sharma 1982 : 299

F.R. Allchin (1982) tries to explain the continued legacy of the Indus civilization by speculating that the Indo-Aryans arrived even when the civilization was flourishing and 'this permits one to postulate a degree of synthesis between the exponents of the Indus great tradition and those of the arriving conquerors'.

On the whole, this is an important volume in Harappan studies, especially when one remembers that except Wheeler's *The Indus Civilization* (3rd edn. in 1968) and Rao's book on Lothal in 1973, there was no volume, till this one was published in 1982, which adequately dealt with the various ramifications of the spate of Harappan discoveries since 1947.

The Settlement-Subsistence System Approach in Prehistory

It was also in 1982 that K. Paddayya (1982) published his *The Acheulian Culture of the Hunsgi Valley (Peninsular India). A Settlement System Perspective*. In his introductory note S.B. Deo, the then Director of the Deccan College which published the volume commented that the Stone Age cultures of the subcontinent 'could be visualised as past living systems', provided the right approaches were adopted. Paddayya's work followed from his early explorations along the course of the Hunsgi stream, a left bank tributary of the Krishna. In 1969 he discovered an Acheulian assemblage at Gulbal in the south-western section of the Hunsgi valley, which, because of its proximity to the limestone-bearing tableland of the region and general freshness, indicated that it was derived from a nearby primary site. In 1974 he undertook a small excavation in the village of Hunsgi (Locality III) obtaining 'clear indications of the primary context of the artefactual assemblage'. This was followed by a programme of excavations at Hunsgi Locality V and Locality VI in 1975-77, resulting in the discovery of Acheulian occupational floors. It was considered unlikely that the Acheulian cultural system would be based on a limited number of sites, organising its year-long activities around them. This in turn led to the consideration of a regional framework for this system. At this point Paddayya points out that he had developed a multi-stage research strategy, involving the 'testing of three hypothetical propositions'.

> The first proposition was that, once the requirements of a suitable terrain and economic resources are fulfilled, even regions lying away from the major or through-flowing rivers could have been occupied by the Stone Age communities. Secondly, it was argued that, since the fluvial processes operating here are much less effective than those connected with major rivers, such areas oould be expected to preserve Stone Age sites in primary or undisturbed condition. The third proposition was that, given the right approach on the part of the archaeologist, these sites could offer a predictive model of the structure as well as the working of the past cultural system. — Paddayya 1982:5

The regional context was established by undertaking an intensive survey of the relevant area, including the distribution of the relevant raw material of silicified limestone and a detailed listing of the wild plant foods available in the area. The availability of a few varieties of wild mammals was also not ignored. Extending the picture of the present vegetation cover into the past it was inferred that the area had a savanna woodland type of vegetation cover in the past and similarly, the palaeoclimate was considered similar to its present climate. The basic postulate was that the element of seasonality must have influenced the Acheulian cultural and economic system here the most, and Paddayya correlated the dispersed character of sites in the valley to the wet season occupation when there was a far greater choice of naturally available food and people could disperse over a wider area in its search. The sites clustered mostly around the natural pools of water in a limited area would reflect occupation during the dry months of the year. He follows up this interpretation with a reference to the dry season aggregation and wet season dispersal of a few modern hunting-gathering groups including the Chenchus living in the lower reaches of the Krishna river about 150 km to the east of Hunsgi.

Realising that his almost exclusive reliance on this ethnographic model may be criticised, especially in view of the fact that his reconstruction of palaeoclimate has left no scope for divergence from the present one, Paddayya goes on to write :

> If nothing else, ethnographic data have the virtue of suggesting a working model or way-out for transforming "knowledge of the archaeological record" into "knowledge of the archaeological past". The settlement system model offered in respect of the Hunsgi valley Acheulian culture is just an instance of this general process of archaeological inference.
>
> — Paddayya 1982 : 94

He fully understands that in the subcontinental prehistory as a whole there will be many regional and/or temporal variants of the adaptational strategy which he has offered for the Acheulian of the Hunsgi valley and that the identifications of such variant settlement systems may be the major task of Indian prehistory for years to come.

Historically, this approach also establishes a close link between pre-historic studies and the land as it exists with all its nuances. In other words, this establishes the relevance of the understanding of modern land to the understanding of its prehistory and vice versa.

THE PERIOD FROM 1983 to 1989

Major Discoveries and Studies in Prehistory

This point was driven home rather dramatically — and more forcefully than any other Indian archaeological discovery that one can think of — by the publication of what was called an upper palaeolithic shrine at Baghor I in Sidhi district by J.M. Kenoyer *et al.*

(1983). The facts that a fertility symbol in the form of a piece of stone bearing naturally formed lamination marks resembling a vulva was found in the centre of a rubble-built small platform certainly dating from *c.* 9000-8000 BC and that such stones and such platforms are still in use in the same village for the worship of a mother goddess took away the breath of all who believe in the continuity of Indian ritual behaviour from a remote pre-historic past. The work in Sidhi in Madhya Pradesh was done jointly by the teams of Allahabad University under G.R. Sharma and University of California, Berkeley, under the leadership of J.D. Clark. The joint report on this work which was edited by them was also published in 1983 (Sharma and Clark 1983) under the title of *Palaeoenvironments and Prehistory in the Middle Son Valley*. The alluvial history of the valley with reference to its four formations in ascending stratigraphic order — Sihawal, Patpara, Baghor and Khetaunhi Formations — and their dates was first worked out by M.A.J. Williams and K. Royce (1983). This was followed by excavation reports on various pre-historic localities — Nakjhar Khurd, Baghor I, Rampur, Baghor II, Baghor III and Ghagharia, the last two being mesolithic occupation localities. The discovery of postholes at Baghor III was important, considering the rarity of such finds in the Indian pre-historic context. In each case there was a detailed emphasis on the quantitative calculation and metrical measurements of artefactual assemblages and on the whole there was a strong awareness of their ethnoarchaeological dimensions. The 'discussion of preliminary results and assessment of future research potential' by J.D. Clark and G.R. Sharma is a major theoretical contribution to the study of Indian prehistory, and some of the things they emphasise are important in historical perspective. The element of technological continuity from the Upper Acheulian of the Sihawal Formation to the Mesolithic-Neolithic of Baghor-Khetaunhi is clearly marked and similarly, the changing site locations of the major phases in response to the changing ecology of the area are clearly brought to the fore. Radiocarbon dates are used to define the chronology of the sequence, at least of the later part of the sequence where the dates are focussed. In view of the 1.5 mya date for the *Homo erectus* fossils from Java, the possibility of early Hominid occurrence in the subcontinent is clearly admitted. The lithic technology of the various phases is stressed in detail, and one of the conclusions which emerges is that by the Mesolithic times the heat treatment of chert and agate was a regular practice. The concluding ethnographic model of the pre-historic behaviour was based on a documented study of the behaviour of the Baigas and the inference was that the groupings were not more than 20-30 individuals and possibly much smaller. The seasonality led to the frequent shifting of settlements but 'they are unlikely to have been moved very appreciable distances'.

There was no doubt a shift in Indian pre-historic studies by the early 1980s. This shift can also be perceived in Erwin Neumayer's synthesis of the current knowledge of pre-historic Indian rock paintings (Neumayer 1983). By this time there was a substantial amount of literature, a good part of it in Hindi, on this topic. One of the major roles in initiating a general interest in Indian pre-historic art was played by V.S. Wakankar who was one of the great explorers of painted rock-shelters of central India (cf. Wakankar and Brooks 1976). The scholars who had been actively involved in this branch of study since the late 1960s also include Rakesh Tewari, Jagadish Gupta, Ajit Das Kesari, S.K. Pandey, A. Sundara, Y. Mathpal, Jerome Jacobson, Giriraj Kumar and others. In 1978 Sankalia produced a book on *Prehistoric Art of India* (1978) which included discussions on rock-paintings. Neumayer's publication in 1983 provided an accessible overall assessment which was accompanied by clearly produced copies of different types of paintings. By way of a footnote one may add that in the annual conference of the Indian Archaeological Society in Jaipur in the winter of 1977 V.S. Wakankar held an exhibition on the copies he made of Bhimbetka paintings and that among those copies he pointed out those done in green as belonging to the upper palaeolithic. Neumayer discusses the issue, points out that 'green Mesolithic paintings of this particular style are always found in the lowest painting strata on the rock walls' and draws attention to Wakankar's find of green faceted colour material in the context of 'microliths of the Upper Palaeolithic tradition' in his excavations of the rockshelter IIIA-28 at Bhimbetka. In a sense Neumayer (1983) set the context for the publication of Yasodhar Mathpal's detailed study of the paintings of Bhimbetka (Mathpal 1984), updating and elaborating his earlier study jointly with V.N. Misra (Misra and Mathpal 1979). Mathpal discusses these paintings primarily as the source of the contemporary lifeways, and being an artist himself, he has been able to throw light on the implications of different painting styles. For the general archaeological setting of the total area, of which Bhimbetka was only a part, Jacobson's study published in 1980 remains a major source.

Articles and books continued to appear on Indian prehistory throughout the 1980s. This is the time when the multidisciplinary pre-historic research organised by V.N. Misra in western Rajasthan comes into clear focus, initially in an article in *Man and Environment* (Misra *et al.* 1982) and then with a series of radiometric dates in 1989 in the same journal (Raghavan, Rajaguru and Misra 1989). Meanwhile Misra, Rajaguru and Raghavan (1988) contributed a definitive article on the prehistory of the area in *Proceedings of the Indian National Science Academy, A.* Soil science played a major role in the investigation of western Rajasthan pre-historic sediments (Wasson, Smith and

Agrawal 1984). In 1981 A.R. Marathe published the results of his investigations in the prehistory of Hiran valley, Saurashtra (Marathe 1981) and a better chronological framework of the Hiran valley sequence appeared in 1986 (Baskaran *et al.* 1986). In 1983 J. Armand published the report of his pre-historic excavations in Durkadi Nala and he described his finds as 'an early Palaeolithic pebble-tool workshop in central India'. In 1981 and 1983 G. Corvinus (1981, 1983) published the details of her survey and excavations at Chirki-on-Pravara in Maharashtra. In 1982 Sheila Misra (1982) offered the hypothesis that the fact of basalt weathering could have an impact on our understanding of the so-called Nevasian industry which might have had its distinct Acheulian tools made of basalt weathered away. This is certainly a new approach to the problem of archaeological sequencing in Indian prehistory. The report of a skull-cap associated with palaeolithic tools in the cliff section of the Narmada at Hathnora (Sonakia 1984, also Badam *et al.* 1986) was obviously an event of momentous significance in Indian pre-historic studies and although their *Homo erectus* status as established by M.A. De Lumley and A. Sonakia is no longer beyond dispute, this discovery by Sonakia, a Geological Survey of India person, has provided us with the first biological window on the early humans in India.

The publication of an edited volume *Recent Advances in Indo-Pacific Prehistory* (Misra and Bellwood 1985) adequately reflects the research trend of the mid-1980s in Indian prehistory. One has never been quite sure of the academic relevance of lumping the prehistory of India and the Pacific region together, but the conferences of the Indo-Pacific Prehistory Association have provided opportunities — thanks to the consistently generous support of the organisers of the conference, especially Peter Bellwood — to a large number of prehistorians from India, particularly of the Deccan College, to present their findings before an international audience. In addition to the more orthodox archaeological material, the section on wild plant foods and their relevance to the understanding of Indian pre-historic subsistence needs a special notice. Malti Nagar (1985) wrote on the use of wild plant foods by the aboriginal communities of central India and M.L.K. Murty (1985a) wrote on the use of wild plant foods by some hunter-gatherer communities of Andhra. Both Nagar and Murty had been interested in this issue for sometime. Relevant in this context are their articles on the ethnoarchaeology of the Bhimbetka region (Nagar 1983) and ethnoarchaeology of the Kurnool cave areas (Murty 1985b). Nagar is not always interested in the archaeological correlates, but Murty keeps archaeology always in mind, and between him and Paddayya they have worked out the frame of a settlement-subsistence approach to Indian prehistory. It may be relevant to draw attention to my earlier comments on this approach :

> The importance of the above-mentioned researches of Paddayya and Murty does not merely lie in their arrangement and interpretation of data within a coherent theoretical framework but in demonstrating in a number of ways that there is continuity between prehistory and the living present in their respective areas. This throws a significant amount of light on the very deep-roorted adjustment of the Indian life to its various ecological niches, leading to an extraordinary variety of human existence on different levels of subsistence behaviour. At the same time this, by implication, also makes one aware of the inevitability of the tremendous amount of chaos and suffering if this ecological equilibrium is disturbed beyond redemption. — Chakrabarti 1988b: 75

From the point of view of understanding the processes of domestication Vishnu Mittre (1985) undertook a more technical study of the use of wild plants in the same Misra-Bellwood volume.

In 1984 B.C. Verma and J.P. Srivastava, two officers of the Geological Survey of India, reported their finds of palaeolithic implements *in situ* in what they considered to be early Pleistocene and even Pliocene deposits. The implication of this publication was completely ignored in the Indian publications on prehistory for a very long period. Verma and Srivastava worked out their sequence mainly in the Suketi fossil park of the Sirmaur area of Himachal Pradesh and fitted well in the Sharma-Clark speculation in 1983 that a Plio-Pleistocene sequence should emerge from the Siwaliks zone. One must give this publication by Verma and Srivastava its due importance in the history of Indian archaeology.

Thermoluminiscent dating in India took a new step with the dating of Rajasthan sand dunes by thermoluminescence (Singhvi, Sharma and Agrawal 1982) and the first report of ESR dating in India was made by V.D. Gogte and M.L.K. Murty (1986) in the upper palaeolithic context of the Kurnool caves. In 1985 Agrawal, Kusumgar and Krishnamurthy (1985) edited the 'proceedings of the international workshop on the late Cenozoic palaeoclimatic changes in Kashmir and central Asia' at the Physical Research Institute, Ahmedabad, in October 1982. Although a few archaeologists attended the workshop and read some orthodox archaeological papers, some of which were subsequently published in *Man and Environment* and although the eighth annual issue of this journal was published from Ahmedabad to coincide with this workshop, the Kashmir Palaeoclimate Project, the nucleus around which this workshop took place, cannot be said to possess much archaeological relevance for the simple reason that the project did not have any specific archaeological component. The only major archaeologicall fall-out of this otherwise important multidisciplinary project was the discovery of an upper palaeolithic industry (Pant *et al.* 1982) in Kashmir (called Sombur industry). In addition, about 30 neolithic sites were explored and their material collected. The project itself drew extensively on the sophisticated scientific techniques to establish stratigraphy and its dates. Both pollen data and dendroclimatic studies played a leading role in this study, but the only strictly archaeological paper in the volume is by G.M. Buth and R.N. Kaw (1985) on the plant husbandry in the neolithic levels of Burzahom.

Around 1985 there were a few articles of methodological significance in Indian prehistory. Prakash Sinha (1985) published on the 'microwear analysis and its scope in the Indian context', following a similar analysis of the Baghor III blade material (P. Sinha 1983, 1989). U.C. Chattopadhyay (1985) undertook an in-depth study of the methods, significance and some general implications of faunal studies in Indian archaeology with special reference to the Belan valley material. A major paper on the geoarchaeology of the southern microlithic industries — 'Quaternary coastal sediments and stratigraphy, south-east India' — was published by Rita Gardner (1986). In the same year there was a methodological study of wood remains from archaeological sites by Farooq Lone, G.M. Buth and Maqsood Khan (1986).

The most important publication in the field of prehistory in the second half of the 1980s, if one ignores the reports on the general pre-historic discoveries (cf. J.N. Pal 1984, 1985, Varma *et al.* 1985, Chakrabarti 1986, Chakrabarti and Lahiri 1987) was by David Raju (1988) : *Stone Age Hunter-Gatherers, an Ethno-archaeology of Cuddapah Region, South-east India.*

> This work aims at a reconstruction of the Stone Age settlement patterns in the Cuddapah region with the help of location and distribution of sites of the different stages of the Palaeolithic against their topographical setting, water sources, raw materials, flora and fauna, and by drawing inferences from the subsistence strategies and settlement patterns of the present day hunter-gatherers living at and around these sites.
>
> — Raju 1988 : 3

After establishing that the region with its wealth of raw material for tools, perennial supply of water and abundance of both animal and plant wild foods was suitable for occupation by pre-historic groups, Raju discusses the distribution and character of his lower palaeolithic sites with a detailed metrical analysis of their tool components. It is a late Acheulian industry where human groups occupied the areas near the water-sources which were about 1-2 km away from the main stream Gunjana. The two middle palaeolithic sites of the area supposedly represented 'transient encampments along braided runnels in a flat gently sloping terrain in a riverine hinterland ecosystem'. The site of Nandipalli was considered the homebase of such groups.The evidence of the upper palaeolithic was the most extensive (10 sites) among the three divisions of the palaeolithic. The areas of upper palaeolithic artefact occurrence are sometime very extensive — over a distance of about 4 km with varying degrees of concentration in different localities in the case of Vodikalu. The industry is analysed in great detail and the conclusion is that the Gunjana upper palaeolithic industry reveals a tendency towards microlithisation and can thus be considered late upper palaeolithic or epi-palaeolithic. The trial excavation at a particular locus also revealed a total of 84 grinding stone pieces, 19 rubbers and 133 split pebbles. By arguing that Vodikalu was a base-cum-work camp on the basis of a detailed analysis of different artefact types suggesting different maintenance and extractive activities, and by employing different ethnographic parallels from among the hunter-gatherers, Raju argues that the site of Vodikalu would have supported about 150-200 hunter-gatherers. His discussion of the ethnographic present was based on a study of the Yanadis, 'the third largest tribe in Andhra Pradesh'. The Yanadi life has been documented with reference to their 'folk life', settlement pattern, house types and subsistence strategies including hunting, fishing, fowling, foraging and collections of honey and minor forest produce.

Among Raju's conclusions, the following is of a great deal of interest :

> Taking clues from the food habits of the Yanadis, it is reasonable to predict that the Upper Palaeolithic hunter-gatherers relied on aquatic food resources for their subsistence as much as on game and wild vegetal foods. All the Upper Palaeolithic sites are located close to perennial water sources. Further, consumption of roots and tubers must have been an important part of the Upper Palaeolithic diet as the Yanadis are known to have lived during seven years (1950-57) of continuous drought mainly on wild yams . . . supplemented to some extent by roots, honey, fish and game. Such habits and practices possibly have a high antiquity and indicate the traditional subsistence patterns among the late Pleistocene hunter-gatherers. — Raju 1988 : 93

In 1989 J.D. Clark and G.S. Khanna undertook a detailed analysis of the neolithic remains found at Kunjhun II in the middle Son valley. Apart from its intrinsic importance as an early neolithic site of the area, this site has an added importance in the sense that a special activity area where heat treatment was applied to the raw material before making tools was identified and excavated here. The special character of the site rested in the fact that it represents six occupational levels (one with two sub-phases), each separated from the next by a sterile layer.

> The horizons have a maximum thickness of 30-50 mm and the dispersal scatters of artefacts and other material suggest only temporary or transitory occupation for two special purposes — the heat treatment of stone and the processing of meat obtained by hunting. — Clark and Khanna 1989 : 30

V.N. Misra's article on Stone Age India in *Man and Environment 14* (1989) offered a good synthesis of pre-historic India on the basis of the data available till the 1980s, although one is not sure of the justifiability of the section on 'Soanian Culture', nor can understand the reason for absence of any reference to the relevant work of the Geological Survey of India in the Siwaliks.

Protohistory and Later

The publications of this period were no less diverse in the field of protohistory. The detailed report on the Aligarh Muslim University excavations at Atranjikhera was published in 1983 (Gaur 1983). Without suggesting any discredit to the earlier publications on the archaeology of the Doab, one is entitled to comment that this was the first major report which provided a detailed and ready window on the archaeology of this region. It is in this report that the cultural details of its various phases — Ochre Coloured Ware, Black-and-Red Ware, Painted Grey Ware and Northern Black Polished Ware — were systematically highlighted, item by item. Whatever one may say about Gaur's theories or explanations, his concern for a clear and methodical documentation of his excavated data deserves nothing but praise.

In 1983 T.N. Roy of Banaras Hindu University published *The Ganges Civilization* which was an archaeological study of the NBPW and PGW phases of the archaeological sequence of the valley. Three years later he focussed only on the material remains of the NBPW phase (Roy 1986). This phase also received attention in an unpublished Ph.D. thesis of this period in Delhi University (Kohli 1984). A similar analytical study of the Black-and-Red Ware was published by H.N. Singh (1982) and K.M. Srivastava (1979).

In 1984 Makkhan Lal (1984a) brought out a book based on his Ph.D. thesis at the Deccan College : *Settlement History and Rise of Civilization in the Ganga Yamuna Doab.* The thesis itself was based on his intensive exploration of sites in 'rural Kanpur', an administrative district called *Kanpur Dehat*. One of the avowed aims of this work was to try to apply the different theoretical tenets of 'settlement archaeology' to this area, and this was the first work of its kind in the field of Indian proto-historic archaeology. There can be many disagreements in detail, but the book is historically significant and generated, as we shall see later, a number of studies along this line. A summary of this work appeared in *Man and Environment* (M. Lal 1984b), and soon there appeared an analysis of the notion of a correlation between the appearance of iron tools, forest clearance and the growth of cities in the Ganga plain (M. Lal 1986).

In 1983 chemical analysis of soils for their phosphate and nitrogen contents made their mark in the context of some proto-historic sites, along with a search for the fluorine content of their bones. In the first area of study the lead role was played by B.C. Deotare (Joshi and Deotare 1983, Deotare 1983, Kshirsagar 1983) and in the second area of study the primary contribution was made by Anupama Kshirsagar (Joshi and Kshirsagar 1986). A number of articles on the archaeology of pre-industrial Indian mining were published during this period, notably by R.K. Tiwari and N.K. Kavdia (1984) on the traces, dates and context of old mining activities at the Agucha lead field of Rajasthan and by P.T. Craddock *et al.* (1985) on the early zinc production in India, as evidenced in the Zawar mines, also in Rajasthan. The scope of the archaeology of pre-industrial mining in India was emphasised by Chakrabarti (1978, 1988). The 1980s were also the time when V.D. Gogte (1984) began the X-ray diffraction analysis of Indian proto-historic pottery. A major piece of research undertaken during this period was R.N. Singh's monograph on ancient Indian glass (1989).

One of the most important publications of this period in Indian protohistory was the volume *Frontiers of the Indus Civilization* edited by B.B. Lal and S.P. Gupta (1984). Like all edited volumes this too has its quota of useful but not-too-exciting articles, but it will not be far from truth if we claim that this volume will be remembered primarily for a detailed study of the distribution of Harappan sites in India by J.P. Joshi, Madhu Bala and Jassu Ram (1984). Their statewise lists of Harappan sites cover Haryana, Panjab, Rajasthan and Gujarat, and in each case these lists are district-wise and grouped into the categories of pre-Harappan, mature Harappan and late Harappan. An important feature is the listing of the Ganeshwar culture sites within the general orbit of the pre-Harappan sites. Although it was Rafiq Mughal's explorations in Cholistan which highlighted the highest concentration of the pre/early Harappan, mature Harappan and late Harappan sites in that sector of the Sarasvati system in Pakistan, it was the maps published with the article by Joshi, Bala and Ram which visually demonstrated for the first time the sheer number and true character of the distribution of the Harappan sites of all phases on the Indian side of the border. Also, it is these maps which demonstrate that the major spread of this civilization was in the ancient Sarasvati-Drishadvati system. Further, the innumerable dots representing Late Harappan sites all over Haryana,

Panjab and the upper part of the Doab demonstrate more than anything else that the during this period the Harappans were on a major move towards the east. More or less the same thing is suggested by the map of Late Harappan Gujarat, from where thrusts towards Malwa and Maharashtra were not merely possible but also to be expected. The fact that the Late Harappan maps of the region from Haryana to the Doab suggest concentration of sites in a number of pockets has been explained by the authors as 'area concentrations' which were the 'outcome of a process in which subsistence self-sufficiency was achieved by a closely-knit interdependent sites'. As far as we can see, these concentrations may also suggest concentrations in the areas where there were major water bodies in the declining stage of the Sarasvati-Drishadvati river system. Both on the alignments of this river system and on the phenomenon of its drying up, Yash Pal *et al.* (1984) and V.N. Misra (1984) contributed important papers to this volume. Regarding the distribution of sites in other areas of India, K.N. Momin (1984) and R.N. Mehta (1984) discuss two situations in Gujarat, with Momin writing on the distribution of small village sites in the Kheda district of the Bhal area of Saurashtra and Mehta on a specific category of Gujarati Harappan sites, i.e., the sites which can be interpreted as 'cattle-breeding sites'. Mehta discussed the evidence from Valabhi and Nesadi near Bhavnagar. On the basis of the excavated data K.N. Dikshit (1984) provides an authoritative review of the Late Harappan situation in the Doab. Mainly on the basis of his fieldwork in Gujarat Chitalwala (1984) speculates on the class structure of this civilization; one of the points he makes is that the multi-roomed structures of Rojdi could suggest that the extended family was the basic economic norm.

There were two general volumes in 1985, both dealing with the developments of Indian archaeology since Independence. The volume edited by Deo and Paddayya (1985) contained the proceedings of a seminar held in the Deccan College in 1983 on the occasion of the 76th birthday of Sankalia. The second volume (Dikshit 1985) contained the proceedings of a seminar held in Delhi in 1982.

In 1985 again, B.K. Thapar published on behalf of the UNESCO a review of *Recent Archaeological Discoveries in India* which contained such sentences as the following ones :

> The period following the end of the Indus Civilization in northern India (the second half of the second millennium BC) was one of continuing eastward expansion of the Indo-Aryan culture.

> A remarkable chronological proximity is noticed between the beginning of the Painted

> Grey Ware and the later Vedic Age. There can, therefore, be no reasonable doubt in ascribing this ware to later Aryans.

What was attempted by T.N. Roy in the context of the NBPW phase of the archaeology of the Ganga plain was attempted by C. Margabandhu (1985) for the dynastic phases of the Satavahanas and the Western Kshatrapas in the archaeology of Maharashtra, Gujarat and Madhya Pradesh. Occasionally the focus shifts away from the book's main concern, but detailed documentation has been put forth for architecture, trade, transport and exchange, art and religion, domestic equipment, toilet, dress and ornaments, games and toys, tools, implements and weapons, technology and fauna and flora. Apart from a list of radiocarbon dates from the relevant excavated sites, the book provides a detailed listing of brick measurements and shapes of stone beads.

Area Studies

There emerged a focus throughout the 1980s on the field-based archaeological study of comparatively small areas and sites. Two major works were published in the context of Assam, one dealing with the Brahmaputra valley (R.D. Chowdhury 1985) and the other about the archaeology of central Assam (N.D. Chowdhury 1985). The extent to which the archaeological development of the Kangra valley was a part of the mainstream Indian archaeological development and the extent to which it had a regional focus formed the subject of a study by Chakrabarti and S.J. Hasan (1984). Earlier, the archaeology of Kumaun was studied by K.P. Nautiyal (1969) and the archaeology of the Lucknow region by S.D. Singh and S.B. Singh (1972), with the latter publishing a study of the Panchala region in 1979 (S.B. Singh 1979). The Bhopal region was investigated by R.K. Sharma and Rahman Ali (1980). D. Kumar (1986) published on the archaeology of Vaishali and B. Kumar (1987) on the archaeology of Pataliputra and Nalanda. R.C. Prasad (1987) wrote on the archaeology of Champa and Vikramshila. There were also publications of this type in Hindi (cf. S.D. Trivedi 1984) and perhaps other regional languages as well. The thoroughness and/or dependability of such studies varied from author to author, but on the whole different geographical units were getting their own archaeological syntheses.

By 1985 the trans-Sarayu area of Uttar Pradesh emerged as an important segment of proto-historic research. First, S.N. Chaturvedi (1985) published the results of the surveys and limited excavations conducted by Gorakhpur University in that region, trying to link it with the developments which had taken place in the Belan valley and the adjacent sectors of the Ganga plain. Secondly, the preliminary field-documentation of the site of Narhan which was excavated by Purushottam Singh in 1983-85 was published in the same year (P. Singh and M. Lal 1985). The important thing about this report is that it contained specialist contributions on coins, crops, faunal remains, etc., including a detailed quantitative study of the ceramic industries (Lal and A.K. Singh 1985).

The publication of the Inamgaon reports (Lukacs and Walimbe 1986a, Dhavalikar, Sankalia and Ansari 1988) along with the publication of the Daimabad report (Sali 1986) were major events in the study of the Deccanese protohistory. Both these reports discuss in detail the house-planning through the different occupational levels with clear plans, and it is also possible to relate antiquities to the individual house units. One may not always agree with the interpretations offered but these reports will always figure as the base on which socio-cultural models of the proto-historic Deccan can be reconstructed. In one sense, the long trend initiated by Sankalia and others in reporting their excavation results at Navdatoli, Nevasa and other places attains a special height in the Inamgaon and Daimabad reports. Dhavalikar's book *The First Farmers of the Deccan* (1988) was an important publication in the sense that in this slim volume he emphatically demonstrated the relevance of this first farming phase to the understanding of modern Maharashtra. The report on the skeletal remains of Inamgaon by J.R. Lukacs and S.R. Walimbe (1986a) well illustrates the new trend of ancient skeletal studies in India. Articles like those by P.C. Dutta (1984), K.A.R. Kennedy (1984) and Lukacs and Walimbe (1984, 1986b) well reflect concern with the issues of population continuity, palaeopathology, palaeodemography, etc. When viewed against the earlier frameworks of skeletal studies with their emphasis on racial identifications, these developments marked a very important trend. In the context of south India U.R. Moorti's *Megalithic Culture of South India — Socio-economic Perspectives* (1994) is a work based on a thorough study of the relevant sources, and puts the south Indian megalithic studies on a level beyond typology and other technical details.

There were two major publications on 'settlement archaeology' in 1988 (Hooja 1988, Erdosy 1988). Erdosy's survey of the sites of the historical period (Erdosy1985) in the Allahabad area took place a little downstream from Makkhan Lal's Kanpur and followed more or less the same approach, although with some extra emphasis on the archaeologically unverifiable and mostly undated literary data. Rima Hooja's focus was on the proto-historic settlements of the Ahar culture in south-east Rajasthan and partly modelled on V.N. Misra's work on the pre- and proto-historic aspects of the Berach basin of the same area. But she made conscious formulations regarding the settlement aspects of the period and tried to obtain insight into them by studying the life of the 'tribal group' of Bhils who inhabit her field-area. Hooja's work provides a definitive base of understanding the results of archaeological excavations in the Mewar sector of Rajasthan.

The history of various discoveries and the development of ideas behind them till 1947 received a systematic treatment on the basis of the published sources in 1988 (Chakrabarti 1988a) which was also the year when some of the theoretical themes or issues of Indian archaeology were discussed threadbare by the same author (Chakrabarti 1988b). The chapters into which the volume was divided were 'changing concerns', 'idea of diffusion as an explanatory model', 'problem of correlation between archaeology and literature', 'geographical approaches', 'prehistory, transition to food-production and urbanisation', 'agriculture', 'metallurgy' and 'trade'. In a sense these chapters aimed to provide fixed moorings in a rather fluid and diverse academic situation in which people have not always been aware of the threads of research and ideas behind them.

Excavations

The following chart outlines the list of excavated sites in *IAR 1983-84* to *IAR 1989-90:*

Chart 2.2: Excavated sites in *IAR 1983-84* to *IAR 1989-90*

Site	*Years*	*Nature*	*State*	*Status*	*Inst.*	*Person*
Gandlur	83-84	neolithic>	Andhra	Unpub.	Nagarjuna Uni	B.R. Subrahmanyam
Vaddamanu	83-85	early hist.>	Andhra	?	Birla Inst.Hyderabad	T.V.G. Sastri
Ramapuram	83-84	chalco>	Andhra	Unpub.	ASI	B. Narasimhaiah
Hazurnagar	83-84	megalithic	Andhra	Unpub.	State Dept	?
Taradih	83-89	neo>	Bihar	Unpub.	State Dept	A.K. Prasad
Paisra	83-87	pre-historic	Bihar	Pub.	BHU	P.C. Pant, V. Jayasawal
Aphsad	83-84	historical	Bihar	Unpub.	State Dept	P.C. Prasad
Manjhi	83-85	early hist.>	U.P.	Unpub.	BHU	T.N. Roy
Velha Goa	83-84	late mediaev.	Goa	Unpub.	ASI	R.G. Pandey
Nageswar	83-84	Harappan	Gujarat	Pub.	MSU Baroda	K.T. M. Hegde
Goraj	83-86	temple	Gujarat	Pub.	ASI	B.M. Pande R.D. Singh
Banawali	83-84,86-88	Harappan	Haryana	Pub.	ASI	R.S. Bisht
Balu	83-87	Harappan	Haryana	Unpub.	Kuruk. Uni	U.V. Singh, S.Bhan
Hampi	83-90	late mediaev.	Karnataka	Unpub.	ASI/State	various
Banahalli	83-87	neo>	Karnataka	Unpub.	ASI	L.K. Srinvasan B. Narasimhaiah
Tenmalai	83-86	mesolithic	Kerala	?	D.Coll	P. Rajan

Site	*Years*	*Nature*	*State*	*Status*	*Inst.*	*Person*
Gilaulikhera	83-84	chalco >	M.P.	Unpub.	State Dept	various
Pipliya Lorca	83-84	chalco>	M.P.	Unpub.	State Dept	various
Udayapur	83-84	temple	M.P.	Unpub.	ASI	?
Bhagimohari	83-84	megalithic	Maha.	Pub.	Nagpur Uni/State	S.B. Deo-A.P. Jamkhedkar
Kandhar	83-84	temple	Maharashtra	Unpub.	D.Coll/State	Dhavalikar Jamkhedkar
Maragoda	83-84	early hist.>	Orissa	Unpub.	State Dept	N.K. Sahu
Sunet	83-84	Hpn >	Panjab	Unpub.	State Dept	G.B. Sharma
Ganeshwar	83-84,87-89	Gan.culture	Rajasthan	Unpub.	State Dept	Kumar Chakravarty
Didwana	83-84	pre-historic	Rajasthan	Unpub.	D.Coll	V.N. Misra
Zawar	83-84	mining site	Rajasthan	Unpub.	MSU Baroda	K.T.M. Hegde
Kambarmedu	83-84	meg?Hist.?	T. Nadu	Unpub.	ASI	P.N. Babu
Palayarai	83-84	historical	T. Nadu	Unpub.	State Dept	D. Thulasiraman
Gangaikonda-	83-84	Chola palace	T. Nadu	Unpub.	State Dept	S. Selvaraj
Kannanur	83-84	historical	T. Nadu	Unpub.	State Dept	P. Arasan
Fatehp.Sikri	83-89	late mediaev.	U.P.	Unpub.	AMU/ASI	R.C. Gaur
Sringaverap-	83-85	chalco>	U.P.	Pub.	ASI/IIAS	B.B. Lal
Khairadih	83-86	chalco>	U.P.	Unpub.	BHU	K.K. Sinha/B.P. Singh
Hulaskhera	83-84/85-87	early hist.>	U.P.	?	State Dept	various
Damdama	83-84/85-87	mesolithic	U.P.	Unpub.	Allh Uni	various
Dihar	83-85	chalco>	W. Bengal	Unpub.	Cal. Uni	A.C. Pal
Ballal Dhipi	83-89	historical	W. Bengal	Unpub.	ASI	various
Ghantasala	84-85	early hist.>	Andhra	Unpub.	ASI	H.N. Singh
Peddavegi	84-87	historical	Andhra	Unpub.	ASI	Bopardikar- I.K. Sarma
Devasthan	84-85	historical	Assam	Unpub.	State Dept	?
Na-nath	84-85	historical	Assam	Unpub.	State Dept	?
Maner	84-90	neo>	Bihar	Unpub.	Patna Uni	B. Narayan, A.K. Singh
Ratanpura	84-85	late Hpn >	Gujarat	Unpub.	MSU Baroda	K.T.M. Hegde
Rojdi	83-86	late Hpn >	Gujarat	Pub.	State/Penn U	Raval-Possehl
Hoyasaleswara	84-85	temple	Karnataka	Unpub.	ASI	B. Narasimhaiah
Atud Khas	84-85	chaco>	M.P.	Unpub.	State Dept	C. Krishna
Tuljap. Garhi	84-85	chalco	Maha.	Unpub.	ASI	B.P. Bopardikar
Daulatabad	84-89	late mediaev.	Maha.	Unpub.	various	various
Kaothe	84-85	chalco	Maha.	Pub.	D.Coll	Dhavalikar
Raipur	84-85	megalithic	M.P.	?	D.Coll	S.B. Deo

Site	*Years*	*Nature*	*State*	*Status*	*Inst.*	*Person*
Pune	84-85	pre-historic	Maha.	?	D.Coll	H.D. Sankalia
Arni	84-85	early hist.>	Maha.	Unpub.	Nagpur Uni	A.M. Sastri
Khalkapatna	84-85	12th-14th c.	Orissa	Unpub.	ASI	J.S. Nigam
Sanghol	84-90	historical	Panjab	Unpub.	State/ASI	G.B. Sharma-C. Margabandhu
Tiruvakkarai	84-85	megalithic	T. Nadu	Unpub.	Madras Uni	K.V. Raman
Auroville	84-86	megalithic	T. Nadu	Unpub.	ASI	P.N. Babu
Shyamsundar	84-85	historical	Tripura	Unpub.	ASI	J.S. Nigam
Thakurani	84-85	historical	Tripura	Unpub.	ASI	J.S. Nigam
Daulatpur	84-85	chalco	U.P.	Unpub.	Aligarh M. U	R.C. Gaur
Padrauna	84-85	historical	U.P.	Unpub.	ASI	Arun Kumar
Narhan	83-87	chalco>	U.P.	Unpub.	BHU	P. Singh
P.Rajar Dhibi	84-85	chalco>	W. Bengal	Unpub.	State Dept	S.C. Mukherji
Adurru	85-86	historical	Andhra	Unpub.	ASI	H.N. Singh
Chandigarh	85-86	Harappan	Chandigarh	Unpub.	ASI	D.P. Rai
Nagwada	85-90	Harappan	Gujarat	?	MSU Baroda	K.T.M. Hegde
Kunal	85-86	pre-Hpn	Haryana	Unpub.	State Dept	J.P. Khatri, M. Acharya
Yediapur	85-86	pre-historic	Karnataka	?	D.Coll	K. Paddayya
Nagaresvara	85-87	temple	Karnataka	Unpub.	ASI	Narasimhaiah
Khajuraho	85-87/88-89	temple	M.P.	Unpub.	ASI	various
Tharsa	85-86	chalco	Maharashtr	Unpub.	Nagpur Uni	A.M. Sastri
Lalitagiri	85-90	historical	Orissa	Unpub.	ASI	G.C. Chauley
Udaigiri	85-89	historical	Orissa	Unpub.	ASI	various
Darasuram	85-87	temple	T. Nadu	Unpub.	ASI	Babu-Poonacha
Khajuri	85-86	chalco>	U.P.	Unpub.	Allh Uni	B.B. Misra
Darau	85-86	PGW>	U.P.	Unpub.	Aligarh M.U.	R.C. Gaur
Jakhera	85-87	chalco >	U.P.	Unpub.	Aligarh. M.U.	M.D.N. Sahi
Mithakhari V	86-87	shell midden	S. Andaman	Unpub.	ASI	B.P. Bopardikar
Rajahmundry	86-87	late mediaev.	Andhra	Unpub.	State Dept	?
Nelakondapalli	86-87	historical	Andhra	Unpub.	State Dept	?
Alampur	86-87	historical	Andhra	Unpub.	ASI	H.N. Singh
Senuwar	86-87	neo>	Bihar	Unpub.	BHU	B.P. Singh
Khokhrakot	86-87	historical	Haryana	Unpub.	MDU, Rohtak	Silak Ram
Sannati	86-89	historical	Karnataka	ASI/Soc. SAS	ASI/Soc.SAS	J. Howell
Sooron	86-87	early hist.>	MP	Unpub.	Jiwaji Uni	R.A. Sharma R.P. Pandey

Site	*Years*	*Nature*	*State*	*Status*	*Inst.*	*Person*
Hirap.Khadan	86-87	pre-historic	M.P.	Unpub.	ASI	B.P. Bopardikar
Maihar-I	86-88	pre-historic	M.P.	Unpub.	Allh Uni	Pandey-Pal
Nadner	86-87	meso>	M.P.	Unpub.	Prach.Nktn	C.B. Trivedi
Walki	86-87	chalco	Maha.	Pub.	D.Coll	Dhavalikar-Shinde
Sravasti	86-89	early hist.>	U.P.	Pub.	ASI/Kansai U	various
Hatikra	86-87	chalco>	W. Bengal	Unpub.	Visvabharati	Ghosh-Nag
Kotasur	86-88	early hist.>	W. Bengal	Unpub.	Visvabharati	Ghosh-Nag
Mangalkot	86-90	chalco>	W. Bengal	Unpub.	Cal. Uni	A.Ray
Mallipadu	87-88	megalithic	Andhra	Unpub.	State Dept	?
Takkelapadu	87-88	historical	Andhra	Unpub.	State Dept	?
Edithanur	87-88	rockshelter	Andhra	Unpub.	State Dept	?
Thothlakonda	87-90	early hist.>	Andhra	Pub.	State Dept	?
Ambari	87-90	historical	Assam	Unpub.	Gau.Uni Anth	T.C. Sharma
Rajmahal	87-89	chalco>	Bihar	Unpub.	State Dept	R.S. Singh
Kushi	87-88	early hist.>	Bihar	Unpub.	ASI	B.K. Saran
Shikarpur	87-90	Harappan	Gujarat	Unpub.	State Dept	M.H. Raval
Umta	87-88	late mediaev.	Gujarat	Unpub.	State Dept	?
Kuntasi	87-90	Harappan	Gujarat	Pub.	D.Coll	Dhavalikar Shinde
Thanesvar	87-89	early hist.>	Haryana	Unpub.	ASI	B.M. Pande
Balikeshwara	87-88	temple	M.P.	Unpub.	ASI	A. Nath
Chandel	87-88	temple	M.P.	Unpub.	ASI	A. Nath
S'ti-kunda	87-88	temple	M.P.	Unpub.	ASI	A. Nath
Eran	87-88	chalco>	M.P.	Unpub.	Sagar Uni	V.D. Jha
Nadner	87-88	early hist.>	M.P.	Unpub.	Prach.Nktn	C.B. Trivedi
Mulchera	87-88	historical	Maha.	Unpub.	State Dept	Jamkhedkar Kawadkar
Ter	87-89	historical	Maha.	Unpub.	State Dept	Jamkhedkar Kawadkar
Kudikadu	87-89	historical	T. Nadu	Unpub.	Madras Uni	K.V. Raman
Jainal-Naula	87-88	megalithic	U.P.	Unpub.	Garhwal Uni	K.P. Nautiyal
N'kondapalli	88-89	historical	Andhra	Unpub.	State Dept	?
Elchuru	88-89	neo>	Andhra	Unpub.	Telegu Uni	K.T. Reddy
Naksaparvat	88-89	13th-16th c.	Arunachal	Unpub.	State Dept	D.K. Bora
Chechk'tbpur	88-89	neo>	Bihar	Unpub.	ASI	B.K. Sharan
Vaishali	88-89	early hist.>	Bihar	Unpub.	ASI	B.K. Sharan
Old Goa	88-90	late mediaev.	Goa	Unpub.	ASI	?
Siyot	88-89	historical	Gujarat	Unpub.	State Dept	?

Site	*Years*	*Nature*	*State*	*Status*	*Inst.*	*Person*
Umta	88-89	temple	Gujarat	Unpub.	State Dept	?
Watgal	88-89	neo>	Karnataka	Unpub.	State/Case Wn Res. Uni	J. Shaffer
Gudnapur	88-90	historical	Karnataka	Unpub.	ASI	K.P. Poonacha
Kotra	88-89	chalco>	M.P.	Unpub.	Prach.Nktn	C.B. Trivedi
Balwara	88-89	pre-historic	M.P.	Unpub.	ASI	S.B. Ota
Sodanga	88-89	historical	M.P.	Unpub.	Vikram Uni	Rahman Ali
Adam	88-90	early hist.>	Maharashtra	Unpub.	ASI	A. Nath
Nagiari	88-89	Harappan	Panjab	Unpub.	State Dept	?
Manmalai	88-89	?	T. Nadu	Unpub.	State Dept	?
Rataura	88-89	historical	U.P.	Unpub.	Garhwal Uni	K.P. Nautiyal
Bandarkhet	88-89	?	U.P.	Unpub.	Garhwal Uni	B.M. Khanduri
Purola	88-89	PGW>	U.P.	Unpub.	Garhwal Uni	?
Srisailam	89-90	historical	Andhra	Unpub.	Telegu Uni	various
Kolhua	89-90	early hist.>	Bihar	Unpub.	ASI	L.C. Singh
Oriyo Timbo	89-90	Harappan	Gujarat	Pub.	State Dept	Chitalwala Rissman
Dholavira	89-90	Harappan	Gujarat	ASI	unpublished	R.S. Bisht
G'mti-ni-khan	89-90	mesolithic	Gujarat	Unpub.	State Dept	Makwana Suman Pandey
Samnapur	89-90	pre-historic	M.P.	Unpub.	D.Coll	V.N. Misra
Banotiwadi	89-90	historical	Maha.	Unpub.	ASI	?
Vetalwadi	89-90	historical	Maha.	Unpub.	ASI	?
Raipur	89-90	megalithic	Maha.	Pub.	D.Coll	Deglurkar-Lad
Barabati Fort	89-90	mediaeval	Orissa	Unpub.	ASI	B.K. Sinha
Manamunda	89-90	historical	Orissa	Unpub.	Samb.Uni	various
Arikamedu	89-90	historical	T. Nadu	Pub.	Madras Uni	B. Vegley
Ehrich	89-90	chalco>	U.P.	Unpub.	ASI	H.N. Singh
Manigara	89-90	pre-historic	U.P.	Unpub.	Allh Uni	B.B. Misra

The state of publications of the excavation reports does not change at all. The new Harappan sites taken up for excavations include Kuntasi, Nagwada, Dholavira and Shikarpur. Sanghol in Panjab and Banawali in Haryana have an earlier history of excavations. A few pre-historic sites, notably Paisra, get excavated during this period. Early historical and later historical sites such as Adam, Srisailam, Peddaveggi, Ehrich, etc., have an importance of their own both in their regional and pan-Indian contexts. A few sites of different characters — Purola, Jainal-Naula and others — also get excavated in the U.P. hills (modern Uttaranchal). In Orissa the two major monasteries of Lalitagiri and Udaigiri are taken up for excavations during this period which also seems to witness the expansion of excavations at the early historic site of Manamuda near Sambalpur. In Bihar three neolithic sites emerge into prominence — Senuar, Maner and Chechar Kutubpur.

Out of about 145 sites listed in the above chart, the number of sites on which full reports are available is roughly 14.

THE PERIOD FROM 1990 to 2000

Publications

Concern with Theory ?

If Malik (1968) wanted the Indian archaeologists to turn to the Euro-American anthropological literature—mostly of the early 1960s and thus free of the impact of 'New Archaeology' — for the explanatory framework of their data, Paddayya urged us to move in the same general direction for the same reason in 1990, having made a preliminary announcement in 1985 (Paddayya 1985). Although by the mid-1980s, theoretical developments in world archaeology had begun to move away from the rigidities of 'New Archaeology', Paddayya does not show much concern for these shifts and takes an inflexible New Archaeological stand instead. One is, in fact, not surprised that 'in 1986 Deccan College, Poona, conducted a month-long course of lectures (with Binford as one of the resource persons) on the New Archaeology for college and university teachers' (Paddayya 1995 : 135-136). In 1988 the Indian Council of Historical Research organised a conference on New Archaeology in Delhi, with participation from Peter Ucko and Ian Hodder among others. These two British archaeologists have played a stellar role in dismantling the edifice of New Archaeology's anti-historicism and lack of concern, if not downright contempt, for the different national traditions of archaeology. The point is that the Indian Council of Historical Research could not really be concerned with the pristine Binfordian New Archaeology when they organised a conference on this topic in 1988. If one remembers correctly, that was the period when Irfan Habib, a historian of Mogul economic history, was the chairman of the Council and instrumental in recruiting Makkhan Lal, an archaeologist, for his university history department of Aligarh Muslim University. It is not difficult to guess that the idea of holding a conference on New Archaeology and the applicability of its tenets to Indian archaeology emanated from Makkhan Lal. The proceedings of this conference were not published, and thus are of no historical significance. One does not know why Paddayya (1995: 136) even mentions this conference in his historical review of 'theoretical perspectives in Indian archaeology'.

Paddayya's book *The New Archaeology and Aftermath, a View from Outside the Anglo-American World* (1990) aptly summarises his views on New Archaeology, but here we are not concerned with what he thinks about New Archaeology but how he tries to relate this to the Indian context. Right in the beginning of his 'chapter 3' where he discusses the problem, one has to disagree with his view that Sankalia made 'single-handed efforts to introduce the New Archaeology into the country' (p. 45). Sankalia's attempts to weave archaeological facts about India together 'to arrive at some patterns' did not lead him to Binford's New Archaeology but to cultural historical premises of the colonial Indological model. Sankalia was further concerned with the reconstruction of ancient lifeways; this was what led him to undertake the Inamgaon excavations with focus on the house-units and settlement patterns. Paddayya's argument that it was undertaken 'to understand the Chalcolithic phase of Western India from a processual point of view' is difficult to accept. Environmental determinism of the authors of the Inamgaon report, their propensity to find 'chiefdom' among the house remains and their argument that the Deccan reverted back to impoverished semi-nomadism in the Late Jorwe do not reflect the New Archaeology style. I, for one, would find a far stronger dose of New Archaeology in Shina Panja's *Mobility Strategies, Site Structure and Settlement Organization : a Case Study of Chalcolithic Sites in the Middle Bhima Valley with Special Reference to Inamgaon* (1995) than in the Inamgaon report. She was forthright in her comment : 'the work on the Chalcolithic phase at Inamgaon was more in the nature of a reconstruction of past life based on environmental determinism rather than a holistic understanding of a system characteristic of a processual approach'. (Panja 1995 : 24) Of all the Indian archaeological works that I know, this is the only work which begins by aiming to test a specific hypothesis — in this case, how mobility strategies can affect site structures and settlement organisation — and pursues that hypothesis relentlessly, although in a very cut-and-dried, cold, unhistorical fashion, till the end.

There is perhaps not much point in taking up issues with Paddayya on various points he raises about Indian archaeology in his monograph or the article published in 1992, but I am sure that, if he had known more about ancient Indian historical tradition he would have been reluctant to find merit in what he calls 'indigenous traditions for studying the past'. The question is not whether there were certain stereotyped ahistorical references to the past in the vast and amorphous body of Indian texts but whether such references can build a base for forming an Indian archaeological research tradition. The answer is a very clear 'no'. Similarly, was Indian epistemological tradition meant to incorporate a modern knowledge tradition such as archaeology ?

Further, Paddayya (1995) takes a negative approach to a critical study of the West's Orientalist enterprise : 'the total debunking of Europe's contribution to the understanding of India's past would amount to throwing baby with the bathwater'. (Paddayya 1995: 111) What is important for us is to realise that the Indological construct of ancient India was something which was determined by the West's need to exercise control over India. It was very much a necessary corollary of the old imperial power structure. The author whom he appreciately cites in this context is Ronald Inden (1990) who does not even bother to raise this issue and the issue of unabashed racism which was — and still is — an essential ingredient of the Indological framework in the West. Inden's critique of the various trends of Western writing on India is nothing more than an internal critique — textual criticism, if one likes — of those writings.

Prehistory

For an idea of the directions of research in Indian prehistory in the 1990s the best source is the range of articles published in *Man and Environment* of this period. The following features stand out. First, the emphasis on the settlement-subsistence system which began in the 1980s continues to be an important feature. Zarine Cooper (1997) has two aims regarding the microlithic assemblages of the Chitrakut Falls area of Bastar, Madhya Pradesh: their contents and internal structure, and the relationship of these contents and internal structures to the environmental setting of the area and the ethnographic documentation of the life of the modern Kuruks in the same area. The Chitrakut Falls lies along the Indravati river, a tributary of the Godavari. The study area covers about 108 sq km where the author's 49 shallow, lithic scatters measure in size from *c.* 20000 sq km to *c.* 25 sq km and located within 1 km of a perennial water source, either of the Indravati or one of the associated rivulets. Some sites show a number of narrowly spaced clusters. Relaivelyl large and widely spaced sites occur along the main river whereas the smaller and less widely spaced sites are found mostly along the small tributaries. According to Cooper's interpretation, the sites along the minor streams may reflect population dispersal during the monsoon when the sheer volume of water in the main channel could have made the task of procuring food along that more difficult. The most important ingredient of the past subsistence system is said to be fish, which is also true of the life of the modern Kuruks. The modern Kuruk life has been described in some detail with reference to fishing, hunting for small game and collection of edible wild plants. Cooper's analysis of the microlithic industry is detailed, put behind a lot of statistical cherts and graphs, and argues that the proximity of a particular type of raw material did not determine the frequency of that material at a particular site. Cooper's Indravati study was based on her Ph.D. thesis at the Deccan College in 1983. Her later work was on the shell middens of the Andaman islands. About 16 radiocarbon dates from different midden and cave sites did not find them more than 2200 years old. Her excavation of the Cauldari mound in the South Andamans showed the predominance of shellfish among the excavated fauna found in association with artefacts made of shell and stone (Cooper 1990). For ethnographic comparisons she studied Onge encampments at South Bay in the Little Andamans (Cooper 1994).

A similar kind of work was undertaken in the Kuntala region of Adilabad in Andhra (N. Rao 1994).

> The model developed for subsistence and settlement on the basis of contemporary ethnographic and ecological evidence in semi-arid Kuntala suggests that human groups would move around the perennial water source of the region in relation to wet/dry seasonal variations. It is suggested that that in the dry season, groups would aggregate nearer the source of perennial water. A further inducement to establish camps would be that fauna would also gather there. Groups would be free to move away from the perennial water source in the wert season as water and therefore fauna would disperse throughout the forest. However, it would be advantageous to retain a camp at the perennial water source in order to exploit the fish abundantly available within it. Thus the model suggests a settlement pattern of long-term bases (associated with settlement debris) near the perennial water source, with temporary camps associated lesswith settlement debris, but more with subsistence activity debris, randomly distributed both near it and farther away within the forest. — N. Rao 1994 : 149

Ajay Pratap's work (2000) was in the Rajmahal hills of eastern India where the focus of his ethnoarchaeological and ethnohistorical work was the sector inhabited by the Mal Paharias. The Mal Paharias still practise shifting cultivation and Pratap tried to determine its archaeological correlates.

On the whole the importance of the settlement-subsistence approach in Indian prehistoric studies is a continuing phenomenon. V.N. Misra's study of the Van Vagris of the Rajasthan desert (Misra 1990) and Malti Nagar's and V.N. Misra's joint study of the hunter-gatherers in the nineteenth-century agricultural setting of the Ganga plains (Nagar and Misra 1989) are among other major examples of this trend.

Secondly, there is a good deal of emphasis on understanding the character of the artefact assemblages in terms of quantitative attributes, often leading to insights into pre-historic behaviour. For instance, M.L. Inizan and M. Lechevallier (1995) have studied the microlithic assemblage from Baghor in Rajasthan and found evidence of pressure debitage technique and heat treatment of chalcedony as raw material. They also find here 'a trend towards standardisation that only a perfectly well-mastered debitage technique could allow'. In the microlithic sites of the Tarafeni valley in the western part of W. Bengal Bishnupriya Basak does not find the evidence of the chief raw materials used at the sites or scatters and in their vicinity. This, and a detailed examination of the industry make her argue that there was no 'on-place reduction of nodules' and that 'partially decorticated cores were imported into the region along with some trimmed nodules which were also used for blade reduction'. She also discerns patterns of variability among sites, which may reflect diverse patterns of use. Asok Datta (1991) selects two upper palaeolithic and three microlithic occurrences of artefact clusters in the Jhargram area of W. Bengal and finds that simple blades and backed blades constitute 54.83 per cent of the sampled material of the upper palaeolithic whereas lunates, simple blades and marginally retouched blades become the dominant (68.58 per cent) micolithic features. The scatter diagrams of the length and breadth frequencies suggest that there is a close relationship between the upper palaeolithic and microlithic assemblages. This conclusion is also supportyed by his study of the maximum, minimum and mean values of length, breadth and thickness of both the assemblages. Difference between them lay principally in the raw materials used : green quartzite for the upper palaeolithic and chert quartz for the microlithic. Datta (2000) further develops this approach and analyses the components of the upper palaeolithic industry of a site in Orissa. P.P. Joglekar and M.S. Vaishampayan (1991) try to lay down 'a systematic protocol of statistical analysis' for stone tools. In a detailed study of the lithic blade assemblage of the Karnataka neolithic site of Watgal Ann S. DuFresne *et al.* (1998) reach certain major conclusions about both the nature of its blade technology and the changed character of the site later in the sequence. After Occupation I which is not related to Occupation II and its subdivisions and later Occupations of the site, the blade production showed increasing use of one raw material — a particular variety of chert (called Ch1 chert) which was not available around the site and had thus to be imported or procured from an off-site occurrence. The blade production in this particular type of chert increases between Occupations IIA and IIB and then becomes stable at 45 per cent of all chipped stones in Occupations IIB, III and IV. Their comment is that 'this intensified use of Ch1 Chert in the production of everyday tools may reflect a technologically-and/or culturally based preference as well as intensified and regular access to an off-site commodity'. There are a few other behavioural implications of this study. The trend towards standardisation of blade length and width in Occupations III and IV may reflect, according to them, the incorporation of the site in a wider economic system, a fact which is also suggested by other finds. In the case of the Kortallayar basin near Chennai. Shanti Pappu (2001) puts emphasis on the complete lithic reduction sequence to study the associated hominid behaviour patterns. Regarding the raw materials her conclusion is that no site is more than 4 km away from their source. Tools made on cobbles and pebbles are more common on the hill slope sites where such materials are near at hand. Modified cobbles/trimmed nodules, which are found at all sites, predominate at sites away from the sources of raw materials. Non-cortical flakes constitute the dominant debitage at most of the sites. Among the finished tools, scrapers and core-scrapers dominate. Her general conclusions provide an insight into the general system :

> . . . In addition to resource structure, the repeated reoccupation of sites through time (from the Acheulian onwards), with the highest tool densities in sites located close to the river, could be tied to anticipation of re-usable raw materials, in particular in those areas where they are scarce. One possible strategy emerging is the seasonal movement of hominids between the river and the hills based on the availability of water and associated game.
>
> — S. Pappu 2001 : 115

Thirdly, there is an increasing emphasis on the geomorphological and related contexts of the pre-historic sites. The debate about the date and context of the volcanic ash deposit at Bori in the Deccan and a few other places including the Son valley is perhaps the most important case in point. The claim of occurrence of lower palaeolithic tools in the lower pleistocene and possibly still earlier contexts of Jammu and Himachal Pradesh Siwaliks is another such case. Similarly, attention may be drawn to the study of the Acheulian quarry at Islampur with reference to its tool-making, tool morphology and behaviours by Petraglia, La Porta and Paddayya (1999) and Paddayya, Jhaldiyal and Petraglia (1999-2000). Islampur has gained further significance because of its ESR dates around 1.5 mya (personal information from Petraglia).

D.P. Agrawal's *Man and Environment in India through Ages* (1992) perhaps provides a convenient focus of palaeoclimatic studies along this line. However, its lopsidedness will also be clear from its exclusive concern with the climatic sequence of Kashmir from about '4 million years ago' onwards. Its multifaceted palaeoclimatic reconstruction, warmly laudable in itself, cannnot hide the fact that its archaeological component is virtually absent. Whatever archaeology is incorporated in this volume occurs in its penultimate chapter and that too cursorily and within a parameter of environmental determinism. The scope of the 'Rajaguru volume' — *Quaternary Environments and Geoarchaeology of India* (Wadia, Korisettar and Kale eds. 1995) — is much wider and it has acquired the status of an important sourcebook in this field. Of all the articles in this volume, the ones by M.A.J. Williams and M.F. Clarke (1995) and by Subrata Chakrabarti (1995) possess clear archaeological correlates. Most of the other articles are primarily exercises in climatic reconstruction of various phases in various areas. The impact of all these hypotheses on our understanding of our known archaeological profiles remains to a great extent unclear to the non-scientists. For instance, the radiometric dating of Late Quaternary levels of the Saurashtra coast (Jual *et al.* 1995) is no doubt an extremely worthwhile piece of research but can we relate this to what is known about the archaeological profile and distribution of sites in the Saurashtra coast? Some idea of the impact of marine transgressions or regressions on the pre-historic and other sites in Gujarat may be obtained from A.R. Marathe's survey (1995) in the same volume, but in many cases climatic research has remained purely on the level of climatic research. Even when the emphasis is not so much on climate as on geomorphology, the result is not in all cases better. The article on the Quaternary formations of Gujarat (Chamyal and Merh 1995) does not even bother to discuss how the definition of these formations will clarify the understanding of the pre-historic sites of the region. Many of these scholars are established professionals in the wide spectrum of the earth sciences, and *prima facie*, archaeology is not their concern. On the other hand, where archaeologists/historians have begun to claim expertise in the earth sciences, the result perhaps is not quite trustworthy. For instance, Basak (1997) in her study of the microlithic sites of the Tarafeni valley of W. Bengal claims that she adopted 'a multidisciplinary approach involving geology and palaeontology'. That an MA in History from Delhi University, could become enough of a geologist and palaeontologist in the course of her Ph.D. work in the Deccan College to adopt a geological and palaeontological approach in the field is certainly an interesting claim and perhaps reflective of the general standard of the geoarchaeological work pursued by the archaeologists of the Deccan College. The academic credentials of these self-styled geoarchaeologists will not bear close scrutiny. What even the best of them generally possess is a 'Pass' degree in science and an MA degree in Ancient Indian History, Culture and Archaeology. One can certainly accept the basic field-observations regarding archaeological stratigraphy from such non-scientists, but there is no reason why their 'explanations' should be accepted too.

On the other hand, publishing pure geological articles without any relationship to 'man' in *Man and Environment* is perhaps not such a good idea.

A development which is certainly disquieting is the glibness with which the geoarchaeologists are trying to take into consideration the unresearched and presumably unfounded observations of historians and archaeologists to explain their data. A good case in point is the article by B.C. Deotare *et al.* (1999) on the environment of a historical site of about AD 500 in western Rajasthan. The basic cultural issue here is not the geological, chemical and radiocarbon studies the authors have made but the long time-gap between the floods, which allowed a settlement to come up in the midst of a wide and shallow water channel. Along with another studied case of a long time-gap between floods in the Narmada valley in central India, which is a long way to the south from western Rajasthan, the west Rajasthan phenomenon is taken as an indication of 'environmental degradation around 1500-1000 bp, possibly coeval with the European Dark Age'. Behind such a remarkably strong desire to seek 'environmental degradation' both in Europe and India in the same period lies a historical/archaeological premise cited in the beginning of this paper. The reference here is principally to a theory of Dhavalikar who is said to have assessed the available historical, archaeological and literary evidence (including travellers' accounts) to argue in favour of an urban decline in India between the fourth and tenth centuries AD. Those who are familiar with the concerned primary data in some depth will immediately see through the remarkable superficiality of this theory. Among other things, there is absolutely no lack of sites of this period throughout the length and breadth of the subcontinent. In fact, it is the sites and remains of this phase which are the most visible aspects of the archaeological landscape in northern India. The point is that citing ill-founded archaeological theories to explain local geoarchaeological findings is not in the best interest of archaeological science. Certain caution has to be exercised by Indian geoarchaeologists in this direction.

This is in no way to denigrate the increasing trend of researching the geomorphological and environmental perspectives of Indian archaeological sites. All that we are saying is that their implications on the understanding of the archaeological cultures or sites concerned should be clearly focussed and that the people doing such studies should not embroil themselves in unfounded archaeological and historical premises. Such studies can also flourish in India without any underlying current of environmental determinism.

It is also apparent that the interpretation of different pre-historic sections has come a long way from the days when similar beds and similar tools were supposed to mean the same segment of time. One of the articles where this is amply highlighted is the one by Sheila Misra and S.N. Rajaguru (1993) on the Bheraghat section of the Narmada near the marble rocks at Jabalpur. Their conclusions are significant even to a non-specialist.

> . . . the lithounits within the Narmada alluvium represent episodes of fluvial activity as do the breaks between them. Given this, correlations of sections would be unjustified. Similar lithounits may belong to quite different time periods. All chronological information, including relative dating criteria such as typology, fluorine/phosphate ratios, weathering of pebbles, diagenesis of the sediments, palaeontology as well as stratigraphic relationships and absolute dates must be taken into consideration in working out the Quaternary stratigraphy of the Narmada. These criteria are usually sufficient to separate Holocene and latest Pleistocene (12-40000 years) units from the earlier Pleistocene deposits. However, pre-latest Pleistocene units are difficult to separate or correlate. . . .
>
> — Sheila Misra and Rajaguru 1993 : 10-11

Considering that the litho units along the Narmada form one of the crucial frames of the study of Indian prehistory, observations such as these make us aware of the vulnerability of the premises which have been made earlier, and at the same time they also underline the emergence of a more critical and truly multi-faceted approach to the understanding of the geomorphological contexts and stratigraphy of Indian pre-historic sites. That geomorphic 'events' can also be related to the distribution of a chain of sites belonging to a wide chronological range has also been suggested by Sheila Misra *et al.* (1999) in the context of the sites along the Narmada in the Nimar region of Madhya Pradesh. It may be proper to point out that they infer a 'reduction in settlements after the early historic period' simply on the basis of the fact that at both Navdatoli and Khaparkheda there was no trace of occupation after this period. There can be various explanations of the so-called 'desertions' of a site : erosion of the top deposits, a new settlement in the adjacent area, a new historical factor which does not favour the continuation of the old settlement at the same spot, and so on. Besides, when people focus on the absence of occupation of a particular phase at a given site, they should also try to assess the evidence from the entire region in its totality. For instance, Dhavalikar's much-trumpeted hypothesis of the onset of aridity in the Deccan and Malwa after the Jorwe phase was unacceptable right at the time when it was offered because he forgot to consider the large number of sites which occurred throughout the Deccan and Malwa showing a continuous sequence from the chalcolithic to the historical periods. More recently, excavations at Chichali have revealed a continuity from the Jorwe phase to the early historical period (Mittra and Shivananda 2000).

Thus on the one hand, such writings are very welcome, but on the other hand, great caution should be exercised regarding their cultural conclusions.

An increased focus on dating, especially of the lower palaeolithic stage, is the fourth major aspect of Indian pre-historic studies in the 1990s. It is gratifying to note that not long after the publication of the article by Raghavan, Rajaguru and Misra (1989), the number of dates available for the lower segment of the Indian pre-historic sections markedly increased (Sheila Misra 1995). Thermoluminescent dating seems to have been fairly effective in dating the dune profiles of the Thar desert, leading to a better understanding of the Thar lithic industries (Chougaonkar *et al.* 1999, Sheila Mishra *et al.* 1999). It has to be acknowledged that A.K. Singvi (cf. Singhvi *et al.* 1987, Chawla and Singhvi 1989, Rao, Bisaria and Singhvi 1997, Singhvi *et al.* 1998) of Physical Research Laboratory, Ahmedabad, has played the leading role in the development of dating techniques based on luminescence in India. A better understanding of the geological contexts of artefacts and a better access to their dating have led to a situation where it is possible to claim that the age of the Indian lower palaeolithic goes well back into the lower pleistocene.

There are also signs of concern with the site formation processes, although the pathways of this study do not seem to be clear. Richa Jhaldiyal's (1998) article is a good example of this concern. However, till now there is no clear case study demonstrating how these processes — studied experimentally or otherwise — can lead to changes in the current interpretations of Indian pre-historic scatters. If it is possible to reconstruct the original deposition pattern of the current scatters through such studies, it should be clearly demonstrated through the study of particular sites. I would still hesitate to consider the site formation studies in Indian prehistory as a distinct trend.

Another tradition which has failed to form a distinct trend is 'probability sampling strategies', a topic on which Prakash Sinha (1988) wrote an article and which he followed up in his precisely and carefully written monograph on the prehistory of the Satna district in M.P. (P. Sinha 1991). This monograph basically belongs to the settlement-subsistence approach in Indian prehistory, but here Sinha (1991) builds his arguments not so much on ethnography as on microwear studies and statistical appraisals of various attributes of the stone industries. In fact, in the Indian context Prakash Sinha seems to be one of the very few persons to have carried out statistical tests on the relevant attributes of the stone tool assemblages. One of the other early examples that come readily to mind is the article by Arun Kumar (1989) on the handaxes and cleavers from Gangapur in Maharashtra.

The issue of pre-historic art, however, has come to constitute a distinct and important trend, especially after B.M. Pande (1971) reported a neolithic hunting scene on a stone slab from Burzahom. The major credit should certainly go to V.S. Wakankar, as we have pointed out earlier. With his involvement in the Indian journal *Rock Art Research* Giriraj Kumar too has played the role of a pioneer in this regard. The scholar who has internationally increased the profile of Indian pre-historic art is an Australian, R.G. Bednarik. His article on 'palaeolithic art in India' (Bednarik 1993) was an eye-opener in this regard and based on a careful and positive evaluation of the evidence (Bednarik 1993). E. Neumayer's *Lines on Stone* (1993) is also a comprehensive publication, offering in a precise and clear fashion, the basic data from all over India. A substantial number of rock art occurrences need not be attributed pre-historic status, but some of them certainly went back to a still undefined 'mesolithic' stage. A more careful study of their locations and more successful attempts at their dating are important in the current situation of Indian rock art studies.

On a regional level *Prehistoric Archaeology of Bihar* by B. Narayan (1996) has been influential in hightening the focus on pre-historic research in eastern India, mainly because of its wide research scope, close familiarity with earlier research and clarity of expression. He followed this up by another monograph in 1999 (B. Narayan 1999). In the same vein one should mention both contemporary and earlier publications like R.K. Chattopadhyay's study of palaeolithic West Bengal (1992), P.C. Pant's study of Uttar Pradesh (1982), Vidula Jayaswal's study of the chopper-chopping component of the Indian palaeolithic (1982), Radha Kant Varma's study of the mesolithic in Mirzapur (1986), etc.

Archaeological Science

The range of scientific studies of the archaeological remains does not seem to have widened much in the 1990s. The situation is somewhat better than the 1980s when K.T.M. Hegde (1985) could write a paper focussing — unjustly, of course — on two of his own works in a review of 'scientific studies in Indian archaeology'. One of these researches was on the dating the buried soil profiles in the plain of Gujarat, although he does not take care to explain how these soil profiles affect our understanding of the archaeology of this plain. The second piece of research that he decided to write about was his work on the history of metallurgy in the Aravallis. One of the arguments is that the superficial shallow gouging of pits was a precursor to the digging of deep shafts for mining. The only problem is that not an iota of archaeological argument was offered in favour of this argument. Hegde was basically an archaeological chemist, and his contribution in the field of archaeometallurgy lay principally in the fact that he analysed a few ancient metal artefact samples from excavations.

P.T. Craddock (1987, 1987-88, Craddock *et al.* 1989) had an extensive series of publications on the history of Indian zinc and brass in the 1980s. In the 1990s he studied the use of firesetting in the granite quarries of south India (Craddock 1996). Lynn Willies followed up his major contribution on the ancient zinc-lead-silver mining in Rajasthan (Willies 1987) by a detailed study of the ancient and post-mediaeval mining sites in the Khetri copper belt of Rajasthan and the Kolar gold field of Karnataka (Willies 1992). The work is in the nature of a preliminary reconnaissance, but as Willies is a specialist mine historian, it is possible to have an idea of how to approach this field of history on the ground. One of his interesting observations in the case of Kolar is that 'working continued in ancient times well below water table'. In Khetri he puts emphasis on the Madhan mines which, be believes, has enormous archaeological potential and calls for a detailed survey of the old workings. What is important is that he tries to offer a brief pre-modern history of the copper working at Khetri : (1) an early phase of selective and near surface mining in gossan; (2) deeper mining of pyritic ores below gossan; (3) reworking below water table; and (4) large-scale use of fire-setting methods.

The first major application of lead isotope studies in the Indian context was published by Sharada Srinivasan (1999), combining these with compositional analysis for 18 elements using inductively coupled plasma optical emission specroscopy. In all 130 objects, mostly metal images belong to the pre-Pallava, Pallava, Early Chola, Late Chola, Vijayanagara and Nayaka-Maratha phases of south Indian history. Lead isotopic investigations were done on 60 objects whereas compositional analysis was done on 115 objects. On 40 objects both kinds of analysis were attempted. As the objects cover a wide time-frame from a relatively homogeneous geographical and cultural area, and as the technical methods of analysis are sophisticated, this study has a special importance in the history of archaeometallurgical studies in India. The cultural conclusions reached are important too.

> The lead isotope and trace element trends of most South Indian bronzes seem to be distinctive from artefacts from other parts of the Indian subcontinent. Lead isotope analysis also indicates that the western Indian deposits such as Ambaji, which was a source of brass for northern India from the late pre-Christian era to the mediaeval period, were also minor sources of lead and brass for mediaeval south India. A remarkable discovery is that, by the early historic period (c. fourth century A.D.), there appears to have been a source of metallic zinc for southern India. . . . One source for southern Indian

> Andhra Satavahana lead from the Early Christian era seems to have been the local Bandalamottu mine in Andhra. Exchange of metal with the Mediterranean is indicated in the early historic period by the finding of a Sardinian source for some Satavahana lead and of a western Indian source (Ambaji) for some Hellenistic brass.
>
> — Srinivasan 1999 : 111

Sharada Srinivasan (1998) has also studied the modern tradition of making high tin bronze bowl makers of Kerala.

More orthodox trace element studies continue to be made. One may take note of P.K. Chattopadhyay's find of tin at a number of early east Indian sites including the chalcolithic levels of Bahiri, Senuar and Dihar (Chattopadhyay 1993-94, Chattopadhyay and Singh 1998, Chattopadhyay 1999-2000). Isolating a consistently high tin alloying (10 per cent tin in a piece of wire from Bahiri, 9 per cent tin in a copper bangle from Dihar and 5.3 per cent and 7.6 per cent in two bangles from Senuar) is a major achievement of Chattopadhyay's work, implying an almost positive proof of the mining of tin sources in the Giridih sector and a trade in tin (including other metals) during, presumably, the second half of the second millennium BC Rajam Sheshadri (1992) undertook a study of the compositional elements, metallography and smithery techniques of an axe and a chisel from the Harappan context of Nagwada. Hari Narain *et al.* (1998) studied 5 copper artefacts between *c.* 400 BC and *c.* AD 300 from Manjhi, a fortified town site on the Sarayu/Ghaghra river in the Saran district of Bihar. Three bangles and a copper rod show both lead and tin alloying, and in the case of the bangles the tin alloying varies between 6 per cent and 8.8 per cent. The whole range of archaeological, literary, geological, metallurgical and ethnographic data on early Indian copper has been critically analysed and integrated by Chakrabarti and Lahiri (1995). This study is on the model of Chakrabarti's earlier study of iron. There have also been studies of tin (Chakrabarti 1980), lead (Nanda and Chakrabarti 1982), silver (Nanda and Chakrabarti 1989) and gold (Nanda 1992) on this model. An important development in the context of Harappan metallurgical studies is a belated archaeological realisation of the fact that there is a rich source of tin in the Tosam area of Haryana which falls in the middle of a rich Harappan distribution area (Kochhar, Kochhar and Chakrabarti 1999). Among the important analyses of copper artefacts are those from Senuar (Singh, Merkel and Singh 1996-97) and Narhan (Singh, Merkel and Singh 1997).

In the case of iron there have been a number of archaeological discoveries which strongly support the earlier premise of Chakrabarti that the beginning of iron technology in India was a polycentric, indigenous and early affair. In West Bengal the occurrence of iron in the so-called chalcolithic level was first highlighted at Bahiri (Chakrabarti and Hasan 1982) and has since then been supported by the finds at Pandu Rajar Dhibi, Baneshwar Danga and Mangalkot (for the data, G. Sengupta ed. 1992, 1993-94). Chakrabarti's premise of the association of Black-and-Red Ware of the upper Ganga plain with iron has also been supported by the finds of iron implements in the Black-and-Red Ware level at Jakhera and Dadupur, with its date at Dadupur going back to *c*.1700 BC (Tewari *et al.* 2001-02). This find gains further support from the date of iron around 1100 BC at Jhusi (Misra, Pal and Gupta 1999-2000). A major recent discovery regarding the presence of early iron in the fringes of the Ganga plain has been obtained from excavations at Raja Nal-ka-Tila in the Sonabhadra plateau where iron appears around 1200/1300 BC. A still more important early find of iron occurs at Malhar in the Karmanasa valley near Banaras where iron has been taken back to *c*. 1600 BC (both for Raja Nal-ka-Tila and Malhar dates, Tewari *et al.* 1999-2000). There is a chain of iron-producing sites around Malhar in the upper part of the Karmanasa valley, and it appears that sites such as these were meant to supply bloomery iron to the Banaras section of the Ganga plain. The range of mostly early historic iron artefacts from various excavated sites has been studied by O.P. Agrawal, Narain and Prakash (1991), Hari Narain *et al.* (1990-91, 1991-92, 1998a, 1998b) and Singh, Glover and Merkel (1998-99), among others. The sites involved are, respectively, Khairadih (U.P.), Soron in Gwalior (Madhya Pradesh), Hulaskhera near Lucknow (U.P.), Manjhi (Bihar), Sringaverpur (U.P.) and Senuar (Bihar). Singh, Glover and Merkel (1998-99), for instance, conducted Electron Probe Microanalyser, Scanning Electron Microscope and metallographic studies of the Senuar iron objects and concluded that layering techniques were used for fabricating the tools and that the smiths were also familiar with the process of infusing carbon (0.2 per cent to 0.4 per cent) by case hardening and lamination. In view of the very wide former prevalence of pre-industrial iron-smelting tradition in India, it is gratifying to note that the Rourkela Steel Plant undertook a project of reviving this tradition in Orissa (N.R. Srinivasan 1998). Till recently, National Research Laboratory for Conservation of Cultural Property in Lucknow played an important role in analysing ancient iron artefacts from excavated sites, and the study of such objects from Khairadih, Soron, Hulaskhera, Manjhi and Sringaverpur was undertaken at this institute. For various reasons the institute has recently lost interest in pursuing this field of study.

The archaeobotanical evidence is on the increase, as more studies of the material from different sites are being undertaken — mostly by the same scholars who were active in the earlier decade. In a wide-ranging archaeological context in the Ganga plains and Panjab — the neolithic of Senuar, the chalcolithic of Narhan and Imlidih, the late Harappan of Hulas, the early historic of Sanghol and others — K.S. Saraswat (cf. 1993, 1994, Pokharia and Saraswat 1999-2000, Saraswat 1992-93) has greatly expanded our knowledge of the agricultural economy of this vast area. His study of the plant remains from the late Harappan contexts of Rohira and Mahorana in Panjab (Saraswat 1986, 1990-91) and early Harappan context of Kunal in Haryana has added new dimensions to the study of Harappan agriculture. On the all-India level the profile of no archaeobotanist has been as extensive, diverse and significant as that of K.S. Saraswat in the 1990s. He is the true and illustrious successor of K.A. Chowdhury and Vishnu Mittre. In the early historical context of the Lucknow region Chanchala's report on the plant remains from Hulaskhera is significant (Chanchala 1991-92). In the 1990s M.D. Kajale remained generally busy with the material from the sites excavated mostly by the Deccan College and the Archaeological Survey of India (cf. Kajale 1996a, 1996b), and partly branched off in the direction of phytolith studies (Kajale 1995, Kajale and Eksambekar 1997).

A better integration between the overall archaeological picture of India and her archaeobotanical remains is reflected well in the writings of Dorian Fuller (1999) whose main focus so far has been on south Indian neolithic. He collected 72 flotation samples from 12 sites, which provided him with a complete chronological and geographical coverage of the south Deccan. His research base, thus, did not begin with the identification of remains from a particular site and was broad-based and focussed right from the beginning of the research. Five pulses were identified — horsegram/*kulthi*, moong, blackgram, arahar and hyacinth bean. Of these two — horsegram and moong — were considered staple crops and their probable region of domestication has been argued to be south India itself. Both blackgram and arahar were of Indian origin but outside the south Indian neolithic zone. Hyacinth bean is of east African origin. If one leaves out the millets described as minor crops or weeds, one is left with 'bristly foxtail millet-grass' which, although never domesticated, was a staple crop and native to south India, and finger and pearl millets which were of east and west African provenances respectively and initially a minor crop in the south Indian neolithic. The crops of west Asiatic origin with their nuclear area of cultivation extending as far east as Baluchistan included wheat (both free-threshing and hulled), barley, cotton and flax. All these were added/minor crops, although the status of cotton is not certain. Rice occurs but as a minor addition. Melon and jujube need not have been domesticated. The status of *parenchyma* fragments or tuber fragments is not decided but they formed a native cultivar and had significant presence. Fuller rightly deduces a dependence on roots/tubers in the south Indian neolithic. On the whole he has tried to offer, on the basis of archaeobotany, a broad historical image of the crop-pattern of the south Indian neolithic with reference to its native and introduced crops. Areca-nut which has been isolated at Watgal is apparently missing from his samples, but there are always exigencies of discovery. Unlike some archaeobotanists who try to reconstruct grand schemes on the basis of a highly limited number of sites and a pre-ordained and highly questionable scheme (cf Weber 1999), Fuller has carefully and painstakingly built up an eminently acceptable frame of analysis. Gail Wagner (1990) and N. Seetha Reddy (1991, 1997) seem to be to two new entrants to the scene. For an integration of the archaeological, literary, botanical, ethnographical and linguistic data Tuk-Tuk Kumar's work on early rice in India (Kumar 1988) is noteworthy.

In the field of archaeozoology Paul Rissman (Rissman and Chitalwala 1990) introduced the method of counting annual rings in tooth *cementum* for age measurement of bones, along with the study of epiphyseal fusion of long bones and tooth eruption and wear. The general conclusion is the following : 'the youngest animals are not well represented, frequent culling of young adults is indicated, while a substantial presence of older adults can be seen'. (Rissman and Chitalwala 1990: 126) It is conclusions like these which make us realise how essential archaeozoological studies are for the reconstruction of economic history. A more recent attempt to contribute to the picture of Harappan economy through archaeozoological studies is that by Arati Deshpande-Mukherjee (1998). Her study of shells from nine excavated Gujarat Harappan sites shows a pattern of utilisation geared both to the manufacture of shell artefacts and collection for food.

> Besides shell working, another important aspect that emerges from this study is the dietary contribution of select molluscs to the Harappan food economy. At the coastal sites of Kuntasi, Shikarpur, Nageswar, Bagasra, etc. seasonal harvesting of shellfish at low tide was carried out all the year round. There was a general preference for bivalves although a few gastropods were also collected. Species like *Meretrix, Paphia* sp., and *Andara* sp. which were harvested then constitute commercially important species even today.
>
> — Deshpande-Mukherjere 1998 : 76

An authoritative review of the post-pleistocene faunal material was undertaken by Thomas and Joglekar (1994). B.P. Sahu (1988) attempted a major historical synthesis by underscoring the role of wild and domestic fauna in ancient Indian economy. For an integrated current approach to the study of the faunal material from a single site P.K. Thomas *et al.* (1995) and Sathe and Badam (1996) provide good examples.

Human skeletal studies have not made much headway in recent years, the monographs by K.A.R. Kennedy *et al.* (1992) and Kennedy, Lovell and Burrow (1986) being some standard examples of the current approach. Still one finds occasional attempts at 'race, culture, language correlation', and it is time biological anthropologists working in India focussed only on the things they can deduce from their studies of ancient skeletons, as Walimbe and Kulkarni (1993, 1994) do in the case of the study of ancient dentition or as Kennedy and his associates do in the case of Mahadaha and Sarai Nahar Rai. As long as biological anthropologists accept the simple idea that biology cannot be combined with historically derived premises of any kind, there is no problem with what they tell us about ancient skeletons. It is only when they digress from their field and begin to argue that their finds support the racist structure of colonial language and population histories, that people without faith in the 'science' of such assumptions have to think about the socio-politics of the concerned biological anthropologists.

The diversity and history of Indian population groups may perhaps be best approached from the DNA study of both modern populations and ancient skeletal material. On the modern populations the DNA study seems to be on the way (Thangaraj, Ramana and Singh 1999). The situation regarding the study of ancient DNA has not yet taken off, although S. Siva Kumar *et al.* (1999) have reviewed the current trends in ancient DNA studies. S. Siva Kumar *et al.* (n.d.) tried to extract DNA from a bone specimen from the chalcolithic level of Kaothe, a site in Maharashtra but was not successful. They conclude that even with further technical developments in extracting DNA from ancient specimens the situation is unlikely to improve in the case of open air sites where exposure to heat and moisture could have adversely affected the survival of endogenous proteins in the bones and thus the possibility of finding DNA in them. According to them 'attempts to obtain ancient DNA from India should instead focus on sites in non-tropical environments and/or cave sites'.

In an article examining 'people of India : biological diversity and affinities' P.P. Majumdar (1998) concludes that 'geographical affinity plays a stronger role than does cultural affinity in determining genetic affinity' but devotes a separate section of his paper to examine the question 'how well do patterns of biological affinities correlate with the culural history of India'. On the basis of outdated archaeological and historical literature the cultural history of India is put up as a succession of migrations of both languages and people and eventually it is concluded that, 'because genes move with peoples, the entry of diverse genetic elements into India must be a major reason for the extraordinary biological diversity of contemporary Indian peoples'. Whether this is true or not is a different matter, but what does a biological anthropologist gain by reviewing and accepting as a fact the colonial model of India's cultural history, especially when they do not bother to examine how this model was built up and with which kind of logic? T. Kivisild (1999) reached the following conclusions by analysing 'about 1000 mtDNA genomes and 400 Y-chromosomes from various locations in India'.

> First, we found that the node of the phylogenetic tree of mtDNA, ancestral to more than 90 per cent of the present-day typically European maternal lineages, is present in India at a relatively high frequency, being also a founder of a large variety of Indian-specific sequence variants. We found them spread rather uniformly all over the Indian Peninsula. Inferred coalescence time of this ancestral node is slightly above 50,000 BP. Second, we found that haplogroup U is the second most abundant mtDNA variety in India as it is in Europe. However, the sub-varieties of the Indian and the European haplogroup U overlap only to a limited extent. Finally, from sequence and RFLP analysis we suggest that there is very little genetic evidence supporting a massive recent Indo-Aryan invasion. At least as far as maternal lineages are concerned. There is indeed a significant haplogroup-level overlap between the European and Indian mtDNA lineages, but the majority of them may date back to times, when Europe was probably not yet inhabited by modern humans. The fraction of lineages that are closely shared with Europeans in India is less than 10 per cent and seems to date back approximately 9000 BP, in average. Summing up, we believe that there are now enough reasons not only to question a 'recent Indo-Aryan invasion' into India some 4000 BP, but alternatively to consider India as a part of the common gene pool ancestral to the diversity of human material lineages in Europe.

Kivisild *et al.* (2000) wrote a fuller paper on this issue.

The point is that the old notions of India's population and language history are not something which biological anthropologists should use to test the non-biological implications of their data. They should realise that many of the linguistic and cultural historical hypotheses about India, which are found in most of the books today, are no more products of scientific reasoning than the political and social climates in which they were offered.

An important approach which still remains to be developed as a field of study is what R.K. Mohanty and S.R. Walimbe (1993) called 'a demographic approach to the Vidarbha megalithic culture'. Regarding the megalithic burials of this region they began with three questions : why were these burials erected and were they meant to be the burial grounds of selected individuals or all people of the group ? And, thirdly, if they were meant for the burials of selected individuals, how were the bodies of the rest of the society disposed of after death ? Mohanty and Walimbe considered the totality of both archaeological and osteological evidence and carried out an experimental study to construct a similar megalith. Their major conclusions are that only a limited number of individuals had acceess to this mode of the disposal of the dead and that the society supporting it was agricultural or semi-agricultural. This is one of the rare examples where skeletal evidence has been consciously used to solve an archaeological problem.

The impact of archaeological science can be seen in a few other areas. V.D. Gogte (1997) undertook a major study on the source of the ancient rouletted ware on the basis of x-ray diffraction analysis. One is not entirely happy with the way Gogte (1996) has argued Balathal to be a trading centre on the basis of x-ray diffraction analysis of pottery, but the application of this technique (cf. Gogte and Shinde 1995) will, hopefully, be more widely accepted in Indian archaeology, thanks to his pioneering efforts. A. Kshirsagar (1995) continues her fluorine content studies, and focusses on chemical analysis of excavated soil profiles as well (Kshirsagar 1996). Vinod Nautiyal *et al.* (1992) have been concerned with the phosphorus content of the excavated soil profiles of some Ganga plain and mid-central Himalayan sites. Similarly, Deotare (1990) continued his interest in archaeological soils. Vinod Nautiyal (personal information) has also published on the isotopic study of excavated animal bones, which is likely to provide clues to animal diet.

This section studies seem to have been generally neglected, the only major exception in this regard being K. Krishnan's attempts in this direction (Krishnan 1986, Krishnan and Hegde 1987), certain new techniques of study are also being developed. Attention must be drawn in this context to a mechanical and instrument-based way of pottery drawing by Vinod Nautiyal *et al.* (1995). Rao, Rao and Rao (1997) have studied two port sites of the Satavahana period — Majeru and Kothapatnam — in Andhra using geomorphic mapping based on remote-sensing. As one of the rare examples of site-specific application of remote-sensing technique in Indian archaeology, this publication has a special significance of its own (for remote-sensing, Sushama Deo and Joglekar 1996; K. Balaji *et al.* 1996). It would be incorrect to claim purely on the basis of S.R. Rao's work at Dwaraka (1987) or that marine archaeology has made a beginning in India, but certainly steps have been taken in that direction (cf. Tripati and Gaur 1997). The establishment of a 'marine archaeology centre' in the National Institute of Oceanography in Goa is a very positive and necessary measure to understand the scope of archaeology along the Indian coast. A considerable credit for this should go to S.R. Rao whose commitment to academic archaeological pursuits contrasts sharply with the political activities of many of his contemporaries.

Protohistory

Excavations at Dholavira have dominated Indus studies in India in the 1990s, although the impact of such a major happening has been considerably offset by disappointment with the lack of a detailed and comprehensive report on it. The isolation of an early Harappan level at Padri, especially the occurrence of Indus script signs on the potsherds of that period, is another major event (Shinde In Press). In the rest of the Indus distribution area there is a kind of stalemate; the excavations at Rakhigarhi being too recent to generate a clear interest in its significance. The Baroda University's work at Bagasra, Loteshwar and other sites in Gujarat is still unpublished in detail. The Kurukshetra University's prolonged work at Balu is unlikely to see the light of the day, and the same can be said about the excavated sites in Panjab. The excavations of two Late Harappan sites — Bhorgarh and Mandoli — in Delhi have an importance of their own because they are within the confines of modern Delhi. Otherwise, the discovery of the Mandi hoard of Late Harappan jewellery in the Muzaffarnagar district of U.P. may be the most significant piece of Harappan discovery on the Indian side in the new millennium. The Indus studies have reached, for some reason, a statemate in India in the 1990s. The concern with its name — the Indus civilization or the Indus-Sarasvati civilization — has not done it any good except making it a political issue, although one notes, with considerable amusement, the use of the completely illogical term *Indus Valley Civilization* in the official mouthpiece of the Indian Archaeological Society, *Puratattva*. This no doubt is a good reflection on the status of the Indus studies in India and the level of the intellectual concern of the current leadership of the Society. There are more things to be studied about this civilization than finding the *Rigveda* in its entirety in it. On a different level, V. Shinde's study of the proto-historic settlement archaeology of the Tapti basin (1998) is a very significant contribution to the study of Indian settlement archaeology in its proto-historic context. D.P. Sharma's study of *Harappan Seals, Sealings and Copper Tablets* (2000) in the National Museum, Delhi, is both a timely and important catalogue of such antiquities. In Gujarat the studies by Sonawane (1994-95), K. Bhan (1992), Kiran Dimri (1998-99) and A. Majumdar (1998-99) are noteworthy.

In the non-Indus sphere the excavations at Balathal and Budihal stand out, one for isolating a village level as early as Kot Diji in the south-eastern section of the Aravallis and the other for proving that ashmounds were not isolated occurrences but parts of the overall settlement complex of the southern neolithic. One looks forward to reading the report on another southern neolithic site, Watgal. In the east there was a report on the area survey of the Chhotanagpur plateau in 1993 (Chakrabarti 1993), trying to examine the base line of the archaeology of this vast area in its totality, with a special emphasis on the possible nature of its interaction with the Ganga plain. Archaeological research in West Bengal has gained a lot with fairly detailed accounts of the work done in the past by its government directorate of archaeology in its journal *Pratnasamiksha* which is edited by G. Sengupta and has been recently accompanied by a journal published in Bengali, *Puravritta*, under the same editorship. Its first issue was published in 2000 and contained many excellent articles with original material. The archaeology of Assam and the north-east as a whole has not yet picked itself up from the morass of plain lethergy which seems to have characterised the archaeological research in that area throughout. The establishment of a separate 'Circle' of the Archaeological Survey of India in Guwahati does not seem to have made any difference. Excavations of neolithic levels at Senuar and Taradih are no doubt the major happenings of proto-historic archaeology in Bihar. One learns that the Senuar report has been prepared by B.P. Singh, and one wishes one could write the same for Taradih excavated by Ajit K. Prasad. One, of course, does not even think that the reports on the three other excavated neolithic sites of Bihar — Chirand, Chechar-Kutubpur and Maner — will ever be published. In Orissa the excavation of Golbai Sasan which has revealed neolithic and chalcolithic levels in the Puri district is a landmark excavation in the context of east India (B.K. Sinha 1999). It is a matter of great regret that with the untimely death of its well-organised and methodical excavator B.K. Sinha, the chances of a detailed report coming out have virtually ceased.

The one area which has stood out in the archaeological research in India in the 1990s is U.P. The first issue of the journal *Pragdhara* which is the official mouthpiece of the U.P. State Archaeological Organisation and edited by Rakesh Tewari was published in 1990-91. Since then it has been published every year, with detailed reports and articles on the excavations and explorations conducted by the Department and a few other bodies in the State. The most prominent among the other bodies is Banaras Hindu University under Purushottam Singh. Among the U.P. areas which have emerged into prominence due to these researches are the Sonabhadra plateau and the trans-Sarayu area. With the publication of a detailed report on Narhan (P. Singh 1994), the identity of a culture characterised by Black-and-Red Ware, a very distinct black-slipped ware with white paintings on a surface with shining polish, absence of microlithic tools and a rich assemblage of bone tools, among other things, in the trans-Sarayu plain fell in place. Singh called this culture Narhan Culture to distinguish it from the other Black-and-Red Ware assemblages of the Ganga valley. The Narhan discovery was immediately followed by excavations at a number of sites such as Imlidih, Waina, Dhuriapar, Lohuradeva, etc., the details of which were regularly published in *Pragdhara*. It was also during this general period that B.R. Mani of the Archaeological Survey of India excavated a site in Basti, which he identified with the site of *Setavya* in Buddhist literature. The excavation programmes in the trans-Sarayu area were accompanied by extensive explorations along the local river valleys such as the Ami, Kuwana, etc., which were in turn published in detail in *Pragdhara*. The internal situation of P. Singh's Department in Banaras Hindu University — or, rather, the people controlling the Department — did not permit him — a well-trained archaeologist with experience not merely in his university but also in the Archaeological Survey and the Institute of Archaeology (London) — to undertake fieldwork for about 13 years, and eventually when he could go out for fieldwork, he excavated Narhan and other sites, built up a band of younger people around him, and generally changed the features of trans-Sarayu archaeology. The power-structure of the work-place has been an important factor in the history of Indian archaeology after Independence, and Purushottam Singh's case has been cited only as an example.

In the case of the Sonabhadra plateau and the adjoining area the credit goes wholly to Rakesh Tewari under whose leadership the U.P. State Archaeological Organisation has undertaken major excavations at Raja-Nal-ka-Tila, Malhar, Dadupur and Lohuradeva and published detailed reports on these sites and the results of their exploration, giving the whole region a sharp archaeological focus. Each of his excavations has been of cardinal importance in understanding the archaeology of the central Ganga plain. In the U.P. Himalayas which now form the bulk of a new state, Uttaranchal, the Garhwal University has a long-running excavation programme; unfortunately the only major publication it has been able to sponsor so far is a monograph by B.M. Khanduri (1994). In the Doab the publication of R.C. Gaur's Lal Qila excavation report is important (Gaur 1995).

Early History

In the field of early historic archaeology the publication of the report on his excavations at the settlement site of Pauni in Maharashtra by Amarendra Nath (1998) is a welcome event, and one hopes that it will be followed by a report on his excavations at Adam, another fortified early historic city-site in the same area. In Orissa the excavations of the Buddhist monasteries at Lalitagiri and Udaigiri by G.C. Chauley are major events in the history of contemporary archaeology in India. It is time some detailed articles began to come out (cf. Chauley 2000). Similarly, considerable importance can be attached to the excavations at the Buddhist monastery and *stupa* site of Jagjivanpur in the Maldaha district, West Bengal. The Jagjivanpur work has been undertaken by Amal Ray of the State directorate of Archaeology of West Bengal (Ray 2000). As far as the early Buddhist *stupa* sites are concerned, there have been a few notable discoveries in recent years : the report of a Bharhut-type *stupa* at Katara near the early historic city-site of Musanagar at an old crossing of the Yamuna beyond Kanpur (Tewari and Srivastava 1990-91), the excavations of the *stupa* at Kanganahalli in Karnataka which have sculptures of the first-second centuries BC (one of the sculptures showing a king flanked by queen and a female cauri-bearer carries the inscribed label 'Asoka' — a discovery of extraordinary significance, cf. Website of the Archaeological Survey of India), and the beginning of excavations at the *stupa* site of Deur Kothar at Sohagi Ghat of the Vindhyas in M.P. Phani Kant Mishra's work at Deur Kothar, undertaken on behalf of the Archaeological Survey of India, has clearly taken its antiquity back to the third century BC and established the element of steady continuity between the Mauryan and Sunga arts (Mishra 2001). This was preceded by R.C. Agrawal's work on the Satdhara and the adjacent *stupa*s of the Sanchi area (1997). Although Banavasi in Karnataka is very important as an early historic site, the results of its excavations are unpublished. In Tamil Nadu there has been a better focus on its Roman contacts after the recent excavations at Arikamedu, but the real breakthrough in the early historic archaeology of Tamil Nadu has been achieved by K. Rajan (1994, 1997) of Thanjavur University who excavated the site of Kodumanal and undertook extensive explorations in a large part of the State. The result is that it is now possible to argue that the beginning of urban growth in the Kaveri delta can be as early as the fifth century BC with evidence of considerable interaction with the river valley areas of the north. In Jammu and Kashmir R.C. Agrawal's work (1998) and B.R. Mani's excavations (1999-2000) have provided much-needed archaeological focus to a number of well-known historical sites. Monica Smith's surface survey of Kaundinyapur (2000) is an important pointer in the direction of systematic surface survey of Indian sites.

Related Problems

In the field of material culture Arundhati Banerji (1994) provides a scholarly analysis of the excavated terracottas of both proto-historic and early historic periods and is generally representative of the recent literature of this genre.

Trade and trade-routes were given a firm footing up to *c.* 200 BC by a careful analysis of the evidence of raw material utilisation at various sites, the geological distribution of such raw materials, the probable areas from which they could have been obtained by the sites concerned, and the probable routes by which they could have been obtained (Lahiri 1992). This was the first work to give a comprehensive archaeological depth to the proto-historic and early historic internal trade of India, and should be followed by an equally in-depth analysis of the later historic internal trade. Routes also formed a major component of Chakrabarti's historical geographical study of the archaeological sites of the lower and the middle Ganga plains (Chakrabarti 2001). Sites as an integrated part of a network and the historical geographical implications of the locations of at least the major sites have been the main thurst of this work. On a different level, the archaeology of a major trunk route of early historic India, the routes which linked the Ganga plain with both east and west Deccan, have been taken up for ground studies (Chakrabarti, Tewari and Singh 2000, 2001). Some attempts have also been made to understand the archaeology of Hinduism both in terms of the archaeological evidence of rituals and the continuity of sacred space in various segments of the Indian landscape (Chakrabarti 2001). In the Buddhist context a focussed and detailed work on the sacred geography of the Sanchi area has been undertaken by Julia Shaw (2000). Early historic urban growth is the subject of a mainly archaeology-based monograph by S.K. Jha (1998). The nature of the Harappan state has formed the subject of a book by S. Ratnagar (1991). In the early historic context, quarrying for stone in the Chunar hills, the transportation of such blocks to Banaras/Sarnath, and eventually their use as raw material for fashioning images have been the subject of a fine piece of archaeological investigation (Jayaswal 1998). The maritime aspect of early historic trade figures in various volumes, especially the volume edited by H. Ray and J-F. Salles (1996). The contact of the Indus civilization with the Gulf area has been freshly examined by Chakrabarti (1998) who argues that both maritime and overland trade should be viewed as parts of the same network even in the proto-historic context. L. Shahani (1997) examines the tradition of *Dhow* trade between the Gulf and the Gujarat coast. Sunil Gupta's subscription to the theory of an Indo-Pacific network of exchange of goods up to Japan (S. Gupta 2000) is an interesting premise. Regional studies of archaeology have received a great impetus with the publication of two volumes on the archaeology of Orissa which have been ably edited by K.K. Basa and Pradeep Mohanty (2000). Basa has a major research focus on India's south-east Asian trade (Basa 1996) and his study of the problem with special reference to his own compositional study of glass beads from various Indian south-east Asiatic sites still remains unmatched. On a different level, the archaeology of European expansion in India, which was based exclusively on trade, has been reviewed in detail in the context of Gujarat by Chakrabarti (In press). A major contribution to the regional archaeology of Tamil Nadu has also been made by Selvaraj (2000). A significant theoretical contribution to both archaeological and ethnographic studies of a Rajasthan village and thus of other comparable villages through detailed ethnographic observations aided by micro-morphological studies of soil have been made by Nicole Boivin (2000). Chakrabarti (1997) published a detailed study of the racist basis of the widely accepted frame of race-language-culture correlation of ancient Indian archaeology and history and argued that the framework came in place as an important ideological ingredient of exercising colonial power in the subcontinent. The reason of this framework still being in place in Independent India is reflective of the position of India as a Third World country *vis-à-vis* the West. This is in sharp contrast to Paddayya's apparent belief in the disassociation between knowledge and power. Sociopolitics of the past is still a marginal aspect of Indian archaeological research, although there is no reason why it should be so (cf. Chakrabarti 2000, Lahiri 2000).

*A recent synthesis : **India — An Archaeological History. Palaeolithic Beginnings to Early Historic Foundations***

In a number of ways this monograph (Chakrabarti 1999) differs from the earlier attempts to survey the spectrum of Indian archaeology as a whole. Among other things, this is the first single-authored work to view the archaeological history of the subcontinent in all its major geographical areas from the palaeolithic stage to *c.* AD 300 as a part of a historical and archaeological narrative which is firmly focussed on the Indian soil itself. Secondly, this narrative is continuous and it smoothly unfolds itself without the interjection of the various external agencies. Thirdly, it takes pains to highlight the fact that the pre-historic roots of India are vitally relevant to the understanding of modern India and Indians. Fourthly, the narrative is closely interwined with the many nuances and dimensions of India's physical geography and geo-politics. Fifthly, it has shown, among other things, how right from the point of its beginning to its decline, and its impact on, and subsequent integration with, the incipient farmers and specialised hunter-gatherers of inner India, the Indus civilization has been a wholly Indian development which has contributed enormously to the shaping of later India.

Its chapter one throws into relief the special significance of archaeological record in the reconstruction of ancient Indian history, the unity among the diversity of Indian geographical and cultural features, the limitations of a mechanical approach to the problem of India regions, the problems of its north-western, northern and south-eastern 'frontiers' and the unsound basis of the various widely popular notions of the subcontinent's population and language history. Chapters two and three examine the pre-historic context mainly with reference to the basic historical informations about them and their historical relevance. After a reference to the problem of the beginning of food production based on different crops in the subcontinent, chapter four puts the Indus civilization in its proper context by undertaking a systematic and region-by-region evaluation of the relevant archaeological data. That the Aravalli region played a major role in the genesis of this civilization along with the various segments of its distribution area has been adequately pinpointed in this discussion. Chapter five explains why Mesopotamia-type canal irrigation system was prevalent in the Indus context too and goes on to summarise the basic known facts about this civilization. It also underscores the fact that the Mature and the Late forms of this civilization had a long chronology, just like the Early Harappan stage and the stage before that. It tries to explain geographically how the Late Harappans were getting merged in the contemporary and later cultures of both the upper Ganga plain and Peninsular India. Chapter six dwells on the vast canvas of proto-historic village life in all the areas outside the Harappan orbit, commenting on their moorings and significance from the point of view of later Indian developments. In the next chapter the beginning of early historic India and the development of major early historic cities have been put in the background of the general elements of political and economic history of the subcontinent. The essential data on arts and architecture and inscriptions and coins have been integrated into the general early historic archaeological scene. Nose has remained buried throughout in the ground but, hopefully, the wider historical waves also have been a perceptible feature of the narrative.

Excavations

Chart 2.3: Excavated Sites in *IAR 1990-91* to *IAR 1994-95*

Site	*Years*	*Nature*	*State*	*Status*	*Inst.*	*Person*
Gangadhara	90-91	temple	Andhra	Unpub.	State Dept	?
N'kondapalli	90-91/93-94	historical	Andhra	Unpub.	State Dept	?
Gopalapatnam	90-94	historical	Andhra	Unpub.	State Dept	?
Thotlakonda	90-93	historical	Andhra	Pub.	State Dept	?
Kolhua	90-94	early hist	Bihar	Unpub.	ASI	L.C. Singh

Site	*Years*	*Nature*	*State*	*Status*	*Inst.*	*Person*
Old Goa	90-93/94-95	church	Goa	Unpub.	ASI	various
Babar Kot	90-91	Harappan	Gujarat	?	State/Penn U	Possehl/Raval
Padri	90-92/93-94	Harappan	Gujarat	Unpub	D.Coll	V. Shinde
Dholavira	90-93	Harappan	Gujarat	Unpub	ASI	R.S. Bisht
Loteshwar	90-91	Harappan	Gujarat	Unpub	MSU Baroda	V.S. Parekh M.H. Sonawane
Thaneshwar	90-91	early hist	Haryana	Unpub.	ASI	B.M. Pande
Hampi	90-95	mediaeval	Karnataka	Unpub.	State/ASI	K.P. Poonacha
Gudnapur	90-91/93-95	historical	Karnataka	Unpub.	ASI	K.P. Poonacha
Cheramangad	90-91	megalithic	Kerala	Unpub.	ASI	Narasimhaiah
Kotra	90-91	chalco>	M.P.	Unpub.	Prach.Nktn	R.G. Pandeya
Karkabhat	90-91	megalithic	M.P.	Unpub.	ASI	A.K. Sharma
Sorar	90-91	megalithic	M.P.	Unpub.	ASI	A.K. Sharma
Adam	90-92	early hist	Maharashtra	Unpub.	ASI	A. Nath
Kanchipur	90-92	?	Manipur	Unpub.	State Dept	S.R. Singh
Setka	90-91/94-95	historical	Manipur	Pub.	ASI/State	Sharma/Singh
Barabati Fort	90-95	historical	Orissa	Unpub.	ASI	Sinha/V. Rao
Golbai Sasan	90-92	neolithic	Orissa	Unpub.	ASI	B.K. Sinha
Arikamedu	90-92	early hist	T. Nadu	Pub.	Madras Uni	Raman-Vegley
Brass	90-92/93-95	historical	Panjab	Unpub.	State Dept	Rishi-Sidhu
Juna Khera	90-91	historical	Rajasthan	Unpub.	State Dept	P. Chakravarty V. Kumar
Mamallapuram	90-91	temple	T. Nadu	Unpub.	ASI	Narasimhaiah
Kodumanal	90-91	early hist	T. Nadu	Pub.	Tamil Uni	K. Rajan
Alangakulam	90-91	early hist	T. Nadu	Unpub.	State Dept	A.A. Majeed
Dhuriapar	90-91	chalco >	U.P.	Pub.	BHU	P. Singh
Chunar	90-91	historical	U.P.	Pub.	BHU	P.C. Pant V. Jayasawal
Sanichara	90-91	temple	U.P.	?	State Dept	R. Tewari
Gudisala	91-92	temple	Andhra	Unpub.	State Dept	?
Pavuralla'knd	91-92	historical	Andhra	Unpub.	State Dept	?
Taradih	91-92	neo>	Bihar	Unpub.	State Dept	A.K. Prasad
Patna	91-92	early hist	Bihar	Unpub.	ASI	?
Maner	91-94	neo>	Bihar	Unpub	Patna Uni	Narayan-Singh
Dulmi	91-92	historical	Bihar	Unpub.	ASI	B.K. Sharan
Ichhagarh	91-92	historical	Bihar	Unpub.	ASI	L.C. Singh
Lal Kot	91-94	mediaeval	Delhi	Pub.	ASI	B.R. Mani
Pithad	91-92	meso/Hpn	Gujarat	Unpub.	MSU Baroda	Parekh-Son'ne

Site	*Years*	*Nature*	*State*	*Status*	*Inst.*	*Person*
Arangpur	91-92	pre-historic	Haryana	Pub.	ASI	A.K. Sharma
Kunal	91-92/93-95	pre-Hpn	Haryana	Unpub.	State Dept	Khatri-Acharya
Budihal	91-92	neo>	Karnataka	Unpub.	D.Coll	Paddayya
Wasvi	91-92	temple	M.P.	Unpub.	ASI	G.T. Shende
Maihar	91-92	pre-historic	M.P.	Unpub.	Allh Uni	Pandey-Pal
Banki	91-92	pre-historic	M.P.	Unpub.	Allh Uni	Pandey-Pal
Shirkanda	91-92/93-94	chalco>	Mahrashtra	Unpub	Nagpur Uni	A.M. Sastri
Arambha	91-92	pre-NBP>	Mahrashtra	Unpub.	ASI	A. Nath
Vodagokugiri	91-92	historical	Meghalaya	Pub.	ASI	A.K. Sharma
Lalitagiri	91-92	historical	Orissa	Unpub.	ASI	G.C. Chauley
Manamunda	91-92	historical	Orissa	Unpub.	Sambp. Uni	Mishra-Pradhan
Nrusimhanath	91-92	temple	Orissa	Unpub.	Sambp. Uni	Panda-Pradhan
Dholbaha	91-92	temple	Panjab	Unpub.	State Dept	?
Sadhwara	91-92	chalco>	U.P.	Unpub.	ASI	Shankar Nath
Jainal-Naula	91-93	megalithic	U.P.	Unpub.	Garhw Uni	K.P. Nautiyal
Ladyura	91-92	megalithic	U.P.	Unpub.	ASI	S.B. Ota
Sravasti	91-94	early hist	U.P.	Pub.	ASI/Kansai U	Aboshi
Imlidih	91-93	chalco>	U.P.	Pub.	BHU	P. Singh
Banars'kalan	91-92	early hist	U.P.	Unpub.	ASI	L.C. Singh
Garapadu	92-94	neo>	Andhra	Unpub.	Birla/Nag'jna	G. Kamalakar
Mayo Hill	92-93	historical	Arunachal	Unpub.	State Dept	?
Suryapahar	92-94	historical	Assam	Unpub.	ASI	D. Bhengra
Moti Pipli	92-93	pre-Hpn ?	Gujarat	Unpub.	MSU Baroda	Parekh-Son'ne
Balu	92-95	Harappan	Haryana	Unpub.	Kuruk Uni	various
Datnagar	92-93	historical	H.P.	Unpub.	ASI	H. Manjhi
Talkad	92-93	historical	Karnataka	Unpub.	State/Mys. U	D.V. Devaraj
Bhawar	92-93	chalco>	Maha.	Unpub.	ASI	A. Nath
Kachargarh	92-93	pre-historic	Maha.	Unpub.	ASI	A.K. Sharma
Pachkheri	92-93	micro>	Mahrashtra	Unpub.	ASI	A. Nath
Pynthorlangt-	92-93	neo.	Meghalaya	Unpub.	ASI	L.S. Rao
Sarnath	92-93	early hist	U.P.	Unpub.	ASI	A.K. Sinha
Dhuliapar	92-93	pre-historic	W. Bengal	Unpub.	State Dept	Sudhin De
Nakshaparvat	93-94	mediaeval	Arunachal	Unpub.	State Dept	D.K. Bora
Taposo	93-94	mediaeval	Arunachal	Unpub.	State Dept	?
Bhorgarh	93-94	Harappan	Delhi	Unpub.	State Dept	P.S.R. Babu
Datrana	93-95	Harappan	Gujarat	Unpub.	MSU Baroda	Parekh-Son'ne
Santhli	93-94	pre-historic	Gujarat	Unpub.	MSU Baroda	Parekh-Son'ne

Site	*Years*	*Nature*	*State*	*Status*	*Inst.*	*Person*
Hap	93-94	historical	Gujarat	Unpub.	ASI	G. Shengde
Sugh	93-94	early hist	Haryana	Unpub.	State Dept	Acharya
Malpur	93-94	neo>	J&K	Unpub.	ASI	R.S. Fonia
Badaga Ka'k	93-94	megalithic	Karnataka	Unpub.	ASI	L.S. Rao
Kotatattu	93-94	neo ?	Karnataka	Unpub.	ASI	L.S. Rao
Hasargundigi	93-94	historical	Karnataka	Unpub.	State/ASI	K.P. Poonacha
Sanchi	93-94	early hist	M.P.	Unpub.	ASI	R.C. Agrawal
Satdhara	93-94	early hist	M.P.	Unpub.	ASI	R.C. Agrawal
Pauni settlm.	93-94	early hist	Maharashtr	Unpub.	ASI	A. Nath
Donder Khera	93-94	chalco>	Rajasthan	Unpub.	ASI	R. Saran
Balathal	93-94	chalco>	Rajasthan	Unpub.	D.Coll	V.N. Misra
Padavedu	93-94	historical	T. Nadu	Unpub.	ASI	Narasimhaiah
Mehtab Bagh	93-94	mediaeval	U.P.	Unpub.	ASI	P. Sengar
Gingee	93-95	mediaeval	T. Nadu	Unpub.	ASI	Narasimhaiah
Dihar	93-94	chalco>	W. Bengal	Unpub.	Cal.Univ	A.C. Pal
Puduru	94-95	historical	Andhra	Unpub.	Birla-Hydera.	Kamalakar
Salimgarh	94-95	mediaeval	Delhi	Unpub.?	ASI	B.R. Mani
Ambakut	94-95	mesolithic	Gujarat	Unpub.	MSU Baroda	A. Prasad
Heggadehalli	94-95	megalithic	Karnataka	Unpub.	State Dept	?
Kanganahalli	94-95	early hist	Karnataka	Unpub.	ASI	K. Poonacha
Sannati	94-95	early hist	Karnataka	Unpub.	ASI	K. Poonacha
Banavasi	94-95	early hist	Karnataka	Unpub.	ASI	K. Poonacha
Pipri	94-95	chalco>	M.P.	Unpub.	ASI	S.B. Ota
Utawad	94-95	chalco>	M.P.	Unpub.	ASI	S.B. Ota
Mansar	94-95	historical	Mahrashtra	Unpub.	ASI	A. Nath
Khalkatapatan	94-95	historical	Orissa	Unpub.	ASI	V. Rao
Jhusi	94-95	early hist	U.P.	Pub.	Allh. Uni	various
Wina	94-95	chalco>	U.P.	Pub.	BHU	P. Singh
Musanagar	94-95	chalco>	U.P.	?	State Dept	R. Tewari

The number of excavated sites in this list is 106, and the number of published reports is 12. The actual publication dates of the relevant issues of *IAR* are the following :

IAR volume	*Actual publication date*
1990-91	1995
1991-92	1996
1992-93	1997

1993-94	2000
1994-95	2000

In no way is this situation different from the situations listed earlier. The publication of reports even in a fairly elaborate form with the basic drawings and other illustrations was never a general rule in Indian archaeology after Independence. Even the publication of the brief annual reports of *IAR* has not been regular for ages. In fact, there is no way of knowing what happened in Indian archaeology in the preceding year simply because the summary report for that year will not be published within the next three/four/more years. There is also no way of claiming that the people who control the issue of excavation licenses have ever been least serious about the basic rule they were supposed to observe, i.e., those who have not published their reports should not be granted permissions to excavate, nor should they apply for permission to dig a fresh site till their report on the earlier site is published.

The 'authorities', of course, do not bother about publications themselves. In the Archaeological Survey officers are transferred according to the rules/system of transfer; for instance, having excavated a site in W. Bengal for two years an officer may find himself transferred to Gujarat where he will not be allowed to transport his excavated material and where other responsibilities will be paramount. One does not know what happens in the States where the senior archaeological officers are not frequently transferred. In most of the universities nobody simply cares.

On the whole this reflects a very interesting ground reality. On the one hand the Nation spends a fair amount of money on excavations in different parts of the country. It maintains a fairly elaborate archaeological machinery on the Central and State levels to do archaeological research as one of their major tasks. This machinery is also supplemented by the archaeological sections and even Departments of a number of educational institutions spread throughout the country. On the other hand, there is no public accountability of any kind of all these efforts. The Nation cannot be said to possess much of an interest in the archaeological activities it spends money on. Slowly we have reached a situation when archaeological publicity material in newspapers or summary statements in general publications including 'felicitation volumes' have come to constitute the primary source material of Indian excavated sites.

AN OVERVIEW OF THE STATE OF PUBLICATIONS OF EXCAVATION REPORTS IN INDIAN ARCHAEOLOGY

Perhaps the best way to achieve such an overview is to undertake a State-wise survey, also highlighting the agencies responsible for archaeological work in the concerned State. If one begins this review with Assam and the other north-eastern states including Tripura, one realises that there is not a single definitive archaeological report from that area. Apart from the Archaeological Survey, there are State archaeological agencies in that region including a regular State Department in Assam. In the other States there are government administrative units devoted to cultural affairs, and they look after archaeology as well. In the regional universities archaeology does not have a worth-mentioning role. During his time in the North Eastern Hill University (a 'Central' university) S.N. Rao, a Deccan College Ph.D., excavated a site called Sarutaru, on which no report exists. Archaeological research in the Department of Anthropology of Guwahati University has a tradition of archaeological work since the days of M.C. Goswami and T.C. Sharma, the historic site of Ambari in Guwahati being its most famous excavated site. There is no report — not even a comprehensive catalogue of the sculptures which were excavated there.

In West Bengal it is a mixed situation. In addition to the Archaeological Survey, the State has a large government department and among the regional universities which have done archaeological fieldwork in the region are Calcutta University (Asutosh Museum of Fine Arts, Department of Anthropology, and an independent Department of Archaeology dating from 1960), Visvabharati (Department of Ancient Indian History, Culture and Archaeology since the mid-1970s), Burdwan University (Museum) and North Bengal University (Department of History). The last-mentioned Department has done some explorations in the sub-Himalayan terrain and published articles. The museum of Burdwan University collaborated with the Archaeological Survey to excavate the site of Bharatpur. There is no report. Visvabharati has done regular archaeological fieldwork including excavations at two sites, but there is no report. The Asutosh Museum of Fine Arts of Calcutta University excavated Chandraketugarh for many years but did not publish a proper report. The Department of Anthropology of this university published a report on its Mayurbhanj work many years ago and a volume on its work in Singhbhum in the early 1970s. The Department of Archaeology of this university has excavated four major sites so far but except an incomplete report (no section on pottery) published for the 1961-62 season, there is no definitive publication by this Department. The State Department of Archaeology also has been active in the field since the early 1960s but never thought it proper to publish a definitive report. The situation has recently changed for the better with the introduction of a new government archaeological journal called *Pratnasamiksha* in English and another journal, *Puravritta* in Bengali. The detailed summaries of work done at various sites by S.C. Mukherjee (cf. Mukherji 1992) are a very positive feature. The Survey's work at Birbhanpur was published but in the last 40-odd years the Survey has not produced any definitive report on the archaeology of the region, although it has excavated four major sites here.

The Survey has a 'Circle' and an 'Excavation Branch' in Bhuvaneshwar, Orissa. The only report it has produced on Orissa after the Sisupalgarh report in 1950 is that on Ratnagiri. Excavations have been done by Sambalpur University (Department of History?) but without any proper report. Utkal University's Department of Anthropology has a tradition of pre-historic research but there is no report on the small-scale excavations done by the Department. The State Department of Archaeology of Orissa has never bothered to publish reports.

Except the early reports on Pataliputra, Vaishali and Sonpur, there is no report on the excavations done in Bihar, either by the State Department or the Archaeological Survey. The same is true of Patna University's Department of Ancient Indian History, Culture and Archaeology and K.P. Jayaswal Institute. No other educational/research institute in Bihar has any history of archaeological field-investigation and/or excavation.

The Survey runs a 'Circle' in Lucknow, the State capital of U.P. and has excavated in the post-Independence period a number of sites, mostly in the upper sector or the Doab. Apart from the reports on Hastinapur and Sringaverapura by B.B. Lal, there is no proper report on any of them. For the last 10 years the U.P. State Department of Archaeology has been undertaking important excavations and publishing them as well. Before the publication of detailed reports in *Pragdhara* the U.P. State Department had no tradition of publishing archaeological reports. Banaras Hindu University has a large Department of Ancient Indian History, Culture and Archaeology and the reports it has published so far on its own excavations are those on Rajghat, Prahladpur, Paisra, Chunar Quarry, Narhan, Imlidih and Waina. The first two of them were published by A.K. Narain and his associates, the third and fourth of them by P.C. Pant and Vidula Jayasawal and the last three by P. Singh and his associates. The Department of Ancient Indian History, Culture and Archaeology of Gorakhpur University excavated a number of sites but without any report. It is only recently that Lucknow and Bareilly Universities have begun to organise archaeological field-research. The record of Allahabad University's

Department of Ancient History and Archaeology is bright in the pre-historic field but dismal in the area of historic archaeology. The primary reports are available on the sites in the Sidhi area of Madhya Pradesh and on Chopani Mando, Mahagara and Mahadaha in U.P. but none on Koldihawa, Sarai Nahar Rai and Damdama. Of the many seasons put up in the excavations at Kausambi, the report is available only for the years 1949-50 and 1957-59. The results of their very recent work at Jhusi have been published in *Pragdhara*.

Aligarh Muslim University (Department of History) has published the reports on their excavations at Atranjikhera, Lal Quila and Fatehpur Sikri but sites like Jakhera and Radhan are unpublished. Garhwal University's Department of Ancient Indian History, Culture and Archaeology has excavated a large number of sites in the U.P. hills but not bothered to publish a single report unless B.M. Khanduri's monograph can be considered a report.

Moving further up, Delhi University (Department of History) excavated two sites under Romila Thapar without any report. Later, it excavated a site (under the present author) in West Bengal in 1982 and published the basic report in the same year. Since then there has been no tradition of excavations by this Department. The two other universities in Delhi — Jawaharlal Nehru and Jamia Milia — never developed a tradition of archaeological field-research. The government of the Union Territory of Delhi has an archaeology department and although it has undertaken excavations, the reports have not been published. Among the sites excavated by the Archaeological Survey in the Union Territory of Delhi, a detailed monographic account is available only for Lalkot.

The only Archaeological Survey report on the neighbouring State, Haryana, is the one on Bhagawanpura; its State Department has never bothered to publish a report, and except the report on Mitathal published in *Journal of Haryana Studies*, there is no report by the Kurukshetra University's Department of Ancient Indian History, Culture and Archaeology on any of the many Harappan and other sites excavated by them. The same is true of the M.D. University, Rhotak, although it is a comparatively new university.

One is hard put to recollect if the Survey has any report on a site in Panjab in the post-Independence years; there is none. The State government department has no report, and neither does the Department of Ancient Indian History, Culture and Archaeology of Panjab University (Chandigarh) which has excavated some sites. No other university or institution of Panjab has been interested in archaeology. In Himachal Pradesh too there is no report either by the Survey or the State, and no university there is interested in archaeology.

It may come as a shock but the truth is that except the excavation report on Ahar, all the excavations in Rajasthan in post-Independence years are unpublished. There is no report from the State department or the Survey. The universities there are not interested in archaeology. An institution known as Rajasthan Vidyapeeth in Udaipur collaborates with the Deccan College.

In M.P. the Deccan College has produced reports on Kayatha and Navdatoli and the Survey on Nagda. The State Department under the direction of K.K. Chakravarty published the report on Dangwada and initiated the journal *Puratan* which contains archaeological articles. Jabbalpur University published the report of their work at Kakrehta and among the Sagar University's report publications only the one on Tumain deserves notice. Vikram University, Ujjain has excavated sites but one is not sure if they have independently published any excavation report. In Maharashtra the Survey has published the report on Daimabad and Pauni. The Deccan College and the State Department have published a good number of reports and the same may be said about the work of Nagpur University during the leadership of S.B. Deo. Marathwada University has excavated sites but, as far as one is aware, without any report. Bombay University has not bothered to develop an archaeological research tradition in the post-Independence years. One is not sure if the Gujarat State Department has published any excavation report; the Survey has not published any report after the ones on Rangpur and Lothal. The task of publishing reports in the Gujarat context has long been handled by the Department of Ancient Indian History, Culture and Archaeology of M.S. University, Baroda, although they have not published all their reports. In the context of Gujarat the combined team of Gujarat State and Pennsylvania University has produced the Rojdi and Oriyo Timbo reports.

Most of the sites excavated by Andhra State — and it has excavated a large number of them — lie unpublished. The Survey has published only the volume on prehistory in its prolonged Nagarjunakonda excavations and it has also published a report on Satanikota. The Birla Institute in Hyderabad has come out with reports on Veerapuram and Vaddamanu. Telegu University, Srisailam, has excavated sites but without any report. The universities in Tirupati and Waltair have an interest in archaeology, but the publication of full reports has not been their concern. The Central university in Hyderabad has an archaeologist professor, but one is not aware if any archaeological field-programme has been taken up by that university.

Under T.V. Mahalingam Madras University published reports on Kanchipuram, sites like Alagarai and perhaps even Urayur but more recently, the substantive report it may be said to have produced is by collaborating with Vimala Vegley at Arikamedu. Apart from the early *Ancient India* reports, the major Survey report on a Tamil Nadu site is the one on Kaveripattinam by K.V. Soundara Rajan. The Madras State has never bothered to publish reports. Tamil University, Thanjavur, has invariably published the results of their archaeological work. The only other significant work is the research in Tamil Nadu neolithic by Narasimhaia.

If any university in Karnatak has produced a definitive report on a site, one does not know about it, and the same thing can be said about the State Department's work with the exception of those on Hallur and Hemmige. Deccan College has published a number of reports on the region and the Survey has produced a report on the *stupa* at Sannati by James Howell (1995). One hopes that the State and Case Western Reserve University (Cleveland) will produce a report on their joint excavations at Watgal (cf. Devaraja *et al.*1995). The megalithic excavations in Kerala have occasionally been published but there is no recent tradition of archaeological research in the State government or any of its universities.

Finally, if one goes through the brief reports on explorations in the successive issues of *IAR*, one realises that there is no paucity of both small-scale and large-scale explorations in different parts of the country. The explorations which were undertaken as parts of Ph.D. dissertations have generally been published in detail. Most of the other explorations were conducted on the levels of the Survey and State departments. Virtually all these explorations remain unpublished in detail.

CONCLUDING REMARKS

There has been no break in the sequence of development of Indian archaeology since 1974. The cumulative research product of the period from 1947 to 1974 was not allowed to die out; on the contrary, the data-base — whether adequately published or not — has greatly expanded. Both in the fields of ideas and methods the phase from 1974 to 2000 has witnessed significant changes. Innovative approaches to the study of Stone Age sequences and tools, a much greater reliance on various scientific methods to reconstruct past environments, in-depth analyses of various proto-historical and historical problems and themes, an increasing dissatisfaction with the erstwhile attempts to view India as an area of colonisation and a determined focus on the understanding of the flow of

Indian archaeological history in its own terms, and finally, the realisation that the course of India's economic and cultural development as reflected in the archaeological record is closely intertwined with the land's geography and that this course is uninterrupted — all these developments have taken archaeological research in India considerably away from the tradition with which it began in 1974. There is a clear image of the internal growth of the discipline throughout, and this may be the most positive message which can be derived from our reasonably close study of the development of the subject since 1947 or even from its very beginning till 1947.

We have no reason to compare the current developmental stage of our discipline with any particular stage in the Euro-American development of the subject; even in Euro-America there is no monolithic tradition or even a particularly dominant one. To argue that Indian archaeology has not advanced theoretically since the days of Mortimer Wheeler, as one has occasionally heard argued, is based on both ignorance and malice. Nor has Indian archaeology been isolationalist, as some people in the West have been known to claim. Such claims are based on an innate refusal on the part of some Western archaeologists to accept a different tradition of work on equal footing and the sooner such claims are ignored by the Indians the better. Over the past fifty years or more — even if one omits the earlier period — Indian archaeology has developed a distinct historical tradition of its own, and there is absolutely no reason to feel shamefaced about it.

At the same time, those who can view the land in its totality, focussing on each of its geographical segments phase by phase and evaluating what is known and what is unknown will feel both impatience and despair at the enormity of the tasks ahead. This feeling of impatience and despair gets worse if one can think of the vast number of sites spread throughout the land, of which only a microscopic proportion has been investigated and a still lesser proportion properly published. If one looks beyond the actual ground and considers the very thinly spread character of archaeological education in the country, one does not feel any better. In the light of all this, the increasingly visible use of archaeology in the battles for identity and politics in the country becomes very difficult to understand. However, all these elements of impatience and despair are also parts of the ground reality of Indian archaeology today. They cannot be wished away; and it is toward their analysis that the rest of this volume will be devoted.

3

Archaeological Heritage Management, Education and Nationalism

INTRODUCTION

THE two earlier chapters may have demonstrated that, although the development of archaeological research in India has been continuous since Independence and internally consistent, it has been very thinly spread and characterised by an almost total indifference to the publication of excavated data. In fact, as we have already emphasised, the detailed publication of one's own excavation and exploration results has been considered totally unnecessary in the post-Independence years for archaeological reputation and career advancement, and this is true of each and every organisation responsible for doing archaeology in the country. Newspaper reports, a few paragraphs or more in *IAR* and occasional articles outlining one's 'theories' are all considered sufficient to prove one's archaeological credentials. Those who have an idea of how the actual artefacts are stored in our archaeological organisations and how difficult it is to have access to them will clearly appreciate the fact that, by keeping their data generally unpublished and by making it virtually impossible for anybody else to have access to them, Indian archaeologists themselves have seriously harmed — and are harming — the cause of archaeological studies and thus the general awareness of archaeological heritage and heritage management in the country.

Money has nothing to do with this situation. On the general planning level, the Government of India has always done its duty. If the planning has in places gone wrong or if some policy has turned out to be a failure, the responsibility rests squarely on the shoulders of the archaeologists who were involved in that planning or the formulation of that policy and given the responsibility of carrying them out. Specific examples may be offered to illustrate the situation. In the early 1980s some universities and possibly a few other educational institiutions of the country received a circular from the UGC, asking for proposals related to 'the development of expertise in archaeology and museums' in those universities and institutions. The committee which was constituted to decide on the merits of the submitted proposals and take policy decisions in these matters included an ancient historian (R.S. Sharma) and two archaeologists (G.R. Sharma and B.K. Thapar). It was an excellent opportunity provided by the Nation to give some serious look at the archaeological research situation and identify areas where further investment could be beneficial. One university submitted proposal for an archaeological science section and got no response. Others were clever and asked for general posts, and money for excavations, etc. Some of them, depending on the relationship of their archaeologists with the members of the committee, got both posts and money. If pursued vigorously with a clear focus based on an appraisal of the fields needing investment, this UGC initiative would have led to significant changes in the dimension of archaeological research in the country. As things stood, it failed to make any noticeable impact on the general situation.

The same is possibly true of the considerable financial support given by the Ford Foundation in the second half of the 1980s to three archaeological programmes in the country. The Ford Foundation got expert reports from J.D. Clark and George Rapp (a geo-archaeologist from Minnesota) and decided on that basis and perhaps also on the basis of other recommendations to support a number of programmes in Deccan College, M.S. University, Baroda and Banaras Hindu University. That was when *Man and Environment* received a large amount of money from the Ford Foundation and was shifted to the Deccan College. In any case, archaeological science was considered one of the priority sectors in this context, and the selected institutions were given substantial grants to develop that. If the input of this Ford Foundation money has made a significant difference in the development of archaeological science in these institutions, we are not aware of it.

The history of Indian archaeology since 1947 cannot, thus, be a mere history of archaeological discoveries and research. Attention has to be drawn to the basic ground reality and as far as possible, that reality has to be explained. The issues which cannot remain neglected in this volume are the current state of archaeological heritage preservation, the current status of archaeology as an academic discipline in the educational system of the country and the way archaeology has begun to be affected by religious fundamentalism and conflict between two opposing power-groups in the general arena of Indian historical studies.

PRESERVATION OF ARCHAEOLOGICAL HERITAGE

As the agency responsible for the conservation and preservation of the 'protected' monuments and sites under its care, the Archaeological Survey of India has an old and established conservation set-up, rules and principles in place. The chain of command passes from the Director General to his Director of Conservation and other conservation-related senior officers in the headquarter and from the headquarter to the Superintendent and officers below him in the 'Circles'. The ground staff comprise 'monument attendants' at nearly all sites, 'custodians' and 'foremen' in the major complexes and 'Conservation Assistants' who are stationed in a few 'sub-circles' within 'Circles'. Under the general care of the Circle Superintendents or 'Superintending Archaeologists', 'Conservation Assistants' are the kingpins of the Survey's conservation and preservation programme. The inclusion of a monument or site in the category of 'World Heritage' sites does not mean any change in this administrative structure; it only means a better input of money to look after that particular monument. The principles which guide the actual tasks of conservation undertaken by the Survey put very strong emphasis on the fact that the original character of the monument to be conserved has to be maintained under all circumstances. If its damaged portions need reconstruction, the original material and techniques have to be used as far as practicable, and the reconstructed portion should be clearly highlighted to let visitors know that this particular portion has been reconstructed.

For the unprotected monuments the responsibility lies with the State departments/directorates of archaeology. Here the situation varies from State to State. On the whole, it may not be correct to claim that the States have yet in place an well-oiled conservation machinery like the Survey. Theoretically conservation is a recognised part of the States' responsibility for the monuments in their jurisdiction. The extent to which they try to fulfil this responsibility depends on the resources, the leadership of the Director and the competence and will of the conservation officers appointed for the purpose. No systematic body of data is available on this issue. For instance, throughout its history the Archaeological Survey has regularly published in *Annual Reports* till the 1930s and in *IAR* since 1953-64 separate sections on the 'Circle-wise' conservation works done during the relevant year. Chemical treatment of both structures and antiquities also plays a major role in the Survey scheme, and if one wants to know the types of work which have been done in a particular year, all that is necessary to do is to refer to the issue of *IAR* in question (provided it belongs to a year which is earlier than the last one for which *IAR* is available). This has given the Survey professional expertise in this field on a level which may not be easily matched in many parts of the world. On the other hand, if one goes through the official publications of the States, it is difficult to come away with the feeling that conservation ever loomed large on the State authorities' mind.

The Role of the Indian Universities and Museums in the Preservation of Archaeological Heritage

A crucial role is played by such institutions, although they are not concerned with preservations of monuments which remain essentially the prerogative of the Survey and the State departments/directorates of Archaeology. Some museums, especially the big ones, have laboratories for conservation and preservation of antiquities, but one would not say that their facilities extend far into this area. There is a National Research Laboratory for Conservation in Lucknow which also possesses Indian Institute of Conservation, the latter being headed by O.P. Agrawal, a major figure in this field in modern India. The Birla Archaeological and Cultural Research Institute in Hyderabad has also been seriously interested in chemical conservation and the scientific analytical studies of artefacts.

Museums are of various kinds : purely governmental ones including the chain of museums run by the Museums Branch of the Survey at various important sites; the National Museums in several places including Delhi, Calcutta (Kolkata), Allahabad, Bombay (Mumbai) and Madras (Chennai); the formal University Museums in a handful of universities like Banaras Hindu University and Calcutta University; the museums in the history/ancient Indian history and/or archaeology departments of a few universities; and finally, museums set-up at the private and municipal initiatives. All of them will have a collection and a staff to look after it. Their resources will vary but on the whole it is fair to say that except the museums directly under the government management and the few proper University Museums, the state of the museums in India is not generally good. Very few universities, for instance, have ever taken the issue of setting up museums — not necessarily only archaeology museums — seriously.

The Legal Framework

The basic legal set-up has a long history going back to the late nineteenth century, but the Act under which the 'protected' monuments are presently governed is The Ancient Monuments and Archaeological Sites and Remains Act, 1958 with an accompanying set of rules under The Ancient Monuments and Archaeological Sites and Remains Rules, 1959. The 1958 Act repealed and replaced The Ancient and Historical Monuments and Archaeological Sites and Remains (Declaration of National Importance) Act, 1951 and section 26 of the States Reorganisation Act, 1956. Further, it repealed and replaced The Ancient Monuments Preservation Act,1904.

A brief historical background may be in order at this place (B.K. Thapar 1984). The earliest Acts on record are the Bengal Regulation XIX of 1810 and the Madras Regulation VII of 1817, both of which empowered the governments of these provinces to stop, if they so wished, the despoilation of ancient buildings. The extent to which these regulations were applied is not known. The Act XX which was passed in 1863 gave the viceregal administration the authority to prevent injuries to ancient buildings of historical and architectural value. The Treasure Trove Act of 1878 allowed the Government to claim possession of any unearthed treasure exceeding ten rupees in value. One of the two directives issued in 1886 by the Government as a follow-up action of the Act of 1878 debarred the public officials from disposing of antiquities acquired or received by them unless they had acquired an official approval to do so. The second directive made the excavations of any ancient remains without the prior approval of the Survey illegal. It has been said that James Burgess, the Director General of that period, also wanted, as an amendment of the Treasure Trove Act of 1878, to make the export of antiquities without an official permit illegal but he could not push this idea through.

The Ancient Monuments Preservation Act of 1904 was aimed

> to provide for the preservation of ancient monuments, for the exercise of control over traffic in antiquities and over excavation in certain places and for the protection and acquisition in certain cases of ancient monuments and of objects of archaeological, historical, or artistic interest.

The Devolution Rules of 1921 under the Montague-Chelmsford Reforms of 1919 classified archaeology as a Central subject, which made all the monuments protected under the Ancient Monuments Preservation Act of 1904 come under Central control, leaving the care of non-protected sites and monuments and the administrative control of the staff of various Circles to the charge of the provincial governments who in these matters were supposed to act as the agents of the Central government. The Government of India Act of 1935 put under the Federal List ancient and historical monuments and archaeological sites and remains without any corresponding entry in the Provincial List, which meant that the Central government came in full control. The actual conservation work used to be undertaken by the Public Works Department in all but two 'Circles'. This system came to an end only in 1944 when the task of monument conservation became a total Survey responsibility. The Constitution of India which came into effect on 26 January,

1950 (Seventh Schedule, Article 246) put the historical monuments and records and archaeological sites and remains which are declared to be of national significance under a law passed by the Parliament under the Central jurisdction, whereas those outside the formally approved category of 'national importance' were kept under the State and joint State-Centre (Concurrent) responsibilities. Under The Ancient and Historical Monuments and Archaeological Sites and Remains (Declaration of National Importance) Act of 1951, all monuments preserved under the Act of 1904 were designated as sites and monuments of national importance and included within its scope over 450 monuments and sites of the former princely states. Under section 126 of the States Reorganisation Act of 1956 some more sites and monuments were declared to be of national importance.

The Act of 1958 and the Rules of 1959 were thus the successors of a long legacy and thus the products of much thought in this matter. The full texts of these Acts are not easy to procure, but the Directorate of Archaeology, Archives and Museum, Government of Madhya Pradesh took the wise decision of publishing these Acts along with the Acts modelled on them and passed by the M.P. Legislative Assembly (A. Srivastava 1998). It also printed The Indian Treasure-Trove Act of 1878. According to the provisions of the last-mentioned Act the finder of any treasure, 'hidden in the soil or in anything affixed thereto' and 'exceeding in amount or value ten rupees', had to notify the Collector in writing and either put the treasure in the Government treasury or give the Collector assurance by depositing a security that the treasure would be produced before him whenever it was required to do so. The Collector could, if he so desired, acquire the treasure for the Government by paying the finder 'a sum equal to the value of the materials of such treasure'.

The Act of 1958 has detailed provisions for putting a monument under the protected category and preserving it, sometimes directly and sometimes with the concurrence and support of its present owner(s). If the protected monument is a shrine or a place of worship, it cannot be used 'for any purpose inconsistent with its character', and the government has to take steps to prevent its pollution or desecration. If it so wishes, the government can also relinquish its rights in a protected monument. It is also laid down that 'subject to any rules made under this Act, the public shall have a right of access to any protected monument'. The second major section of the Act deals with the protected areas where no person can 'carry on any mining, quarrying, excavating, blasting or any operation of a like nature'. According to the third section, archaeological excavations in both protected and unprotected areas are not permitted 'except with the previous approval of the Central government and in accordance with such rules or directions, if any, as the

Central government may make or give in this behalf'. The final section deals with the protection of antiquities.

The Rules of 1959 under the Act of 1958 as a number of 'chapters' dealing with various eventualities such as 'access to protected monuments', 'construction and other operations in protected areas', 'excavation in protected areas', 'excavation in unprotected areas', excavated antiquities, moving of antiquities from certain areas, 'mining operation and construction near protected monuments' and 'copying and filming of protected monuments'. For excavations in a protected area, a license has to be granted by the Director General

> if he is satisfied that having regard to the status of the applicant, the competence of the director of excavation operations, the adequacy of the staff to be employed and other relevant factors, the license may be granted to the applicant.

If the application is refused, the Director General will offer 'reasons to be recorded in writing'. There are various rules associated with the holding of a license to excavate in a protected area, and if a person makes an unlawful excavation in a protected area or contravenes any of the conditions of a license, he/she 'shall be punishable with fine which may extend to five thousand rupees'. In the case of excavations in unprotected areas, the Rules say that

> every State government intending to undertake or authorise any person to undertake any archaeological excavation or other like operation in any area which is not a protected area shall intimidate its intentions to the Central Government at least three months prior to the proposed date of the commencement of the excavation or operation

and supply some specified items of information. The Central government will consider the proposal and 'may either approve it or advise the State government to modify it or abandon it altogether'. The Central government may also send one of its own archaeological officers to an excavation under the State government or one of its authorised persons in an inspecting and advisory capacity. Interestingly, Chapter III of the Rules has some provisions regarding the publication of the results of excavation in protected sites and areas. The first of these provisions (Chapter III, 16 (j)) is that 'the licensee shall, within three months of the completion of excavation operations, submit to the Director General a summary report of the results of the excavation'. Chapter III, 21 lays down that the Director General shall not, without the consent of the licensee, publish the results of the excavation unless the licensee has failed to publish the results within the period specified by the Director General in this behalf'. Interestingly, Chapter IV which is about 'excavation in unprotected areas' does not mention the publication of the results of excavation in any way.

The set of Rules 1959 is also accompanied by a number of 'schedules' and 'forms'. For instance, there are forms to apply for license for excavation in a protected area and the issue of such a license by the Director General. The application for license to excavate in a protected area, if the form is an indication, is to be made on behalf of the Institution which makes the application, and the form should bear the signature of the head of the Institution which, in the case of an university, will mean the Registrar. The Director General personally signs the license which, interestingly, names the Director of excavations, tying apparently both the institution and the employee directing the excavations on behalf of the institution together.

The Antiquities and Art Treasures Act, 1972 (Act No. 52 of 1972) governs the Government of India's policy regarding antiquity trade. This was meant

> to regulate the export trade in antiquities and art treasures, to provide for the prevention of smuggling of, and fradulent dealings in, antiquities, to provide for the compulsory acquisition of antiquities and art treasures for preservation in public places and to provide for certain other matters connected therewith or incidental or ancillary thereto.

The term 'antiquity' has been defined in detail; basically this meant anything 'which has been in existence for not less than one hundred years'. In the case of 'any manuscript, record or other document' of 'scientific, historical or aesthetic value' the period has been brought down to 75 years. This Act prohibited any unauthorised person 'to export any antiquity or art treasure'. Further,

> no person shall, himself or by any other person on his behalf, carry on the business of selling or offering to sell any antiquity except under and in accordance with the terms and conditions of a license.

The proper procedure of applying for, and the issue of, such a license is clearly laid down, including the appointment of licensing officers. License is for a specified period but can be renewed or revoked. 'Registration of antiquities' means registration of only those antiquities which have been specified in the Official Gazette and its provisions are aimed to take care of the following factors:

> or are likely to, contribute to the safeguarding of the cultural heritage of India

(i) the necessity for conserving the objects of art;

(ii) the need to preserve such objects within India for the better appreciation of the cultural heritage of India;

(iii) such other factors as will, — Section 14

The procedures for applying for registration and grant of the certificate of registration by 'Registering Officers' are all laid down. The antiquities 'owned, controlled or managed by the government' were given exemption from registration.

This Act gives power to Central government 'to compulsorily acquire antiquities and art treasures' and lays down the procedure of giving payment compensation for such compulsorily acquired objects. This Act also gives authorised government officers the power of entry, search, seizure, etc. In this connection such authorised officers are empowered to

(i) enter and search any place;

(ii) seize any antiquity or art treasure in respect of which he suspects that any provision of this Act has been, is being, or is about to be, contravened and thereafter take all measures necessary for securing the production of the antiquity or art treasure so seized in a court and for its safe custody, pending such production.

— Section 23

The power to determine if an object is antiquity/art-treasure or not rests wholly with the Director General of the Archaeological Survey or an officer not below the rank of a Director in the Survey and authorised for this purpose by the Director General.

The Antiquities and Art Treasure Rules were framed by the government on 31 August 1973. These 'Rules' essentially deal with the sanction of licenses to deal in antiquities. However, Rule 11 specifies that

> every application for a certificate of registration . . . shall be made in Form VII to the registering officer having jurisdiction on the area in which the applicant resides. Further, every such application shall be accompanied by four copies of photographs in post-card or large size in sharp focus, of each antiquity in the applicant's possession, and if so required by the registering officer, by an equal number of photographs of different sides, or facts of such antiquity.

It is important to note that these Acts and Rules did not bar the various State governments from passing their own Acts and framing their own Rules on the Central model. For instance, the Madhya Pradesh Legislative Assembly passed 'The Madhya Pradesh Ancient Monuments and Archaeological Sites and Remains Act, 1964' with an amendment in 1970. In fact, the amended Act is called 'The Madhya Pradesh Ancient Monuments and Archaeological Sites and Remains (Amendment) Act 1970'. Similarly, there was a set of rules under 'The Madhya Pradesh Ancient Monuments and Archaeological Sites and Remains Rules, 1975' (for Madhya Pradesh, A. Srivastava 1998). One is not sure if the other States too had passed Acts and framed Rules in this regard. It may be assumed that many of them now possess their own sets of Acts and Rules.

The preceding sections were aimed to argue that India has a long-established and well-knit structure and a comprehensive legal framework to deal with the problem of the conservation and preservation of archaeological and other cultural heritage. The legal framework may have developed inadequacies with the changing times, and it may be useful to point them out at this stage. B.K. Thapar (1984) outlined these inadequacies, and considering that as the Director General of the Survey he was closely familiar with them, we prefer to cite him at length on this point :

> The concept of an isolated historic building now belongs to the past. Today a historic building is regarded as a part of its setting — an ensemble; even vernacular architecture is regarded as forming part of the architectural heritage. The present Act is silent on these matters, with the result that secular or vernacular architecture in historic towns is fast disappearing under the pressure of modernization. Because of pressure on land in big cities, high-rise buildings are constructed in close proximity to protected monuments, thus changing both the historic character and setting. Civic legislation is therefore an urgent necessity to safeguard this aspect of the architectural heritage and to integrate modern architecture so as to comply with aesthetic and historical requirements.
>
> Likewise, there is no provision in the existing Act to control the location of industrial units in close proximity to protected monuments and to shield them from atmospheric and environmental pollution. The location of the oil refinery at Mathura is a case in point, despite the remedial measures taken by the Government to reduce atmospheric pollution in and around Agra.
>
> As regards portable cultural property, the provisions of the Antiquities and Art Treasures Act 1972 seem to be all-embracing and should yield fruitful results. The smuggling of antiquities out of India through clandestine means, however, still continues, probably because of demand in the illicit international market. This illicit traffic could perhaps be reduced, if not completely stopped, by the establishment of an agency authorised by the

> Government to export antiquities. The present Act already contains a provision to this effect, but the agency has not yet been set up. Foreign buyers would always prefer an open transaction through an official agency to an illicit deal. The class or grade of antiquities intended for the export market could be monitored by a Committee of Experts, constituted for the purpose by the Government. — B.K. Thapar 1984 : 71

What Thapar does not point out is that the Act has no provisions to deal with the destruction of monuments and sites which are not under the protection of the Survey or the concerned State government. Similarly, it lays stress on prohibiting archaeological excavations but is silent about the spoilation of sites by digging for earth or for any other purpose. It is also doubtful if the international market will remain satisfied with the quality or the grade of the antiquities formally exported through a governmental agency, as Thapar suggests that the setting up of a similar agency with its own body of formally appointed experts will stop the illicit trade in antiquities.

The INTACH and Other Heritage Agencies

It is not easy to have detailed information about such non-governmental agencies. The Indian National Trust for Art and Cultural Heriage (INTACH), established in 1984, is the most prominent of them. Initially at least it received strong political patronage, and possibly it does so even now, having the economically and politically powerful people of different areas associated with its various chapters which are now spread throughout India. Its source of funding is not clear to the present author, but one assumes that, in addition to the governmental or Public Sector subsidies and grants, it enjoys a strong support among the concerned grant-giving international agencies. It has people of various backgrounds on its boards and receives active participation from architects. It is not possibly a rigidly centralised institution, which means that in some areas it is likely to enjoy the services of motivated, high quality professionals. The *INTACH* consultants prepare 'heritage plans' for different areas; the implementation of these plans is not possible without the governmental support. Their focus of interest is not only archaeological — in fact, their role on the archaeological side has perhaps been minimal. The main thrust is towards the demarcation of areas which need conservation because of their historical and architectural characters. An interesting case study can be had in Nalini M. Thakur's article 'Archaeological Park at Mehrauli, Delhi' (1999).

It apparently grew out of a larger study of the 'Integrated Conservation of Mehrauli Heritage Zone', a document commissioned by the Delhi Development Authority (DDA) and prepared by Thakur herself on behalf of the Delhi Chapter of the INTACH. The physical boundaries of the Park have the Qutb complex, Mehrauli settlement and Chhatarpur at its northern, western and eastern boundaries respectively.

> Contents of the Park include many structures of historical importance and mounds that represent the walls of the deserted capitals Lalkot and Rai Pithora. It also includes Thomas Meltcalf's nineteenth century Dilkhusha grounds and landscape garden, the Chaumukha Darwaza of Lal Kot and the Jamali Kamali mosque (sixteenth century). This area incorporates remnant historic orchards as well as contemporary landscaping, and picnic and play areas that are heavily used by local residents.
>
> — Thakur 1999 : 187

Apparently, the concept of a heritage park like this with its focus on the historical aspects cuts through various segments of time in a given area and

> is a giant step from the current system of heritage management, which is still very outdated (quaintly Victorian), and depends upon a very selective scope of the heritage. The Park emerges as a concept that can be duplicated in many situations all over India, provided that the technical and management procedures are worked out from fundamental principles. This will go a long way towards working out a way of heritage management in a country which still clings to colonial legislation. — Thakur 1999: 188

One of the major supports of this concept was the development of a suitable data-base where the information recorded fell into the four categories of legal, architectural, artistic and historical, condition and threats, and infrastructure. The entire data-base can be used as a tool for heritage management.

To be a success such a heritage park concept in an overpopulated Indian metropolis will obviously call for a tremendous amount of input from, and collaboration among, a large number of concerned government agencies, including the Archaeological Survey of India. Even if it fails, it will lead to the creation of a heritage awareness among these agencies, which in itself may be a very positive thing. It is unlikely that the various government agencies will fully wake up to the needs of creating heritage parks in the midst of all other pressures on its time, resource and commitment, but no useful purpose is served by contrasting the 'energy and direction' of Thakur's Western experts with the 'indifference and discouragement' seen by her in India. (Thakur 1999: 194, fn. 5) The main thing is to take the message across to the people living in the area and not to allow it to be reduced to a show meant exclusively for the elite.

Apart from the INTACH there are other 'heritage or conservation societies' in some places like Calcutta, Bombay, Ahmedabad, etc. In all these places motivated young architects are actively involved. This certainly is a good development.

In recent years the Indian Archaeological Society also has stepped into the area of conservation, and among the tasks it has already completed is a 'Report on Agra monuments and Mathura Refinery — a regional environmental plan for controlling pollution' (Dikshit 1997). The project was taken up at the behest of the Indian Oil Corporation and submitted nine specific recommendations to reduce the impact of atmospheric pollution on the Taj Mahal and other monuments of Agra. This trend also augurs well for the future.

Funding

The funding of the Survey and the State-level departments and other organisations comes from different items of the governmental budget expenditure. In whichever way one views it, the funding of Indian heritage management can eventually be related to the government-sanctioned budgeted expenditure. Even with the induction of the INTACH and similar other smaller bodies the situation does not seem to have changed much, although in the case of the INTACH some input of foreign money seems to be an accepted feature.

One is not sure if the establishment of the National Culture Fund (NCF) as a non-profit Trust by the Ministry of Culture in 1996 has brought about any significant change in the pattern of government funding. It is supposed to draw contributions from the corporate bodies of the country and its initial corpus of Rs. 25 crore is to be augmented by a recurring annual contribution of Rs. 10 crore and the income from tourist facilities. It is supposed 'to preserve and promote heritage, in partnership with community and corporate, and undertake donor-specific projects which provide visibility and accountability'.

Along with the NCF one must consider the institution of the Indian Oil Fund (IOF) created by Indian Oil as a non-profit Trust which will be exclusively funded by Indian Oil and in a close collaborational relationship with the Archaeological Survey of India and NCF. The IOF will adopt at least one heritage site in every State and Union Territory and the archaeological works will be funded by the IOF through the NCF to the Survey. One is not quite sure if the NCF is at present merely a conduit to receive money from the IOF for the Survey. The IOF is further supposed to take up beautification and upkeep of the sites and develop world-class tourist facilities at the each of the sites on land allotted or assigned by Archaeological Survey of India.

Again, theoretically this is an important development, but one has to note that there is no element of community or corporate initiative here except that money should come on a recurrent basis from the Corporate sector.

This is also the place to record that the Government of India's recent decision to make the non-Indian visitors to some of the more visible and famous monuments of the country, particularly those in, or in the vicinity of, big towns and cities, in terms of the rupee equivalents of USA dollars carries with it an undesirable implication which has not been carefully looked into. Many persons of Indian origin hold non-Indian passports and are thus, 'non-Indians'. Among the visitors to Indian monuments there are many 'non-Indians' of this kind. And yet, unless one asks for people's passports, there is no way of distinguishing such 'non-Indians' from 'Indians'. Thus, virtually all non-Indians of this type can get away by paying the normal 'Indian' fees, and eventually, the only people who end up paying fees in terms of the USA dollars are those with the tell-tale white colour of the skin. The Government of India certainly did not want this to happen. A reasonable across-the-board increase in entry fees to the 'protected' monuments is both justified and desirable but not any discriminating increase of this type.

Those who have been familiar with Indian monuments over a long time will appreciate the fact that money may not be the most important factor in maintaining the good quality of their conservation and preservation. Proper attitude and a better enforcement of the discipline among the people kept at the government expense to maintain them are more important than the money which is already available. World Heritage Sites should not have financial problems of any kind, but how does one explain the dirt in their compounds and the absence of the normal guidebooks in their 'ticket counters' ?

THE GROUND REALITIES OF INDIAN ARCHAEOLOGICAL HERITAGE PRESERVATION

Without trying to denigrate in any way the elaborate structure of agencies, funding and legal framework of Indian archaeological heritage preservation and the hard work of many motivated people in this connection, it remains our duty to point out that the ground realities contrast in many cases strongly with the official image. In many such cases, however, the ground officers concerned are not responsible. In some cases, of course, the responsibility rests directly with them.

Most of the protected sites have their quotas of watchmen, but whether those watchmen can be found at the sites or not will depend on the general vigil maintained by the people senior to them. One has come across many cases of protected sites where even the fences are missing and jungle, among other things, has been allowed to take over both the monument and its compound. Removal of bricks by the locals or the use of the structures and the compound as a general meeting place of the unsavoury elements among the local populace is increasingly becoming more common than many archaeological officers will be willing to admit. In the less accessible areas the standard and extent of the conservation work undertaken at various monuments leave much to be desired. To some extent this has to be related to the Circle's annual budget for conservation, but this is also rooted in the absence of a carefully rotating annual conservation programme. Notwithstanding these well-known drawbacks, I would maintain that the Survey has been generally successful in looking after the monuments in its care.

The Survey officers cannot be blamed for situations which are beyond their control. The situation outlined below in the context of the temples of Bhuvaneshwar in Orissa may highlight the limitations of the powers of the Survey. This is quoted from Reuben Banerjee's article entitled 'temples of doom' in *India Today*, dated 31 January 2000. The state of affairs expressed by the following extract is more or less true of the heritage preservation reality all over India.

> Take the Eshno temple, overshadowed by the . . . Lingaraj temple. Standing alone in a bare field . . . the temple serves as a garbage dump for the local municipal hospital adjacent to it. Most of its carvings have disappeared, stray dogs fight over blood-stained bandages strewn around. . . . On the road leading to the Lingaraj temple is another structure known as the 'Traffic Mahadev'. Having been rebuilt and replastered haphazardly, the 400-year-old temple now stands uncomplainingly as a road divider. . .
>
> The ASI has taken over 27 city's temples while another 15 are under the State Archaeology Department. The ones officially protected, however, fare no better than the ones left to their fate. Ananta Basudev, a 13th century temple . . . is a case in point. Its status as a protected shrine has not deterred sevayets cooking bhog (prasad) inside the temple. . . . Similar fate has befallen many others. . . .
>
> The 9th century Taleswar temple in Kedar Gowri Chowk . . . bears the ignominy of a neighbourhood club's signboard. Another serves as a wood supplier's stockyard, while the 900-year-old Baba Mangaleswara temple houses a garage. An encroacher built a house around the Param Guru temple. . . . An influential local minister hosted his daughter's reception inside the 13th century Rameswar temple despite the monument's protected status. . . . During the past decade no less than 500 FIRs were filed with various Police

> stations against trespassers. Not once have the Police acted upon these FIRs, encouraging more blatant violations of conservation rules.

All that the local Survey officers can do in the case of encroachments in their monument compounds is to seek legal redress. They cannot also do much in the case of political pressures on allowing a protected monument to be re-used as a centre of worship and prevent its gradual taking over by an unscrupulous and politically powerful section of the worshippers. The Survey officers cannot do much to prevent the disfigurement of monuments by the increasing levels of pollution in the Indian metropolises. One does not even remember when one last saw the famous *Diwan-e-Khas* of Delhi's Red Fort in a reasonably unpolluted condition. Of course, they could prevent fume-spewing buses from being parked near the famous *Gangavatarana* relief at Mahabalipuram or take steps to ensure that the area of the only complete and free-standing Asokan pillar at Lauriya Nandangarh remained free of water-logging. On the whole, they do not have control over the general conditions affecting monuments in the country.

Similarly, they do not have control over the fast pace of destruction of unprotected archaeological sites and monuments throughout the country, which is essentially a matter of population pressure and apathetic attitude of the people in general to them. In many cases, the people at the top do not even bother. As long as their general power structure is intact they are happy. One may offer numerous examples but the one recorded at the door-step of Delhi and mentioned in print by R.C. Sharma, a former Director General of the National Museum, Delhi, is a convenient example to cite.

Sharma writes about a large mound in Mathura :

> When the present writer took over as Curator of the Mathura Museum, the site looked very imposing, potential and intact. It was lying in an area, more than a kilometre in length and about three-fourth of a kilometre in breadth. Repeated efforts were made to persuade the authorities of the Archaeological Survey of India to declare the entire land as protected area and to start excavations at the earliest. Meanwhile the Govindnagar Housing Society got its project of house building approved and the devastation picked up a terrific speed. Three hundred labourers were engaged for levelling the spot rapidly.
>
> — Sharma 1984 : 92-93

The cases where the destruction of well-known archaeological sites has been ignored by the Survey are many.

The Survey has also been completely uninterested in building up a national register of sites and antiquities. India does not have any organised archaeological data-base. The Survey has recently begun to bring out small volumes on the protected monuments and sites of their 'Circles'. To a great extent this is unnecessary because a little search in the libraries would produce these data on the protected sites which in any case are reasonably well-known. Secondly, this does not serve the purpose of a national data-base. If one considers the Survey's indifference to the destruction of even well-known archaeological sites and the building up of a national archaeological data-base along with the fact that the need to publish excavation results in full has long been completely irrelevant in the general scheme of Indian archaeology, one has to admit that something is very seriously wrong in the pursuit of archaeology as a research profession in post-1947 India. It is with considerable sadness that I write this and wrote the following in 1999 :

> So, what does the elaborate organisational and legal machinery lead to ? Again, I write on the basis of a long personal familiarity with the ground realities in this context : the whole system has long been exercised both crudely and mindlessly without much consideration for the progress of archaeological research in the country. The rules are directed only towards the retention of bureaucratic and authoritarian control over all kinds of archaeological research in India. In view of the rapidly increasing population and the consequent pressure on land, it is not easy to keep archaeological sites and monuments out of danger and eventual destruction, and the archaeology officialdom in India does not have the necessary energy and commitment. The easiest thing to opt for, in such a situation, is to ensure that archaeological research is impossible without its approval and thus retain its grip over archaeologists beyond its chosen circle. It does not care if a huge chunk of mound is dug up by a Housing Society in broad daylight, but does care if a professional archaeologist from a university or elsewhere attempts a rescue operation. . . . After all, that becomes an issue of retaining 'power'.
>
> Purely from the point of view of a wider dissemination of archaeological research in India — from the point of view of making this research far more broad-based than it is today — I would say that the bureaucratic constraints on carrying out archaeological field-investigations in India are far too many and centralised, leading to the very negation of the spirit and purpose of such constraints. Besides, it is a very inefficient bureaucracy which drags its feet over coming to a decision. One would rather see sites vandalised and destroyed than allow research students and professionals to carry out research on them. One does not understand why statutory bodies such as Indian universities and State directorates of archaeology cannot, independently or collaboratively, organize field-research merely by formally informing the relevant authorities in Delhi and keeping them aware of the findings. One would think that in view of the enormity of research problems and the scale of destruction of archaeological sites in the country, what one

> needs is a free-moving and joyous academic spirit concentrating on work alone without having to run the gauntlet of a fairly elaborate and over-zealous bureaucracy, which has been built up to deal with this issue over the years. I would certainly give the Central body its power to stop any ongoing work if it fails to live up to the requisite standard, but first, people should be given a chance to work. As far as international collaborations go, there must be an efficient and quick system to deal with the related issues, with the needs of archaeological research in the country in mind. — Chakrabarti 1999: 20-21

Finally, I would draw attention to a comparatively new but rapidly increasing trend in the work of structural conservation done by the Archaeological Survey of India. In the name of conservation some officers have begun to undertake large-scale reconstruction work without clearly showing the difference between the ancient surface and the modern reconstructed surface. I know a site which revealed traces of an ancient road alignment. What the conservator of the site has done is to reconstruct the entire road-system of that site, without taking the trouble to demarcate between the section or sections of the original road surface which he found and the sections which he reconstructed. In Bagh where ancient caves have been remorselessly given a thoroughly new look, the only surviving panel of ancient painting has been removed from the wall and placed in the local office of the Survey without leaving any sign at the site that a painted panel has been removed from a marked area. Examples can be multiplied, but the point is that the days when we could take pride in the professional standard of the conservation work done by the Archaeological Survey of India seem to be over.

The Big Dams and Impact on Archaeology

The issue is to understand how Indian archaeologists have coped with 'rescue archaeology' in the areas submerged or likely to be submerged by the various dams which have been constructed, or are being constructed, in various parts of India. The first major example of archaeology of this type is the excavation project at Nagarjunakonda in Andhra. The area involved was 23 sq km, and the dam was constructed about 10 km downstream of Nagarjunakonda. The decision to build the dam was taken in 1952 and the archaeological project was initiated in 1954. Intensive survey and excavations were conducted for about 6 years and a large number of sites including many Stone Age ones were documented in this area. The excavations were focussed mainly on the Ikshvaku capital of Nagarjunakonda with its magnificent assemblage of city-planning, temples, *stupas*, monasteries, bathing *ghats*, canals, etc. It was decided that there would be a reconstruction of some of the original features of the site on the top of the

Nagarjunakonda hill which would not be submerged by the lake created by the dam and feature as an island. A subsidiary area chosen for the purpose was Anapu on the eastern bank of the reservoir. Among other things, nine large and prominent monuments were rebuilt in their original form and alignment. In 1960 the Government decided to create a dam on the Krishna, affecting about 100 villages on the river bank in the Kurnool and Mehbubnagar districts of Andhra. The project had its focus at Srisailam. On the basis of the survey work between 1962 and 1972 the Survey drew up a comprehensive salvage plan which involved the transplantation of about 20 major temples, the most famous of which is perhaps the Papanasi group of temples. The work of dismantling and transporting this group of temples began in 1980 and its major part was completed towards the end of 1986 (for a general survey, Batra 1996 : 30-40). It must forthwith be stated that the salvage works of this kind are a stupendous achievement for all the archaeologists and conservation experts involved.

However, this field achievement should not blind us to two glaring limitations. First, these works are not suitably published. For more than 40 years the report on the historic period archaeology of Nagarjunakonda has been lying unpublished. The report on the survey of the Kangsavati valley, for instance, has not been published in detail for about the same period. The Srisailam project has not fared any better. Those who are familiar with the water shortage in Gujarat are unlikely to join the Human Rights activists about the Narmada river project, but the area to be submerged needs massive surveys and excavations. Some of it has been undertaken by the Archaeological Survey (Ota 1992), but this is something for which various agencies including the non-governmental ones should have been inducted. If the Survey made any attempt in this direction, that was not publicised enough. Secondly, virtually no attention has yet been paid to the concept of 'rescue archaeology' in the country, which has long been an established feature of archaeology elsewhere. If a certain percentage of the estimated cost of a big civil project involving earth removal could be mandatorily reserved for archaeological research in the affected area before hand, that would have infused a fair amount of money in 'rescue archaeology' and made the rapid execution and publication of very focussed archaeological jobs a reality in the country. It is time field — archaeology began to be run on somewhat commercial lines in India instead of depending on government financing for ever. This would also give rise to the commercially run laboratories for archaeological science. Free dating is no longer possible elsewhere; there is no reason why Indian archaeologists should get their dates free and not have a specific heading for obtaining scientific analytical and dating work in their excavation budget.

The Looting of Antiquities

The restitution of cultural property and trade in illegally acquired archaeological objects are both seriously discussed in modern archaeological literature. Only the governments of nation states can take formal positions on the first issue, and as far as I know, there is no Government of India policy document in this matter. There is no reason to believe that the bureaucrats of Shastri Bhavan, National Museum and the Archaeological Survey have given any thought to the matter. The issue also remains undebated among the Indian art and archaeology circles. The second issue, i.e., illegal traffic in antiquities which in the Indian context generally means art objects, has been taken more seriously by our authorities. As we have pointed out in the section on the legal framework, a regulatory mechanism with a set of well-defined rules in the background has long been in place, and if one knows correctly, there is a special section of the Indian Central Bureau of Investigation to deal specifically with this problem. I shall later try to examine the extent to which the Government of India's policy in this regard has been successful, but it would be relevant to look into its international dimension first.

A secure current baseline of approaching the issue globally is *Culture without Context,* a half-yearly newsletter of the Illegal Antiquities Research Centre of the McDonald Institute for Archaeological Research at Cambridge. It documents and discusses the relevant global material, besides drawing attention to many publications, resolutions and conferences within its frame of reference. Between 22 and 25 October 1999, it also held, jointly with J. Paul Getty Museum of Los Angeles, an international conference on *Illicit Antiquities : The Destruction of the World's Archaeological Heritage.*

The scale and endemicness of this destruction, which the papers read in this conference brought out, are, in fact, quite shocking. Not many parts of the world — not even the well-looked-after Mediterranean lands — are apparently immune. Many Classical objects on display in the Western world — Cycladic figures or Apeulian vases — do not have any context. In the less developed parts of the world, it is plain looting and destruction of archaeological sites, aided in all cases by population pressure, inadequate laws, and greed for easy money both on the part of ordinary people unaware of the need for preserving heritage and corrupt officials. Occasionally it can be something more than that. For instance, in 1993 the looters used rocket-launchers and handgrenades to attack the Angkor Conservation Compound in Cambodia. Antiquities are also looted to finance civil unrest, as in Mexico and Somalia. In China the local authorities are known to have helped the looters. Listening to these papers made one realise the truth of the following observation :

> The most single source of destruction of the archaeological heritage today is through looting : the illicit, unrecorded and unpublished excavation to provide antiquities for commercial profit. This constitutes an unmitigated and continuing catastrophe for the world's archaeological heritage. — Renfrew 1999: 6

The Indian situation was summed up in the Cambridge conference by a paper sent by Ajai Shankar (2001), the then Director General of the Archaeological Survey of India, although he himself could not attend the conference. His paper — *Threat to cultural sites in India from illegal excavations etc. : case study — problems and solutions* — began by giving three examples of the looting of archaeological sites by illegal excavations. He mentioned the theft of the Gupta period carved bricks and inscribed *Ramayana* panels from Katingra in Etah (U.P.) and the illegal excavations conducted by villagers to acquire antiquities of the early historic period at the centrally protected sites of Bilsar (Etah, U.P.) and Chandraketugarh (Twenty-four Parganahs,West Bengal). In the second section of his paper he outlined the salient features of the Antiquities and Art Treasures Act of 1972, as an indication of the Government of India's concern to stop illegal traffic in antiquities. He also said that it was a matter of global concern and that the relevant international bodies such as the UNESCO should be more involved in laying down the specific preventive and regulatory measures. The third and final part of his paper dealt with the successful cases of retrieval of Indian antiquities from abroad, both as a result of victory in court cases and bilateral negotiations. Ten specific cases were cited : Sivapuram Nataraja (restitution to India under an agreement in the wake of prolonged litigation in U.K. and USA), Tamluk *Yakshi* (out-of-court settlement), Tiruvilakkudi Nataraja (out-of-court settlement), Nalanda stucco (out-of-court settlement), Amin pillars (victory in court ?), Pathur Nataraja (victory in court), Bodh-Gaya Buddha (out-of-court settlement), and *Krishnajanma* sculpture of the Dhubela museum, Chhatarpur, M.P. (out-of-court settlement).

As an ordinary Indian academic, miles away from any corridor of power, I would not put the entire blame of looting India's antiquities at the door of the unlicensed/licensed antiquity dealers and the general public unmindful of the country's heritage. I would put the blame partly at the door of India's policy-makers too. It is well-known that antiquities have acquired their market-value because of the demands of the international market, but it is unlikely that the bottom will ever drop out of this market and that the looting of antiquities will some day cease to be commercially viable. We should accept this unfortunate fact of life that the international market of antiquities will continue to operate, and the sooner we make our own laws more transparent, more realistic and more enforceable, the better. We have to assume that there will always be people interested more in money than in their national heritage, and our aim should be to stamp out the element of profit as much as possible. Crying aloud in international conferences will not protect one's national heritage.

In south Asia as a whole, the scale of the looting of antiquities is still not on the scale in which it is pursued in some other parts of the world. It is only in the Northwestern Frontier Province of Pakistan that there may be gun-toting gentlemen to drive away inquisitive archaeologists, but let us remember that even there it was possible for the government to recover a Kushana period gold necklace weighing 27 kg. In the rest of the subcontinent I can think of only two cases where armed robbers looted government museums. One of these cases was in India when the museum of Bodh-Gaya was looted, and in the second case, the government museum of Mainamati in Bangladesh was robbed of its old bronzes.

The desirable south Asian things in the international market comprise mostly objects of art in various forms. There is no noticeable market for normal archaeological objects such as pottery, lithic or metal tools, etc. I know of no case where the artefacts of the Indus civilization and the Neolithic-chalcolithic cultures have been deliberately looted and smuggled out.

The hub of the regulatory framework in India is, as we have already seen, The Antiquities and Art Treasures Act of 1972, with various ordinances and notifications associated with it. This act is fairly Draconian. It is Draconian in the sense that it virtually makes the possession of an antiquity by a god-fearing Indian a criminal offence. The onus of registering everything with the government and that too in triplicate, with three copies of photographs and within a very short time-frame lies entirely with the individual. In a country with limited literacy the effectiveness of such a piece of legislation can easily be imagined.

A detailed analysis of this Act is out of place here. All that I would say is that people should be given some chance to feel clean in the eyes of the law. It is the illiterate and poor peasants ploughing their land, who make most of the antiquity finds in India. One does not expect them to forego labour and spend money on a trip to the nearest large city to hand over, without any remuneration, what he has found to a government officer. I cannot think of a single reason why he should not hand it over to a wandering agent of the area's antiquity dealers and earn a little money. I may draw on my memory to describe how the system operates — or used to operate — at the grass-roots level. A *panawala* of Allahabad told me that he had a small sum invested as 'advance' among ordinary people in the countryside. If those people had found anything while ploughing their land, they would take that, in their next trip to town, to my *panawala*. A small sum would change hands, and perhaps an umbrella or a school text would be bought. If the government makes at least a gesture of paying for such antiquities, and if the concerned archaeological officers make regular trips to the village level, most of the people would be willing to hand over antiquities to the government, rather than to the agents of commercial dealers. The source of antiquity supply to the dealers would at least begin to partly dry out.

In his paper the Director General of the Survey refers to the illegal diggings at certain sites. One of these sites has long been known to me. This site, Chandraketugarh, is about an hour's bus-journey from north Calcutta and one of the richest early historical city sites of the country. It has been known since early twentieth century; desultory excavations without any detailed report took place in the mid-fifties and sixties. Meanwhile, breathtakingly lovely terracottas and ivories have been discovered by villagers ploughing their lands here for the last forty years. If the Director Generals for the last forty years or even the local officers had bothered about this site, it would have been properly investigated and the Director General would have found it unnecessary to mention it in an international conference on the looting of antiquities. One cannot let such sites remain shoddily investigated and feel distressed about their looting at the same time. With a better awareness of the monetary value of antiquities in the countryside, the cases of fradulent excavations will no doubt increase in future, and a liberal policy in allowing 'rescue-archaeology' by non-governmental organisations will be necessary to stop this menace in the bud. However, the concept of 'rescue-archaeology' by private organisations is unknown and still unacceptable in India.

The Indian villagers with their simple religiosity consider any old stone image a deity and thus worthy of protection and care. It is a different proposition altogether with the elite. The elite of south Asia are not known for their concern with the country's heritage. Archaeology hardly figures in the scheme of Indian historical education. Here I recollect the case of the Department of History of Delhi University which, for many years, kept its collection of more than 300 Mogul, Rajasthani and Pahari miniature paintings in steel cupboards in a room where the summer temperature frequently exceeded 50° Celsius. The problem is not of money but that of attitude. There has been no lack of Czars and Czarinas in post-Independence India in the realm of culture. What has been largely missing is educated commitment and professionalism. The Delhi University situation which we have cited is, in a sense, reflective of this University's attitude to the needs of heritage preservation. For instance, in response to a letter to M. Raza, the Vice-chancellor, the Registrar of the university (Letter No. SPA/R-40, dated 24 March 1988) communicated an official decision to the effect that the Head of the Department of History was in 'overall control of the museum and archaeology unit of the Department of History' and that he could 'assign this function to any teacher or any member of the staff at his discretion'. Thus, according to a Delhi University official communiqué, the task of archaeological research and museum care could be assigned to any teaching or non-teaching member of the Department at the discretion of the Head of the Department of History. Examples like this are fairly common in the Indian university set-up but serve the purpose of our argument that the Indian elite are not really bothered by the issue of heritage preservation, even within the precinct of a university department.

Eventually we would do much better if we could involve *Panchayat* and District Board level leadership in keeping an eye on the antiquities and monuments of their respective areas. The example of Madhya Pradesh which has set-up district level archaeology committees may be worth emulating in this regard. The system of historical education in the country should change too and inculcate some curiosity in the history of the land that we see around us. Thirdly, it should be possible for any Indian to build a collection of his/her own and *publish* it without incurring anybody's wrath. There should also be a far more liberal policy of export for the general run of antiquities, but for outstanding pieces there should be exemplary vigilance. Vandalising monuments and objects of art should be speedily detected and punishable. For instance, the people responsible for putting a coat of gold on the third century BC 'Bodhi throne' at Bodha-Gaya and on the Kushana period *parinirvana* Buddha at Kusinara must be brought to book. Finally, there must be a governmental system of monitoring the international market in our antiquities.

As a footnote to this discussion it may be pointed out that in the past few years the Government of India seems to have introduced a little more liberal excavation policy for the non-governmental organisations. To begin with, it has allowed the Indian Archaeological Society to collaborate with a university in Venice on the excavations of the famous early historic city site of Kampil (Dikshit 1999-2000). Further, *bodhisattva* Nagarjuna Smarak Sanstha Va Anusandhan Kendra of Nagpur was allowed to organise excavations at Sirpur in modern Chhattisgarh (Joshi and Sharma 1999-2000a) and at Mansar near Nagpur in modern Maharashtra (Joshi and Sharma 1999-2000b). Both these are Buddhist sites and the desire of a Buddhist organisation to arrange for excavations of such sites is understandable. Although these two sites and Kampil were technically excavated by non-governmental agencies, their actual excavators — K.N. Dikshit, J.P. Joshi and A.K. Sharma — are all retired Archaeological Survey of India officers, and one suspects that this development has been possible because of their personal influence. Still, it is the sign of a good development, and one hopes that many non-governmental organisations will be interested in doing excavations.

Archaeological Heritage and Identity

Whatever may be said about the archaeological heritage and national identity elsewhere, it is difficult to assert that archaeology has ever played a major role in the formation of Indian national identity. One really should not attach any particular significance to the fact that the Mauryan lion-capital of the third century BC is one of the most important Indian national emblems. This shows that the modern Republic of India aspires to emulate the ideal behind the lion-capital of the Mauryan monarch Ashoka, but this does not mean that the archaeological image of ancient India plays a role in the formation of the Indian national identity. Most of the educated Indians do not have any idea of what archaeology is about and how this can be the base of a concept of the past which can be shared by all categories of Indians. The strongest evidence of this hypothesis lies in the marginal role archaeology has in the scheme of Indian education. As I have argued elsewhere (Chakrabarti 2000, see 'appendix' of this book), the most important ingredient of Indian identity has been based on the Colonial Indological mix of race, language and culture. This mix is both illogical and undesirable, but archaeology has still a long way to go before it can supplant this frame. The younger section of the current Indian elite does not have much to do with the vernacular literary tradition of the country; one has to go to the classrooms of Indian universities to realise that there are two distinct classes of Indian students — one that was bred in the homespun 'native' literature and the other which has been educated essentially in English and will find it difficult even to read the famous literary authors of their own regions. It is the latter class which is powerful in modern India, and archaeology plays a role in the consciousness of this class only to the extent that it is fashionable these days to talk about things like heritage and conservation. The Indians who participate in panel discussions on such issues as 'fundamentalism and heritage' in India International Centre in Delhi and mouth pious platitudes (R. Thapar 2001) are most unlikely to be people who have supported the cause of archaeological research and education in the institutions they serve or have served. As far as the issue of identity is concerned, for the vast mass of 'native' Indians it is still the tradition derived from the epics, the stories of the religious books and teachers of diverse kinds.

As David Lowenthal (1996) wrote, 'populism notwithstanding, heritage normally goes with privilege : elites usually own it, control access to it, and ordain its public image'. According to him, 'British heritage above all seems an elite domain'. Or,

> Elite apologists are not confined to Britain. Noble names festoon Europa Nostra, the Continental historic buildings lobby. The American Heritage Foundation is a bastion of reaction, and America's built legacy still largely a WASP preserve. Most historic houses the world over focus on eminent lives untainted by manual toil.
>
> — Lowenthal 1996 : 93

To appreciate the validity of Lowenthal's sentiments, an Indian has only to recollect the names of various people associated with the INTACH Chapters ! The problem is that the Indian elite are a very neo-colonial elite. Ancient India is not relevant to them as long as it is not served with some kind of Euro-American academic association or a strong dose of Euro-American sociology/anthropology. Ancient India is a marginal subject in the institutions where they go to study; their historians study essentially the history of British India on the basis of the sources written in English. The number of people who specialise in the history of pre-British India are decreasing at an alarming speed in the country. The study of ancient India played a role, perhaps an important role, during the nationalist period of Indian historical research. In modern India this has declined into being an almost irrelevant subject. Much of the malaise of Indian archaeology — the dichotomy between the framework and the ground reality, to which we have repeatedly drawn attention in this volume — springs from this fact. The Survey, the State departments/directorates of archaeology, the few university departments of ancient Indian history, culture and archaeology — all these cannot really be viewed outside the general web of Indian education and its priorities and values.

ARCHAEOLOGY IN INDIAN EDUCATION

Between 28 February and 1 March 1992, the Indian Council of Historical Research organised a workshop on 'Archaeology, Education and Training'. The proceedings were not published, and the papers themselves could not offer any in-depth analysis. An exception in this regard was the paper on 'archaeology in school education' by Arjun Dev of National Council of Educational Research and Training (NCERT). According to Dev there is a common structure of school education all over India : 10 years of general education followed by 2 years of more specialised study. The syllabus guidelines in different subjects are provided at the national level. In practice, the individual States can bring about modifications according to the perceptions and decisions of their own educational committees. According to Dev 'elements directly or indirectly related to archaeology education are integrated into school curriculum at different stages of school education'. At the primary (grades 1 to 5) level the national guidelines for 'Social Studies' suggest introducing a sense of chronology for human cultural development. At the upper primary (grades 6 to 8) and secondary (grades 9-10) levels History is taught as a separate Social Science subject.

> Various elements connected with archaeology are integrated into the history curriculum at these stages. The general framework of history courses comprises the study of Indian history from prehistoric times at the upper primary stage and the history of civilization from prehistoric times at the secondary stage. One of the objectives of teaching history specified at the upper primary stage is to develop an awareness of the necessity of and participation in the work of preservation of historical remains. The guidelines also recommend that a part of the school time allotted to the teaching of History should be devoted to practical activities and project work . . . including the study of local monuments and participation in the work of their observation and preparing museum kits.
>
> — Dev 1992

At the Higher Secondary (grades 11-12) level archaeology has been claimed to form a significant component of the course dealing with the history of ancient India which is one of the four courses prescribed at this stage for students who opt for History as an elective subject at this stage.

Theoretically there is nothing wrong with this nationally approved framework of History education, in the formulation of which persons like Dev have played a leading role. However, the situation will vary from State to State, and no State-wise study of this framework seems to be available. One understands that in States like West Bengal it is difficult for persons with an M.A. degree in Ancient Indian History and Culture (let alone Archaeology) to get teaching jobs in schools. One would think that in some States the study of ancient India including an archaeological knowledge of that period is not much encouraged. Secondly, the Indian school education cannot be viewed separately from the multitude of 'teachers' training programmes' run by various universities. If historical informations based on archaeology are not a part of such programmes, it is unlikely that in the school-level teaching of History, such informations will play any visible role. Thirdly, the students' participation in local history, monuments, etc., for their 'project works' depends to a great extent on the resources of the schools. An inordinately high percentage of Indian schools outside the major cities does not have any resource to spend on 'Social Science' subjects like History. Among other things, the school libraries will not have the type of books which are required to generate an interest in the subject in the young minds.

In his paper Dev emphasises how archaeology-based information constitutes an important part of the textbooks commissioned and published by the NCERT. He is right, but only up to a point. To begin with, the authors selected to write such books which have very large sales possibilities are 'political authors' in the sense that they are selected mainly because of their political connections with the ruling or powerful political group. This means that they have distinct political agendas as the authors of these school textbooks. I am familiar with the books produced on ancient India by the NCERT. They no doubt contain some archaeological informations, but as the authors do not have anything to do with archaeology, their selection of this information leaves much to be desired in many cases. The educational purpose would have been much better served if the NCERT had left the production of textbooks to the enterprise of individual authors and publishers. The students and teachers should have been given a choice in the selection of their books on History. This, of course, would not have served any political agenda, nor would it have offered any opportunity to the political authors to cry out in the name of secularism/communalism every time their books were criticised.

The situation gets widely diluted on the level of B.A. course (Pass/Honours) in History. Very few universities offer any kind of archaeological information at this level, even as a part of their 'ancient India' component. Even where some archaeological topics are included in the general course structure of 'ancient India', as they are in Delhi University, normally the teaching of these topics is avoided by the concerned teachers, most of whom find archaeology of little relevance to the understanding of ancient India. Also, 'ancient India' is something the students finish in the first year of their three-year degree course and has little long-term impact on the students' minds. Some universities which seem so far restricted generally to U.P. offer a full subject of Ancient Indian History, Culture and Archaeology at the B.A. level. Any subject can be introduced at the B.A. level but the point is that, unless it is accepted at a large number of undergraduate colleges, this will not have any impact, nor will it have any quality base. The important thing about the U.P. universities is that many undergraduate colleges affiliated to these universities offer a study of Ancient Indian History, Culture and Archaeology. Calcutta University, for instance, has Ancient Indian History and Culture at the B.A. level but only at one affiliated college ! Visvabharati (Santiniketan) runs a separate Department offering this undergraduate programme, but this institution does not have any affiliated college. It must be clearly understood that in the Indian context a subject is never a part of the mainstream education unless it is taught widely in undergraduate colleges. Except in the State of U.P. Ancient India is not a part of Indian mainstream education, not even of the mainstream historical education.

At the M.A. level the situation is equally diverse. Some universities run separate Departments of Ancient Indian History and Culture, combined in some cases with Archaeology. Most of the universities offer 'ancient India' as an optional group/paper in the general subject stream of History. Very few universities still retain an independent Department of Archaeology. Further, in the Indian context a subject cannot be considered mainstream unless the multitude of colleges and schools in the country has needs of teachers in the subject. Considering that there is no need for 'ancient India teachers' in India outside U.P., ancient India (let alone Archaeology) is not a 'hot option' in most of the States.

Some comments on the general structure of historical education in India may not be inappropriate at this place. It has its major emphasis on the history of British India with a background of European history. Full papers in European history are taught throughout the vast multitude of Indian educational institutions on the basis of ill-digested information derived from books of abysmally low quality. It is also expected that the students will know all about British India. It is never expected, of course, that the students will have a rational understanding of what the study of the Indian past is about. At the turn of the twentieth century Tagore wrote that the type of history that was taught in India brought about a separation of the people from the country. Even after about a hundred years nothing about the basic character of Indian historical education has changed.

As long as this situation persists we do not expect Archaeology to develop as an academic subject in India. The Indian past is still an 'excluded past'. In their comments on 'why is there an 'excluded past' in education' Peter Stone and R.S. Mackenzie (1990: 3-4) isolates four reasons.

> First, school curricula are already overcrowded, and educational decision-makers argue that time cannot be allowed to a 'new' subject when the survival of many long-established subjects is now threatened by the increasing domination within curricula of job-related education and training. . . . Second, teachers have allowed important aspects of the past to be excluded through their own ignorance. The little of the 'excluded past' that is included

> in syllabuses is taught only with great difficulty. . . . Third, the study of the 'excluded past' is often seen as an indulgent luxury that has no direct bearing on today's society. . . . Finally, aspects of the past may be excluded for overtly political or ideological reasons.

All these factors are true in the Indian context where one has to consider, in addition, the essentially neocolonial character of the Indian elite, especially the Indian historians.

NATIONALISM

It is not easy to define relationship between archaeology and nationalism in India. This is an area of study which will need detailed investigations in future. Only some general points can be made here. First, in the pre-Independence period archaeology did not play a conscious role in the archaeological investigations undertaken by Indians in the country. The pursuit of archaeological research and the task of heritage preservation was limited to the Survey. It was the Government of India which was responsible for whatever was done in the field of archaeology. It is possible that the nationalist image of the 'glories of ancient India' derived some support from the excavations of ancient cities like Sravasti, Rajagriha, Pataliputra, Taxila, etc., and Buddhist *stupas* and monasteries. These places were important in the textual records of Buddhism, and the image of Buddhist India was perhaps heightened in the Indian national consciousness by these excavations. Tagore, for instance, wrote evocative poems in the setting of Buddhist India. There are two well-known cases where Indians contributed to the cost of excavations. The House of the Tatas contributed to the early excavations at Pataliputra and Sarat Chandra Ray of the House of Dighapatiya in Bengal financed or partly financed the first excavations of the Paharpur *stupa* and monastery in Bengal under D.R. Bhandarkar of Calcutta University. This trend did not take off. The conscious Indian interest in the archaeological ruins of the countryside does not seem to be common in the nineteenth century or even in the early part of the twentieth century. As far as Bengal is concerned, the literary monthlies like *Bharatavarsha* and *Prabasi* used to publish a substantial number of articles on the Indian antiquities, especially those in Bengal, in the 1930s and later. In English *Modern Review* was the place where such articles used to get published. I am not aware of the extent to which the earlier journals like *Manasi*, *Marmabani*, etc., published articles incorporating field-investigations of archaeological ruins and structures. The literary monthlies in other regional languages remain to be researched from this point of view.

It was the literary genre built around ancient India and the later phases of Indian history which served as the main focus of Indian national consciousness in pre-Independence India. There was a whole series of Bengali translations of ancient Sanskrit texts, including not merely the *Rigveda* and such other texts but also literary works, in Bengal in the nineteenth century. The translation of the *Mahabharata* in Bengali by Kali Prasanna Sinha still remains as one of the pivots of Bengali literature and many Bengalis still have their first introduction to the works of such authors as Bhavabhuti and Kalidasa through excellent nineteenth-century Bengali translations. Many of these translators were not professional scholars; they were essentially *Bhadralokas* — the Bengali gentry — of the time. Historical novels had their roles too. Ramesh Chandra Datta wrote a couple of famous novels set in the contexts of Rajasthan and Maharashtra — *Rajput Jiban Sandhya* and *Maharashtra Jiban Prabhat*. Bankim Chandra Chattopadhyay set Bengali hearts aflame by authoring a number of highly evocative historical novels including *Durgesanandini* and *Anandamath*. Hara Prasad Sastri wrote *Bener Meye*, perhaps the most authentic of such novels from the historical point of view. Rakhal Das Bandopadhyay who is better known as an archaeologist wrote a series of historical novels set mostly in the context of the Gupta and Pala periods. His most famous piece perhaps is *Pashaner Katha* which happens to be the history of ancient India as seen by a block of stone in the body of the *stupa* of Bharhut (for a perceptive analysis of the beginning of consciousness of ancient Indian past in Bengal, Nag 1996).

What is important is that by the late nineteenth and early twentieth centuries there was in Bengali literature a conscious image of ancient and beautiful India spread in all her geographical splendour from Jamrud and Khyber in the north-west to Cape Comorin or Kanya Kumari in the south. The travel literature of this period, written in many cases in chaste sonorous Bengali and drawing unconsciously on the imageries of the classical Sanskrit literature, introduced its readers to the geographical beauties of the land — the sombre and pure dazzling whiteness of the high Himalayan peaks, the long meandering courses of the Ganga, Kaveri, Sindhu, Godavari, Yamuna and Brahmaputra through their vast and green plains, the beauty of their water and that of the waves breaking on the myriads of beaches along the long coast-line, the silence of virginal and deep forests, and the ruins of innumerable historical places strewn around the country. One of the best examples of this literary genre is *Bharat Bhraman*, a heavy and well-illustrated volume written and published by Dharani Kanta Lahiri Choudhury, a rich landholder of Kalipur, Mymensingh (Lahiri Choudhury1317 Bengali Samvat/ 1910). This 800-page volume contains an account of the author's visit to about 102 major places scattered throughout the subcontinent, and what is important from the present point of view is that in each case he gives proof of his familiarity with the basic archaeological information then available about them.

The relationship between the study of ancient India and the growth of Indian nationalism is well acknowledged and obvious in many directions, but archaeology was not closely related to it. In fact, as far as Indian nationalism is concerned, I would say that one of its most serious limitations lay in the fact that it did not lead to determined quests in different parts of the country to relate history to the ground. The relationship between archaeology and nationalism in post-Independence India is perhaps more overt. The rapidity with which the outline of pre-historic and proto-historic India was formulated after Independence is a clear pointer in this direction. In a sense, an inexplicable concern to find the archaeological roots of Indian tradition, as we have seen in many archaeological writings after 1947, is a reflection of this nationalism too. Still, it is the textual image of ancient India which constitutes the most important historical cornerstone of Indian nationalism. One of the most important manifestations of this concern is the recent trend to understand the scientific perceptions embedded in the *Rigveda* (cf. Kak 2000) and other texts. The various unedifying debates about the Aryan theory are manifestations of this concern too. A fair percentage of such debates is perhaps completely unnecessary, but the fact that such debates are taking place is a good sign. It shows that some Indians at least are no longer happy with the frame of understanding they were given by Colonial Indologists. The Indian concern with the Rigvedic river Sarasvati, which seems to have reached almost an uncontrollable concern now among certain quarters may appear to be completely unnecessary to many of us archaeologists, but the concern is understandable in view of the fact that this river is the holiest river of Hinduism and had witnessed the genesis of the Indus civilization on its banks.

What is not understandable, of course, is episodes like the recent (23 February 2001) UGC circular to universities offering full-fledged university departments for the study of Hindu rituals or what it calls *karmakanda* or *paurohitya*. Hindu rituals are controlled by the *Dharmashastra* texts, for whose study there are Sanskrit 'Departments' in virtually all undergraduate and post-graduate colleges and universities in the country. Further, it is difficult to find any reason for the study of only Hindu rituals in publicly funded educational bodies which should put emphasis, if necessary, on the study of the rituals of all Indian religions and beliefs. The fact that the Indian UGC has issued such a circular only regarding the Hindu rituals may justifiably be interpreted as a sign of religious bigotry on the part of the people who were a party to this decision. The way the circular offered a justification for this UGC proposal strengthens the justification of such an interpretation.

> Our ancient Indian culture believes in *Jnan* (knowledge), *Karma* (action) and *Upasana* (worship). The ancient Indian texts related to these three are rooted in the Vedas. Every true human being believes in the practice of his *Dharma* (duty) which enables him to live a happy and moral life. In order to achieve a moral life and fulfilment of goals of life, knowledge, action and worship are true means. . . . 'Karmkanda' covers the whole life of an individual. Starting the courses in Karmkand in universities will produce a trained group of young scholars with proficiency in rituals and other cognate subjects and they in turn will meet the requirement of a large segment of the society desirous of knowing and practising the path of action (Karma) coupled with Jnana (Knowledge) and Bhakti (worship).

Interestingly, what this UGC circular sent to the Vice-Chancellors of different Indian universities does not make clear if the non-brahmanas too would be admitted to the proposed university Departments of *paurohitya*, because in Hinduism only the brahmanas are supposed to be priests or *purohits* !

Among the signs of modern self-confident Indian nationalism in archaeology one may consider emphasis on various issues which were ignored earlier : the formation of an Indian identity on the basis of the archaeological story of human adaptation to the land, the understanding of the land both in terms of geography and the archaeological continuities, the need to relate Indian history to the land, the detailed nuances of the land and its ecological history to understand the archaeological patterns, the preoccupation with the analytical details of the archaeological data, etc. A lot remains to be achieved and pursued in this direction, and one of the grievously detrimental features of modern archaeological research in India is that it does not have any core of strategic leadership.

Whatever leadership emerged in this field after 1947 and effectively continued up to the early 1970s has currently deteriorated into coteries of purely self-seeking, and mostly old, individuals.

The overall impact of nationalism on Indian archaeology has been very limited in the past, and it is limited even now. The topic would need a lot of further research. What has been offered here is only a possible outline of the issues involved.

CONCLUDING REMARKS

In this chapter we tried to go beyond the general history of archaeology in post-Independence India and underline the different components of this structure. There are no doubt many positive features, but one of the most important points that we would like to make is that archaeology has failed to grow as an academic subject in India.

Officially this is an approved part of the Indian educational scene, but in practice it has not made any country-wide impact. This problem is intimately linked to the mind-set of a large section of the Indian elite who are still happy to see their endeavours in the Humanities and Social Sciences as a minor footnote to the Euro-American tradition in these fields. The history of British India on the basis of the sources written in English still dominates the field of Indian historical education because this is relatively easy to do and this is what is mostly studied in the framework of Indian Studies in Euro-America anyway. There is some truth in my assertion that the Indian elite are unlikely to find archaeology significant and attractive for the study of ancient India until archaeology becomes a significant component of the Euro-American establishment of Indian Studies. The second major point is that the present notion of the Indian past is dominated by an essentially literary image — the image based on the Vedas, epics and myriads of other religious or semi-religious texts. The sort of evidence of the past that only modern archaeological research can provide does not play any role in it. Again, this is a product of Colonial Indology.

The dichotomy that we have noticed between the official framework and the ground reality of the archaeological practice in India is rooted in the failure of the subject to grow up as an academic discipline in the country.

4

Religious Fundamentalism, Archaeology and the Problem of the Preservation of Archaeological Heritage in Modern India

INTRODUCTION

THIS problem has assumed a direct visibility since December, 1992 when the sixteenth-century mosque built in the U.P. town of Ayodhya during the reign of the Mogul king Babur at a place which, according to the belief of the Hindu devotees, marks the birth-place of Rama, a Hindu god and the hero of the Hindu epic *Ramayana*, was pulled down by an irate Hindu mob. The demolition was the culmination of a prolonged period of agitation to build a Hindu temple at the place after removing and re-erecting the mosque at another place acceptable to the Muslim community. The agitation came to receive support from the Bharatiya Janata Party (BJP), one of the largest political parties of modern India. The demolition of the mosque understandably led to Hindu-Muslim riots all over the country, and in retaliation Hindu temples were destroyed in the neighbouring Muslim-majority countries of Pakistan and Bangladesh.

This incident had impact in other directions too. First, this apparently helped the BJP to be elected to power at the centre. Secondly, this led to a serious concern with the possibility of the secular values of modern India being at risk. Even some of the international academic archaeological literature expressed this concern in some form, although the tone of much of this literature was patronising and arrogant. Thirdly, the position of the various Indian participants in the World Archaeological Congress (WAC) in December, 1994 in Delhi *vis-à-vis* the incident of mosque demolition in Ayodhya led to serious disputes among them, which led to both unpleasant incidents and chaos at the conference, negating the international image of Indian archaeology in turn. Fourthly, there are some grounds to claim that Indian archaeological thought has begun to be affected by issues which are not strictly archaeological or academic.

The ramifications of all these developments cannot be ignored in a book devoted to the history of Indian archaeology since Independence, and the purpose of the present chapter is to highlight the tangled web of issues behind them. We begin with the recent case of the destruction of the Bamiyan Buddhas in Afghanistan because this has shown in very clear terms the danger posed by fundamentalism in the preservation of archaeological heritage in this part of the world. We try to show the chain of historical situations which led to this development and point out the basic complexity involved. We do the same for the Ayodhya incident of 1992 and the turn of events in the WAC in Delhi in 1994. Thirdly, we point out the essential ideological argument of the so-called 'Hindu fundamentalist lobby' in Indian archaeology and the position taken by its political opponents. Finally, we highlight some of the hitherto ignored dimensions of heritage preservation in the country.

Fundamentalism is not an exclusive feature of any particular religious group. The Ayodhya incident has made the issue visible in India, but what is generally forgotten that the subcontinent was divided in 1947 in the name of religion, with a rich history of communal strife and tension both before and after that. I find it impossible to believe that the preservation of archaeological monuments remained completely immune to such a cataclysmic event as the Partition. We simply have not researched the evidence. Further, the 'living monuments', i.e., the religious monuments in active worship, were allowed to remain in the hands of the worshipping communities even when such monuments came under the general protection of the Archaeological Survey of India, and in all such cases the relationship between the dictates of conservation by the Survey and the intransigence of the religious committees of the place was a delicate one. Drawing on one's memory one further discovers that the Survey has long been under pressure of various kinds to allow Friday prayers, etc., in 'dead' monuments under its care. I clearly recall a protected terracotta temple in West Bengal which had no priest living in it when I saw it but has now passed into the care of a priest. Many years ago I learnt from the late H.B. Sarkar, a very senior officer of the Survey, that a well-known public school in Delhi had an unprotected Mogul monument in its compound destroyed to construct a new building.

The issue of this chapter is not to engage in pious disputations about the merits and demerits of fundamentalism but to judge the extent to which fundamentalism poses danger to the monuments and other forms of heritage or if it only provides a convenient façade for political expediency of all kinds.

THE CASE OF THE BAMIYAN BUDDHAS

Afghanistan lies at the junction of west, central and south Asia, and this simple geographical fact has been well reflected in its archaeological record. Archaeological research here has more or less been in abeyance since the late 1970s when the Soviet troops moved in.

The unsettled political conditions apparently encouraged clandestine diggings, and it seems that the ancient Bactrian region, centred in the Oxus valley which lies to the north of the Hindukush range, has been a good source of trade in illicit antiquities. In fact, the looted Bactrian graves, or rather, their antiquities surfacing in the western market, have been the major factor behind the postulate of an Oxus Civilization from the second half of the third millennium BC to about the middle of the second millennium BC. The richness of Bactria in the historical period may be inferred from a discovery made in 1978 by a Russian-Afghan expedition to a site called Tillya Tepe. More than 20000 gold ornaments dating from 100 BC to AD 100 were excavated from six burials and shown to an international conference on the Kushana dynasty in 1978 and to the Diplomatic Corps in Kabul in 1991. The collection, reputedly placed in 1991 in a vault of the National Bank inside the Presidential palace in Kabul, is, as far as I know, unpublished.

Antiquity-wise, the archaeology of the historical period in Afghanistan, which may be said to begin in the sixth century BC with the Achaemenid occupation of the region, is incredibly rich. From the early centuries AD to about seventh-century AD Afghanistan was a major hub of the Buddhist world, and the Buddhist religious complexes with their assortment of religious architecture, sculptures and paintings dot the country, particularly along the trade routes joining the main Silk Route from China to Rome from India. One such site is Bamiyan, located in the Bamiyan valley of the Hindukush at an elevation of about 2600 m. The archaeological site has many Buddhist caves cut into the hill-sides. Some of them contain fresco paintings linking them with the contemporary painted caves of Sinkiang and India. However, Bamiyan is principally known for its two extraordinarily large Buddha images hewn out of the live rock and finished with plaster. These sculptures are earlier than *c.* AD 400 when Fa-Hian, a Chinese pilgrim to India, saw them. They are about 53 m and 35 m high. These two 'Bamiyan Buddhas' which overlook one of the trade routes passing through the Hindukush, the central mountain range of Afghanistan, stand as the most impressive fixed points in the history of the spread of Buddhism from India to China.

The archaeology of Afghanistan at the peak of the trade along the Silk Route and its southern feeders is best exemplified by the antiquities from the site of Begram near Kabul. The Begram collection, discovered in 1939 and dating from the first two centuries AD, consisted of 1800 lacquers, bronzes, ivories, statuettes and glassware items which show trade links with Italy, Greece, India, China, Egypt and central Asia, the Indian craftmanship being particularly noticeable in the ivories. The Begram ivories are a legend in the history of ancient south Asian art.

My purpose here is not to offer a resume of Afghanistan archaeology but to draw attention to two things which have happened to it. First, the national museum in Kabul which was inaugurated in 1924 and the most important repository of the excavated material from Afghanistan, has been systematically looted. To put this looting in its proper perspective we have to consider some recent events of Afghan political history. The Soviet troops were in Kabul in 1979 to protect the pro-Communist government of the Democratic Republic of Afghanistan. In late 1988 or early 1989 these troops went back to Russia, after fighting a losing war against the Afghan rebel groups or the Mujahideen who were liberally supported by Pakistan and the USA. The Islamic State of Afghanistan was established in April 1992, but there was no love lost among the rival factions of the Mujahideen. Kabul witnessed considerable fighting, and in the ensuing chaos the museum was looted, perhaps on several occasions. In an article ('museum under siege') in *Archaeology* in 1996 Nancy Dupree (1996), a well-known American scholar on Afghanistan, offered a list of the important looted material. This amounts to about 70 per cent of the museum's material comprising most of its vast gold and silver coin collections, stone statuaries and ivories and also the famous Islamic metalwork of the Ghaznavid dynasty. Dupree's analysis clearly suggests that 'the museum was not plundered by rampaging gangs of illiterate Mujahideen'.

> The looters in 1993 were discriminating in what they took and apparently had both the time and the knowledge to select the most attractive, saleable pieces. For example, they removed from wooden display mounts only the central figures (depicting voluptuous ladies standing in doorways) of the delicate Begram ivory carvings. It is also telling that although some 2000 books and journals remain in the library, volumes with illustrations of the museum's best pieces are missing. — Dupree 1996 : 46

In another place she roundly accuses the organised antiquity trade in the neighbouring state of Pakistan :

> You have to remember that the items that have been stolen from the Museum or have

> been plundered, are not owned by only one person and usually not only by Afghans. It is usually one or two Afghans with five or six Pakistani partners. And the underground stolen art business in Pakistan is just as well organised and it is just as dangerous as the drug business. In fact, I have heard some people say that as far as the end-result is concerned, it's even more profitable than drugs. — Dupree 2000

The loss of the Begram ivories caused considerable excitement, and people have tried to trace their possible movements and price in the international art market. Emily Hayes, a former archaeology student at Girton, who spent a year teaching English in Japan, told me that she saw three Begram ivory pieces in in the Miho Museum in Shiga prefecture (near Kyoto).

The second incident is more recent and has been widely reported in the newspapers in the first week of March 2001. According to an Agency report dated Kabul, March 4, anti-aircraft weapons were used by the soldiers of the Taleban, the then ruling power of Afghanistan, to try to bring down the Bamiyan Buddhas. It was a part of the general Taleban offensive against the pre-Islamic idolatrous heritage of Afghanistan and rockets, tanks and explosives are said to have been used to get rid of the statues in other parts of the country too. According to another newspaper report, the Taleban chief Mulla Mohammad Omar urged the Muslim world to support the destruction of ancient Buddhist icons and unite behind his vision of Islam. In a report published in the British newspaper *Guardian* of 17 November 2000, one gets an idea of the background of this development. I quote from the Guardian report :

> Part of the problem is the Taliban's hostile attitude towards Afghanistan's non-Islamic heritage. As a movement, it does not accept the portrayal of any living form, whether human or animal. Two years ago (i.e., in 1998) the Taliban seized from a rival faction the remote Bamiyan valley. . . . A Taliban commander then blew up the head of the smaller Buddha with explosives, and fired rockets at the groin and dress of the larger Buddha. The attack damaged frescos that had withstood an assault from Gengis Khan. The commander later returned to dump two burning tyres on the larger Buddha's lip. Hardline elements within the Taliban are equally opposed to Kabul museum showing Buddhist sculptures.

What that Taleban commander began in 1998 was accomplished in March 2001. The decree ordering the destruction of all statues in Afghanistan including ancient pre-Islamic figures, which was issued by Mulla Mohammad Omar on 26 February, 2001, was, in fact, based on the verdict of the clergymen and the decision of the Supreme Court of the Islamic Emirate. According to an Agency report of February 27, Omar said the following:

> The breaking of statues is an Islamic order and I have given this decision in the light of a fatwa of the ulema (clerics) and the supreme court of Afghanistan. Islamic law is the only law acceptable to me.

However, if Nancy Dupree (1996) is to be believed, the recent decree and its execution came in the wake of a prolonged looting of antiquities by the Mujaheedin.

> While I have seen a few museum pieces for sale in Afghanistan, there are a number of artifacts on the market that have recently been dug up in Afghanistan. Mujaheedin commanders in all parts of the country are involved in this illicit activity, most notably in the east near the Hadda museum. An important Buddhist pilgrimage site in the second through seventh centuries, Hadda has been totally stripped of its exquisite clay sculptures in the Gandhara style, which combines Bactrian, Greco-Roman, and Indian elements. Looted artifacts from Faryab and Balkh provinces in the north allegedly include jewel-encrusted golden crowns and statues, orbs (locally described as 'soccer balls') studded with emeralds and all manner of exotic ephemera, as well as fluted marble columns similar to those found at Ai Khanoum in the northeastern province of Takhar. These are being carted away to embellish the houses of the newly powerful, according to witnesses.

When and how the acquisitive and commercial instinct gave way to a destructive frenzy mixed with religion is not clear. A number of points may be considered here. First, the Taleban Islamic movement of Afghanistan developed in the background of a long-drawn unsettled condition in the country when millions of people died amidst a general scene of devastation and heart-rending deprivation. Why should an average Afghan nurtured in this kind of scenario have a special concern for heritage, and that too of the pre-Islamic variety ? The second point has been raised by Nancy Dupree, and I give her great credit for that, because this is something I have raised too in the context of India.

In an interview dated 26 February 2000 she (Dupree 2000) said that very often it was not the fault of the community.

> They just don't know. It is the fault of the education system that was in place before the war. The system was heavily secularised. They had history and geography. But nobody ever taught children about the glories of Afghanistan's monuments and handicrafts. It was not part of the curriculum. So now there are very few people who even remember what the Kabul Museum, for instance, stood for. There are two generations of Afghan children who have been raised in refugee camps in Pakistan and Iran. They do not know what their country is all about.

Third, the mass-scale looting of artifacts both from museums and sites would not have happened if there was not an organised and well-connected international art market willing to pay for them. The uninhibited expression of this commercial greed seems to have played a role in the Taleban decision. The following sentence has been put in the mouth of the Taleban chief : 'I would like to ask you, do you prefer to be called statue-destroyers or statue-sellers'. Obviously, he preferred to be a statue-destroyer.

Fourth, this Taleban decision has also been explained as an act of defiance against the sanctions imposed by the U.N. Security Council Resolution No. 1333 on 19 January 2001. Although said to be Taleban-specific, according to an Agency report,

> the sanctions couldn't have been more inopportune: Afghanistan is reeling under a harsh winter and the worst drought of the last 30 years, aggravating the problems of a population which has had no respite from the bloody civil war. This was further compounded by supreme Taliban leader Mulla Mohammad Omar banning poppy cultivation, the mainstay of Afghanistan's war-shattered economy and its farmers.

The fundamentalism which has so seriously affected Afghanistan's archaeological heritage is, thus, the product of a specific and tragic historical situation, with the Taleban clerics providing its general farade. Whatever the background or the general façade, the destruction of monuments has suddenly become an aim of unstable human elements.

THE AYODHYA INCIDENT

The second major example of religious fundamentalism affecting archaeological heritage in south Asia is the demolition of a mosque built in the sixteenth century at Ayodhya in north India in December 1992. The mosque was built at the order of Babur, the first Mogul king of India, at a spot which has traditionally been identified as the place where Rama of Indian mythology and the epic *Ramayana* was born. The Hindus consider Rama as an incarnation of Vishnu, one of their supreme gods. Further, the Indian literary tradition is consistent in associating Rama with Ayodhya. There is nothing that will prove that Rama was a historical figure. But this lack of historicity does not rob him of tremendous veneration by the Hindus, especially at the village level in northern India. The epic *Ramayana*, of which he is the hero, developed over an uncertain segment of time, and the consensus is that the text, as we know it now, emerged between the second century BC and the early centuries AD. By the early centuries AD the Rama cult was in place. Rama's hold over the Hindu masses can be guessed from the fact that the Indian roads used to look deserted at the hours when the various episodes of the epic were serialised and put on the air by the Indian T.V.

If Rama is important, so is his capital Ayodhya as an archaeological site. This site which stands on the left bank of the Ghaghra, a tributary of the Ganga/Ganges is a massive site protected by a high and broad mud rampart. Excavations at the site have been desultory, but the sequence goes back to the Northern Black Polished Ware phase of the archaeology of northern India, the beginning of which may now be put in the seventh or eighth century BC. It was one of the two capitals of an early and large political unit called Kosala, and had major pan-Indian significance as a trading place. Today it is a minor administrative centre but very important as a place of pilgrimage, mostly for the Hindus but for the Jains and perhaps the Buddhists as well.

The dispute between the Hindus and the Muslims over the possession of the spot where the now-demolished sixteenth-century mosque stood is not a recent dispute. It can be traced throughout the nineteenth century, with a particularly virulent Hindu-Muslim riot recorded in 1855. Up to 1857 the Hindus and the Muslims worshipped in the same building, but after 1857 an outer enclosure was put up for the Hindus to use and the inner enclosure was reserved for the Muslims. Legal wrangling and bitterness for the possession of the property continued well into the modern period.

The genesis of the developments leading to the demolition of the mosque on 6 December 1992, with consequent disturbances all over India and in Pakistan and Bangladesh where some comparatively recent Hindu temples were demolished in retaliation, can be traced back to 1991. This genesis was mostly due to a demand for the construction of a temple on a plot of land adjacent to the mosque in Ayodhya. A vast mass of Hindus came out or were mobilised in support of the construction of the proposed temple and eventually the local law and order machinery crumbled, leading to the demolition of the mosque built in 1528-29 at the supposed place of Rama's birth.

Given a certain amount of goodwill on both sides, Hindu and Muslim, the mosque and a temple would have stood side by side at this spot. Temples were destroyed during the reign of the Mogul dynasty founded by Babur at two of the holiest places of Hinduism — Banaras and Mathura. Temples have since then come up at both the places, but without destroying the eighteenth-century mosques standing on the spots of the original temples. In the case of Ayodhya neither the Hindus nor the Muslims were willing to soften their stands, and whatever had to happen happened.

I doubt if Ayodhya got media headlines only because of the mosque's demolition and the consequent Hindu-Muslim riots leading to the loss of life and property in various parts of the subcontinent. These factors have certainly played an important part but one has to admit that the long-drawn controversy between two groups of Indian historians and archaeologists over the existence or non-existence of a temple at the site of the mosque has played a role too in this wholly condemnible affair. The notoreity of this affair is also partly due to the way in which this Indian 'intellectual' controversy affected the proceedings of the World Archaeological Congress in Delhi in 1994.

As far as I am concerned, I find no reason to doubt the inscriptional and other evidence which suggests that there was a Vishnu temple at the disputed spot in the twelfth century AD. It is most possibly this temple which was pulled down in 1528-29 and a mosque built in its place. This was not an unusual happening in mediaeval India. However — and this is the crucial point — this fact does not in any way justify the destruction of a building which was built in the sixteenth century and has thus become a part of India's monumental heritage. A monument of that period should not have been made the focus of a religious frenzy.

I am sure that the historians and archaeologists who wrote thousands of partisan pages arguing either for or against the existence of a temple at the disputed site were fully aware of the point I have just made. The question is : was it only to assuage their own partisan religious feelings or was there something more to this ?

The most important division among the Indian historians and archaeologists is that between the so-called 'progressives' and the so-called 'reactionaries'. The historical circumstances of this division which may be traced back to the 1970s were once clearly expressed by me (Chakrabarti 1990).

> Criminalisation of Indian higher education should form the theme of a national debate to which people of different subjects should contribute by underlining the general factors behind the decline of ethics and the rise of criminality in their respective subjects.
>
> In the field of Indian historical studies, this process began in an organised fashion in the early seventies when a teacher-cum-politician with specialisation in history was given charge of the education ministry. Reputedly a 'progressive' in the CPI (Communist Party of India) tradition, this gentleman of great personal charm and qualities was very loyal to his political cause.
>
> A number of things were orchestrated right at the beginning. A new governmental organisation called the Indian Council of Historical Research was established with powers to offer money and patronage to historians and a person of the same political hue was brought over from Patna to head the ICHR and the history department of Delhi University.

> A historian with similar ideological leanings was put in charge of the UGC. The Indian Historical Congress was brought under the control of this group. Next, the selection committees were infiltrated and fellow-travellers inducted. Finally, with the Delhi-Aligarh base well-secured, they cast their net far and wide, establishing bases in Calcutta, Calicut, Baroda, Allahabad and elsewhere.
>
> Most of us worshipped at this altar of 'progress'. We denigrated historians like R.C. Majumdar who spent their lives in understanding the Indian historical sources. We sang hymns in praise of the bullies who could neither read an original ancient text nor decipher an inscription. We were given sermons on the glory of the Marxist approach and the value of diverse sociological and anthropological models. Dissidents were quickly dubbed rightist reactionaries.

The 'reactionaries' had to lie low throughout this phase, but when the Ayodhya dispute burst through, they saw their chance to increase their profile and began to argue that there could not be any doubt about the existence of an earlier Hindu temple at the site. On the other hand, the 'progressives' could not let slip such a chance of getting media and political publicity and began to argue with equal vehemence that no temple was pulled down when the Ayodhya mosque was built. The conflict between these two groups was well reflected in the 1994 WAC in Delhi. The question was the issue of control over a major international happening in the Indian capital with contributions from the government pouring in alongside the individual participants' fees.

With the coming of the BJP to power, the 'reactionaries' seem to have won for the present. They too have begun the process of filling up the crucial educational and cultural posts with their friends and are in no way behind their 'left' predecessors in filling up crucial academic posts with their own people. It is doubtful if the Indian archaeological heritage ever seriously mattered or matters to any of these two groups, but if the occasion arises, they will do their best to derive some advantage out of that.

THE ARYANS

The historical controversy which is being waged at present in India between the 'progressives' and the 'reactionaries' has shifted from Ayodhya to the Aryans. The issue is related to the speculation about the language/languages spoken by the people of the Indus civilization. The general opinion, although without any specific evidence in its favour except a chain of speculations, is that it was a language of the Dravidian language family. Doubts have been expressed about this opinion from time to time, but there has been an archaeological development in recent years, which has exacerbated the debate.

It is now an accepted archaeological fact that the most dense distribution of Indus civilization sites of all phases is a limited geographical area along the course of the dried-up bed of the modern Hakra or the ancient Sarasvati river in the Bahawalpur area of modern Pakistan. There is no reason to doubt that the Indus civilization originated in this area. What has made this fact interesting is that this area along the ancient Sarasvati is considered in the ancient Indian literary tradition as falling in the holiest land of Hinduism. The Sarasvati river, for instance, received great praise in the *Rigveda*, some of which must have evolved as a literary piece on the banks of this river. The origin of the Indus civilization on the bank of the Rigvedic Sarasvati may logically lead to the postulate that this particular text was composed in the subcontinental soil and that the people of the Indus civilization possibly spoke a language belonging to the Indo-Aryan family.

I have no difficulty with the argument so far, but the 'reactionary' view of things did not stop with this. They went a lot further. After all, the *RV* is the earliest surviving Indo-Aryan text. The Aryans were residents on the bank of the Sarasvati, and from here they moved elsewhere outside India. India was the Aryan homeland. They fully accept the validity of the Aryan premise but simply reverse the direction of the Aryan movement. The 'progressives' too believe in the existence of a group of people called the Aryans, but according to them, their homeland cannot be in India. In fact, making a claim like this, according to them, is an act of Hindu fundamentalism. Those who consider the Aryan idea to be a plain racist myth — as I do — are not intrigued by the opinion of either groups.

The notion that India was the Aryan homeland is not a novel idea. The history of this idea goes back to the nineteenth century, if not earlier. The idea was not then considered an example of fundamentalist ideas. Why an apparently harmless academic opinion should be labelled as fundamentalist now ?

What is relevant in the present context that quirky academic opinions would not have been matter of 'progress versus reaction' or 'secularism versus communalism' in modern India unless there was a struggle between the ruling BJP and their 'leftist' opponents to dominate the power structure of Indian historical studies. As the left has currently been dislodged from certain central points in this power-structure, they have been crying out the loudest.

MONUMENTS AND RELIGIOUS GROUPS

The third example that I am going to cite is rooted in the way the concept of archaeological conservation developed in India. By the early twentieth century the Government of India had a conservation policy in place. Its main architect was the viceroy Lord Curzon who was assisted by the Director General of the Archaeological Survey of India, John Marshall, the holder of a Cambridge tripos in archaeology and classics. As far as the technical details of the structural conservation are concerned, Marshall's *Conservation Manual* still remains unsurpassed. But one policy matter, dictated perhaps by political considerations, was flawed. The deserted monuments or 'dead' monuments — at least the more significant of them — were taken over directly by the government and 'protected'. The 'living' monuments or those which were still in use as religious places were allowed to maintain the *status quo*, but with some government control of things which could be done or not done to the structures and the precincts. If such a religious place stood on the land of a person of different religion, the government devised ways to get it back to the worshipping religious group. In this way the Buddhists came in the possession of the Bodh-Gaya temple at the turn of the century. On the other hand, if the authorities found the task of preservation of the beauty of a monument too important to be left to the taste of a particular religious community, measures were taken to throw the community out of that. The case of the sixteenth-century Sidi Sayyid mosque is famous in this context. The government threw out its undesirable owners and took direct control. I would not say that the conservation policy of the Government of India was a particularly consistent policy, but on the whole it served the country well. Most of the south Indian temples have been in active worship since they were built. They are usually managed by 'temple committees' in which there are government representations, and religious enthusiasm has not yet begun to play havoc with the structure.

I do not know why, but over the years I have seen some 'protected' religious monuments falling in the grip of fairly unscrupulous religious persons. I do not know whether this is the result of a conscious demand by various religious groups to be given back their right of worship in the monuments built by their fellow religionists and the relenting by the Archaeological Survey of India under political pressure, but this is most likely to be the case. I have a suspicion that some of these monuments have also been 'deprotected' and vagrants have been allowed to take possession in the name of religion.

Whether such monuments are being taken over by vagrants or people with whom it is possible to have a dialogue will depend entirely on the general level of poverty in the area and the extent to which the community leadership will go in the name of religion. The problem is not yet particularly acute in the villages, but in some of the major modern cities with a great Islamic building tradition, the problem seems to have got completely out of hand. I would put the blame squarely on the political and administrative leadership of the concerned areas. They should never have succumbed to pressures in the case of the protected monuments.

I have recently read of the Friday prayers being held in the precinct of Taj Mahal. I can only hope that it is not true. I have seen the community grip being tightened in the case of some mediaeval monuments of Delhi. The enormity of the problem, however, has been driven to me only recently in Ahmedabad.

In the fourteenth, fifteenth and even sixteenth centuries the local rulers of Gujarat embellished their kingdom — especially the capital Ahmedabad — well, creating some of the most appealing structural complexes that I have seen anywhere in India. The Archaeological Survey of India alone is supposed to have 52 'protected' monuments in Ahmedabad. To cut a dismal story short, the whole lot seems to have gone into the effective possession of a bunch of people who have not merely put up electric fans on their ceilings and actually live inside these monuments but also constructed urinals and compound walls in the immediate vicinity. As far as I could make out, the authorities have decided not to protest.

Ahmedabad is only an example. But what is crystal clear is that there is a lot of pressure on the heritage monuments in the urban areas, with religious communities laying claim to what they consider to be 'their' monuments. To some extent, this is due to keenness on the part of the unscrupulous to make some money out of the gullible worshipping public; to some extent this is due to the encouragement of the local mafia and politicians who need their support banks, but this is also a quest to assert identities. The renewal of identities of different kinds is a major ongoing process in modern India, and among other things, the former *Dalits* are creating new monuments in honour of people whom they consider to be their own heros.

CONCLUDING REMARKS

I have discussed, although briefly, three specific situations which may be linked *prima facie* to religious fundamentalism of one kind or other and have posed serious challenge to the efficacy of archaeological heritage preservation in south Asia. What is also interesting is that in each case we find the problem linked to issues which go beyond religious fundamentalism. The chaos, unrest and killings which Afghanistan has witnessed since 1979 have obviously taken their toll of the Afghan heritage. In the case of Ayodhya in India it was a case of political expediency mixed with the crass opportunism of the rival groups of Indian historians and archaeologists to consolidate their power. In the case of the mediaeval monuments of Ahmedabad and elsewhere, there is an aggressive urge to reaffirm identities. In some cases, as in the case of the Hindu or Buddhist pilgrims smearing ancient statues with gold, oil or vermillion, depending on the available resources, it is religious fervour mixed with crass ignorance. It is unlikely that the situations we have outlined are going to change for the better in south Asia. In fact, they are likely to get worse. Different kinds of past are in the process of being created in response to various social and political demands in modern south Asia, and competing claims and destruction are to some extent inevitable.

Competing models of the past do not necessarily imply deliberate destruction and misuse of archaeological heritage monuments. The fact that such destructions and misuse are being increasingly common in India are essentially because of the insignificance of archaeology and all that it stands for in Indian historical education. That, however, is a different theme and has been outlined in the preceding chapter.

5

The Common Denominators of Third World Archaeology

India as an Example

The title of this book suggests that the history of Indian archaeology and the related issues that we have outlined so far reflect some general features of archaeological research in the modern Third World countries among which India is one. It also implies that Archaeology, as practised in the Third World countries, has theoretical priorities and issues which may be different from the theoretical priorities and issues currently discussed in the First World. It is towards the examination of these two propositions that this concluding chapter is devoted.

DEFINING THE THIRD WORLD

The term dates from the 1950s (Dickenson *et al.* 1983 : 1), and the chief criterion of including a country in this category is the per capita estimate of its annual gross national product (GNP). There is apparently no specific yardstick of the latter. Accepting an arbitrary upper limit of 600 USA dollars, A.B. Mountjoy (1978 : 13) finds that

> the Third World embraces about 100 nations. It comprises 60 per cent of the earth's surface and is the home of about 70 per cent of the human race, some 2800 million people.

This was written in 1978. In 1981 the World Bank listed 38 countries — 25 in Africa, 12 in Asia and 1 in Latin America — as the poorest countries of the world, all with GNP figures per capita below \$ 370 (Dickenson *et al.* 1983 : 11). If we take this as the cut-off point, we discover that according to a set of data published in a geographical atlas in 1997, the number of such countries is 40.

Their distribution is interesting. Europe and the Middle East have one country each — Albania (\$360) and Yemen (\$280). The whole of central and east Asia has two countries : Tadjikistan (\$350) and Mongolia (\$340). The Americas also possess two countries :

Nicaragua ($330) and Haiti ($220). In the whole of Oceania there is only one country of this type — a 26 sq km island ($326). Of the six south Asian states, four — Bhutan (less than $200) Bangladesh ($230), Nepal ($200) and India ($310/ $370?) — belong to this category. In southeast Asia there are four such states — Cambodia ($200), Laos ($320), Myanmar ($200) and Vietnam ($190). In northern Africa they are Eritrea ($115), Ethiopia ($130), Somalia ($150) and Tanzania ($100). In western Africa it is Benin ($370), Burkina ($300), Gambia ($360), Guinea-Bissau ($240), Mali ($250), Sierra Leone ($150), Togo ($320) and Niger ($230). The distribution is similarly extensive in central Africa : Burundi ($150), Central African Republic ($370), Chad ($190), Nigeria ($280), Rwanda ($201), Sao Tome and Principe ($250), Uganda ($200) and Zaire ($220). In the southern belt of Africa Madagascar ($230), Malawi ($140), Mozambique ($80) and Zambia ($350) fall in this group. The total number of population of all these countries is in the region of 1.7 billion.

It is not necessary to vouch for the 100 per cent accuracy of such data to claim that they are fairly representative. These countries are the poorest of the poor, getting by with about one US dollar a day per person. However, in all of them there is a severe inequality of income, and this means that an overwhelming majority of their citizens have to live on a much smaller daily budget. Translated into human reality, the level of poverty we are talking about — the level of poverty which currently affects 40 countries and about 1.7 billion people — can be upsetting. Here is a series of facts mentioned recently by an Indian journalist about India :

> 52.7 per cent Indians live on less than a dollar a day; 71 per cent have no access to sanitation; 19 per cent have no access to clean drinking water; 15 per cent have no access to health services. Over 35 million of India's children in the 6-10 age group do not attend primary school.
>
> — *India Today*, 7 December 1998, p. 31

With some variations, this is the general Third World economic and social scenario at its bottom level, i.e., an average daily income level of about one US dollar per person. If one adds about 37 cents to this income, i.e., raise our per capita GNP yardstick of $370 to $ 500, the total population involved becomes almost double, with Pakistan ($440) and China ($490) alone contributing about 1.3 billion.

Our focus here is only on the lowest rung of the Third World — the segment with per capita GNP of less than $370. This segment is also known as the Fourth World.

THE SCOPE OF THE PRESENT CHAPTER

If the development of archaeological research is well-grounded in social realities — as everybody says it is — which kind of archaeological research is expected to emerge out of this context or what, in fact, has emerged? Is there any commonality between the different national traditions of Third World archaeological research?

Further, at which level should the aims of such research be targeted? Should the myriads of theoretical explorations characterising archaeology in the Western World be accepted without demur by the Third World professionals or should they be selective and focus on problems and issues which they have historically inherited and which are perhaps more relevant to the social and educational needs of their own contexts?

Archaeological literature has focussed on diverse ramifications of the socio-politics of the past and the notion of the 'other', but there is no specific theoretical concern with archaeological research in the Third World *per se*, although the gap, both in scale and methods of this research between the First and Third Worlds, is increasing at an alarming speed. The least an archaeologist from the Third World can do is to spell out some specific Third World issues, examine their commonality and focus on some dimensions which may be commensurate with the individual national goals of the Third World.

THE COMMON DENOMINATORS OF THIRD WORLD ARCHAEOLOGY

The Colonial Background

Most of these countries are former colonies. This fact has coloured archaeological research in their territories in several ways and imparted some common features to it.

(1) The first thing to note is that the archaeological notion of the past is an European import in these countries. I find no virtue in claiming that the ancient Indian texts displayed a sense of archaeological time or that 'structural conservation of monuments and repairs to mutilated sculptures were being undertaken in India since early times and continued till the nineteenth century'. (Paddayya 1995 : 118) Similarly, the oral tradition of various places may show how archaeological features of the landscape were explained on the indigenous level, but such explanations are in no sense conveyors of historical realities. I cannot think of any archaeological mound in India, which is not associated with the Indian epics. This is simply the Indian villagers' way of explaining and assimilating something in his landscape, which, otherwise, he has no reason to understand.

(2) Secondly, the tradition of archaeological research in the Third World was imposed from above. In each case it was a deliberate decision on the part of the government,

motivated to undertake this non-revenue-earning task because of a combination of historical circumstances including representations from a section of its own officers. The way the native intelligentsia accepted, or rather reacted to, this new tradition of looking at, and after, their country's past, remains by and large an unresearched theme.

(3) Thirdly, during the growth of nationalism in these countries there was no special quest to know the land in terms of its monuments, sculptures, mounds or prehistoric relics. It certainly was not an issue with the Indian nationalists who were quite happy with their reconstruction of a text-based past which to this day remains essentially devoid of archaeology. This feature must be considered a serious limitation of the Third World nationalism during the colonial period. And this is the reason why there has never been a serious attempt to link its countryside to its texts. To understand the enormity of this situation one has only to remember that in a country like England such attempts date from the sixteenth century.

(4) Fourthly, during the colonial period archaeologists did not play any significant role in the development of a negative image of the Third World's past. Basically, such an image was established to drive home the point of the Third World's inferior and lower status on the rungs of human achievement. As far as India is concerned, the responsibility of creating such an image may, very clearly, be laid at the door of Indologists and historians of various kinds. Archaeologists had no special responsibility in this matter. All that I am trying to say is that the government archaeologists of different Third World countries during the colonial period had perhaps little to do with the manipulation of the past of their respective countries. Even in the case of the controversies regarding the ruins of Zimbabwe, the framework within which the controversy took place was within a framework of race and language theories, in the evolution of which archaeologists had hardly any say. They certainly wrote within this framework but they were not responsible for putting that in place. It is in the post-Colonial situation that archaeologists, irrespective of their 'world' contexts, have been far more damaging to the study of the Third World past by drawing on the earlier race-language-culture framework for interpretations and theories. As far as India is concerned, I would, most strongly, defend the honour of persons like John Marshall and Mortimer Wheeler as long as they served as the Director General of the Archaeological Survey of India, whereas I would take a dim view of many of the archaeological

theories and approaches propounded in the context of south Asia after 1947-48.

(5) Fifthly, archaeology had hardly any place in the general educational scheme of the Third World countries. Although there was a substantial participation of the native intelligentsia in the structure and organisation of the universities of their countries, there was no development of archaeological field-tradition in these universities. Even when the colonial government tried to encourage this tradition, the universities showed remarkable apathy.

To sum up, the Third World archaeology in the colonial context was a small government-run affair which hardly played any role in its educational systems or in nationalist movements. Working archaeologists no doubt made discoveries but these discoveries were interpreted in historical terms within a framework of race-language-culture correlation, itself tied to the notion of a hierarchy of races. One of the striking examples of the latter approach was the way the discovery of the Indus civilization was accepted in India. The thrust of theoretical interest in this civilization, apart from the pride generated by south Asia's inclusion in the geography of the First civilizations and the quality of Mohenjo-Daro's drainage and sanitation system, lay in determining if this was an Aryan or pre-Aryan civilization.

The Situation after Independence

(1) The organisational framework of doing archaeological research, which was laid down during the colonial era, continues unchanged, although with a considerable amount of expansion. The government regulations controlling archaeolgical research have increased. This has in no way prevented the wilful mass destruction of archaeological sites or illicit trade in antiquities but has certainly ensured that archaeological enterprise remains a directly bureaucratic affair or at least something blessed by bureaucracy. What is further intriguing is that these rules are not printed in accessible public documents; most of the people have no way of knowing what they are. Basically this is a system which is subject to manipulation of all kinds.

As far as India is concerned, even this system led to an unprecedented increase in the quantum of archaeological research in the post-Independence period. The reason was the quality of archaeological leadership provided by a few enlightened persons. The situation has been sadly different over the last two decades. The bureaucratic stranglehold, of course, remains.

(2) Archaeology has not also been able to carve a space for itself in the Third World educational system. Where it is studied at the universities, it is usually a part of larger History departments. There would have been no problem with this, if only the historians were interested in earlier periods. The problem is that they are seldom interested in anything but comparatively recent or contemporary history. I would point out that in the case of a country like India, not even 20 per cent of the historians working in university History departments research anything earlier than the nineteenth century. The blame cannot be laid at the door of the government or the UGC. If anything, they have been leniently supportive of historical research. The basic reason is that archaeology still plays no great role in the formulation of the national consciousness of its past. I shall cite an Indian example. A large research institute which is funded exclusively by the Ministry of Culture of the Government of India has recently been set-up under the directorship of a social scientist to specialise in central Asian studies. Archaeology, or even ancient history has not been considered a part of central Asian studies at this institute. In fact, it is worth putting on record that, despite a long Indian interest in west, south-east and central Asia, and the Mediterranean lands including Egypt, there is no specialised Indian institute or university department to specialise in the archaeology and ancient history of these regions. The only major exception in this regard is the Department of Ancient History and Culture of Rohilkhand University, Bareilly (U.P.) which, under the leadership and inspiration of U.P. Arora, runs a specialised centre of Graeco-Roman studies and has been publishing since 1991 an annual jounal called *Yavanika*, journal of the Indian Society for Greek and Roman Studies. There are a few individual scholars in other fields but there is no organised focus in those areas.

(3) From time to time one hears about the role of archaeology in the identity-formation in the Third World countries. Nothing can be further from the truth. The quest for identity is prominent only among those people who have traditionally felt deprived. Despite some strains of nationalism, the influential section of the Third World intelligentsia is interested mostly in acquiring political power and money. They are not interested in defining their national identities in the post-colonial context when they already have their own nation-states and done reasonably well for themselves. There is hardly any emotive quest for the past in the modern Third World. Occasionally, the past has no doubt been put to political use, but that is of no major consequence. For instance, the image of the

past, which has no doubt been profitable for a vocal section of Indians, is not something based on archaeology but relates to a hypothetical context when the land was full of Aryan mendicants sitting cross-legged and teaching spirituality.

(4) The question of identity-formation is important but on a different level. Most of the Third-World nation states have their multiple ethnic groups, and because of uneven access to the nation's resources, there is a built-in element of tension between them. The way these ethnic groups think of their past is largely unresearched, but one can assume that this will depend on the way the historical framework of the nation-state, of which they are a part, has been built up. An issue of considerable theoretical interest to these multi-ethnic states of the Third World is to develop a non-sectarian image of their past in which their current ethnic groups are not related to a superior/inferior hierarchy. This may turn out to be the most important future task of Third World archaeology.

(5) Another general feature of Third World archaeology is the general absence of the concept of rescue-archaeology. The main reason is that there is no law for mandatory archaeological survey before major public works are undertaken. No builder is under obligation not to destroy archaeological remains that may be discovered in the course of building work. The only way the government departments and the builders can be persuaded to get something done before everything is destroyed is to build up a newspaper publicity. About two years ago some structural remains were unearthed in the deep foundation trenches laid for a high-rise building in one of the government colleges of Calcutta (Chakraborty and Biswas 1998-99). Everybody was very willing to ignore the whole thing, but an enthusiastic history teacher and her students managed to create some commotion in the local newspapers, which led to the temporary closure of building work at the site, much to the dismay of the building contractor and the college officials. The State government archaeology officials came, peered down the foundation trenches and declared that everything dated from the nineteenth century. They felt rather unhappy with me when I suggested that the date might be about five hundred years earlier! In the Delhi University (South) campus there was a section of pre-historic gravel which I used to study from time to time with my students. It has been destroyed since then.

(6) There is another little-noticed but none the less major unifying feature of Third World archaeology. The results of archaeological research are mostly published

in one of the dominant languages of the colonial period (English in the case of India) and are thus disassociated from the vast majority of people. If anything gets published in regional languages, that hardly joins the mainstream archaeological literature of the country.

DISCUSSION

There are thus about eleven common denominators of Third World Archaeology, as we have argued above both in the context colonial and Independent contexts. These may not make pleasant reading, but in the context with which I am personally familiar, I am not unlikely to take back a single sentence, and in other contexts too it is likely to be correct, with some variations from country to country. What is striking about this picture is not its individual components but the element of uninterrupted continuity between the colonial and post-Independence situations. As far as the Third World is concerned, this continuity is apparent not merely in the Third World itself but also in the arena of Third World studies in the First World. It would be unwise of me to explore this matter further; let me only state that archaeology has hardly any place in the 'area studies' scheme which has evolved in the First World and which includes Third World studies within its orbit.

On the other hand, it would be incorrect to claim that no archaeology gets done in the Third World or that the Third World archaeologists are unfamiliar with what the High Priests of the subject have been writing about it for the past three decades. A fair amount of archaeology, in fact, gets done, although within the restrictive context I have outlined.

However, which kind of archaeology is expected to have emerged out of this context? This is one of the questions we put before ourselves at the beginning.

As everybody knows, and as some First World archaeologists never tire of reminding us, the primary focus of this archaeology is the reconstruction of archaeological culture history with emphasis on surveys and excavations oriented towards the establishment of stratigraphy, typology, distribution and dating. The most visible progress of Third World archaeology in the post-Independence context has been in these fields. There are two good reasons for this. This is the kind of work which can be done with a limited amount of resource and intellectual moorings in historical studies. It is at a more-than-ordinary level of funding that one can think of multi-disciplinary work or at least harbour thoughts of getting the bones and crops identified, but then, the problem would be to find two people with suitable expertise. There is no lack of botanists and zoologists in the Third World because these two subjects are taught at virtually all educational institutions, but once they decide to specialise in archaeo-botany or archaeo-zoology, they damage their chances of career advancement. It is only at the highest level of funding and managerial ability that one can turn to the investigations of pollens, multiple methods of dating, palaeo-environment and such other issues. Is there any radiocarbon laboratory in the Third World? There are two in India, but both of them, if the drying-up of their publications is any indication, are somewhat moribund.

It is not that other kinds of work beyond the calls of culture history are not undertaken in the Third World. The language of modern Anglo-American archaeology is widely disseminated, but the emphasis is still on the building up of a proper historical perspective.

Our second question was : at which level should Third World archaeological research be targeted? Without being prescriptive, and first making the statement that any piece of research is welcome as long as it has a logical structure, I would try to argue that it is a good thing for Third World archaeology to have a firm niche in the scheme of historical studies. There are two arguments in favour of this idea.

The first argument is that archaeology has traditionally been a part of historical studies in the Third World countries, and if it has to strike deeper roots in their educational system, it can do so far more effectively as a part of the general province of history than in isolation. As far as India is concerned, I am positive that archaeology cannot get down to the level of school and undergraduate curricula without being a part of the overall History syllabi. Archaeology seems to be a strong component of the discipline of History in Africa too (Robertshaw 1990 : 87). Basil Andah (1995: 96) emphasises the need for 'a proper understanding of African *cultural history*' (emphasis ours). For a very long time historians have been concerned both with events and processes, and there really is no point in throwing the term 'particularistic' in a derogatory sense against the study of history.

My second argument stems from what I argued earlier : the task of linking the texts to the countryside remains seriously incomplete in the Third World countries. This is a serious limitation of their national liberation movements.

Even rather elementary things like locations, political geography and routes are basically unworked in detail. Fieldwork without involving excavation was once described as 'one of the peculiar and distinctive traits of British archaeology' by Stuart Piggott

(Fowler 1972: 36), a trait he found 'inherent in the eighteenth century attitude that accepted antiquarianism as a part of the Romantic movement'. (Piggott 1985 : 12) On an ideal level, one would love to see this attitude developing as a mass movement in the Third World. This kind of affordable fieldwork may lead to a new orientation of not merely of archaeology in the Third World but also of the general range of its historical studies. Among other things, this will lead to a much better understanding of geography in relation to archaeology and history in these countries. This seems to be a well-accepted approach in the modern Classical studies where this has a significant palaeo-environmental component. But the other kinds of geographical and historical sources which the Classicists use to offer a continued history of settlements in various geographical units can be inexpensively applied to the Third World.

Such a new orientation of historical and archaeological studies based on close investigations of what can be observed on the ground is desperately needed in the Third World to lead to a well-defined consciousness of its historical landscapes. It was earlier noted that the whole conception of the modern sense of archaeological and historical past was imposed on these countries from above. It never got down to the grass-roots. An important need in the social and educational context of the Third World is to change this situation, and even with low per capita GNP this can be done. If any particular element of the task of archaeological reconstruction needs highlighting as being the most suitable in this connection, I would highlight the field defined by a Cambridge archaeologist as early as 1953 as 'economic approach to prehistory'. Hunger is the most important thing at the grass-roots level of the Third World; if archaeological consciousness has to be taken there to the grass-roots level, archaeologists had better tell people something about the essential framework of living.

Finally, I would point out that the study of the socio-politics of its past can be an important arena of Third World archaeological research. I have underlined the element of uninterrupted continuity between the colonial context and the post-Independence status of archaeology in the Third World. Things cannot change unless the old framework of race-language-culture-based past is dismantled. First, as any historiographical review will show, there is nothing 'scientific' about this frame, and secondly, for multi-ethnic Third World countries the persistence of such models is dangerous because it excludes a large section of their own population. Even within their internal modern frameworks the study of the socio-politics of archaeological writings will prove to be immensely rewarding. Although there is no lack of studies of this type in the current First World archaeology, virtually all such studies, in so far as they relate to the Third World, are simplistic, pompous, and ignore the local and regional complexities. In the case of the multi-ethnic, and even multi-religious countries it is imperative to carefully dissect the myriad strands of interpretations, attitudes and biases that have gone into the making of the perception of their past by different ethnic and religious groups.

In the case of the multi-ethnic Third World societies a major challenge of the future will be to assess the implications of the DNA studies on the current notions of their population histories. In the case of India we cite below the abstract of an article entitled 'Genetic Evidence on the Origins of Indian Caste Populations' (*Genome Research*, June 2001). The principal author of this multi-authored article is Michael Bamshad of the Department of Paediatrics of the University of Utah.

> The origins and affinities of the ~1 billion people living on the subcontinent of India have long been contested. This is owing, in part, to the many different waves of immigrants that have influenced the genetic structure of India. In the most recent of these waves, Indo-European-speaking people from West Eurasia entered India from the Northwest and diffused throughout the subcontinent. They purportedly admixed with or displaced indigenous Dravidic-speaking populations. Subsequently they may have established the Hindu caste system and placed themselves primarily in castes of higher rank. To explore the impact of West Eurasians on contemporary Indian caste populations, we compared mtDNA (400 bp of hypervariable region 1 and 14 restriction site polymorphisms) and Y-chromosome (20 biallelic polymorphisms and 5 short tandem repeats) variation in ~265 males from eight castes of different rank to ~750 Africans, Asians, Europeans, and other Indians. For maternally inherited mtDNA, each caste is most similar to Asians. However, 20%-30% of Indian mtDNA haplotypes belong to West Eurasian haplogroups, and the frequency of these haplotypes is proportional to caste rank, the highest frequency of West Eurasian haplotypes being found in the upper castes. In contrast, for paternally inherited Y-chromosome variation each caste is more similar to Europeans than to Asians. Moreover, the affinity to Europeans is proportionate to caste rank, the upper castes being most similar to Europeans, particularly East Europeans. These findings are consistent with greater West Eurasian male admixture with castes of higher rank. Nevertheless, the mitochondrial genome and the Y chromosome each represents only a single haploid locus and is more susceptible to large stochastic variation, bottlenecks, and selective sweeps. Thus, to increase the power of our analysis, we assayed 40 independent, biparentally inherited autosomal loci (1 LINE-1 and 39 Alu elements) in all of the caste and continental populations (~600 individuals). Analysis of these data demonstrated that the upper castes have a higher affinity to Europeans than to Asians, and the upper

> castes are significantly more similar to Europeans than are the lower castes. Collectively, all five datasets show a trend toward upper castes being more similar to Europeans, whereas lower castes are more similar to Asians. We conclude that Indian castes are most likely to be of proto-Asian origin with West Eurasian admixture resulting in rank-related and sex-specific differences in the genetic affinities of castes to Asians and Europeans.

What even a non-specialist like the present author understands from the above abstract is that the nineteenth century idea of race-languguage-culture correlation is buttressed by the way the scientific findings have been interpreted here. The interpretation that the upper caste Indians are 'more similar to Europeans, whereas lower castes are more similar to Asians' has an underlying implication of superiority and inferiority, which has always been the underlying implication of the Aryan/non-Aryan dichotomy too. One further wonders if terms such as 'Europeans' and 'Asians' indicate homogeneous population groups with distinct biological markers. In any case, the implications of such DNA studies have to be very carefully assessed by competent people because the way these studies can be interpreted will lead to a greater consolidation of fissiparous tendencies of various kinds in a multi-ethnic Third World society like India.

Another important focus of Third World archaeology should be to assess how the First World archaeologists who work in the Third World generally interpret that past and the degree of contempt and condescension with which Third World scholarship is viewed or treated by them. With the rapid globalisation of the economic order of the world, the control of the Third World pasts will be one of the major areas of conflict between the First and the Third World scholarships. Till now there has hardly been any conflict in this area; it is the First World frame of the Third World past which has remained so long virtually unchallenged in different parts of the Third World. It is very likely that this frame will be increasingly challenged and consequently there will be more signs of stress between the First World and Third World scholarships. India offers a suitable example in this regard. The framework of the ancient Indian past, as we understand it today, was laid down by Colonial Indology. For an increasing number of Indians this past and its overtly political purpose are something which should now be subject to very close scrutiny. This has, in fact, begun to happen in modern India. A particularly refreshing trend that one can observe is the care and concern with which many Indian scientists and technologists have begun the process of rethinking about the ancient Indian past. The following comment by Subhas Chandra Kak, one of the

Indian Institute of Technology products, may be taken as a sober and sincere reflection of this trend :

> In the colonial state, the idea of profit was replaced by that of service of the British empire. The new system of education was instrumental in the socialization of this view. The idea of the other-worldly Indian was promoted. Those, especially in the cities, who learned about India from textbooks soon came to hate their past. After Independence, socialists seized control of institutions of education and the process set forth by the British was much accelerated. It is only now, fifty years after political Independence, that an objective understanding of the foundations of Indian culture is beginning to emerge. — Kak 2001

A part of this challenge is no doubt still bigoted, but the very fact that this is happening is good for the country, and I am not surprised that this has upset a particular class of Indians and their patrons in the Western campuses.

As far as the subcontinent is concerned, I would say that most of the Euro-American archaeologists working in that region have, regretfully, been unable to forget that they work in the backward Third World and to them and their compatriots, it is only their work which constitutes 'scientific' knowledge and represents the truth for that part of the world. It is always 'us versus them'.

The 'us versus them' syndrome is, of course, the most visible element of the scenario of 'Indian Studies' in the West. The following comment by Koenraad Elst seems to reflect this situation.

> In spite of all the 'multiculturalism' and 'globalization' buzz-words, numerous Westerners still treat Indians as a lesser breed which is not to be taken seriously. Professor Ulrich Libbrecht, the Flemish pioneer of Comparative Philosophy, told me how at an international conference in Honolulu on that subject, multicultural par excellence, the average American participant treated the lectures by Indians as coffee breaks. I too have noticed many times that proposals for talks or publications by Indians are dismissed without a proper hearing on the assumption that Indians are cranks unless they have an introduction from a Western institution. (footnote 102 of the section 1.3.3 of a web-site entitled 'Update on the Aryan invasion debate by Koenraad Elst, Aditya Prakashan, New Delhi')

Almost an identical opinion has been voiced by Nayanjot Lahiri (2001) :

> First World academics frequently fail to consider Third World scholars as "agents of knowledge" whose views about their own history need to be taken seriously at all. Even

> before the onset of globalisation, this asymmetry was there for all those who cared to look. For instance, in a paper called "Trade mechanisms in Indus-Mesoptamian interrelations", C.C. Lamberg-Karlovsky . . . examined the stimulus behind the creation of the Harappan civilisation. Karlovsky's paper, published in 1972, did not think that such writings or issues were important to the question of the formation of the Indus civilisation. In fact, his citations would suggest that as far as he was concerned, there had been no writings by Indians on the civilisation since 1949 — the only two Indian scholars cited there, those of Madho Sarup Vats and M.G. Dikshit, were published before 1950.

What the Third World archaeologists must also not forget is that, when the Western archaeologists work in areas like India, most of them do it, not in terms of the archaeological tradition of the land they have gone to but in terms of the Euro-American tradition which has accumulated in relation to that land. The knowledge which gets generated is put in the latter context and need not necessarily relate to what the regional archaeological research tradition considers important, or even desirable. There is also a distinct First World tradition of academic intolerance and/or contempt for any contrary opinion emerging from the Third World. An element of conflict between the two traditions is, thus, implicitly present, which, from the Western side is generally taken care of by throwing carrots to the local elite who in return are expected to feel respectful to whatever opinion emanates from that quarter. This may be understandable, as long as the Third World remains the Third World, but there should also be a common meeting ground. As far as I can judge it, that common meeting ground is still far way, at least not until there is a larger Western participation in Third World archaeology at the level of the young undergraduates and graduates who as a group generally provide a refreshing and open-minded intellectual stimulation across the national boundaries.

Another important common platform may be provided by the large-scale induction of 'landscape archaeology' in its best sense in the Third World with Western collaboration. The fact that an archaeological site can be made alive, so to speak, in its original natural setting and in relation to the other archaeological sites of the area with the help of diverse science-based investigations of the landforms around the site is perhaps the most important ground truth of modern Western archaeology. For example, archaeological research of this type is pursued quietly in the British countryside by its innumerable commercially run 'archaeology units', local 'Societies', museums, amateurs and the university departments — thousands of rather taciturn young men and women and their superiors. It is in this archaeology and the hundreds of publications that go with it lies the basic strength of Western archaeology. The Third World archaeology — Indian archaeology in particular — is aeons away from this. Reading Binford — or whichever High Priest one prefers — will not bring this most important ground reality of Western archaeology any closer to the Indian archaeological world. If we are keen on bringing it about, a sizeable part of our conception of archaeology as a subject and our notion of the past has to change, and along with it, the academic background of a substantive group of its practitioners. Unless our landscapes are studied on small regional scales in a time sequence and unless we see our sites as a dynamic part of those landscapes, a tremendous amount of our history will remain locked to us. The sooner we realise this the better. It is in developing this area of archaeological research in the Third World that Western archaeology can play a very significant role and this may be the most important meeting ground of these two increasingly separate traditions. It is on the basis of this kind of collaborative research that the true foundations of 'One World Archaeology' can be laid.

The element of tension between the First World and Third World archaeologies has been almost invariably neglected in the general archaeological literature which has also neglected the tension between the work done by the First World archaeologists in the Third World and the work done by its own archaeologists. In his introduction to the first volume of *Encyclopaedia of Archaeology, History and Discoveries* edited by him, Tim Murray speaks of 'the tensions between local and global archaeologies', and this is a rare acknowledgement of this fact in the mainstream archaeological literature. Similarly, in the same *Encyclopaedia* Kathleen Deagan (2001) openly acknowledges the issue in the context of the Caribbean :

> "Ownership" of the past becomes an increasingly central issue in the use of history in nationalist ideology and political manoeuvring, and particularly in attempts to establish a postcolonial identity in much of the Caribbean. This problem is underscored — and in part inspired by — the marked inequity in resource distribution between North American and Caribbean practitioners of archaeology, particularly in terms of access to public and private funds for archaeology. The increasingly expensive requirements of what has become standard multidisciplinary archaeology — equipment, analytical techniques, consultants, libraries, collections, travel to meetings, and the like — exacerbate imbalances between many Caribbean and North American researchers. Developing joint strategies to mitigate, if not eliminate, these imbalances, while at the same time acknowledging and respecting the national interest and local perspectives of Caribbean communities, is probably the greatest challenge facing archaeologists in the region at the beginning of the new millennium.
>
> — Deagan 2001 : 514

In the context of the French-dominated Africa R.J. McIntosh (2001) speaks of a conflict between the French archaeological tradition in the region and the tradition of 'those returning with an American Ph.D.'. He also writes that 'local prehistorians accuse the large French-funded projects of the late 1970s and 1980s of overwhelming African national research priorities'.

A major achievement of the 'One World Archaeology' movement, which was initiated only in 1986, has been to incorporate multiple strands and traditions of archaeology by reaching into various recesses all over the globe. However, as far as Third World archaeology is concerned, till now it is largely a question of highlighting 'indigenous' and socio-political issues, inviting Third World archaeologists to participate in conferences and contribute to expensive 'First World' volumes, and establishing a patronage network in the Third World academia through a judicious distribution of largesse of various kinds which are in most of the cases controlled by individuals and powerful lobbies having an interest in particular areas of the Third World. The national governments of the Third World countries do not have any say in the matter. Some Third World archaeologists no doubt appreciate this wind of change and fiercely compete among themselves to get the attention of their patrons, but it is also time it was realised that Third World archaeology had its own compulsions, objectives and perhaps even an intellectual tradition. It is certainly time the Third World archaeologists and their governments understood the full implications of the patronage network which is one of the key elements of the Third World studies in the First World. Further, we Third World archaeologists must also know which kind of archaeology we should now try to learn from the First World.

In an article on 'science for the have-nots' A.H. Zewall (2001) ascribes the poor scientific research tradition in the Third World to a cluster of four factors :

(1) the general failure of the educational systems to train people properly,

(2) the limited use of human resources largely due to hierarchical dominance, strong seniority systems and the centralisation of power, all of which suppress collective human thought and undermine human potential,

(3) the mix-up of state laws and religious beliefs, and

(4) an incoherent vision for science and technology. Apart from the factor of a mix-up of state laws and religious beliefs, of which India is free, the other debilitating circumstances are all present in India and on an abstract level, explain the Indian archaeological situation too.

Bibliography

Agrawal, D.P., 1964, 'New evidence for a shorter Harappan chronology', *Science* 143 : 950.

———,1966, 'Harappan chronology : a re-examination of the evidence', *Studies in Prehistory : Robert Bruce Foote Memorial Volume* (D. Sen and A.K. Ghosh, eds), Calcutta, pp. 139-48.

———, *Copper-Bronze Age in India*, Delhi.

———, 1982, *The Archaeology of India*, London.

———, 1992, *Man and Environment in India through Ages*, Delhi.

———, and Ghosh, A., eds., 1973, *Radiocarbon and Indian Archaeology*, Bombay.

———, and Kusumgar, Sheela, 1974, *Prehistoric Chronology and Radiocarbon Dating in India*, Delhi.

———, and Pande, eds., 1977, *Ecology and Archaeology of Western India*, Delhi.

———, Bhandari, N. and Singhvi, A.K., 1979, 'Thermoluminiscent dating — an Indian perspective', *M&E,* 3 : 78-82.

———, and Sood, R.K., 1982, 'Ecological factors and the Harappan Civilization', In G.L.Possehl, ed., *Harappan Civilization*, Delhi, pp. 223-32.

———, Kusumgar, Sheela and Krishnamurthy, R.V., eds., 1985. *Climate and Geology of Kashmir, the Last 4 Million Years*, Delhi.

Agrawal, O.P., Narain, Hari and Prakash, J., 1991, 'Metallographic studies of iron artifacts of domestic use, tools and weapons from Khairadih, U.P.', In M.C. Ganorkar and N. Rama Rao, eds., *Role of Chemistry in Archaeology*, Hyderabad, pp. 103-11.

Agrawal, Ramesh Chandra, 1997, 'Stupas and monasteries : a recent discovery from Satdhara, India', In R. and B. Allchin, eds., *South Asian Archaeology 1995*, Delhi, pp. 403-15.

———, 1998, *Kashmir and its Monumental Glory*, Delhi.

Agrawala, R.C., 1979, 'More copper finds from Rajasthan', *M&E,* 3 : 91-92.

———, 1980a, 'Khurdi(?) copper hoard from Rajasthan', *M&E,* 4 : 89-91.

———, 1980b, 'More copper celts from Rajasthan', *M&E,* 4 : 92.

———, and Kumar, V., 1982, 'Ganeshwar-Jodhpura culture : new traits in Indian archaeology', In G.L. Possehl, ed., *Harappan Civilization*, Delhi, pp. 125-34.

Agrawala, V.S., 1948, 'The terracottas of Ahichchhatra', *AI,* 4 : 104-79.

Allchin, B., 1966, *The Stone-Tipped Arrow*, London.

———, Goudie, A. and Hegde, K.T.M., 1978, *The Prehistory and Palaeogeography of the Indian Desert*, London.

Allchin, B., and Allchin, F.R., 1968, *The Birth of Indian Civilization*, Harmondsworth.

———, 1982, *The Rise of Civilization in India and Pakistan*, Cambridge.

Allchin, F.R., 1960, *Piklihal Excavations*, Hyderabad.

———, 1961, *Utnur Excavations*, Hyderabad.

——, 1963, *The Neolithic Cattlekeepers of the Deccan, a Study of the Deccanese Ashmounds*, Cambridge.

——, and Chakrabarti, Dilip K., eds., 1979, *Source-Book of Indian Archaeology*, Volume I, Delhi.

Alur, K.R., 1973, 'Significance of faunal remains in archaeological studies', In *Radiocarbon and Indian Archaeology* (D./P. Agrawal and A. Ghosh, eds), Bombay, pp. 111-17.

Ahmad, N., 1984, *'The Stone Age Cultures of the Upper Son Valley'*, Delhi.

Andah, B., 1995, 'European encumbrances to the development of relevant theory in African archaeology', In P. Ucko ed., *Theory in Archaeology, a World Perspective*, London, pp. 96-109.

Ansari, Z.A., 1970, 'Pebble tools from Nittur (Mysore State)', *Indian Antiquary (Bombay)*, 4 : 1-7.

Armand, J., 1983, *'Archaeological Excavations in Durkadi Nala : an Early Palaeolithic Pebble-tool Workshop in Central India'*, Delhi.

Asthana, Shashi, 1979, 'Harappans' interest in Kirman', *Man and Environment*, 3 : 56-60.

Babu, B.S.R., 1994-95, 'Excavations at Bhorgarh', *Puratattva*, 25 : 88-90.

——, 1996, 'Mandoli, a late Harappan settlement in Delhi', In C. Margabandhu and K.S. Ramachandran, eds., *Spectrum of Indian Archaeology*, Delhi, pp. 98-104

Badam, G.L., 1979, *'Pleistocene Fauna of India with Special Reference to the Siwaliks'*, Poona.

——, Ganjoo, R.K., 'Salahuddin and Rajaguru', S.N. 1986. Evaluation of fossil Hominid — the maker of late Acheulian tools at Hathnora, Madhya Pradesh, India', *Current Science*, 55 : 143-45.

Bajpai, K.D., and Pande, S.K., 1978. *Malhar 1975-78*, Sagar.

Balaji, K., Suresh, L.S., Raghavaswamy, V. and Gautam, N.C. 1996, 'The use of remote sensing in monitoring changes in and around archaeological monuments — a case study from Hyderabad, Andhra Pradesh', *M&E,* 21(2):63-70

Banerjee, N.R., 1965, *The Iron Age in India*, Delhi.

——, 1956, 'The megalithic problem of Chingleput in the light of recent exploration', *AI*, 12 : 21-34.

——, and Soundara Rajan, K.V., 1959, 'Sanur 1950 & 1952 : a megalithic site in District Chingleput', *AI*, 15 : 4-42

Banerji, Arundhati, 1994, *Early Indian Terracotta Art, Circa 2000-300 B.C., (Northern and Western India)*, Delhi.

Basa, K.K., 1991, 'The Westerly Trade of Southeast Asia from c.400 B.C. to c.A.D.500 with Special Reference to Glass Beads', Unpublished Ph.D. thesis, London University.

Basa, K.K., and Mohanty, P., eds., 2000, *Archaeology of Orissa*, Delhi.

Basak, Bishnupriya, 1997, 'Microlithic sites in the Tarafeni valley, Midnapur district, West Bengal : a discussion', *M&E,* 22 (2): 11-28.

Baskaran, M., Marathe, A.R., Rajaguru, S.N. and Somayajulu, B.L.K. 1986, 'Geochronology of palaeolithic cultures in Hiran valley, Saurashtra, India', *Journal of Archaeological Science*, 13 : 505-14.

Batra, N.L., 1996, *Heritage Conservation*, Delhi.

Bednarik, R.G., 1993, 'Palaeolithic art in India', *M&E*, 18(2): 33-40.

Bhan, Kuldeep, 1992, 'Late Harappan Gujarat', *The Eastern Anthropologist*, 45: 173-92.

Bhan, S. and Shaffer, J.G., 1978, 'New discoveries in northern Haryana', *M&E*, 2 : 59-68.

Bharadwaj, H.C., 1979, *Aspects of Ancient Indian Technology*, Delhi.

Bisht, R.S., 1982, 'Excavations at Banawali 1974-77', In G.L. Possehl, ed., *Harappan Civilization*, Delhi, pp. 113-24.

——, 1991, 'Dholavira: new horizons of the Indus civilization', *Puratattva*, 20 : 71-82.

Boivin, N., 2000, 'Life rhythms and floor sequences: excavating time in rural Rajasthan and neolithic Catalhoyuk', *World Archaeology*, 31: 367-88.

Bose, N.K. and Sen, D., 1948, *Excavations in Mayurbhanj*, Calcutta.

Bose, N.K., Gupta, P.C. and Bose, A., 1960, 'Palaeoliths from Monghyr district, Bihar', *Man in India*, 40 : 68-75.

Braidwood, R.J., ed., 1962, *Courses toward Urban Life*, Chicago.

Brunswig, R.H., 'Prospective tree-ring calibration of Indus civilization radiocarbon chronology', *Man*, 8 : 543-54.

Buth, G.M. and Kaw, R.N., 1985, 'Plant husbandry in neolithic Burzahom, Kashmir', In *Climate and Geology of Kashmir and Central Asia : the Last 4 Million Years* (eds., D.P. Agrawal, Sheela Kusumgar and R.V. Krishnamurthy), Delhi, pp. 109-13.

Chakrabarti, Dilip K., 1968, 'The Aryan hypothesis in Indian archaeology', *Indian Studies : Past and Present*, 9 : 343-58.

———, 1972-73, 'Concept of the Urban Revolution and the Indian context', *Puratattva*, 6 : 27-32.

———, 1976, 'The beginning of iron in India', *Antiquity*, 50 : 114-24.

———, 1977, 'India and west Asia — an alternative approach', *M&E*, 1 : 25-38.

———, 1978, 'Reserved Slip Ware in the Harappan context', *Puratattva*, 8 : 158-65.

———, 1979, 'The problem of tin in early India — a preliminary survey', *M&E*, 3 : 61-74.

———, 1982, 'Long barrel-cylinder beads and the issue of pre-Sargonic contact between the Harappan civilization and Mesopotamia', In G.L.Possehl, ed., *Harappan Civilization*, Delhi, pp. 265-70.

———, 1986, 'The lithic industries of the Santal Parganas with notes on the Damin industry', *M&E*, 10 : 143-49.

———, 1986, 'The preindustrial mines of India', *Puratattva*, 16 : 65-72.

———, 1988, 'The old copper mines of eastern India', In *The Beginning of the Use of Metals and Alloys* (ed. R. Maddin), Boston, pp. 230-44 .

———, 1988a, *A History of Indian Archaeology from the Beginning to 1947*, Delhi.

———, 1988b, *Theoretical Issues in Indian Archaeology*, Delhi.

———, 1990, *The External Trade of the Indus Civilization*, Delhi.

———, 1990, 'Archaeology in Indian universities', In *The Excluded Past* (P. Stone and R. Mackenzie, eds.)' London, pp. 24-32.

———, 1990, 'National debate on universities required', *Onlooker (April 1-15)*, 52 (7) : 4-6.

———, 1992, *The Early Use of Iron in India*, Delhi.

———, 1995, *The Archaeology of Ancient Indian Cities*, Delhi.

———, 1997, *Colonial Indology: Sociopolitics of the Ancient Indian Past*, Delhi.

———, 1998, 'The Indus civilization and the Arabian Gulf : an Indian point of view', In C.S. Phillips, D.T. Potts and S. Searight, eds., *Arabia and Its Neighbours; Essays on Prehistorical and Historical Developments presented in honour of Beatrice de Cardi*, Brepols, pp. 303-14.

———, 1999, 'Documenting heritage : some observations on the Indian situation', In H.J. Hansen and G. Quinne, eds., *Our Fragile Heritage. Documenting the Past for the Future*, Copenhagen, pp. 15-22.

———, 1999, *India — an Archaeological History. Palaeolithic Beginnings to Early Historic Foundations*, Delhi.

———, 2000, 'Colonial Indology and identity', *Antiquity*, 74 : 667-71.

———, 2001a, *Archaeological Geography of the Ganga Plain : the Middle and the Lower Ganga*, Delhi.

———, 2001b, 'The archaeology of Hinduism', In T. Insoll, ed., *Archaeology and World Religion*, London, pp. 33-60.

———, In press, *The Archaeology of European Expansion in India : Gujarat, c.16th-18th Centuries AD.*

———, and Hasan, S.J., 1982, 'The sequence at Bahiri (Chandra Hazrar Danga), District Birbhum, West Bengal'. *M&E*, 6: 111-49.

———, and Hasan, S.J., 1984, *The Antiquities of Kangra*, Delhi.

———, and Lahiri, Nayanjot, 1987, 'A preliminary report on the Stone Age of the Union Territory of Delhi and Haryana', *M&E,* 11: 109-16.

———, and Lahiri, 1996, *Copper and its Alloys in Ancient India*, Delhi.

———, Tewari, R. and Singh, R.N. 1999-2000, 'The archaeology of the Deccan route : a preliminary report on the field work in 1999', *Pragdhara*, 10 : 121-33.

Chakrabarti, S., 1995, 'Late Quaternary stratigraphy and an upper Acheulian occupation site in the Kalubhar valley, Saurashtra', In S. Wadia, R. Korisettar and V. Kale, eds., *Quaternary Environments and Geoarchaeology of India*, Bangalore, pp. 277-81.

Chakraborty, Uttara and Biswas, Swati, 1998-99, 'Archaeology of Calcutta : evidence from Bethune College', *Puratattva,* 29: 83-88

Chakravarti, N.P., 1949, Notes, *AI*, 5 : 1-3.

———, 1950, Notes, *AI,* 6 : 1-3.

Chamyal, L.S. and Merh, S.S., 1995, 'The Quaternary formations of Gujarat', In S. Wadia, R. Korisettar and V. Kale eds., *Quaternary Environments and Geoarchaeology of India*, Bangalore, pp. 246-57.

Chanchala, 1991-92, 'The fruit and seed remains from ancient Hulaskhera, district Lucknow, U.P. (*c.* 700BC- 500 AD)', *Pragdhara,* 2 : 65-80.

Chattopadhyay, P.K., 1993-94, 'Bahiri : a protohistoric manufacturing centre in West Bengal', *Pratna-Samiksha,* 2-3 : 159-68

———, 1999-2000, 'Copper objects from Dihar : archaeotechnical studies', *Puratattva*, 30 : 151-54.

———, and Singh, B.P., 1998, 'Metallographic and chemical study of copper artifacts from Senuwar', In V. Tripathi, ed., *Archaeometallurgy in India*, Delhi, pp. 20-26.

Chattopadhyay, R.K., 1992, 'Palaeolithic West Bengal', *Pratna Samiksha,* 1 : 27-60.

Chattopadhyay, U.C., 1985, 'Faunal studies in archaeology : current trend in methods and concepts', *M&E,* 9 : 3-20.

Chaule, G.C., 1999, 'Excavated remains at Lalitagiri, a Buddhist site in Orissa', In K.K. Basa and P. Mohanty, eds., *Archaeology of Orissa*, Delhi, pp. 441-55.

Chawla, S. and Singhvi, A., 1989, 'Thermoluminiscence dating of archaeological sediments', *Naturwissenschaften,* 76 : 416-18.

Childe, V.G., 1948, 'Megaliths', *AI*, 4 : 4-13.

Chitalwala, Y.M., 1982, 'Harappan settlements in the Kutch-Saurashtra region : patterns of distribution and routes of communication', In G.L. Possehl, ed., *Harappan Civilization*, Delhi, pp. 197-204.

———, 1984, 'The problem of class structure in Indus civilization', In *Frontiers of the Indus Civilization* (eds. B.B. Lal and S.P. Gupta), Delhi, pp. 211-15.

Choudhury, N.D., 1985, *Historical Archaeology of Central Assam*, Delhi.

Choudhury, R.D., 1985, *Archaeology of the Brahmaputra Valley*, Delhi.

Chougaonkar, M.P., Raghav, K.S., Rajaguru, S.N., Kar, A., Singhvi, A.K. and Nambi, K.S.V., 1999, 'Luminiscence dating results of dune profiles from the margins of the Thar desert and their implications', *M&E*, 24(1) : 21-26.

Chowdhury, K.A. and Ghosh, S.S., 1951, 'Plant remains from Harappa 1946', *AI*, 7 : 1-2.

———, 1952, 'Wood remains from Sisupalgarh', *AI*, 8 : 28-32.

Clark, J.D. and Khanna, G.S., 1989, 'The site of Kunjhun II, middle Son valley and its relevance for the neolithic of central India', In J.M. Keonoyer, ed., *Old Problems and New Perspectives in the Archaeology of South Asia*, Madison, pp. 29-46.

Clason, A.T., ed., 1975, *Archaeozoological Studies*, Amsterdam.

Cooper, Z., 1990, 'Archaeological evidence for resource exploitation in the Andaman islands', *M&E*, 15(1) : 73-81.

———, 1994, 'Abandoned Onge encampments and their relevance in understanding the archaeological record in the Andaman islands', In B. Allchin ed., *Living Traditions, Studies in the Ethnoarchaeology of South Asia*, Delhi, pp. 235-63.

———, 1997, *Prehistory of the Chitrakot Falls, Central India*, Pune.

Corvinus, G., 1981, *A Survey of the Pravara River System in Western Maharashtra, India Vol. 1 : the Stratigraphy and Geomorphology of the Pravara River System*, Tubingen.

———, 1983, *A Survey of the Pravara River System in Western Maharashtra, India, Vol. 2 : the Excavations of the Acheulian Site of Chirki-on-Pravara, India*, Tubingen.

Craddock, P.T., 1987, 'The early history of zinc', *Endeavour (New Series)*, 11 : 183-91.

———, 1987-88, 'The early history of zinc and brass', *Wiener Berichte uber Naturwissenschaft in der Kunst*, 4/5 : 225-45.

———, 1996, 'The use of firesetting in the granite quarries of south India', *Mining History : the Bulletin of the Peak District Mines Historical Society* 13 : 7-11.

———, Freestone, I.C., Gurjar, L.K., Hegde, K.T.M. and Sonawane, V.H. 1985, 'Early zinc production in India', *Mining Magazine* (January), pp. 45-52.

———, Freestone, I.C., Gurjar, L.K., Middleton, A. and Willies, L. 1989, In A. Hauptmann, E. Pernicka and G.A.Wagner, eds., *Old World Archaeometallurgy*, Bochum, pp. 51-69.

Dasgupta, P.C., 1965, *Excavations at Pandu Rajar Dhibi*, Calcutta.

Datta, Asok, 1991, 'Blade and blade tool assemblages of the upper palaeolithic and mesolithic periods — a case study from the mid-Kasai valley in the Jhargram subdivision of Midnapur district, West Bengal', *M&E*, 16(1) : 23-31.

———, 2000, 'The context and definition of upper palaeolithic industries in Panchpir, Orissa, India', *Proceedings of the Prehistoric Society* 66 : 47-59.

Deagan, Kathleen 2001, 'Historical archaeology in Florida and the Caribbean basin', In Murray 2001, pp. 500-20

Deo, S.B., ed., 1972, *Archaeological Congress and Seminar Papers*, Nagpur.

———, and Paddayya, K., eds., 1985, *Recent Advances in Indian Archaeology*, Pune.

Deo, S. and Joglekar, P.P., 1996, 'Satellite remote sensing in archaeology', *M&E*, 21 (2): 59-62.

Deotare, B.C., 1983, 'Determination of the extent of settlement area by Phosphate analysis', *Bulletin of the Deccan College Post-Graduate and Research Institute*, 42 : 40-48.

———, 1990, 'A chemical study of anthropic soils from chalcolithic Tuljapur Garhi', *M&E*, 15(2) : 61-62.

———, Kajale, M.D., Kusumgar, Sheela and Rajaguru, S.N. 1999, 'Late holocene environment and culture at Bari Bavri, western Rajasthan, India', *M&E*, 24 (1) : 27-38.

Deshpande, M.N., 1959, 'The rock-cut caves of Pitalkhora in the Deccan', *AI*, 15 : 66-93.

Deshpande-Mukherjee, Arati, 1998, 'Shellfishing and shell crafts during the Harappan period in Gujarat', *M&E*, 23 (1): 63-80.

Dev, Arjun, 1992, (unpublished) 'Archaeology in school education', In *ICHR workshop on Archaeology, Education and Training*, 28 February-1 March, 1992, Delhi.

Deva, K., 1959, 'The temples of Khajuraho in central India', *AI,* 15 : 43-65.

Devaraja, D.V., Shaffer, J.G., Patil, C.S. and Balasubramanya, 1995, 'The Watgal excavations : an interim report', *M&E,* 20 : 57-74.

Dhavalikar, M.K., 1978, 'Settlement archaeology of Inamgaon', *Puratattva*, 8 : 44-54.

———, 1979a, 'Early farming cultures of central India', In *Essays in Indian Protohistory* (D.P. Agrawal and D.K. Chakrabarti, eds), Delhi, pp. 229-45.

———, 1979b, 'Early farming cultures of the Deccan', In *ibid*, pp. 247-65.

———, 1988, *The First Farmers of the Deccan*, Pune.

Dickinson, J.P., Clarke, C.G., Gould, W.T.S., Hoskins, A.G., Prothero, R.M., Siddle, D.J., Smith, C.T., Thomas-Hope, E.M. 1983, *A Geography of the Third World*, London.

Dikshit, K.N. 1982, 'Hulas and the late Harappan complex in western Uttar Pradesh', In G.L. Possehl, ed., *Harappan Civilization*, Delhi, pp. 339-52.

———, 1984, 'Late Harappans in north India', In *Frontiers of the Indus Civilization* (eds. B.B. Lal and S.P. Gupta), Delhi, pp. 253-69.

———, ed., 1985, *Archaeological Perspective in India since Independence*, Delhi.

———, 1996-97, 'Report on Agra monuments and Mathura refinery — a regional environmental plan for controlling pollution', *Puratattva*, 27 : 122-24.

———, 1999-2000, 'Report of the first archaeological campaign at Drupad Tila (Kampilya)', *Puratattva*, 30 : 164-72.

Dikshit, M.G., 1952, 'Beads from Ahichchhatra, U.P', *AI*, 8 : 33-63.

Dimri, Kiran, 1998-99, 'Assessing the distribution of Harappan culture in northeastern Saurashtra : a preliminary report', *Pragdhara*, 9 : 27-44.

DuFresne, Ann S., Shaffer, J.G., Shivashankar, M.L. and Balasubramanya, 1998, 'A preliminary analysis of microblades, blade cores and lunates from Watgal : a southern neolithic site', *M&E*, 23(2) : 17-43.

Dupree, Nancy H., 1996, 'Museum under seige', *Archaeology*, 49 : 42-51.

Dupree, Nancy H., 2000, 'Interview. http://www.afghan-xgeneration.com/Interview.htm'.

During-Caspers, E.C.L., 1971, 'Etched carnelian beads', *Bulletin of the Institute of Archaeology* (*London*), 10 : 83-98.

Dutta, P.C., 1983, *The Bronze Age Harappans : a Bio-Anthropological Study of the Skeletons Discovered at Harappa*, Calcutta.

Enzel, Y., Ely, L.L., Mishra, S., Ramesh, R., Amit, R., Lazar, B., Rajaguru, S.N., Baker, V.R. and Sandler, A., 1999, *Science*, 284 (cf. Lahiri 2000).

Erdosy, G., 1985, 'Settlement archaeology of the Kausambi region', *M&E*, 9 : 66-79.

———, 1988, *Urbanisation in Early Historic India*, Oxford.

Fairservis, W.A., 1971, *The Roots of Ancient India*, London.

Fowler, P.J., 1972, 'Field archaeology in future', In, P.J. Fowler, ed., *Archaeology and the Landscape*, London, pp. 96-126.

Fuller, D. Q., 1999, *The Emergence of Agricultural Societies in South India : Botanical and Archaeological Perspectives*, Unpublished Ph.D thesis. Cambridge University.

Gairola, T.R., 1950, 'The red paint, lime-washes and plasters on Bhuvaneswar and Konarak temples', *AI*, 6 : 103-7.

———, 1951, 'The weights of the punch-marked coins from Barwani', *AI,* 7 : 79-85.

———, 1956, 'Bidri ware', *AI,* 12 : 116-18.

——, 1957, 'Preservation of a textile and miniature painting', *AI*, 13 : 143-45.

——, 1962, 'Preservation of a miniature and a wall-painting', *AI*, 16 : 85-88.

Gardner, Rita, 1986, 'Quaternary coastal sediments and stratigraphy, southeast India', *M&E*, 10 : 51-72.

Gaur, A.S., Sundaresh, Gudigar, P., Trpati, S., Vora, K.H. and Bandodkar, S.N. 2000, 'Recent underwater explorations at Dwaraka and surroundings of Okha Mandal', *M&E*, 25 (1): 67-74.

Gaur, R.C., 1983, *Excavations at Atranjikhera*, Delhi.

——, 1995, *Excavations at Lal Qila, a Habitational O.C.P. Site and a Unique Copper Hoard Site from Kiratpur*, Delhi.

——, 2000, *Excavations at Fatehpur Sikri, a National Project*, Delhi.

Ghosh, A.K., 1970, 'The palaeolithic cultures of Singhbhum', *Transactions of the American Philosophical Society*, 60 (1) : 1-68.

Ghosh, S.S., 1950, 'Re-examination of wooden post from Kirari, Madhya Pradesh', *AI*, 6 : 17-20.

Ghosh, A., 1951, 'Rajgir 1950', *AI*, 7 : 66-78.

——, 1952, 'The Rajputana desert — its archaeological aspect', *Bulletin of the National Institute of Sciences in India* 1:37-42.

——, 1954, 'Notes', *Indian Archaeology 1953-54 — a Review*, Delhi.

——, 1954-55, 'Notes', *AI*, 10-11 : 1-3.

——, 1956, 'Notes', *AI*,, 12 : 1-3.

——, 1957, 'Notes', *AI*, 13 : 1-3.

——, 1958, 'Notes', *AI*, 14 : 1-3.

——, 1959, 'Notes', *AI*, 15 : 1-3.

——, 1962, 'Notes', *AI*, 16 : 1-3.

——, 1963, 'Notes', *AI*, 18-19 : 1-3.

——, 1967, 'Notes', *AI*, 20-21 : 1-3.

——, 1973, *The City in Early Historic India*, Simla.

Gogte, V.D., 1984, 'X-ray diffraction analysis (Part I) of chalcolithic pottery from Inamgaon', *Bulletin of the Deccan College Post-Grasuate and Research Institute* 43 : 53-56.

——, 1996, 'Chalcolithic Balathal — a trading centre as revealed by the XRD study of ancient pottery', *M&E*, 21(1): 103-10.

——, 1997, 'The Chandraketugarh-Tamluk region of Bengal : source of the early historic rouletted ware from India and southeast Asia', *M&E*, 22 (1) : 69-85.

——, and Murty, M.L.K., 1986, 'ESR dating of Kurnool caves, south India', *M&E*, 10 : 135-40.

——, and Shinde, V., 1994-95, 'Chalcolithic Walki : a satellite settlement of Inamgaon — a study by X-ray diffraction of pottery', *Puratattva* 25 : 62-63.

Gordon, D.H., 1950, 'The stone industries of the Holocene in India and Pakistan', *AI*, 6 : 64-90.

Gordon, D.H., 1954-55, 'The pottery industries of the Indo-Iranian border : a re-statement and tentative chronology', *AI*, 10-11 : 157-91.

——, 1958, *The Prehistoric Background of Indian Culture*, Bombay.

Gupta, S., 1999-2000, 'From eastern Indian ocean to the Yellow Sea interaction sphere : Indo-Pacific beads in Yayoi, Japan', *Puratattva* 30:93-98.

Gupta, S.P., 1979, *Archaeology of Soviet Central Asia and the Indian Borderlands*, 2 vols., Delhi.

Guzder, S., 1980, *Quaternary Environment and Stone Age Cultures of the Konkan, Coastal Maharashtra, India*, Pune.

Hammond, N., 1973, *South Asian Archaeology 1971*, London.

Hegde, K.T.M., 1985, 'Scientific studies in Indian archaeology', In S.B. Deo and K. Paddayya, eds., *Recent Advances in Indian Archaeology*, Pune, pp. 100-9.

Hooja, Rima, 1988, *The Ahar Culture*, Oxford.

Hora, S.L., 1954-55, 'Angling in ancient India', *AI,* 10-11:152-56.

Howell, J.R., 1995, *Excavations at Sannathi 1986-1989*, Delhi.

Hutchinson, J., ed., *Evolutionary Studies in World Crops, Diversity and Change in the Indian Subcontinent*, Cambridge.

Inden, R., 1990, *Imagining India*, Oxford.

Inizan, M.L., and M. Lechevallier, 1995, 'Pressure debitage and heat treatment in the microlithic assemblage of Bagor, Northwest India', *M&E*, 20 (2): 17-21.

Isaac, N., 1960, *Stone Age Cultures of Kurnool*, Unpublished Ph.D thesis, Poona University.

Jacobson, J., 1970, 'On palaeolithic occupation floors in India', *Current Anthropology* 11 : 483.

——, 1975, 'Early Stone Age habitation sites in eastern Malwa', *Proceedings of the American Philosophical Society*, 119: 280-97.

——, 1980, 'Investigations of Late Stone Age cultural adaptations in the central Vindhyas', *M&E*, 4 : 65-82.

——, 1979, 'Recent development in south Asian prehistory and protohistory', *Annual Review of Anthropology* 8: 467-502.

Jayaswal, V., 1982, *Chopper-Chopping Component of Palaeolithic in India*, Delhi.

——, 1998, *From Stone Quarry to Sculpting Workshop : a Report on the Archaeological Investigations around Chunar, Varanasi and Sarnath*, Delhi.

Jha, S.K., 1998, *Beginnings of Urbanization in Early Historic India*, Patna.

Jhaldiyal, R., 1998, 'Surface wash processes and their impact on Stone Age sites', *M&E,* 23(1) : 81-91.

Joglekar, P.P., and Vaishampayan, M.S., 1991, 'Some basic issues related to the metrical analysis of stone tools', *M&E*, 16 (1): 109-14.

Joshi, J.P., Bala, M. and Ram, J., 1984, 'The Indus civilization : a reconsideration on the basis of distribution maps', In *Frontiers of the Indus Civilization* (eds., B.B. Lal and S.P. Gupta), Delhi, pp. 511-30.

——, and Sharma, A.K., 1999-2000a, 'Excavations at Sirpur, district Mahasamund, Chhattisgarh', *Puratattva* 30:110-16.

——, and Sharma, A.K., 1999-2000b, 'Excavation at Mansar, district Nagpur, Maharashtra — 1997-2000', *Puratattva* 30 : 127-31.

Joshi, M.C., 1978, 'Archaeology and Indian tradition — some observations', *Puratattva*, 8 : 98-102.

Joshi, R.V., 1955, *Pleistocene Studies in the Malaprabha Basin*, Poona.

——, 1961, 'Stone-Age industries of the Damoh area, Madhya Pradesh', *AI*, 17 : 5-36.

——, 1978, *Stone Age Cultures of Central India : Report on the Excavations of Rock-Shelters at Adamgarh, Madhya Pradesh*, Poona.

——, and Khare, M.D., 1966, 'Microlith-bearing deposit of Adamgarh rock-shelter', In *Studies in Prehistory, Bruce Foote Memorial Volume* (eds. D. Sen and A.K. Ghosh), Calcutta, pp. 90-95.

——, Rajaguru, S.N., Pappu, R.S. and Bopardikar, B.P. 1974, 'Quaternary glaciation and palaeolithic sites in the Liddar valley (Jammu- Kashmir)', *World Archaeology* : 369-79.

——, and Deotare, B.C., 1983, *Chemical Analysis of Archaeological Deposits from India*, Pune.

——, and Kshirsagar, Anupama, 1986, *Chemical Analysis of Archaeological Bones from India : Fluorine and Fossilization Process*, Pune.

Jual, N., Pant, R.K., Bhushan, R. and Somayajulu, B.L.K., 1995, 'Radiometric dating of late Quaternary sea levels of the Saurashtra coast, western India : an experiment with oyster and clam shells', In S. Wadia, R. Korisettar and V. Kale, eds., *Quaternary Environments and Geoarchaeology of India*, Bangalore, pp. 372-79.

Kabir, H., 1950, 'Preface', *Archaeology in India*, Delhi : Ministry of Education.

Kajale, M.D., 1977a, 'On the botanical findings from the excavations at Daimabad, a chalcolithic site in western Maharashtra', *Current Science*, 46 : 818-19.

——, 1977b, 'Plant economy at Inamgaon', *M&E,* 1: 64-66.

——, 1996a, 'Palaeobotanical investigations at Balathal : preliminary results', *M&E*, 21(1) : 98-102.

——, 1996b, 'Palaeobotanical investigations on chalcolithic Tuljapur Garhi', In B.P. Bopardikar, *Excavations at Tuljapur Garhi 1984-1985*, Delhi, pp. 47-61.

——, Mulhollad, S. and Rapp, G. Jr., 1995, 'Applications of phytolith analysis : a potential tool for Quaternary environmental and archaeological investigations in the Indian subcontinent', In S. Wadia, R. Korisettar and V. Kale, eds., *Quaternary Environments and Geoarchaeology of India,* Bangalore, pp. 530-44.

——, and Eksambekar, S.P., 1997, 'Application of phytolith analyses to a neolithic site at Budihal, district Gulbarga, south India', In A. Pinilla, J. Juan-Tresseras and M.J. Machado, eds., *Estado Actual de Los Estudios de Fitolitos en Suelos y Plantas*, Madrid, pp. 219-29.

Kak, S.C., 2000, *The Astronomical Code of the Rigveda*, Delhi.

Kak, S.C., 2001, Unpublished Mss, *The Wishing Tree*, Baton Rouge.

Kennedy, K.A.R., 1975, *The Physical Anthropology of the Megalith-Builders of South India and Sri Lanka*, Canberra.

——, 1980, 'Prehistoric skeletal record of man in south Asia', *Annual Review of Anthropology*, 9 : 391-432.

——, 1984, 'Biological adaptations and affinities of mesolithic south Asians', In J.R. Lukacs, ed., *The People of South Asia : the Biological Anthropology of India, Pakistan and Nepal*, New York, pp. 29-57.

——, Lovell, N.C. and Burrow, C.B., 1986. *Mesolithic Human Remains from the Gangetic Plain : Sarai Nahar Rai*, Cornell.

——, Lukacs, J.R., Pastpor, R.F., Johnston, T.L., Lovell, N.C., Pal, J.N., Hemphill, B.E. and Burrow, C.B., 1992, *Human Skeletal Remains from Mahadaha : a Gangetic Mesolithic Site*, Cornell.

Kenoyer, J.M., Clark, J.D., Pal, J.N. and Sharma, G.R., 1983, 'An upper palaeolithic shrine in India?', *Antiquity*, 57: 88-94.

Khanduri, B.M., 1994, *The archaeology of Alaknanda Valley* (*Central Himalaya*), Delhi.

Khatri, A.P., 1958, *Stone Age Cultures of Malwa*, Unpublished Ph.D thesis, Poona University.

——, 1962, 'Mahadevian : an Oldowan pebble culture in India', *Asian Perspectives* 6 : 186-96.

Kivisild, T., 1999, 'An Indian ancestry : a key for human diversity in Europe and beyond', In Katie Boyle and Peter Forster, compiled, *Human Diversity in Europe and beyond : Retrospect and Prospect. The Third Biennial Euroconference of the European Human Genome Diversity Project, 9-13 September 1999*, Abstracts, Cambridge.

Kivisild, T., Papiha, S.S., Rootsi, S., Parik, J., Kaldma, J., Reidla, M., Laos, S., Metspa;lu, M., Pielberg, G., Adojaau, M., Metspalu, E., Mastana, S.S., Wang, Y., Golge, M., Demirtas, H., Schnakenberg, E., Franci di Stefano, G., Geberhinot, T., Claustres, M. and Villems, R., 2000, 'An Indian ancestry : a key for understanding human diversity in Europe and beyond', In Colin Renfrew and Katie Boyle, eds., *Archaeogenetics : DNA and the Population Prehistory of Europe*, Cambridge, pp. 267-75.

Kochhar, N., Kochhar, R. and Chakrabarti, Dilip K., 1999, 'A new source of primary tin ore in the Indus civilization. *South Asian Studies,* 15 : 115-18.

Kohli, D., 1984, *The Material Culture of Northern India during the Northern Black Polished Ware Phase*, Unpublished Ph.D thesis, Delhi University.

Krishnan, K., 1986, *Chemical and Petrological Studies in Ancient Pottery*, Unpublished Ph.D thesis, M.S.University, Baroda.

———, and Hegde, K.T.M., 1987, 'Chemical and petrographic stuidies in pottery of Harappa culture in Gujarat', *Journal of the M.S.University of Baroda (Humanities)*, 35-36 (1) : 27-56.

———, V.D., 1947, 'Stone Age India', *AI*, 3 : 11-57.

———, 1949, 'Megalithic types of south India', *AI,* 5 : 35-45.

———, and Soundararajan, K.V., 1951, 'The lithic tool-industries of the Singrauli basin', *AI*, 7 : 40-65.

———, 1953, 'Progress in prehistory', *AI*, 9 : 53-79.

———, 1962, 'The neolithic pattern of India', *AI*, 16 : 25-64.

Kshirsagar, Anupama, 1983, 'Nitrogen contents of the sediments from chalcolithic Inamgaon', *Bulletin of the Deccan College Post-Graduate and Research Institute* 42: 99-101.

———, 1993, 'The role of fluorine in the chronometric dating of Indian Stone Age cultures', *M&E*, 18 (2): 23-32.

———, 1996-97, 'Ladakh : relative time frame for neolithic culture by fluorine analysis', *Bulletin of the Deccan College Post-Graduate and Research Institute* 56-57 : 37-39.

Kumar, A., 1989, 'A metrical analysis of handaxes and cleavers from the Acheulian site at Gangapur, Nasik district, Maharashtra', *M&E,* 13 : 49-63.

Kumar, B., 1987, *Archaeology of Pataliputra and Nalanda*, Delhi.

Kumar, D., 1986, *Archaeology of Vaishali*, Delhi.

Kumar, Giriraj, Sahni, A., Pancholi, R.K. and Narvare, Geeta, 1990, 'Archaeological discoveries and a study of late pleistocene ostrich egg shells and egg shell objects in India', *M&E*, 15(1) : 29-40.

Kumar, Tuk-Tuk, 1988, *History of Rice in India — Mythology, Culture and Agriculture*, Delhi.

Lahiri, Nayanjot, 1990, 'Harappa as a centre of trade and trade routes : a case study of the resource-use, resource-access and lines of communication in the Indus civilization', *Indian Economic and Social History Review* 27:405-44.

1992, *The Archaeology of Indian Trade Routes (up to c. 200* BC), Delhi.

———, 1995, 'Indian metal and metal-related artefacts as cultural signifiers : An Ethnographic Perspective', *World Archaeology*, 27 : 116-32.

———, 2000, 'Archaeology and identity in colonial India', *Antiquity*, 74 : 687-92.

———, ed., 2000, *The Decline and Fall of the Indus Civilization*, Delhi.

———, 2001, 'Are you Aryan and elite ? A provocative study that intends to mitigate Indological McCarthyism', Review of E. Bryant, 'The Quest for the Origins of Vedic Culture', *India Today* November 19, p. 71.

———, and Sharma D.P., In press, 'Harappan settlers of the Ganga-Yamuna Doab', *Marg*.

Lahiri Chaudhuri, 'Dharani Kanta, 1317 B.S./1910 AD' (in Bengali), *Bharat Bhraman*, Calcutta.

Lal, B.B., 1949, 'Sisupalgarh 1948 : an early historical fort in eastern India', *AI,* 5 : 62-105.

———, 1950, 'The Painted Grey Ware of the upper Gangetic basin : an approach to the problems of the Dark Age', *Journal of the Royal Asiatic Society of Bengal (Letters)*, 16 (NS) : 89-102.

———, 1951, 'Further Copper Hoards from the Gangetic basin and a review of the problem', *AI*, 7 : 20-39.

——, 1953, 'Protohistoric investigation', *AI,* 9 : 80-102.

——, 1954-55, 'Excavation at Hastinapura and other explorations in the upper Ganga and Sutlej basins 1950-52', *AI,* 10-11 : 5-151.

——, 1956, 'Palaeoliths from the Beas and Banganga valleys, Panjab', *AI,* 12 : 58-92.

——, 1958, 'Birbhanpur, a microlithic site in the Damodar valley, West Bengal', *AI,* 14 : 4-48.

——, 1962, 'From the megalithic to the Harappa : tracing back the graffiti on the pottery', *AI* 16 : 4-24.

——, 1963, 'A Picture Emerges — An Assessment of the Carbon-14 datings of the protohistoric cultures of the Indo-Pakistan subcontinent', *AI,* 18-19 : 208-21.

——, 1964, *Indian Archaeology since Independence*, Delhi.

——, 1981, 'The two Indian epics *vis-à-vis* archaeology', *Antiquity* 54 : 27-34.

——, and Gupta, S.P., 1984, eds., *Frontiers of the Indus Civilization*, Delhi.

Lal, B.B. (Dr). 1952, 'Examination of some ancient Indian glass specimens', *AI,* 8 : 17-27.

——, 1953, 'Archaeological Chemistry and Scientific Studies', *AI,* 9 : 199-206.

——, 1956, 'An examination of some metal images from Nalanda, *AI,* 12 : 53-57.

——, 1958, 'Examination of rods of glass-like material from Arikamedu', *AI,* 14 : 139-143.

——, 1963, 'Chemical preservation of ancient objects', *AI,* 18-19 : 230-50.

——, and Lal, S.B., 1961, 'The microlithic site of Birbhanpur : A Geochronological Study', *AI,* 17 : 37-45.

Lal, M., 1984a, *Settlement History and Rise of Civilization in the Ganga Yamuna Doab*, Delhi.

——, 1984b, 'Summary of four seasons of explorations in Kanpur district, Uttar Pradesh', *M&E,* 8 : 61-80.

——, 1986, 'Iron tools, forest clearance and urbanisation in the Gangetic plains', *M&E,* 10 : 83-90.

Leshnik, L. S., 1966, 'Early settled farmers of central India', *Year Book of the South Asia Institute, Heidelberg*', pp. 43-55.

——, 1974, *South Indian 'Megalithic' Burials*, Weisbaden.

Lone, F .A., Buth, G.M. and Khan, M., 1986, 'Wood remains from archaeological sites', *M&E,* 10 : 73-78.

Lowenthal, David, 1996, *The Heritage Crusade and the Spoils of History,* London.

Lukacs, J.R., 1978, 'Biocultural interaction in prehistoric India: culture, ecology and the pattern of dental disease in neolithic-chalcolithic populations', In S. Vatuk, ed., *American Studies in the Anthropology of India*, Delhi, pp. 425-44.

——, and Walimbe, S.R., 1986a, *Excavations at Inamgaon,* Vol. 2, Pune.

Madella, Marco, 1999, *Morphological Analysis of Phytoliths : a Botanical Tool for the Interpretation of Archaeological and Geological Sediments from Eurasia*, Unpublished Ph.D thesis, Cambridge University.

Majumdar, A., 1998-99, 'Early Harappan settlements in north Gujarat', *Pragdhara,* 9 : 15-25.

Majumdar, P.P., 1998, 'People of India : biological diversity and affinities', *Evolutionary Anthropology*, pp. 100-10.

Malik, S.C., 1959, *Stone Age Industries of Bombay and Satara Districts*, Baroda.

——, 1968, *Indian Civilization : the Formative Period*, Simla.

Mani, B.R., 1996-97, 'Recent archaeological investigations in trans-Ghaghra plains and identification of some city sites of Kosala', *Puratattva* 27 : 10-18.

——, 1997, *Delhi : Threshold of the Orient — Studies in Archaeological Investigations*, Delhi.

——, 1999-2000, 'Excavations at Kanispur : 1998-99 (district Baramulla, Kashmir)', *Pragdhara,* 10 : 1-21.

Marathe, A.R., 1981, *Geoarchaeology of the Hiran Valley, Saurashtra, India*, Poona.

——, 1995, 'Prehistory and Quaternary sea level changes along the west coast of India : A summary', In S. Wadia, R. Korisettar and V. Kale, eds., *Quaternary Environments and Geoarchaeology of India*, Bangalore, pp. 405-413.

Margabandhu, C., 1985, *Archaeology of the Satavahana Kshatrapa times*, Delhi.

Mathpal, Y., 1984, *Prehistoric Rock Paintings of Bhimbetka, Central India*, Delhi.

McIntosh, R.J., 2001, 'Francophone Africa', In Murray 2001, pp. 21-35.

Mehta, R.N., 1974, 'Urban Surat :an archaeological, topographical and toponymical perspective', *Journal of the Maharaja Sayajirao University of Baroda,* 22-23 : 81-92.

——, 1975, 'Khambat (Cambay) : topographical, archaeological and toponymical perspective', *Journal of the Maharaja Sayajirao University of Baroda* 24 : 17-29.

——, 1979, *Mediaeval Archaeology*, Delhi.

——, 1984, 'Valabhi — a station of Harappan cattle-breeders', In *Frontiers of the Indus Civilization* (eds. B.B. Lal and S.P. Gupta), Delhi, pp. 227-30.

Mishra, Phani Kanta, 2001, 'Deorkothar stupa : new light on early Buddhism', *Marg*, pp. 65-74.

Mishra, Sheila, 1982, 'On the effects of basalt weathering on the distribution of lower palaeolithic sites in the Deccan', *Bulletin of the Deccan College Post-Graduate and Research Institute* 41 : 107-15.

——, 1994, 'The south Asian lower palaeolithic', *M&E,* 19 (1): 57-71.

——, 1995, 'Chronology of the Indian Stone Age : The impact of recent absolute and relative dating attempts', *M&E,* 20 (2): 11-16.

——, and Rajaguru, S.N., 1993, 'Quaternary deposits at Bedaghat near Jabalpur, Madhya Pradesh', *M&E,* 18(2): 8-12.

——, Ota, S.B., Shete, G., Naik, Sonali and Deotare, BC 1999, 'Late Quarternary alluvial history and archaeological sites in the Nimar region of western Madhya Pradesh', *M&E,* 24(1) : 149-57.

Misra, V.D., Pal, J.N. and Gupta, M.C., 1998-99, 'Further excavations at Jhusi (1998-99)', *Pragdhara,* 10: 23-30.

Misra, V.N., 1961, 'Palaeolithic culture of western Rajputana', *Bulletin of the Deccan College Post-Graduate and Research Institute*, 21: 85-116.

——, 1967, *Pre and Prooi-History of the Berach Basin, South Rajasthan*, Poona.

——, 1973, 'Bagor : A Mesolithic Settlement in Northwest India', *World Archaeology* 5 : 92-110.

——, 1990, 'The Van Vagris — "lost" hunters of the Thar desert', *M&E,* 15(2) : 89-108.

——, 1984, 'Climate, A Factor in the Rise and Fall of the Indus Civilization — evidence from Rajasthan and beyond', In *Frontiers of the Indus Civilization* (eds. B.B. Lal and S.P. Gupta), Delhi, pp. 461-82.

——, and Mate, M.S., eds., 1965, *Indian Prehistory : 1964*, Poona.

——, and Mathpal, Y., 1979, 'Rock art of Bhimbetka region, central India', *M&E,* 3 : 27-33.

——, Rajaguru, S.N., Raju, D.R., Raghavan, H. and Gaillard, C., 1982, 'Acheulian Occupation and Evolving Landscape around Didwana in the Thar desert, India', *M&E,* 6:72-86.

——, and Bellwood, P., eds., 1985, *Recent Advances in Indo-Pacific Prehistory*, Delhi.

——, Rajaguru, S.N. and Raghavan, H., 1988, 'Late Pleistocene Environment and Acheulian Culture around Didwana, Rajasthan', *Proceedings of the Indian National Science Academy*, 54 A, pp. 425-38.

——, Shinde, V., Mohanty, R.K., Dalal, K., Mishra, A., Pandey, L. and Kharakwal, J., 1995, 'The excavations at Balathal : their contribution to the chalcolithic and Iron Age cultures of Mewar', *M&E,* 20(1) : 57-80.

Mitra, Debala, 1972, *Excavation at Tilaurakot and Kodan. Exploration in the Nepalese Tarai*, Delhi.

Mittra, S.K. and Shivananda, V., 2000, 'Chalcolithic settlements at Chichali', *Puratattva,* 30: 45-49.

Mohanty, R.K., 1999, 'Significance of a bead manufacturing centre at Mahurjhari, district Nagpur, Maharashtra, India', *M&E,* 24 (2): 79-89.

Mohanty, R.K. and Walimbe, S.R., 1993, 'A demographic approach to the Vidarbha megalithic culture', *M&E,* 18 : 93-103.

Mohapatra, G.C., 1962, *The Stone Age Cultures of Orissa*, Poona.

———, 1966, 'Preliminary report of the exploration and excavation of Stone Age sites in eastern Punjab', *Bulletin of the Deccan College Post-Graduate and Research Institute*. 25 : 221-37.

Momin, K. N., 1984, 'Village Harappans in Kheda district of Gujarat', In *Frontiers of the Indus Civilization* (eds. B.B. Lal and S.P. Gupta), Delhi, pp. 231-34.

Morrison, Kathleen, 2000, *Fields of Victory, Vijayanagar and the Course of Intensification*, Delhi.

Mountjoy, A.B., ed., 1978, *The Third World Problems and Perspectives*, London.

Mukherji, S.C., 1993-94, 'Excavation at Banesvar Danga, district Barddhaman, West Bengal', *Pratna Samiksha,* 2-3 : 80-143.

Murray, Tim, ed., 1999, *Great Archaeologists*, Santa Barbara.

———, ed., 2001, *Encyclopaedia of Archaeology — History and Discoveries*, 3 Volumes, Santa Barbara.

Murty, M.L.K., 1966, *Stone Age Cultures of Chittoor District*, Unpublished Ph.D thesis, Poona University.

———, 1975, 'Late pleistocene fauna of Kurnool caves, south India', In *Archaeozoological Studies*, Amsterdam, pp. 132-38.

———, 1981, 'Hunter-gatherer ecosystems and archaeological patterns of subsistence behaviour on the southeast coast of India : an ethnographic model', *World Archaeology,* 13 : 47-58.

———, 1985a, 'The uses of plant foods by some hunter-gatherer communities in Andhra Pradesh', In *Recent Advances in Indo-Pacific Prehistory* (eds. V.N. Misra and P. Bellwood), Delhi, pp. 329-36.

———, 1985b, 'Ethnoarchaeology of the Kurnool cave areas', *World Archaeology* 17 : 192-205.

Nagar, Malti, 1983, 'Ethnoarchaeology of the Bhimbetka region', *M&E,* 7 : 61-69.

———, 1985, 'The use of wild plant foods by aboriginal communities in central India', In *Recent Advances in Indo-Pacific Prehistory* (V.N. Misra and P. Bellwood, eds.), Delhi, pp. 337-42.

———, and Misra, V.N., 1989, 'Hunter-gatherers in an agrarian setting : the nineteenth century situation in the Ganga plains', *M&E,* 13 : 65-78.

———, 1990, 'The Kanjars — a hunting-gathering community of the Ganga valley, Uttar Pradesh', *M&E,* 15 (2): 71-88.

Nagpall, J.C. and Agrawal, O.P., 1959, 'Examination and preservation of a painted stucco head', *AI,* 15 : 94-99.

Nanda, Rajni, 1992, *The Early History of Gold in India*, Delhi.

———, and Chakrabarti, Dilip K., 1985, 'Lead in early India : a study of the geological, archaeological and literary data', *Indian Historical Review,* 7: 1-18.

———, and Chakrabarti, Dilip K., 1989, 'Silver in early India', *Calcutta Review.*

Nag, A.K., 1996 (in Bengali), *Pratnatattva o Pratikriya*, Academy Patrika, Paschimbanga Bangla Academy (April issue), pp. 52-70.

Narain, Hari, Srivastava, Prakash, J. and Agrawal, O.P., 1990-91, 'Metallographic studies of iron implements and weapon from Soron 600 BC 100 AD, Uttar Pradesh', *Pragdhara,* 1 : 163-71.

———, Prakash, J., Agrawal, O.P. and Nair, M.V., 1991-92, 'Technical studies of iron artifacts from Hulaskhera (Uttar Pradesh) 400 BC — 500 AD', *Pragdhara,* 2 : 81-88.

———, Prakash, J , Nair, M.V. and Agrawal, O.P., 1998, 'Metallographic studies of copper antiquities from Manjhi (district Saran, Bihar), 400 BC — 300 AD', In V. Tripathi, ed., *Archaeometallurgy in India*, Delhi, pp. 27-35.

———, Prakash, J., Agrawal, O.P., and Nair, M.V., 1998, Metallographic studies of iron artifacts of domestic use, tools and weapons from Sringaverapura (250 BC — 600 AD)', In, V. Tripathi, ed., *Archaeometallurgy in India*. Delhi, pp. 44-53.

Narayan, B., 1996, *Prehistoric Archaeology of Bihar*, Patna.

———, 1999, *Emerging Issues of Prehistory in Bihar*, Calcutta.

Nath, A., 1998, 'Rakhigarhi : A Harappan metropolis in the Sarasvati-Drishadvati divide', *Puratattva* 28 : 39-45.

———, 1998, *Further Excavations at Pauni 1994*, Delhi.

Nautiyal, K.P., 1969, *The Archaeology of Kumaon (including Dehradun)*, Varanasi.

Nautiyal, V., Farawan, Y.S. and Rawat, J.S., 1992, 'Phosphorus analysis of soils from archaeological sites in the mid-central Himalayas and Ganga-Yamuna Doab', *M&E,* 17(1) : 41-50.

Nautiyal, V., Nautiyal, K.P., Khanduri, B.M., Nautiyal, S. and Negi, J., 1995, 'The optical plotting technique using the reflex metrograph : a new approach to ceramic drawing', *M&E,* 20(2): 91-96.

Neumayer, E., 1983, *Prehistoric Indian Rock Paintings*, Delhi.

———, 1993, *Lines on Stone*, Delhi.

Ota, S.B., 1992, 'Archaeological investigations in the submergence area of the Narmada Sagar dam, Madhya Pradesh : a reconnaissance survey', *M&E,* 17(1) : 97-103.

Paddayya, K., 1975, 'The faunal background of the neolithic culture of south India', In *Archaezoological Studies* (A.T. Clason, ed), Amsterdam, pp. 329-34.

———, 1978, 'New research designs and field-techniques in the palaeolithic archaeology of India', *World Archaeology* 10 : 94-110.

———, 1982, *The Acheulian Culture of the Hunsgi Valley (Peninsular India), A Settlement System Perspective*, Poona.

———, 1990, *The New Archaeology and Aftermath, a View from Outside the Anglo-American World*, Pune.

———, 1995, 'Theoretical perspectives in Indian archaeology : an historical view', In P.J. Ucko, ed., *Theory in Archaeology, a World Perspective*, London, pp. 110-49.

———, Thomas, P.K. and Joglekar, P.P., 1995, 'A neolithic animal butchering floor from Budihal, Gulbarga district, Karnataka', *M&E,* 20(2) : 23-31.

———, Jhaldiyal, R. and Petraglia, M., 1999-2000, 'The significance of the Acheulian site of Islampur, Karnataka, in the lower palaeolithic of India, *Puratattva,* 30 : 1-24.

Pal, J.N., 1984, 'Epi-palaeolithic sites in Pratapgarh district, Uttar Pradesh', *M&E,* 8 : 31-38.

———, 1985, 'Some new light on the mesolithic burial practices of the Ganga valley : evidence from Mahadaha, Pratapgarh, Uttar Pradesh', *M&E,* 9 : 28-37.

Pal, Yash, Sahai, B., Sood, R.K. and Agrawal, D.P., 1984, 'Remote sensing of the lost Saraswati river', In *Frontiers of the Indus Civilization* (eds. B.B. Lal and S.P. Gupta), Delhi, pp. 491-97.

Pande, B.M., 1971, 'Neolithic hunting scene on a stone slab from Burzahom', Kashmir', *Asian Perspectives* 14 : 194-98.

Panja, Shina, 1995, *Mobility Strategies, Site Structure and Settlement Organization : A Case Study of Chalcolithic Sites in the Middle Bhima Valley with Special Reference to Inamgaon*, Unpublished Ph.D thesis, Deccan College.

Pant, P.C., 1967-68, 'Typology in prehistory', *Puratattva,* 1 : 61-67.

Pant, R.K., 1979, 'Microwear studies on Burzahom neolithic tools', *M&E,* 3 : 11-18.

———, Gaillard, Claire, Nautiyal, V., Gaur, G.S. and Shali, S.L. 1982, 'Some new lithic and deramic industries from Kashmir', *M&E,* 6 : 37-40.

Pappu, R.S., 1974, *Pleistocene Studies in the Upper Krishna Basin*, Poona.

Pappu, Shanti, 2001, 'Middle palaeolithic stone tool technology in the Kortalayar basin, south India', *Antiquity,* 75 : 109-17.

Petraglia, M., La Porta, P. and Paddayya, K., 1999, 'Islampur, the first Acheulian quarry in India : stone tool manufacture, biface morphology and behaviours', *Journal of Anthropological Research* 55 : 39-70

Piggott, S., 1985, *William Stukeley, an Eighteenth Century Antiquary*, London.

Pokharia, A.K. and Saraswat, K.S., 1999-2000, 'Wood charcoal remains from ancient Sanghol, Punjab (*ca* 100-300 AD), *Pragdhara* 10 : 149-71.

Possehl, G.L., 1980, *Indus Civilization in Saurashtra*, Delhi.

———, ed., 1982, *Harappan Civilization*, Delhi.

Pratap, A., 2000, *The Hoe and the Axe: an Ethnohistory of Shifting Cultivation in Eastern India*, Delhi.

Prasad, R.C., 1987, *Archaeology of Champa and Vikramasila*, Delhi.

Puri, B.N., 1966, *Cities of Ancient India*, Delhi.

Raghavan, H., Rajaguru, S.N. and Misra, V.N., 1989, 'Radiometric dating of a Quaternary dune section Didwana, Rajasthan', *M&E,* 13 : 19-22.

Rajan, K., 1994, *Archaeology of Tamil Nadu (Kongu Country)*, Delhi.

———, 1997, *Archaeological Gazetteer of Tamil Nadu*, Thanjavur.

Raju, D., 1988, *Stone Age Hunter-Gatherers, an Ethnoarchaeology of Cuddapah Region*, Pune.

Ramasamy, Venkatasubramanian, V. Abdullah, S.R. and Balaji, S. 1992, 'The phenomenon of river migration in northern Tamil Nadu — evidence from satellite data, archaeology and Tamil literature', *M&E,* 17(1) : 13-25.

Rao, K.N., Rao, Ch.U. and Rao, K.S., 1997, 'Significance of remote sensing for geomorphic mapping in archaeological investigations', *M&E,* 22(2) :67-72.

Rao, Nandini, 1994, 'Subsistence and associated settlement patterns in central India : an ethnoarchaeological analysis', In B. Allchin, ed., *Living Traditions, Studies in the Ethnoarchaeology of South Asia*, Delhi, pp. 143-68.

Rao, M.S., Bisaria, B.K. and Singhvi, A.K., 1997, 'A feasibility study towards absolute dating of Indo-Gangetic alluvium using thermoluminiscence and infrared-stimulated luminiscence techniques', *Current Science* 72: 663-69.

Rao, S.N., 1966, *Stone Age Cultures of Nalgonda District, Andhra Pradesh*, Unpublished Ph.D thesis, Poona University.

Rao, S.R., 1963, 'Excavation at Rangpur and other explorations in Gujarat', *AI,* 18-19 : 5-207.

———, 1973, *Lothal and the Indus Civilization*, Bombay.

———, 1990, 'Excavation of the legendary city of Dvaraka in the Arabian sea', *Journal of Marine Archaeology,* 1: 59-98.

Ratnagar, S., 1981, *Encounters*, Delhi.

———, 1991, *Enquiries into the Political Organization of Harappan Society*, Pune.

Ray, Amal., 2000, (in Bengali), 'Samprati abishkrita bauddhavihar : Jagajjivanpur', *Puravritta,* 1 : 145-66.

Ray, H.P. and Salles, J-F., eds., 1996, *Tradition and Archaeology : Early Maritime Contacts in the Indian Ocean*, Delhi.

Ray, Niharranjan, 1963, 'Archaeology in India today', *AI,* 18-19 : 222-29.

Reddy Seetha, N., 1991, 'Archaeobotanical investigations at Oriyo Timbo (1989-90): a post-urban site in Gujarat', *M&E,* 16 (1): 73-83.

——, 1997, 'If the threshing floor could talk : integration of agriculture and pastoralism during the late Harappan context in Gujarat', *Journal of Anthropological Archaeology* 16 : 162-87.

Renfrew, Colin., 1999, *Loot, Legitimacy and Ownership : the Ethical Crisis in Archaeology*, Amsterdam.

Richards, F.J., 1933, 'Geographical factors in Indian archaeology', *Indian Antiquary* 62 : 235-53.

Rissman, P.C and Chitalwala, Y.M., 1990, *Harappan Civilization and Oriyo Timbo*, Delhi.

Robertshaw, P., 'A history of African archaeology: an introduction', In P. Robertshaw, ed., *A History of African Archaeology*, London, pp. 3-12.

Roy, Sourindranath, 1961, *The Story of Indian Archaeology*, Delhi.

Roy, T.N., 1983, *The Ganges Civilization*, Delhi.

——, 1986, *A Study of Northern Black Polished Ware*, Delhi.

Sahi, M.D.N., 1979, 'Iron at Ahar', In *Essays in Indian Protohistory* (D.P. Agrawal and D.K. Chakrabarti, eds.), Delhi, pp. 365-68.

Sahu, B.P., 1988, *From Hunters to Breeders*, Delhi.

Sali, S.A., 'The Harappans of Daimabad', In G.L. Possehl, ed., *Harappan Civilization*, Delhi, pp. 175-84.

——, 1986, *Daimabad 1976-79*, Delhi.

Sankalia, H.D., 1951, 'Ancient and prehistoric Maharashtra', *Journal of the Bombay Branch of the Royal Asiatic Society*, 27 : 99-106.

——, 1952, *The Godavari Palaeolithic Industry*, Poona.

——, 1956, 'Animal-fossils and palaeolithic industries from the Pravara basin at Nevasa, District Ahmednagar', *AI,* 12 : 35-52.

——, 1960, 'Houses and habitations through the ages', *Bulletin of the Deccan College Post-Graduate and Research Institute*, 20 : 140-63.

——, 1962, *Prehistory and Protohistory in India and Pakistan*, Poona.

——, 'Preface', In *Indian Prehistory: 1964* (eds. V.N. Misra and M.S. Mate), Poona.

——, 1977, *The New Archaeology: Its Scope and Application to India*, Lucknow.

——, 1978, 'Prehistoric colonization in India : archaeological and literary evidence', *Puratattva,* 8 : 72-86.

——, 1978, *Prehistoric Art of India*, Delhi.

——, Subbarao, B. and Joshi, R.V., 1950, 'Studies in the prehistory of Karnatak', *Bulletin of the Deccan College Post-graduate and Research Institute*, 11 : 56-82.

——, and Dikshit, M.G., 1952, *Excavations at Brahmapuri (Kolhapur), 1945-46*, Poona.

——, Subbarao, B. and Deo, S.B., 1958, *The Excavations at Maheshwar and Navdatoli 1952-53,* Baroda.

——, Deo, S.B. and Ansari, Z.D., 1960, *From Prehistory to History at Nevasa (1954-56)*, Poona.

Sarkar, H., 1962, 'Some aspects of the Buddhist monuments at Nagarjunakonda', *AI,* 16 : 65-84.

Sarkar, S.S., 1964, *Ancient Races of Baluchistan, Panjab and Sind*, Calcutta.

Saraswat, K.S., 1986, 'Ancient crop economy of Harappans from Rohira, Punjab (*c.* 2000-1700 BC)', *The Palaeobotanist,* 35: 32-38.

——, 1990-91, 'Crop economy at ancient Mahorana, Punjab (*c.* 2100-1900 BC)', *Pragdhara* 1 : 83-88.

——, 1992-93, 'Seed and fruit remains of Imlidih Khurd, Gorakhpur : A preliminary report', *Pragdhara,* 3 : 37-41.

——, 1993, 'Plant economy of late Harappan at Hulas', *Puratattva,* 23 : 1-12.

———, Sharma, N.K. and Saini, D.C., 1994, 'Plant economy at ancient Narhan', In P. Singh, *Excavations at Narhan (1984-1989)*, Banaras, pp. 255-346.

Sastry, T.V.G., Bai, M.Kasturi and Rao, J.V., 1984, *Veerapuram, a Type Site for Cultural Study in the Krishna Valley*, Hyderabad.

Sathe, Vijay and Badam, G.L., 1996, 'Animal remains from the neolithic and chalcolithic periods at Senuwar, district Rhotas, Bihar', *M&E,* 21 (2) : 43-48.

Selvakumar, V., 2000, 'Investigations into the Iron Age- early historic cultures of the upper Gundar basin, Madurai district, Tamil Nadu, India', *South Asian Studies,* 16 : 116-32.

Semans, Cheryl A., 1981, 'Analysis of an Acheulian collection from Peera nullah, Narmada valley', *M&E,* 5 : 13-31.

Sen, D., 1955, 'Nalagarh palaeolithic culture', *Man in India* 35 : 177-84.

———, and Ghosh, A.K., 1960, 'On the occurrence of palaeoliths in Singhbhum', *Man in India* 40 : 178-91.

Sen, D.K., 1967, 'Ancient races of India and Pakistan — A Study of Methods', *AI,* 20-21 : 178-205.

Sengupta, G., ed., 1992, *Pratna-Samiksha 1*, Calcutta.

———, ed., 1993-94, *Pratna-Samiksha 2-3*, Calcutta.

Shaffer, J.G., 1978, 'Bronze Age iron from Afghanistan : Its implications for south Asian protohistory', Mss.

———, 1982, 'Harappan Culture : A Reconsideration', In G.L. Possehl, ed., *Harappan Civilization*, Delhi, pp. 41-50.

Shahani, Lajwanti, 1997, 'Ethnoarchaeology of Harappan sea trade — a preliminary study', *M&E,* 22(1) : 9-18.

Shankar, A., 2001, 'The threat to cultural sites in India from illegal excavation', In N. Brodie, J. Doole and C. Renfrew eds., *Trade in Illicit Antiquities : the Destruction of the World's Archaeological Heritage*, Cambridge, pp. 33-36.

Sharma, I.K., 1967-68, 'Patpadu revisited : A New Painted Pottery Culture of Southeast India', *Puratattva,* 1 : 68-84.

———, 1970, 'Southeast Asia, India and west Asia', In S.B. Deo, ed., *Archaeological Congress and Seminar Papers*, Nagpur, pp. 95-112.

Sharma, A.K., 1974, 'Evidence of horse from the Harappan settlement at Surkotada', *Puratattva,* 7 : 75-76.

———, 1982, 'The Harappan cemetery at Kalibangan : A Study', In G.L. Possehl, ed., *Harappan Civilization*, Delhi, pp. 297-300.

Sharma, Chhaya and Chauhan, M.S., 1991, 'Palaeovegetation and palaeoenvironmental inferences from the Quaternary palynostratigraphy of the western Indian plains', *M&E,* 16 (1): 65-71.

Sharma, Deo Prakash, 2000, *Harappan Seals, Sealings and Copper Tablets*, Delhi.

Sharma, D.V., Prabhakar, V.N., Tewari, R. and Srivastava, R.K., 1999-2000, 'Harappan jewellery hoard from Mandi', *Puratattva,* 30 : 36-41.

Sharma, G.R., 1973, 'Mesolithic lake cultures in the Ganga valley', *Proceedings of the Prehistoric Society*, 39 : 129-46.

———, Misra, V.D., Mandal, D., Misra, B.B. and Pal, J.N. 1980, *Beginnings of Agriculture*, Allahabad.

———, and Clark J.D. eds., 1983, *Palaeoenvironment and Prehistory in the Middle Son Valley (Madhya Pradesh, North Central India)*, Allahabad.

Sharma, R.C., 1984, *Buddhist Art of Mathura*, Delhi.

Sharma, R.K., ed., 1982, *Indian Archaeology, New Perspectives*, Delhi.

———, and Ali, Rahman, 1980, *Archaeology of Bhopal Region*, Delhi.

———, and Misra, S.N., 1992, *Excavations at Kakrehta (Rupnath)*, Delhi.

Sharma, T.C., 1966, *Prehistoric Archaeology of Assam — A Study on Neolithic Culture*, Unpublished Ph.D. thesis, London University.

Sharma, Y.D., 1953, 'Exploration of historical sites', *AI,* 9 : 116-69.

——, 1956, 'Rock-cut caves in Cochin', *AI,* 12 : 93-115.

——, 1982, 'Harappan complex on the Sutlej(India)', In G.L. Possehl, ed., *Harappan Civilization*, Delhi, pp. 141-66.

Shaw, Julia. n.d., *The Sacred Geography of Sanchi Hill : the Archaeological Setting of Buddhist Monasteries in Central India*, Unpublished Ph.D. thesis, Cambridge University.

Sheshadri, Rajam, 1992, 'The composition and smithery techniques of copper artefacts from Nagwada — a preliminary study', *M&E,* 17(1): 7-12.

Shinde, V., 1991, 'A horn-headed human figurine on a Harappan jar from Padri Gujarat', *M&E,* 16(2) : 87-89.

——, 1992, 'Excavations at Padri — 1990-91 : a preliminary report', *M&E,* 17(1): 79-86.

——, 1996, 'A preliminary report of the second season's excavation at Padri', In R.K. Sharma and R.C. Agrawal, eds., *Krsna Smrti: Studies in Indian Art and Archaeology*, Delhi, pp. 40-45.

——, 1998, *Early Settlements in the Central Tapi Basin*, Delhi.

——, and Kar, S.B., 1992, 'Padri Ware : A New Painted Ceramic found in the Harappan levels at Padri in Gujarat', *M&E,* 17(2) : 105-10.

——, and Thomas, E., 1993, 'A unique Harappan copper fish-hook from Padri, Gujarat', *M&E,* 17(2) : 105-10.

Singh, H.N., 1982, *History and Archaeology of Black-and-Red Ware (Chalcolithic Period)*, Delhi.

Singh, P., 1970, *Burial Practices in Ancient India,* Banaras.

——, 1994, *Excavations at Narhan (1984-89)*, Delhi.

——, and Lal, M., 1985, 'Narhan 1983-85 : A Preliminary Report', *Bharati* (New Series). 3 : 113-88.

Singh, Rameshwar, 1965, *Palaeolithic Industries of Northern Bundelkhand*, Unpublished Ph.D. thesis, Poona University. (Dr Singh joined the Department of Anthropology, Delhi University, as a lecturer in pre-historic archaeology in the mid-1960s. Soon afterwards, he was killed during an attack by bandits on his village home. I remember him as a quiet , scholarly and hospitable gentleman.)

Singh, R.N., 1989, *Ancient Indian Glass : Archaeology and Technology*, Delhi.

Singh, R.N., Merkel, J.F. and Singh, B.P., 1996-97, 'Analysis of copper objects from Senuar', *Bharati,* 23 : 154-56.

——, Merkel, J.F. and Singh, A.K., 1997, 'SEM and EPMA analysis of copper objects from Narhan', *Pragdhara,* 7: 123-24.

——, Glover, I and Merkel, J.F., 1998-99, 'Scientific studies of some iron objects from Senuwar', *Pragdhara,* 9 : 123-28.

Singh, S.B., 1979, *Archaeology of Panchala Region*, Delhi.

Singh, S.D. and Singh, S.B., 1972, *The Archaeology of Panchala Region*, Lucknow.

Singhvi, A.K., Sharma, Y.P. and Agrawal, D.P., 1982, 'Thermoluminiscence dating of sand dunes in Rajasthan, India', *Nature*, 295 : 313-15.

——, Bronger, A., Pant, R.K. and Sauer, W. 1987, 'Thermoluminiscence dating and its implications for the chronostratigraphy of loess-paleosol sequences in the Kashmir valley (India)', *Chemical Geology (Isotope Geoscience Section)* 65 : 45-56.

——, Wagner, G.A. and Korisettar, R. 1998, 'Techniques for the chronometry of the palaeolithic : evidence for global colonization', In Petraglia, M. and Korisettar, R., eds., *Early Human Behaviour in Global Context*, pp. 23-83.

Sinha, B.K. 2000, 'Golabai : a protohistoric site on the coast of Orissa', In K.K. Basa and P. Mohanty, eds., *Archaeology of Orissa,* Delhi, pp. 322-55.

Sinha, B.P., ed., 1969, *Potteries in Ancient India*, Patna.

Sinha, Prakash, 1985, 'Microwear analysis and its scope in Indian context', *M&E,* 9 : 21-27.

———, 1988, 'Probability sampling strategies in archaeology', *M&E,* 12: 153-68.

———, 1991, *Model for Land-Use in Late Acheulian Tradition* (*Satna District, M.P.*), Allahabad.

Sinha, Surajit, 1951, 'Discovery of some prehistoric tools in south Manbhum', *Science and Culture* 17 : 164.

Siva Kumar, S., Nasidze, I., Walimbe, S.R. and Stoneking, M., In press, 'Discouraging prospects for ancient DNA from India'.

Siva Kumar, S., Subramanian, V., Walimbe, S.R. and Singh, Lalji, 1999, 'Current trends in 'ancient DNA studies', *Current Science* 76 : 879-85.

Smith, M.L., 2000, 'Systematic surface survey at the early historic site of Kaundinyapura, India', *M&E,* 25 : 75-87.

Sonakia, A., 1984, 'The skull-cap of early man and associated mammalian fauna from the Narmada valley alluvium, Hoshangabad area, Madhya Pradesh, India', *Geological Survey of India, Records,* 113 : 159-72.

Sonawane, V.H., 1998-99, 'Harappan civilization in Gujarat : A recent perspective', *Pragdhara* 9 : 1-13.

———, and Ajitprasad, P., 1994, 'Harappa culture and Gujarat', *M&E,* 19(1) : 129-39.

Soundara Rajan, K.V., 1952, 'Stone Age industries near Giddalur, District Kurnool', *AI,* 8 : 64-92.

———, 1958, 'Studies in the Stone Age of Nagarjunakonda and its neighbourhood', *AI,* 14 : 49-113.

———, 1961, 'Quaternary pebble, core and flake cultures of India — an appraisal of the data', *AI,* 17 : 68-85.

Spate, O.H.K., 1954, *India and Pakistan. A Regional Geography*, London.

Srinivasan, K.R., 1958, 'The Pallava architecture of south India', *AI,* 14 : 114-38.

———, and Banerjee, N.R., 1953, *AI,* 9 : 103-15.

Srinivasan, N.R., 1998, 'Revival of rural iron-making in Orissa', In V. Tripathi, ed., *Archaeometallurgy in India*, Delhi, pp. 228-40.

Srinivasan, S., 1999, Lead isotope and trace element analysis in the study of over a hundred south Indian metal icons', *Archaeometry* 41 : 91-116.

———, and Glover, I. 1997, 'Wrought and quenched, and cast high-tin bronzes in Kerala State, India', *The Journal of the Historical Metallurgical Society,* 29 : 69-88.

Srivastava, A., 1998, *Archaeological Acts and Rules*, Bhopal.

Srivastava, K.M., 1979, *Community Movements in Protohistoric India*, Delhi.

Stone, P. and Mackenzie, R., eds., *The Excluded Past, Archaeology in Education*, London.

Subbarao, B., 1948, *Stone Age Cultures of Bellary*, Poona.

———, 1956, *The Personality of India*, Baroda (1st edn.).

———, 1958, *The Personality of India*, Baroda (2nd edn.).

Sundaresh and Gaur, A.S., 1998, 'Archaeology of Bet Dwaraka island', *M&E, 23*(2) : 77-86.

Supekar, S.G., 1968, *Pleistocene Stratigraphy and Prehistoric Archaeology of the Central Narmada Basin*, Unpublished Ph.D. thesis, Poona University.

Takahasi, T., Yamaoka, T., Yoneda, F. and Uesogi, A., 1999-2000, 'The ancient city of Sravasti : its significance on the urbanisation of north India', *Puratattva,* 30 : 74-92.

Tewari, R. and Srivastava, R.K., 1990-91, (in Hindi), 'Katar-Umarharg ke bauddha stup ke avasesh', *Pragdhara,* 1 : 9-13.

———, and Srivastava, R.K., 1996-97, 'Excavation at Raja Nala-ka-Tila (1995-96), district Sonabhadra (U.P.) — preliminary observation', *Pragdhara,* 7 : 77-95.

———, and Srivastava, S.K., 1997-98, 'Excavation at Raja Nala-ka-Tila (1996-97), district Sonabhadra — preliminary observations', *Pragdhara* 8 : 99-105.

———, Singh, P.K., Srivastava, R.K. and Singh, G.C., 1998-99, 'Archaeological investigations in district Mirzapur, *Pragdhara,* 9 : 163-223.

———, Srivastava, R.K., Saraswat, K.S. and Singh, K.K., 1999-2000, 'Excavations at Malhar, district Chandauli (U.P.)', 1999: 69-98.

———, Srivastava, R.K. and Singh, K.K., 2002, 'Dadupur Excavations 1999-2000-2001, district Lucknow, Uttar Pradesh: a preliminary report', *Pragdhara,* 12.

Thakur, Nalini M., 1999, 'Archaeological park at Mehrauli, Delhi', In H.J. Hansen and G. Quinne, eds., *Our Fragile Heritage Documenting the Past for the Future*, Copenhagen, pp. 187-94.

Thangaraj, K., Ramana, G.V. and Singh, Lalji, 1999, 'Y-chromosome and mitochondrial DNA polymorphisms in Indian populations', *Electrophoresis,* 20: 1743-47.

Thapar, B.K., 1952, 'Porkalam 1948 : excavation of a megalithic urn-burial', *AI,* 8 : 3-16.

———, 1957, 'Maski 1954 : A chalcolithic site of the southern Deccan', *AI,* 13 : 4.

———, 1967, 'Prakash 1955 : A chalcolithic site in the Tapti valley, *AI,* 20-21 : 5-167.

———, 1974, 'Editorial notes', *Puratattva,* 7.

———, 1984, 'India', In H. Cleere, ed., *Approaches to the Archaeological Heritage*, London, pp. 63-72.

———, 1985, *Recent Archaeological Discoveries in India*, Paris.

R. Thapar, 2001, Comments made as part of a panel discussion on 'Fundamentalism and Heritage', India International Centre, Delhi, 27 March 2001, *Seminar 501(May)* : 57-58.

Thomas, P.K., 1975, 'Role of animals in the food economy of the mesolithic culture of western and central India. In *Archaeozoological Studies* (A. T. Clason, ed.), Amsterdam, pp. 322-28.

———, and Joglekar, P.P., 1994, 'Holocene faunal studies in India', *M&E,* 19(1-2) : 179-203.

———, Joglekar, P.P., Misra, V.D., Pandey, J.N. and Pal, J.N., 1995, 'A preliminary report of the faunal remains from Damdama', *M&E,* 20(1) : 29-36.

Tiwari, R.K. and Kavdia, N.K., 1984, 'Ancient mining activity around Aguncha village, Bhilwara district, Rajasthan', *M&E,* 8 : 81-87.

Todd, K.R.U., 1950, 'The microlithic industries of Bombay', *AI,* 6 : 4-16.

Tripati S., 1999, 'Marine investigations in the Lakshadweep islands, India', *Antiquity,* 73: 827-35.

———, and Gaur, A.S., 1997, 'Onshore and nearshore explorations along the Maharashtra coast with a view to locating ancient ports and submerged sites', *M&E,* 22(2): 73-83.

Tripathi, Vibha, 1976, *The Painted Grey Ware — an Iron Age Culture of Northern India*, Delhi.

Trivedi, S.D., 1984, (in Hindi), *Bundelkhand-ka-Puratattva*, Jhansi.

Vats, M.S., 1951, 'Notes', *AI,* 7 : 1-2.

———, 1952, 'Notes', *AI,* 8 : 1-2.

Varma, R.K., Misra, V.D., Pandey, J.N. and Pal, J.N., 1985, 'A preliminary report on the excavations at Damdama', *M&E,* 9 : 45-65.

Verma, B.C. and Srivastava, J.P., 1984, 'Early palaeolithic sites of the outer Siwalik belt in Sirmur district, Himachal Pradesh, — their age and stratigraphic position', *M&E,* 8 : 13-19.

Vishnu-Mittre, 1985, 'The uses of wild plants and the processes of domestication in the Indian subcontinent', In *Recent Advances in Indo-Pacific Prehistory* (eds. V.N. Misra and P. Bellwood), Delhi, pp. 281-91.

———, 1989, 'Forty years of archaeobotanical research in south Asia', *M&E,* 14(1) : 1-16.

Wadia, S., Korisettar, R. and Kale, V. eds., 1995, *Quaternary Environments and Geoarchaeology of India*, Bangalore.

Wagner, Gail, 1990, 'Plant remains from Oriyo Timbo', In P.C. Rissman and Y.M. Chitalwala, *Harappan Civilization and Oriyo Timbo*, Delhi, pp. 127-38.

Wakankar, V.S. and Brooks, R., 1976, *Stone Age Paintings in India*, Bombay.

Walimbe, S.R., 1986, 'Palaeodemography of protohistoric Daimabad', In S.A. Sali, *Daimabad 1976-79*, Delhi, pp.641-740.

———, and Kulkarni, S.S., 1993, *Biological Adaptations in Human Dentition : an Odontometric Study on Living and Archaeological Populations in India*, Pune.

———, and Kulkarni, S.S., 1994, 'Dental anthropology in India : a review', *M&E,* 19(1-2) : 205-16.

Wasson, R.G., Smith, G.I. and Agrawal, D.P., 1984, 'Late Quaternary sediments, minerals, and inferred geochemistry of Didwana lake, Thar desert, India', *Palaeogeography, Palaeclimatology, Palaeoecology* 46 : 345-72.

Weber, S., 1999, 'Seeds of urbanism : palaeoethnobotany and the Indus civilization', *Antiquity,* 73 : 813-26.

Wheeler, R.E.M., 1948a, Notes, *Ancient India* 4 : 1-3.

———, 1948b, 'Brahmagiri and Chandravalli 1947 : megalithic and other cultures in Mysore State', *AI,* 4 : 180-310.

———, 1949, 'Archaeological fieldwork in India : planning ahead', *AI,* 5 : 4-11.

———, 1954, *Archaeology from the Earth*, Harmondsworth.

Wiiliams, M.A.J. and Royce, K., 1983, 'Alluvial history of the middle Son valley, north central India', In *Palaeoenvironment and Prehistory in the Middle Son Valley* (G.R. Sharma and J.D. Clark, eds)., Allahabad, pp. 9-23.

———, and Clarke, M.F., 1995, 'Quaternary geology and prehistoric environments in the Son and Belan valleys, north central India', In S. Wadia, R. Korisettar and V. Kale, eds., *Quaternary Environments and Geoarchaeology of India*, Bangalore, pp. 282-308.

Willies, Lynn, 1992, 'Ancient and post-mediaeval mining sites in the Khetri copper belt and Kolar gold field, India', *Bulletin of the Peak District Mines Historical Society*, 11 : 285-95.

Willies, Lynn, 1987, 'Ancient zinc-lead-silver mining in Rajasthan, India — interim report', *Bulletin of the Peak District Mines Historical Society*, 10 : 81-123.

Willies, L., 1984, 'Ancient lead and zinc mining in Rajasthan, India', *World Archaeology.*

Worman, E.C., 1949, 'The neolithic problem in the prehistory of India', *Journal of the Washington Academy of Sciences* 39 : 181-201.

Zeuner, F. E., 1950, *Stone Age and Pleistocene Chronology in Gujarat*, Poona.

———, 1952, 'The microlithic industry of Langhnaj, Gujarat', *Man,* 52.

———, and Allchin, Bridget, 1956, 'The microlithic sites of Tinnevelly district, Madras State', *AI,* 12 : 4-20.

Zewall, A.H., 2001, 'Science for the have-nots. *Nature*', 12 April, p. 741.

Index

Appendix

Towards a Nationalist Archaeology of India*

INTRODUCTION : COMMENTS ON THE THEME OF 'NATIONALISM AND ARCHAEOLOGY' IN ARCHAEOLOGICAL LITERATURE

THE relationship between archaeology and politics is a well-worn theme of theoretical studies of archaeology now, and the category, which has come in for close scrutiny in recent years for its supposedly baleful influence on the practice of archaeology and the interpretation of archaeological data, is nationalism. Apart from the much-cited case of Nazi Germany, convenient examples have always been easy to come by in the less developed parts of Europe, despotic Middle East, Hindu India, Communist and post-Communist Russia, Communist China, and rigidly homogeneous Japan and Korea. With the exception of Hindu India which seriously figured in this context in the wake of the demolition of a sixteenth-century mosque by a Hindu mob in Ayodhya in December 1992, case-studies from the other areas form the staple of the volumes edited by Philip Kohl and Clare Fawcett (1995) and Lynn Meskell (1998). Kohl and Fawcett (1995 : 5) write that, although 'one can admire the positive role of an ethnically inspired archaeology that helps build justifiable pride in a specific cultural tradition and stimulates research into the past development of that tradition', the essays they have compiled and edited in their volume are principally concerned with the *abuses* (their italics) of the relationship between nationalist politics and archaeology and the related problems of racial superiority/inferiority and questionable political agendas.

There are some problems with this approach. The fact which has not been adequately emphasised in these two volumes is that nationalism can also act as a great cultural force persuading people to undertake the study of not merely archaeology but also history, literature, folk-lore, language and innumerable other expressions of their national culture. Those who have time to think of nationalism as a great historical and cultural driving force will not shudder every time archaeological data are viewed through the lense of

* *Originally the annual lecture of the Ashin Dasgupta Institute of Tribal History, Calcutta, in 2002.*

national pride and self-respect, especially when this lense does not detract from the parameters of an objective assessment of the archaeological data. Further, when the role of nationalism in the development of archaeological researches in a given area is considered, that may not be done in isolation but in the general context of development in these other fields. The link with the romantic movement is important too, at least in Europe where this movement led to a shift of interest from the Classical Mediterranean lands to the features of their own countryside. Bruce Trigger (1995 : 268-269) writes :

> Romantically inclined western European intellectuals called on all to take pride in their nation state and regard the historical, cultural and biological heritage that its citizens shared as being more important than the class antagonisms that were threatening the social order.

One is not sure that the romantic movement, as it manifested itself in literature and even in archaeology, was only an intellectual method to stem the tide of class antagonism which was a social consequence of the Industrial Revolution in Britain (1760-1820) and later elsewhere in Europe.

Trigger (1995 : 269) further writes :

> Under the impetus of nationalism, archaeology abandoned a primary focus on evolution and concentrated on interpreting the archaeological record as the history of specific peoples.

It is doubtful if this is universally true. The texture and fabric of nationalism depended on the history of the nation state in which it flourished and the political circumstances in which this particular nation-state was born. If the catalyctic factor behind its genesis was an overriding feeling of ethnic identity within its territorial limits, it is quite natural that there would be a lot of emphasis on the so-called historicity of this ethnicity. Ethnicity, however, is only a historical reconstruct based on the exigencies of specific historical situations in which this identity is formulated. There is nothing absolute or sacrosanct about ethnic identities. If one has to cite a convenient example, I would cite the case of Bangladeshi ethnic identity which is accepted as a case of separate ethnic identity in modern Britain. As a nation state Bangladesh emerged in 1971, mainly as a consequence of the dissatisfaction of the Bengali-speaking people of the province of East Pakistan of the state of Pakistan which was born on the basis of religion in 1947. The way this nation state was born in 1971 depended specifically on the way in which the dissatisfaction of the Bengali-speaking populace of East Pakistan was handled by the central state structure of Pakistan. The rallying force of the clamour for a separate nationhood by this populace was the Bengali language which emerged in its modern form only within the last two hundred years. One would also say that the Bengali language has had its own story of development in the former East Pakistan and modern Bangladesh, which is not quite the same with its development in the neighbouring Indian state of West Bengal since 1947. Ethnicity is not an immutable thing and hardly susceptible to close historical and archaeological enquiries. This does not mean that a nation-state whose main pillar is a perceived feeling of commonness of language, religion, or whatever, cannot take pride in the antiquity and glory of archaeological finds within its limits. As an example, the interest which the simple find of prehistoric fossilwood tools in Bangladesh in 1989 generated among its journalists comes readily to mind. The antiquity and richness of historical finds within the territorial limits of modern Bangladesh have also been matters of pride to the general run of its intelligentsia. There is no reason why such cases of simple pride should be run down in the name of an unwarranted political dimension of archaeology.

On the other hand, as we all know, there are many multi-ethnic states. Again, the concept of the past these multi-ethnic states may follow cannot be pinned down merely to the question of the dominance of a particular ethnic group over the other ethnic components of their population. The case of Turkey, as propounded by Mehemet Ozdogan (1998) is a pointer in this direction.

> In creating a nation out of the ruins of the Ottoman Empire, it was essential to formulate an ideology that would assure national pride, give moral direction and identity. Most of the elite of the time were utterly desparate and had lost confidence as a result of the events that led to the collapse of the Ottoman system. They took a more retrospective view by looking back to the glorious days of history and to their Turkic origins in Central Asia. Thus, they promoted the Pan-Turkist ideology.
>
> Ataturk was one of the few, if not the only person, who rejected Pan-Turkism and still had confidence in Anatolia. He developed an antithesis to the prevailing anti-Turkist ideology and insisted upon Anatolia being the homeland. To substantiate this totally new concept, an ethnohistorical theory was formulated, relating Sumerians and Hittites to the Turks, and integrated into the ideological framework of the new state. This approach considered Anatolia and the present population as an ethnic amalgamation of thousands of years. Pan-Turkists, who later became the ideologists of the racist movements of the present times, were rather pleased with the idea of affiliating Sumerians and Hittites to Turkish origins, but they never accepted a pre-Turkish history of Anatolia as a part of their

> heritage. In some respects, conflict between 'Anatolianism' and Pan-Turkism continues to the present day — although there was some consensus, at least in history books, by stressing both the Anatolian heritage and over-stressing Central Asian origins. The latter, particularly in books written in the 1930s under the impact of prevailing nationalistic trends of its time, posited a Turkish exodus from Asian steps. Ataturk's view, summoning all the pasts of Anatolia — regardless of ethnic origin — as national, was incorporated into the ideology of the modern state. — Ozdogan 1998 : 116-17

As we shall see later, the Turkish situation has a similiarity with the Indian case. Both are multi-ethnic states with deep roots in history, and a past acceptable to all sections of populace is important to both of them.

The complexity in building up a nationally acceptable sense of the past in modern Egypt has been analysed by Fekri Hassan (1998). In the late nineteenth and early twentieth centuries the first Egyptian nationalists looked toward Pharaonic Egypt for inspiration. Hassan points out how, after the revolution of 1919, the sense of national solidarity 'was legitimized by an appeal to "eternal Egypt", "young Egypt" and, above all, Pharaonic Egypt' and how pyramids were invoked in a genre of nationalistic poetry and historical plays. The concept of 'Arab nationalism' propounded by Gamal Abdel-Nasser in the 1950s undermined this emphasis, and under Anwar Al-Sadat in the 1970s there was a reawakening of an *Egyptian* identity. According to Hassan (1998 : 212)

> A stable political future of Egypt depends upon an ability to integrate its pasts and recognise its Pharaonic, Hellenistic, and Islamic heritage, and to place that variegated heritage within the course of a global civilization.

Hassan does not suggest the base on which this integration can be achieved.

What is important is that neither Ozdogan nor Hassan mentions any specific misuse of archaeology in the service of Turkish and Egyptian multi-ethnic nationalism. The way a nation views its past — the significance it attaches to its heritage — is a yardstick of its self-respect and identity, but the fact that a nation takes pride in its past does not necessarily mean that this serves as the base of its territorial aggrandisement or means the domination of one of its ethnic groups over others.

China seems to be more than concerned than Turkey and Egypt about maintaining a single 'ethnicity' with the label of 'Chinese'.

> Within the ongoing scholarly and political discourse, the unity and homogeneity of the Chinese nation is axiomatic, and formulations that might conjure up questions of ethnic

> identity in the present era are strictly taboo. Historians and archaeologists concur that all the nationalities mentioned in the ancient texts were long ago fused into the Han nationality. When concentrating their efforts on enhancing an ancient nationality such as Jin, then archaeologists are not claiming that present-day inhabitants of Shanxi are in any way ethnically distinct from other Chinese. Neither should, for example, one scholars's attempt to derive the origins of the Shang dynasty from the far-away north-eastern provinces of China . . . be misread as questioning the 'Chinese' ethnicity of the Shang royal house. At issue is, instead, the historical importance of a particular region in the formation of Chinese civilization, which, symbolically reified in archaeological cultures, is conceived as a metonym of the present-day power and prestige of the political unit that happens to contain that region, and of its ruling authorities.
>
> — Falkenhausen 1995: 210-11

Even in this case, where the ethnic label remains single and uniform over a vast geographical area and more than a billion of people, one fails to see how archaeology is being put to misuse. It may serve as an ideological underpinning of the nation-state of China's necessity to retain a homogeneous Chinese identity but wilful distortion of archaeological facts does not seem to be on its agenda. Similarly, in the case of Japan, 'the notion of the Japanese people as a cohesive and homogeneous "ethnic" group' has been claimed to be the central theme of archaeology from the late 1960s, aimed at creating 'a sense of cohesion and homogeneity among the Japanese people and to deny internal social conflict'. (Fawcett 1995 : 245) Does this national objective have to be viewed in a pejorative sense ? In a different area, democracy might not have flourished in Portugal in 1932-68 when Antonio de Oliveira Salazar was the prime minister, but can he be accused because he 'strove to restore the confidence and nationalistic pride of the Portugese by reminding them of their historic "golden ages" '. (Lillios 1995 : 67)

One of the reasons why ethnicity figures so frequently in the current discussions on the relationship between archaeology and nationalism is the fact much of the European past or much of the past of different European countries was conjured in terms of such groups — Celts, Anglo-Saxons, Slavs, and so on. This has been succintly expressed by Ian Banks (1996 : 6) :

> Historically, the appeal to ethnic origins has featured strongly in European nationalist projects. The ethnic groups with which many modern nations declare their ancestral links are commonly those which can be identified as distinctive peoples in the periods when early historical records first appear.

But even in Europe the situation varies from country to country. In France, for instance, the significance of archaeology was realised rather late, the discipline being considered for a long time a mere 'servant of history' (Schnapp 1996). In Spain modern archaeology has to contend with the regional aspirations of the Andalusians, Basques and Catalans (Diaz-Andreu 1996). M.L.S. Sorensen (1996) emphasises that the link between the past and the present in Denmark was to legitimatise and naturalise the territorial form that Denmark took in the wake of the Napoleonic war and the loss of her colonies.

Since the 1990s there has been a clear, and perhaps increasing, emphasis on finding links between archaeology and nationalism. A good part of this emphasis is to enquire into the socio-politics of archaeological writings within their national contexts, but by and large, as we have pointed out before, there is a strong undercurrent of negative attitude against any kind of equation between the nation and the archaeological data. On the other hand, this is also the phase when common elements are being consciously sought among the pasts of the nation-states within European Union.

Attempts to establish an European identity as opposed to the developments in west Asia, for instance, go clearly back to Gordon Childe's *The Prehistory of European Society* (1958) where the freedom of the itenerant smiths in the European Bronze Age were contrasted with their subordinate role in the context of the Oriental Bronze Age society. In 1994, in the now-powerful context of European Union, Colin Renfrew (1994) took up the theme again. He points out that

> The real problem in the archaeology of Europe today is that to a considerable extent we are still answering yesterday's problems, and in some cases continuing to fight battles whose outcome should long ago have been determined. It is difficult to underestimate the extent to which the broad beliefs of earlier decades about the European past — the myths of archaeology if you like — continue to dominate our thinking.
>
> — Renfrew 1994 : 164

He identifies three 'myths' : the myth of ethnic predetermination based on the notion that 'ethnicity may be assumed from early times, and certainly for the Mesolithic and subsequent periods'; the myth of economic predetermination based on the belief that the European Bronze Age was the result of a dissemination from the west Asian Bronze Age; and finally, the myth of spiritual predetermination associated with the bearers of 'Indo-European speech, mythology, religion, and social structure, whose male-oriented, militaristic values supposedly came to dominate, and whose tripartite social and religious structures (according to Dumezil) came widely to prevail'.

Renfrew acknowledges that it is difficult to root out these myths because they have so long provided the framework of the understanding of the prehistory of Europe. However, 'rather than assailing these myths further' — and, according to him, 'that task is indeed a useful one' — he decides to indicate what he feels 'are some of the more important questions'.

> It is out of these new and intriguing issues that we should, I believe, be formulating *our new narratives, the new myths (if you prefer), which we should be using to provide a fresh framework for the prehistory and early history of Europe over the next few decades*.
>
> — Renfrew 1994 : 165-166 (italics added)

The details of the new issues formulated by Renfrew — paths to urbanisation and the foundations of barbarian Europe with its own complement of sub-issues such as 'value and metallurgy', 'the gods of war' and 'the different roles of men and women in the emerging societies of barbarian Europe' — do not concern us, but what is important and relevant to our point of view is that there can be a reorientation of questions asked of the past of an area and that there should be a new narrative to go with it.

It may also be important to emphasise that there is a clear line of distinction between such new narratives and the use and/or manipulation of archaeological data for specific political agendas of territorial claims, aggrandisement and the suppression of dissenting political groups. The distinction has to some extent got blurred in modern archaeological literature. We further believe that 'misuses of archaeology' have been most frequent where ethnogenesis — the so-called formation of somewhat immutable ethnic identities — has been taken to be a primary goal of archaeological research. This is one of the major end-products of a very old and not-so-worn-out paradigm of race-language-culture correlation. This paradigm is not dead yet; it is easily possible to cite archaeological literature emanating from the liberal Euro-American contexts, which is a distinct throw-back to the essentially nineteenth-century notions of this kind. Why we should be so concerned at present about establishing correlates between biology, modern language groups and archaeological cultures is a question I leave to those archaeologists who are far more familiar with the complexities of the global socio-political realities than myself.

The highly volatile relationship between nationalism, politics and the practice of archaeology in the Caucasian region, which Kohl (1993) demonstrates with precision, is mostly due to the preoccupation of this region's archaeological tradition with questions of ethnogenesis. One fully agrees with him when he writes :

> Ethnic identifications extending back over millennia, which are a favourite form of nationalist interpretation, are problematic and hazardous. . . . The professional responsibility of the archaeologist confronted with such interpretations is straightforward : Emphasize that the identification is uncertain and tenuous and stress the real epistemological limits that circumscribe our ability to people the remote prehistoric past.
>
> — Kohl 1998 : 241

There can also be no disagreement with the following opinion :

> Ethical standards for accepting or rejecting nationalist uses of archaeology may vary in specific cases, but they should ideally satisfy the following three criteria : (a) the construction of one group's national past should not be made at the expense of others; (b) all cultural traditions should be recognized as worthy of study and respect; and (c) the construction of a national past should not be made at the expense of abandoning the universal anthropological perspective of our common humanity and shared past and future. . . .
>
> — Kohl 1998 : 243

Three more points may be emphasised in this 'introduction'. First, there is absolutely no reason why nationalist archaeology should be preoccupied primarily with ethnogenesis. This may be true in some cases, as in the case of the Caucasian region and the Balkan states of Europe, but that certainly is not the concern of nationalist archaeology everywhere. Secondly, the fact that national symbols have been borrowed from the monuments or archaeological objects in the nation-state's territory does not necessarily mean that archaeology is used for political reasons there and that archaeology occupies an important part of the nation's historical consciousness or historical education. This is a point which, in their enthusiasm to list traces of sins in this direction, the writers on this theme have consistently ignored. Thirdly, a lot of the harking back to the past is fairly innocuous. By staging his coronation ceremony in the ruins of Persepolis the last Shah of Iran was no doubt suggesting that his dynasty was an inheritor of the Achaemenid tradition of Iran. Whether this was true or not is a different matter, but as far as the harking back to old traditions goes, it is far more innocuous and less threatening than such terms as 'traditional Western viewpoint', 'dominant Western view', etc., which are increasingly becoming common in the Euro-American writings on Indian archaeology.

It is within this framework of archaeological literature and postulates on the theme of nationalist archaeology that we discuss the complexities of the Indian archaeological tradition in this regard and argue that we need a new 'nationalist' archaeological agenda and narrative. Interestingly, M-A Kaesar (2001) tries to conclude that 'our discipline is not intrinsically nationalist' because institutions like The International Congress of Prehistory, 'founded in 1865, almost four decades before any national body emerged' played a role in the emergence of prehistory as a discipline. While it is true that this 'Congress' played a role in influencing colonial administrators to take an interest in the prehistory of such regions as Africa, India or south-east Asia, it cannot be said to have played any role at all in the development of archaeology on the level of the national states of those regions. Secondly, the very fact that a claim is now being made to delink the roots of archaeology from nationalism is simply an indicator of the changing political climate of Europe with emphasis on European Union as a superbody.

THE UNACCEPTIBILITY OF THE CURRENT CONCEPT OF THE ANCIENT INDIAN PAST

The Indian identity, as built within the colonial Indological framework of race, language and culture and its Aryan-non-Aryan dichotomy, is unacceptable to modern India and Indians. It is unacceptable because its emphasis on the notion of Aryan invasion, and the subjugation of, and interaction with, the native population as the key elements of ancient Indian history, culture and archaeology keeps a vast segment of Indian population away from a sense of positive participation in the country's past. Further, the key ingredient of this notion is the Indian Vedic literature, which thus makes it primarily a textual notion, and as long as this notion persists, the Indian upper castes who *ipso facto* are given a place in the Aryan ruling order, have no special reason to seek a primarily archaeology-based past for themselves. However, before we examine these twin formulations in some detail, it might be useful to look at how the question of identity is emerging as a major phenomenon in India in current years.

Some Aspects of the Socio-politics of the Indian Past

There are many 'tribal', originally hunting-gathering groups in India, but as there has been a continuous process of their absorption in the fold of Hindu caste society, such indigenous groups never felt quite cut off from the social and economic forces operating around them. For instance, they figure in various ways in the Indian epics and mythology, often with virtuous roles being attributed to them. In many of the relevant areas there was also a process of secondary state formations (cf. Sinha 1962), which continued down to the Mogul period in the sixteenth to eighteenth centuries. The rulers of these states invariably claimed a descent from the great legendary dynasties of India, and there was no difficulty at all in their being parts of the general 'princely' society of the country.

Thus, whilst there is no shortage of groups who have a 'tribal' identity, none have as yet used it to question the archaeological interpretation of treatment of its past.

However, India has her problems, and these have been aggravated in recent years by the inability of the economic growth to keep pace with the growth in population. Clamours for an increased share in the national cake are the most persistent and strident noise in modern India, and such clamours are strengthened by appeals to caste, regional and religious identities. In some cases, especially along the borders where separate political niches can be carved out reasonably easily, much is made of ethnic differences. Group identities, as we know, are multi-dimensional and multi-level, and on the whole there is a great play about them in modern India.

There is much scope of investigating the emergence of different kinds of secondary identities, as apart from the basic historical identity of the nation, in the modern socio-economic and political contexts of India, especially with reference to the notions of the past which these identities claim for themselves. For instance, with the consolidation of the untouchables as a strong political power group (Bahujan Samaj Party or BSP) in the state of Uttar Pradesh under the leadership of Kanshi Ram and Mayavati, there has been a strong interest on the part of the untouchables or *Dalits* to discover powerful historical figures among their own communities. Their current identity, and the political language of the BSP which goes with it, are being built around such figures as Maharaja Bijli Paasee and Jhalkari Bai. The first one fought against the Muslim invaders while the second one fought against the British in the rebellion of 1857 (Narayan 1998).

However, movements such as these should not detract our attention from the ways in which the ancient Indian past has been viewed in post-Independence India by different sections of the Indian elite. How, for example, do historians and archaeologists of different socio-economic, educational and institutional backgrounds view the Indian past ? In the course of a long teaching career in two Indian metropolitan universities — Calcutta and Delhi — I have myself witnessed the expansion and consolidation of a group of students and teachers who feel more at home in English than in their native languages and literature and consequently are isolated from their own literary and other related streams of cultural heritage. It is this group which is increasingly forming the bulk of India's dominant educational and bureaucratic elite *vis-à-vis* the 'native' students who pursue their education in their mothertongues and find themselves disadvantaged while trying to seek whatever riches the 'system' has to offer.

The sense of the past of these two groups — or even the way they approach the study of the past — is not the same. For instance, 'Hinduism : one or many' is not an issue with India's ordinary populace; we are quite happy to follow the traditional way of life of a 'Hindu' within the over-arching framework of Brahmanism. However, the 'elite' class we have referred to finds no difficulty in arguing that Hinduism existed primarily as an amalgam of different sects before the Western Indologists invented it, so to speak, as an unified religion (Thapar 1989). The fact that very early in India's religious history emphasis was put on monism despite a plurality of gods and goddesses and the fact that most of the devout Hindus worship gods and goddesses of all these 'sects' in the course of their journey through life mean hardly anything to this class. Apart from such instances of 'Hindu-baiting', one may also point out that most of the historical research in modern India is focussed either on the contemporary issues or on the history of the last 200-odd years. In both cases the sources written in English constitute the basic historical documentation. The point is that the different ways in which the sense of India's past has affected different socio-economic and other groups of Indians and the implications they have for the future of the study of the Indian past is something which provides a singular field of research.

The Present Argument

The present argument is rooted in this context. It seeks to outline the kind of past which has so long been offered to Indians and define why this past is unsuitable for providing a common historical platform to all Indians. My focus is on a notion of India which has been built up by about two centuries of Indological research since the late eighteenth century.

The history of this research can be undertaken both in terms of different subjects and different themes. However, there is also an underlying conceptual framework which, in the course of its long history, has no doubt seen some modifications and undergone some variations in emphasis, but is still in place. In a study undertaken in 1994-95 I defined this framework as being based essentially on racism and the premise of race-language-culture correlation (Chakrabarti 1997). Edward Said (1978 : 322) pointed out that racism was a scarcely concealed part of Orientalism. He himself did not elaborate on the issue, nor has there been any detailed examination of this premise in Indology. One can dispense with 'racism' in the present context, although I must say that the boundless arrogance and the claims to superiority which the Western Indological writings have frequently arrogated to itself have already led to a situation where the Western

Indologists — and not infrequently Western archaeologists specialising in India too — write essentially for other Western Indologists and archaeologists. There should be a very clear awareness of this in India. However, the thrust of my present paper is not to elaborate this argument which I have done in some detail in my *Colonial Indology : Sociopolitics of the Ancient Indian Past* (Chakrabarti 1997). The emphasis here is only to show how the theoretical framework of race-language-culture correlation emerged in the context of India and how the Indian historians accepted it.

The Race-language-culture Framework in Colonial India

By the beginning of the nineteenth century scholars in Europe had already infused a language element into the concept of race. The idea of a masterful race of people coming down from the heights of Caucasus or other highlands of central Asia and marching towards Europe gained currency during that period (Poliakov 1974 : 187-91). Perhaps nobody did more to take this group of people to India than F. Max Muller around the middle of that century. According to him, there were at least two races of men in India, 'distinct in mind as well as in body' (Max Muller 1854 : 342) — the Aryan settlers and the aboriginals. In fact, the idea that the 'immigrant Brahmanical races' drove the earlier inhabitants of India into the jungles can be traced much earlier in a book by the French missionary, J.A. Dubois. The book was published around 1820 by the British Indian government but its manuscript was ready by 1806 (Pope 1879). In 1849 Brian Hodgson (1849) preferred to put all non-Aryans under the category of a 'Tamulian race' and he argued that the unity of this race was demonstrable through linguistic means, just it had been the case with the Aryans. In 1856 Robert Caldwell (1875) speculated about the 'Dravidian physical type'. Ethnological studies began in right earnest with people like George Campbell (1866) who in his classification of Indian population considered physical appearance, language, laws, manners and moral characteristics. He wrote of three main physical types : Caucasian, Mongolian and Negrito. He was not enthusiastic about introducing a separate 'Dravidian' group to the scene; he attributed Caldwell's Dravidian premise to 'his amiable enthusiasm for his beloved Dravidians', this being an illusion to the fact that Caldwell was a missionary in Madras.

Craniological studies based on the cephalic and nasal indices and supplemented by the studies of the type of hair and the colour of the skin came into sharp focus by the 1880s. Throughout the 1880s, 1890s and later H.H. Risley published extensively on the Indian situation (cf. Risley 1903; for a detailed discussion on Risley and the roots of his ideology, Chakrabarti 1997 : 116-29). He established seven main Indian physical types, all with some linguistic implications; Mongoloid, Mongolo-Dravidian, Aryo-Dravidian, Indo-Aryan, Scytho-Dravidian, Turco-Iranian and Dravidian.

As far as the notions of Indian racial types, their history and the issues of racial links with different aspects of Indian culture are concerned, Risley's publications consolidate the earlier hypotheses, offer a forceful image of India's racial components and history on the basis of anthropometric measurements, and formulate, in fact, an authoritative version of India's past (Chakrabarti 1997 : 122).

The Risley framework remained for long the essential framework of Indian racial studies. The most important attempt to modify and elaborate Risley's scheme was by B.S. Guha and J.H. Hutton in 1933 (Hutton 1933). It is also important to mention that the first detailed linguistic survey of India by G.A. Grierson (for a summary, Grierson 1909) was undertaken at the time when Risley was conducting his ethnological survey. Incidentally, Grierson repeatedly uses such terms as 'Dravidian ethnic characteristics'.

The Acceptance of the Race-language-culture Framework by Indian Historians and Archaeologists

It is only in the 1880s that one can detect the first major *Indian* statements about the ancient Indian past. This fact has to be viewed in the context of the nascent nationalism among the Indian upper class of that period. The Indian National Congress, a political party requesting more self-rule, was founded in 1885. The first major publication in this regard was a three-volume study of *A History of Civilization in Ancient India Based on Sanskrit Literature* by R.C. Dutt (1889), a member of the Indian Civil Service. There is a considerable emphasis on 'wonder that was India' in these volumes, but this was accompanied by a constant refrain that all the 'wonder' lay only in the 'intellectual and religious life of the Hindus' and there was a sad 'absence of genius in the people at large in the ordinary pursuits and trades, — in mechanical inventions and maritime discoveries, in sculpture, architecture and arts, in manifestations of popular life and the assertion of popular power'. (Dutt 1889, vol. I : 5) This is a complete and mindless acceptance of the attitude of Max Muller and other Western Indologists of the time to India. Secondly, it was assumed to be the story of 'a gifted Aryan people'.

The Aryan hypothesis bound the ruling Englishmen and the upper castes or the ruling elite of the Hindus together. Attention has been drawn to the report of an Indian exclaiming in a Calcutta newspaper in 1874 : 'we were niggers at one time. We now become brethren'. On the English side, the Aryan heritage made them appear as the inheritors of an ancient tradition to regenerate or re-educate the now-degenerated brothers or cousins just as the early group of Aryans introduced civilization in the land.

Colonial Indology led to the formation of this Indian identity. All subsequent proto-historic discoveries, including the discovery of the Indus civilization, were fitted into the Aryan-non-Aryan framework. The tradition continues (cf. Singh 1995). The proselytisation of the Aryan idea by Max Muller was, in fact, a watershed in the formation of Indian upper class identity. It is this identity which has since then been resplendent in Indian mind. We may cite three well-spaced post-Independence examples :

> (1) The history of India is mainly that of the Aryans of India. — Mookerji 1956 : 48
>
> (2) The foundation of the civilization of India was truly laid in the glorious epoch when the people who called themselves 'Aryas' colonized one district after another of this country. — Bhargava 1971 : 1
>
> (3) The horse is an animal which is not native to India and was brought in by the Aryans from Iran and Central Asia. . . . The Aryans, when they settled in various parts of north India, were hostile to the indigenous people whom they referred to as 'Dasas' and 'Dasyus'. — Thapar 1997 : 41

Archaeologists have not fared any better. The Aryan-Dravidian scheme provided the most significant theoretical focus of post-Independence Indian archaeology till the late 1960s and early 1970s and is still very much on the mind of sundry practitioners of the subject. Colonial Indology is still far from being dead in the portals of south Asian archaeology.

The Need of a Different Past in Modern India

It has to be made clear that the Aryan identity held no charm for the depressed among the Indian castes. Many great Indian nationalist leaders had no appetite for racial theories because of their divisive character; usually we find no reference to such ideas in the writings of, say, a person like Mahatma Gandhi. Opposition came from the leader of the depressed castes, B.R. Ambedkar (1946, 1970 reprint : 73-74) who criticised this theory on two grounds. First, he found the theory based on 'nothing but pleasing assumptions and the inferences based on such assumptions'. Secondly, according to him, it is 'preconceived and facts are selected to prove it'. He also underlined the role of Indian upper castes in the perpetuation of this theory in India.

> The Brahmin believes in the two-nation theory. He claims to be the representative of the Aryan race and he regards the rest of the Hindus as descendants of the non-Aryans. The theory helps him to establish his kinship with the European races and share their arrogance and superiority. He likes particularly that part of the theory which makes the Aryan an invader and a conqueror of the non-Aryan native races. For it helps him to maintain and justify his overlordship over the non-Brahmins.

B.R. Ambedkar was the law member in the Viceroy's Executive Council, chaired the drafting committee of the Constitution of modern India, and led the neo-Buddhist movement of the 1950s.

It is, however, not enough to dismantle the old colonial Indological identity of India. It is imperative to put in its place a sense of identity which can be shared by all categories of Indians. The knowledge, on which this new sense of identity should be based, can only be archaeological knowledge, because, whatever may be the religious and philosophical significance of our ancient textual corpus, it cannot yield in necessary detail any time-bound and area-bound perspective of the history of the Indian people. However, it is precisely this sense of over-riding importance of archaeological data in the reconstruction of ancient India which had been by and large ignored in our nationalist tradition. This point will need a brief but pointed analysis.

MARGINAL POSITION OF ARCHAEOLOGY IN THE INDIAN NATIONALIST TRADITION: A CASE-STUDY OF BENGAL

Because of my personal limitations, I can discuss the theme only with reference to the nationalist tradition in Bengal and the related Bengali literature. Other regional literary traditions should also be analysed by archaeologists from this point of view. However, even in my limited context I can discuss the theme only in its outline. The importance of monuments and similar other remains was no doubt realised by people like Rajendra Lal Mitra by the late nineteenth century, — and Henry Vivian Derozio (1809-31), a noted Anglo-Indian poet of Calcutta who wrote in English, composed a poem on the rock-cut monument of Jahangeera by the side of the Ganga at Sultanganj between Bhagalpur and Munger in Bihar — but it would be wrong to claim that archaeological data *per se* played a role in the contemporary national consciousness. In his attempt to trace 'the genealogy of modern historiography in Bengal' Partha Chatterjee (1994) has pointed out how by 1878 the emphasis on the idea of the Hindus as being of *Arya-Vamsa*

(Aryan lineage) was fully in place in such Bengali writings as Tarinicharan Chattopadhyay's *Bharatvarsher Itihas* ('History of India').

> What distinguishes the giant from the dwarf or the mighty from the frail is nothing compared to the difference between the ancient and the modern Hindu. In earlier times, foreign travellers in India marvelled at the courage, truthfulness and modesty of the people of the Arya *Vamsa*; now they remark mainly on the absence of those qualities.
> — cited in Chatterjee 1994 : 28

Further,

> In ancient times, when virtually the whole world was shrouded in the darkness of ignorance, the pure light of learning shone brightly in India. The discoveries in philosophy which emanated from the keen intellects of ancient Hindus are arousing the enthusiasm of European scholars even today. — Chatterjee 1994 : 29

It is an interesting reflection of the spirit of the times that the nationalist Indian Tarinicharan decided to produce certificates from the colonial Indologists to claim that ancient Indian philosophy was glorious.

Chatterjee (1994 : 29) writes :

> If the nineteenth-century Englishman could claim ancient Greece as his classical heritage, why should not the English-educated Bengali feel proud of the achievements of the so-called Vedic civilization.

The point of difference is that 'the nineteenth-century Englishman' and his eighteenth-century ancestors contributed enormously to the building up of the notion of a pure 'classical heritage' through original studies including extensive antiquarian field-investigations, whereas Tarinicharan and his ilk were happy enough only to brandish testimonials from their colonial masters. The only offshoot of this Bengali interest was the translation of some Sanskrit texts including the *Rigveda* in Bengali. As far as archaeological field-investigations are concerned, one is not sure if these nationalists, with the exception of people like Rajendra Lal Mitra, were particularly aware of the significance of the work of Alexander Cunningham and others in this direction. There was also hardly any excavation conducted in India in the nineteenth century.

Towards the end of the nineteenth century, there was a shift of interest in the Bengali nationalist writings on history, language and culture from the 'Vedic civilization' to the far more mundane items of Bengali heritage — mainly literature and folklore.

The establishment of *Bangiya Sahitya Parishad* as a continuation of the Bengal Academy of Literature (established on 23 July 1893, at the house of Maharajkumar Binay Krishna Bahadur at 2/2 Raja Nabakrishna Street, Sobhabajar, Calcutta) was a milestone in this regard. The aim of the Bengal Academy of Literature, established mainly due to the initiative taken by L. Leotard and Kshetrapal Chakrabarti, was to improve, and attain the spread of, Bengali literature with the help of English and Sanskrit literatures. The proceedings of the Academy began to be published — mostly in English — in a monthly magazine of the same name. The emphasis on English to improve the lot of Bengali led to a debate, and the Bengali version of the Academy's name, Bangiya Sahitya Parishad, was proposed by U.C. Batabyal and generally accepted. For a time the monthly magazine of the Academy was published under both the English and Bengali titles — Bengal Academy of Literature in English and Bangiya Sahitya Parishad in Bengali. In April, 1894 the English name was dropped and the Academy began to meet under its Bengali name. This reconstitution owed much to the efforts of Sarat Chandra Das, Hirendranath Datta and Maharajkumar Binay Krishna Bahadur. The first chairman of the Parishad was Ramesh Chandra Datta (already cited by us as R.C. Dutt), with Nabin Chandra Sen and Rabindra Nath Thakur as Deputy Chairmen and Debendra Nath Mukhopadhyay and L. Leotard as Secretaries. According to the first clause of the rules of the Parishad, '*Bangiya Sahitya Parishad* will discuss Bengali books or Bengali language and literature', and according to the second clause anybody with an interest in Bengali literature could be a member.

The foregoing details are available in the first annual statement of the Parishad, which was published by its Executive Committee from 2/2 Raja Nabakrishna Street in BS 1302. Almost right from the beginning there was emphasis on introducing Bengali as a medium of examination in the lower levels and listing technical words of chemistry, botany and mathematics in Bengali.

In the first part of the Parishad's journal in 1894 Ramesh Chandra Datta wrote the following :

> Fifty years ago we used to get educated in Western learning — even now we are educated in that and hope that this will continue for a long time. Fifty years ago we had no riches of our own; we used to move about like beggars. However, today we have a little wealth of our own. Madhusudan (Datta) and Bankim Chandra (Chattopadhyay) are its main collectors. Now we speak of Bengali literature with pride, care for it with affection and tend it filial devotion. With wealth we have gained a little strength; whatever we think of — politics, ancient history, literature, ancient religion —, we have learnt how to take

pride in our own wealth in these matters. Today we are no mere panegyrists of foreigners; we are not averse to our own manners and way of life; we are not fools in the field of our history, and we do not neglect our religion. It is as if we have gained a little strength, developed a little courage, recognized our national wealth and learnt the spirit of our national religion. This is a sign of progress and also a sign of goodness. May we continue to move forward along this path.

Archaeology — Pratanatattva — is missing from this list. In consonance with the Parishad's spirit, the betterment of the vernacular literature was the main cry, and whatever progress or modernity was achieved in this direction by 1894 was not more than 50 years old.

The need for learning in vernaculars was not realised only by people like R.C. Dutt but also by some contemporary British administrators of India. The annual convocation address of Calcutta University delivered by the vice-chancellor Alfred Croft on 3 February 1894 is one of the clear indications of this trend. In the course of his address he cites the following opinion of one of his predecessors and extends to it his own warm support.

The Bengali language has now a rich literature that is well worthy of study . . . I firmly believe that we cannot have any thorough and extensive culture as a nation, unless knowledge is disseminated through our own vernaculars. Consider the lesson that the past teaches. The darkness of the middle ages of Europe was not completely dispelled until the light of knowledge shone through the medium of numerous modern languages. So in India, notwithstanding the benign radiance of knowledge that has shone on the highest levels of our Society through one of the clearest media that exist, the dark depths of ignorance all around will never be illumined until the light of knowledge reaches the masses through the medium of their own vernaculars. — Croft 1894/1301 BS

It is also in the same issue of the journal that Debendra Nath Mukhopadhyay wrote on the necessity of a 'national literature'. The only thing related to ancient history in this volume is an anonymous summary of what was already published in English on the Gupta period Susunia rock inscription of Bankura. Any mention of the importance of antiquarian investigations is missing in the early volumes of the Parishad's journal, although there is a conscious emphasis on the collection of old Bengali manuscripts to discover the history of Bengali literature. This substantiates my claim that archaeology or the need to relate ancient Indian texts and history to the ground formed no part of the Indian nationalist thought.

From this point of view, Rabindranath's essay on *Bharatvarsher Itihas* (Bharatvarsha's

History) in BS 1309 (1902) is a remarkable and inexplicable exception which does not fit in with anything written by his contemporaries about the Indian past and foreshadows much of what is being perceived by nationalists about a hundred years later. He wrote that in the history of India that he read there was no place for Indians and that it brought about a sense of separation between Indians and India. 'A complete history of India' — that was what he hoped for.

The literary specialists in Rabindranath's writings should systematically analyse and contextualise his thoughts on Indian history. As I look around, I find that the period which occupies most of the Indian historians' attention is only the history of the country under the British rule, and that too, on the basis of sources written in English. The historical research related to the earlier periods has become virtually moribund in modern India. If one goes beyond various sectarian views and does a stock-taking of historical research on the pre-British period throughout the country, one realises that there is not much current work based on a well-developed expertise to handle primary sources in original.

It is not wholly true that the spirit reflected in the establishment of Bangiya Sahitya Parishad did not find any expression in the antiquarian field-research. To some extent, the district-subdivision — village level enquiries which have been undertaken by ordinary Bengalis since the late nineteenth century and published in Bengali is related to this spirit. Tarapada Santra (BS 1407) has provided a thorough list of such writings, and it may be useful to research the extent to which they are based on original field-investigations and the extent to which they owed their structures and contents of the various relevant District Gazetteers brought out by the Government. However, it was primarily in the literary field that there were major achievements and perhaps it is not a matter of surprise that the most important multifacetted volume on Bengal's past — *Brihat Banga* (1935) — was published by Dines Chandra Sen whose scholarly reputation is based on his contributions to the study of the history of Bengali literature. This tradition of historical research has continued till today among the students of Bengali literature, some examples (cf. *Rabi-Jibani* by Prasanta Kumar Pal; the writings of Sudhir Chakrabarti on various obscure religious sects still surviving in the countryside) being based on grass-roots investigation and of outstanding merit. In the historical field I remember the volumes of *Kausiki* which was founded by Tarapada Santra and is currently under the editorship of Indrajit Chaudhuri. I am not familiar with the journal *Itihas* published by Paschim Banga Itihas Sanshad but have been told by Jayanta Sengupta that it has developed a tradition of publishing articles based on a knowledge of the local Bengali sources. In the same vein I recall the excellent web-site set-up by Ambarish Goswami on Chandraketugarh, the first site-focussed web-site of its kind in India. What is important to note is that this tradition has flourished completely away from the mainstream historical research tradition of the country. I would even say that the study of Indian history is unlikely to move out its neocolonial ruts till there is a much wider awareness among the general educated public, especially the scientists, that historical research is a part of the general curiosity about the land and should not be considered the exclusive preserve of different coteries of our professional historians.

SOME INGREDIENTS OF A NATIONALIST INDIAN ARCHAEOLOGY

The themes will vary from person to person and are also likely to be multi-layered. The fundamental thing, as far as I can understand it, is to view the archaeology and history of the land mass of *Bharatavarsha* in its own terms.

(1) The first major theme should aim at a better understanding of the nuances of the interrelationship between geography and history in understanding south Asia's 'foreign' contacts. This land mass must have constantly interacted with her neighbouring regions, but there has to be a clearly defined geographical framework of this interaction. A clear distinction may be made between the direct 'foreign impacts' such as those created by the British rule and those of the earlier centuries when both the origins and the nature of such 'impacts' were mediated by some geographical parameters. In other words, a distinction has to be made between 'foreignness' and what emanates from the neighbouring, historically linked areas with decided geopolitical ties to the subcontinent. According to this argument, the Arab invasion of Sind was a foreign invasion but the whole series of the so-called 'foreign' inroads from the Indo-Greeks to the Moguls reflected only the significance of the close geopolitical ties of the subcontinent with the region stretching up to eastern Iran and the southern part of central Asia. On geopolitical considerations, this region cannot be considered 'foreign' in Indian history. The same thing may be said about the Ahom invasion of the Brahmaputra valley because the area from which the Ahoms moved to the Brahmaputra valley lay virtually at the doorstep of this riverine plain with which it had close traditional links. What we are trying to say is that there has to be a clear understanding of the difference between the 'frontiers' and 'boundaries' in the understanding of Indian history. 'Boundaries' are political constructs, subject to the vicissitudes of historical events. 'Frontiers'

are more abiding historical realities and cannot be considered 'foreign' to the core area.

This simple geographical premise seems to impart a different perspective to our understanding of many so-called foreign invasions of the country. In 1977 (Chakrabarti 1977) I argued that, in view of the constant political and economic interconnections between its component areas, the Indus valley, the eastern rim of Iran, the southern part of central Asia, Afghanistan and the Kashmir-Ladakh region constituted a distinct geopolitical orbit in the archaeology and history of the subcontinent. It was also argued that this premise had a number of historical implications. First, no component of this broad zone was 'foreign' to India. It was perfectly natural for any ambitious political power of the southern part of central Asia to think of the greener pastures of the Indus valley and beyond. However, to realise his ambition, he would have to consolidate his base first in the south of the Hindukush. The interesting point is that the southern side of the Hindukush is the natural frontier of *Bharatavarsha* in this sector, the Durand Line, the current boundary between Pakistan and Afghanistan, being a political product of only 1893. So, once a power has consolidated itself on the southern flanks of the Hindukush, that can hardly be called a 'foreign' power in the subcontinental context, whatever might have been its original roots. Heliodorus was the emissary of an 'Indo-Greek' king based in Taxila; the content of his inscription shows that he was as much Indian as Greek — in all likelihood more Indian than Greek. Secondly, the extent to which the thrust of power from the Indus-Oxus geopolitical orbit would be successful in moving out to the inner orbit of the Gangetic and Peninsular India would depend on the strength of the political powers based in those regions. On many occasions the Gangetic power stretched itself right up to the southern side of the Hindukush. Further back in time, the mature Indus civilization which extended up to the upper Doab and Gujarat up to the Tapti was the most important factor to reckon with in a vast zone of southern central Asia. Without trying to amplify the theme further in the present context, I would claim that the course of Indian history is in a sense the story of interaction between the two geopolitical orbits of the Indus-Oxus and Gangetic and Peninsular India. The idea is rooted in T.H. Holdich's *The Gates of India* (1910); I elaborated the concept in 1977 and showed its implications on assessing some diffusionary postulates in Indian archaeology. The details will certainly need more careful and detailed research, and among other things, this has the merit of showing that many of the 'foreign' invasions of India cannot be considered 'foreign' at all.

In 2001, on the basis of L.W. Shakespear's *History of Upper Assam, Upper Burmah and North-Eastern Frontier* (1914) I woke up to the significance of the Patkoi route to the Brahmaputra from the Hukong valley watered by the upper Chindwyn in northern Myanmar. It is from this region that the Ahoms migrated to the Brahmaputra valley in the thireteenth century AD and later. Geopolitically the Hukong valley lies at the mouth of the Patkoi route and constitutes a part of India's 'frontier' zone on the east. To this extent, the Ahoms were not 'foreign' either.

About the vast northern Himalayan zone our inference is simple: there are always links between the two saddles of a mountain, as there are traditional links between the Tibetan plateau on the north and the Nepal-India-Bhutan slopes on the south in the case of the Himalayas. The evidence of such links need not be construed as events of subcontinental significance, although the significance of Tibet in the artistic and religious history of Nepal, Bhutan and eastern India and a similar impact of eastern India, Nepal and Bhutan on Tibet need not be denied.

The point we have been trying to make is that in any nationalist scheme of Indian archaeology the different nuances of the subcontinent's interaction with the frontier zones on the north-west, north and east cannot be ignored. These nuances have to be understood in detail, area by area and period by period.

(2) Our second point is also geographical, but this time within the strict limits the subcontinent. Each area has its traditional historical linkages and interacts within the orbit thus created. In its turn, an individual orbit interacts with other orbits, leading thus to an image of many historically interacting orbits within the limits of the subcontinent. To some extent, such orbits are geopolitical; in 1999 I pointed out the similarities between the patterns of Satavahana and Maratha expansions, separated by about 2000 years but both with base in the upper Godavari valley (Chakrabarti 1999 : 29-30). However, this is more than a geopolitical issue. The linkages, both on the local and subcontinental levels, need close scrutiny. A study of these linkages will demonstrate two things. First, the pan-Indian interaction has been far more rapid than has been thought. In 1996 Nayanjot Lahiri and I argued that the 'Copper Hoard' implements of the upper Ganga

plain were technologically rooted in the north-eastern Rajasthan and the related parts of Haryana, that they reflected a 'late Harappan' tradition and that were disseminated along properly defined routes to Gujarat on the one hand and central India, the Deccan and the southern peninsula up to Ramanathapuram district of Tamil Nadu and Kerala on the other. This is not an isolated example. It is now possible to argue for an urban growth in the Kaveri delta and its adjecent region as early as *c.* 500 BC, and K. Rajan, on the basis of whose excavations (1997 : 75-90) it is now possible to make this claim, argues that there was clear evidence of contact between the Kaveri delta and north India during this period. How many of us have thought that the diagnostic types of early historic pottery are singularly uniform all over the Gangetic valley right up to the Himalayas. The early historic pottery that I found at Ror in Kangra one season was identical with the pottery that I found next season in the cliff of the Damodar at Pokharna in Bankura, West Bengal. Such spreads — such signs of pan-Indian dissemination of cultural traits and other forces — still remain to be studied in detail and their implications emphasised.

(3) Our third point is geographical too. Within the limits of *Bharatavarsha* there is hardly any major geographical impediment to the movements of people and goods. This point was driven home to me while following the routes between the Ganga plain and the Deccan (cf. Chakrabarti *et al.* 1999-2000). The lines of movement are still clearly traceable, and although at certain points the terrain is difficult, there is no evidence on the ground to suggest that these occasional difficulties ever stood in the way of human movements along them. The so-called north-south divide in terms of the Vindhya range and the Agastya Muni tradition cannot be considered as anything but a myth. The link between the Konkan coast and the hinterland was not easy, but everywhere the geographical lines of linkages are clearly defined. Such lines of linkages all over the subcontinent can be understood at the grass-roots level and this understanding will certainly lead to an easier appreciation of its archaeology in its own terms. We do not accept the proposition that some sections of the subcontinent did not fulfil any major role in the mainstream development of its archaeology and history. While working on a sketchy but coherent survey of the Chhotanagpur plateau as a whole (Chakrabarti 1993), I realised that as the most important source of different types of raw materials to the west and south of the lower and middle Ganga plain, this has to be given a major role in the archaeological

development of this vast section of the plain. We have found Black-and-Red ware of pre-1000 BC in Singhbhum, which possibly denotes the penetration of the chalcolithic settlers of the plain in this section in search of metals including tin. More extensive evidence of Black-and-Red ware settlements in the plateau has recently been found by R.K. Chattopadhyay, especially in Giridih and Santal Parganas. The so-called 'Asur' sites of Sarat Chandra Roy denote perhaps an organised political unit in the Ranchi plateau and its adjacent territories in the late centuries BC and early centuries AD — a political unit which, if the finds of semiprecious stone beads, Kushan coins, etc., are any indication, was well-linked with the developments in the alluvium below. The plain-plateau interaction was mostly in the form of exchange/trade of raw materials, and the hill valleys precluded large-scale settlements there, but by no stretch of imagination can our jungle tracts be called isolated areas. This is a geographical dimension well worth bearing in mind. Rakesh Tewari's work at Malhar in the upper Karmanasa valley and at Raja Nal-Ka-Tila in the upper Belan valley (cf. Tewari *et al.* 1999-2000) has highlighted the significance of this 'isolated' zone near Banaras as a major supplier of iron to the Banaras area of the Ganga plain as early as the first half of the second millennium BC. The mid-fifth century BC date for the NBP at Wari Bateshwar in the Meghna delta to the east and northeast of Dhaka (personal information from S.S.M. Rahman of Jahangirnagar University) amplifies that it is very unwise to judge the archaeological significance of an area on the basis of our perception of its geographical position *vis-à-vis* mainstream development. There must be innumerable examples of this kind from different areas of the subcontinent, and one of the specific angles of nationalist Indian archaeology may be devoted to this theme. According to my perception the core-periphery concept is not particularly relevant to Indian archaeology, each area having contributed significantly to the make-up of the core.

(4) I shall make a final point in the context of geography. The interaction between the different sections of the country — the interdependence between them for raw materials — is far more ancient than we realise. If one follows Nayanjot Lahiri's work (1996) — if one follows the spread of objects made of different raw materials at various archaeological sites and then turns to the possible webs of links between the areas where these sites are located and the areas from where it was possible to get the relevant raw materials — one realises that the country was far more closely intertwined than we are willing to admit and that the

history of this intertwining is very deeply rooted in Indian protohistory. In the same connection, I would point out that the location of individual sites throws in many cases insight into its geographical linkages or possibilities, such as I have argued for Mahasthangarh (Chakrabarti 2001 : chapter 2), among others. This is a trend which can be followed in depth all over the land and may just demonstrate the truth of what Nirmal Kumar Basu wrote on the basis of his close familiarity with the way people actually live in our villages : 'There is more unity in India's variety than one is likely to admit in moments of forgetfulness' (Bose 1961).

(5) One of the basic things which need highlighting in nationalist archaeology of the country is that there is a firm and continuous archaeological sequence running through the land and that this process began perhaps as early as the lower palaeolithic. This does not mean that India was never exposed to interactions with outside areas. This simply means that there is a demonstrable thread of continuity in India's cultural development right from the very beginning. Anybody who has looked at our palaeolithic stratigraphies in the field knows that there is a steady stratigraphical and typological continuity through them. The early hominid movements must have affected India; all that we are saying is that India may have her own story to tell even in this context. The date of 2 million years ago (mya) for the stone tools from Riwat in the Potwar plateau, the date of 1.8 mya for the tools from the Pabbi hills to the east of the Indus, the date of 1+ mya for the extensive Acheulian spread at Islampur and a few other dates going back to 3/4 hundred thousands years ago have gone a long way to establish the significance and antiquity of the Indian lower palaeolithic. Above all, some of its features now categorically show the evidence of cognition : R.G. Bednariks's claim (Bednarik) that the cup-marks and the narrow, meandering groove associated with them in a rockshelter at Bhimbetka near Ubaidullaganj in Madhya Pradesh belong to the middle palaeolithic or the upper part of the lower palaeolithic level of the site and that this may be the earliest example of such cup-marks in the world is worth thinking about. The proof that the Acheulian stage hominids as early as 1 mya (personal information from Michael Petraglia) were quarrying for the raw material used for making their tools at Islampur demonstrates once again that the story of the Indian lower palaeolithic is in all likelihood far more interesting than we are willing to concede. Dates are more easily available for the middle and upper palaeolithic, and everywhere there is a great variety, evolution and spread of artefacts, although in cultural terms the

evidence is still sketchy, mostly because of the lack of suitable excavations of many of these spreads. However, the insight, which has been obtained into the possible ways of using the resources of their landscape by the upper palaeolithic people by carefully studying the available 'wild' food-sources of these areas and the ways in which the modern-day hunting and gathering activities in the same area still use them, has in fact been invaluable in appreciating the significance of this phase — something which has also been highlighted by the discovery of an upper palaeolithic shrine at Baghor in Sidhi in Madhya Pradesh and the finds of the Lohanda Nala (Belan valley) bone harpoon, designs on the excavated ostrich egg shells at Patne (Maharashtra), etc. The cultural and economic image of hunting-gathering is more sharp with the mesolithic phase, of which there is a great deal of evidence, including a wide range of rock-art, of different chronologies in many parts of the subcontinent. Similarly, the beginning of food-production in different areas of the country is now a far more complex issue than was previously realised; things have moved much beyond such simplistic beliefs as the diffusion of wheat-barley cultivation from west Asia, of millets from Africa and of rice from China/south-east Asia. The primary point in all these prehistoric cases is the fact of richness, depth, variety and continuity of India's prehistory. This is something which our nationalist archaeology should consciously strive to highlight and focus on, because now we have advanced far enough in our research to know that many aspects of the grass-roots of modern India are rooted in prehistory. Further, there is no break whatsoever in the Indian prehistoric development; the basic story is that of adaptation of pre-historic people to different areas. A conscious aim of nationalist research should be to understand this adaptation in all its regional varieties. Mercifully, this aim can remain uncluttered by the ambiguities of our literary tradition.

The field of proto-historic discoveries in the subcontinent is far-reaching, ranging from the first wheat-barley-based settlements dated *c.* 7500 BC in Baluchistan to the beginning of the historic period in the Ganga plain and elsewhere around 700 BC and later. The Indus civilization is basically the Bronze Age culmination of the wheat-barley-based neolithic tradition in India, although this civilization could have significantly incorporated other agricultural traditions too, such as those based on rice and millets. Further, there could be earlier pockets of incipient cultivation, possibly in the form of slash-and-burn and digging sticks tradition, in the zone not directly within the distribution area of the Indus/Harappan civilization. However, the growth of wheat-barley based cultivation, which was certainly aided by ploughs in the first half of the third millennium BC, in the Harappan area, must have had impact on its adjacent territories or the general range of territories with which the mature form of this civilization had contacts for the procurement of raw materials. From this point of view the Harappan tradition contributed to the development of plough-based agricultural tradition of the non-Harappan India. This contribution must have become more direct as the civilization declined and eventually moved on a large scale towards Gujarat, south of the Tapti and the Doab. Throughout the second millennium BC we see a large-scale growth of village settlements in all the major agricultural areas of the subcontinent, and we believe that this derived strength from the dissemination of the Harappan plough-based agricultural tradition in inner India. Viewed from this angle, there is a strong, connecting thread of continuity between the different geographical orbits and phases of India's proto-historic development, linking up the Harappan tradition and the tradition before that, with the tradition of the neolithic-chalcolithic communities of inner India, which culminated in the growth of the early historic period. This point of view makes it possible to view the Indus civilization as the fountainhead of civilization in India. Archaeologically this is an eminently justifiable view, and both in my *The Archaeology of Ancient Indian Cities* (1995) and *India — an Archaeological History. Palaeolithic Beginnings to Early Historic Foundations* (1999) I have shown that this does no injustice to the current archaeological data. On the other hand, this makes it possible for us modern subcontinentals to view ourselves as the lineal descendants of the Harappan civilization, although with a lot of input from the various regional archaeological streams.

In an earlier section I have summed up my arguments why the notion of an Aryan invasion towards the end of the Indus civilization is a myth with singularly unpleasant implications for us. In fact, the invocation of archaeological data in favour of this invasion — and there have been many invocations of this kind — has been the worst abuse of archaeological data in the Indian context. An increasing number of archaeologists and other scholars is coming round to this view.

The world of Indo-European and Indo-Aryan linguistic scholarship is a bewildering mass of often contradictory, ambiguous and subjective arguments — a will-o-the wisp obligingly eager to mislead the archaeologist into linguistic quicksands —, and if Edwin's Bryant's lucid review of the Indo-Aryan migration debate (Bryant 2001) has told us anything, it is that there can be no acceptable rapport between archaeology and comparative philology in this area and that any suggested rapport can only be an article of faith and not the product of any clear and coherent archaeological reasoning. Our nationalist archaeological position does not have any place for any superior group of people known as the Aryans. This is something which can be clearly asserted without bending the archaeological evidence in any way, and I am happy that an increasing number of scholars is coming round to this opinion. My first questioning of the Aryan premise is dated 1968 (Chakrabarti 1968), and if anything, my understanding of the racism behind it and the damage it has done for a grassroots understanding of Indian history has become increasingly sharper over the years.

(6) A related theme is about the beginning of various technological innovations in India. Not enough attention has yet been paid to assessing India's part in the story of the major technological developments in the country's archaeological sequence. Far too often the origin of every development of this kind has been equated to the real or imaginary cultural impulses and/or movements of people from west Asia and beyond. On the other hand, recent archaeological research has categorically shown that in the two most important areas of such innovations, i.e., agriculture and metallurgy, India's own role has been crucial. As far as agriculture is concerned, Harappan agriculture can no longer be considered a mere offshoot of the dissemination of wheat-barley agriculture from Iran, central Asia or elsewhere. The significance of the early Baluchistan development as an independent subcontinental development in this regard is well understood, although we do not for a moment deny the possible significance of the interactions of the contemporary Baluchistan with the other components of such early agricultural development in Iran, central Asia and Afghanistan. What does need detailed attention is the way in which the entire gamut of proto-historic agriculture in the subcontinent took shape and developed. The richness and diversity of pre-industrial Indian agriculture — the richness and diversity of its crops, animal-uses and husbandry practices — remain to be explained in detail, especially with reference to their history. This can be one of the most useful arenas of nationalist archaeological research in the subcontinent. Similarly, the richness and antiquity of early Indian metallurgy form another significant arena of research of this

kind. Whatever little has been done in this field suggests the importance of this research, although in this case the focus should be, not on the rummaging of mostly puerile and stereotyped textual data but on the actual laboratory work on the excavated specimens and different ore bodies. The laboratory work should, of course, be accompanied by excavations of metallurgical sites and in-depth field investigations of pre-industrial mining remains. In short, the story of India's technological achievement is a vast field of nationalist archaeological enquiry.

It has been far from my intention to try to isolate all the areas and approaches of such a nationalist enquiry. I have only tried to highlight some themes, in the enunciation of which I have been personally involved. What I have tried to do, however, is to argue that the pursuit of a nationalist goal in archaeology is entirely justified as long as this does not bend archaeological data and is not used as an intellectual support for chauvinism. Further, in such multi-ethnic nation-states as India the notion of the ancient past should not be based on the perceived and historically evolving and changing ethnic, linguistic and other differences but on the story of their interactions and common achievements. A positive archaeological attitude to these achievements is both necessary and justified.[1]

---

1. After I wrote the paper I read Nathali Richard's article on 'archaeological arguments in national debates in late nineteenth century France : Gabriel de Mortillet's *La Formation de la nation francaise* (1897)' in *Antiquity*, March 2002. There are some similarities between what I have argued in this paper and what de Mortillet, who is better known as the person who offered a detailed classificatory scheme of the French palaeolithic, wrote in his book on the formation of the French nation in 1897.

   First, according to him, 'the nation is exclusively a geopolitical entity . . . in which the diversity of ethnic and linguistic origins is overcome by the unifying power of shared sentiments'. Secondly, only prehistory (in our case, archaeology) 'can appreciate and make evident' that the roots of the nation's past (the French nation in the de Mortillet and the Indian nation in my case) are 'incredibly deep'. I now quote from Richard's analysis of de Mortillet's idea in this regard.

   > The depth of pre-historic time appears then as the warranty of national unity, a unity that transcends the original diersity of the populations inhabiting the national territory. . . . With these arguments, the prehistorian added another theme to the classic definitions of the nation — that of the continuity of the past as a guarantee of national unity . . . de Mortillet stressed the overwhelming continuity of development across the Palaeolithic. From the first arrival of a human race on the national territory to the end of the Neolithic, all the physical transformations and development in stone tool industries were strictly autochthonous and totally continuous.

   Finally, de Mortillet was very critical of the soundness of arguments derived from history and linguistics. Archaeological knowledge had to be given the first priority in the scheme of reconstruction of the nation's history. This is also something which I have argued.

REFERENCES

Ambedkar, B.R., 1946, *Who were the Sudras ?* Bombay.

Banks, I., 1996, 'Archaeology, nationalism and ethnicity', In Atkinson, J., Banks, I, Sullivan, J'O eds., 1996, *Nationalism and Archaeology, Scottish Archaeological Forum*, pp. 1- 11, Glasgow.

Bhargava, P.L., 1971, *India in the Vedic Age*, Lucknow.

Bryant, E., 2001., *The Quest for the Origins of Vedic Culture. The Indo-Aryan Migration Debate*, New York.

Caldwell, R., 1875, *A Comparative Grammar of the Dravidian or South Indian Family of Languages*, London.

Campbell, G., 1866, 'Ethnology of India', *Journal of the Asiatic Society of Bengal*, special no.1 : 1-152.

Chakrabarti, Dilip K., 1968, 'The Aryan hypothesis in Indian archaeology', *Indian Studies : Past and Present*, 9 : 343-58.

———, 1977, 'India and west Asia — an alternative approach', *Man and Environment* 1 : 25-38.

———, 1993, *Archaeology of Eastern India : Chhotanagpur Plateau and West Bengal*, Delhi.

———, 1997, *Colonial Indology : Sociopolitics of the Ancient Indian Past*, Delhi.

———, 1999, *India : an Archaeological History. Palaeolithic Beginnings to Early Historical Foundations*, Delhi.

———, 2001, *Archaeological Geography of the Ganga Plain — the Lower and the Middle Ganga*, Delhi.

———, and Lahiri, Nayanjot, 1986, 'The Assam-Burma route to China', *Man and Environment* 10 : 123-34.

———, and Lahiri, Nayanjot, 1996, *Copper and Its Alloys in Ancient India*, Delhi.

———, Tewari, R. and Singh, R.N., 1999-2000, 'The archaeology of the Deccan route : a preliminary report on the field work in 1999', *Pragdhara*, 10 : 121-33.

Chatterjee, P., 1994, 'Claims on the past : the genealogy of modern historiography in Bengal', In, Arnold, D. and Hardiman, D., eds., *Subaltern Studies VIII, Essays in Honour of Ranajit Guha*, pp. 1-49, Delhi.

Croft, A., 1894/1301, 'Bengali Samvat. Address delivered at the Annual Convocation of the Calcutta University for conferring degrees, on the 3rd February', 1894 *Sahitya Parishad Patrika*, 1(1) : 7-26 (translated into Bengali under the title *Amader Visvavidyalay*).

Diaz-Andreu, M., 1996, 'Islamic archaeology and the origin of the Spanish nation', In Diaz-Andreu and Champion eds. 1996, pp. 68-89.

Dutt, R.C., 1889, *A History of Civilization in Ancient India, Based on Sanskrit Literature,* vol. 1, Calcutta.

Falkenhausen, L.V., 1995, 'The regionalist paradigm in Chinese archaeology', In Kohl and Fawcett 1995, pp. 198-217.

Grierson, G.A., 1909, *The Imperial Gazetter of India*, vol. 1, Oxford.

Hassan, F., 1998, 'Memorabilia : archaeological materiality and national identity in Egypt', In Meskell 1998, pp. 200-16.

Hodgson, B., 1849, 'A brief note on Indian ethnology', *Journal of the Asiatic Society of Bengal*, 18 : 238-46.

Hutton, J.H., 1933, *Census of India,1931, Report 1, Part 1*, Calcutta.

Kohl, P.L., 1993, 'Nationalism, politics, and the practice of archaeology in Soviet Transcaucasia', *Journal of European Archaeology* 1 : 11-88.

———, 1998, 'Nationalism and archaeology : on the constructions of nations and the reconstructions of the remote past', *Annual Review of Anthropology*, 27: 223-46.

———, and Fawcett, C., eds., 1995, *Nationalism, Politics, and the Practice of Archaeology*, Cambridge.

Lahiri, Nayanjot 1992, *The Archaeology of Indian Trade Routes* (*up to c.200 BC*), Delhi.

Lillios, K.T., 1995, 'Nationalism and Copper Age research in Portugal during the Salazar regime (1932-1974)', In Kohl and Fawcett 1995, pp. 57-69.

Meskell, L., 1998, ed., *Archaeology under Fire, Nationalism, Politics and Heritage in the Eastern Mediterranean and Middle East*, London.

Mookerji, R.K., 1956, *Ancient India*, Allahabad.

Muller, F.M., 1854, 'Ethnology *v.* phonology', In Bunsen, C.C., ed., *Outlines of the Philosophy of Universal History Applied to Language and Religion,* 1, pp. 349-53, London.

Narayan, B., 1998, 'Determining relations : memory, history and politics', *Studies in Humanities and Social Sciences,* 5 : 113-28.

Ozdogan, M., 1998, 'Ideology and archaeology in Turkey', In Meskell 1998, pp. 111-23.

Poliakov, L., 1974, *The Aryan Myth*, London.

Pope, G.U., ed., 1879, *A Description of the Character, Manners and Customs of the People of India, and of Their Institutions and Religions*, Madras.

Rajan, K., 1997, *Archaeological Gazetteer of Tamil Nadu*, Thanjavur.

Renfrew, C., 1994, 'The identity of Europe in pre-historic archaeology', *Journal of European Archaeology,* 2 : 153-73

Risley, H.H., 1903, *Census of India, 1901,* vol.1, Calcutta.

Said, E., 1978, *Orientalism*, London.

Santra, Tarapada, 1407 B.S., (2000), *Banglar Anchalik Itihas Charcha : Ekti Samiksha, Puravritta* 1 : 70-114.

Schnapp, A., 1996, 'French archaeology : between national identity and cultural identity', In Diaz-Andreu, M. and Champion, T., eds., 1996, *Nationalism and Archaeology in Europe*, pp. 48-67, London.

Sinha, Surajit, 1962, 'State formation and Rajput myth in tribal central India', *Man in India,* 42 : 35-80.

Singh, B., 1995, *The Vedic Harappans*, Delhi.

Sorensen, M.L.S., 1996, 'The fall of a nation, the birth of a subject : the national use of archaeology in nineteenth-century Denmark', In Diaz-Andreu and Champion, eds., 1996, pp. 24-47.

Tewari, R., Srivastava, R.K., Saraswat, K.S. and Singh, K.K., 1999-2000, 'Excavations at Malhar, district Chaundauli (U.P.) 1999 : a preliminary report', *Pragdhara,* 10 : 69-98.

Thapar, R., 1989, 'Imagined religious communities? Ancient history and modern search for a Hindu identity', *Modern Asian Studies,* 23 : 209-31.

———, 1997, *Ancient India*, Delhi.

Trigger, B., 1995, 'Romanticism, nationalism, and archaeology', In Kohl and Fawcett 1995, pp. 263-79.